To my 365 students at the

University of Delaware

who helped me to appreciate better

the impact and joy of museums

Museums in Motion

AMERICAN ASSOCIATION FOR
STATE AND LOCAL HISTORY BOOK SERIES

About the Series:

The American Association for State and Local History Book Series publishes technical and professional information for those who practice and support history and addresses issues critical to the field of state and local history. To submit a proposal or manuscript to the series, please request proposal guidelines from AASLH headquarters: AASLH Book Series, 530 Church Street, Suite 600, Nashville, Tennessee 37219. Telephone: (615) 255-2971. Fax: (615) 255-2979.

About the Organization:

The American Association for State and Local History (AASLH) is a non-profit educational organization dedicated to advancing knowledge, understanding, and appreciation of local history in the United States and Canada. In addition to sponsorship of this book series, the association publishes the periodical HISTORY NEWS, a newsletter, technical leaflets and reports, and other materials; confers prizes and awards in recognition of outstanding achievement in the field; and supports a broad educational program and other activities designed to help members work more effectively. Current members are entitled to discounts on AASLH Series books. To join the organization, contact: Membership Director, AASLH, 530 Church Street, Suite 600, Nashville, Tennessee 37219.

MUSEUMS IN MOTION

An Introduction to the History and Functions of Museums

Edward P. Alexander

Formerly Director of Museum Studies
University of Delaware

Foreword by William T. Alderson

A Division of
ROWMAN & LITTLEFIELD PUBLISHERS, INC.
Walnut Creek • Lanham • New York • Oxford

ALTAMIRA PRESS
A Division of Rowman & Littlefield Publishers, Inc.
1630 North Main Street, #367
Walnut Creek, CA 94596
www.altamirapress.com

Rowman & Littlefield Publishers, Inc.
4720 Boston Way
Lanham, MD 20706

12 Hid's Copse Road
Cumnor Hill, Oxford OX2 9JJ, England

Originally published by the American Association for State and Local History.

Initial publication of this book was made possible in part by funds from the sale of the Bicentennial State Histories, which were supported by the National Endowment for the Humanities.

Author and publisher make grateful acknowledgment to David McCord for permission to quote, in full, the poem "History of Education," from *And What's More*, by David McCord. Copyright 1941 by Coward, McCann; copyright 1973 by David McCord.

British Library Cataloguing in Publication Information Available

Library of Congress Cataloging-in-Publication Data

Alexander, Edward P. (Edward Porter), 1907–
Museums in motion : an introduction to the history and functions of museums / Edward P. Alexander : foreword by Walliam T. Alderson.
p. cm. — (American Association for State and Local History book series)
Originally published : Nashville, Tenn. : American Association for State and Local History. 1979.
Includes bibliographical references and index.
ISBN 0-7619-9155-7 (acid-free paper)
1. Museums. 2. Museums—History. 3. Museums—Philosophy. I. American Association for State and Local History. II. Title. III. Series.
AM5.A38 1996
069—dc20 95-48343

Printed in the United States of America

™ The paper used in this publication meets the minimum requirements of American National Standard for Information Sciences—Permanence of Paper for Printed Library Materials, ANSI/NISO Z39.48–1992.

Contents

Illustrations

Foreword

Much has been said in recent years about the emergence of the museum profession. Those of us who have devoted careers to the field have regarded with satisfaction the development of some unmistakable attributes of a profession—standards of performance incorporated in an accreditation program, the development of a code of ethics, the emergence of formal programs of academic training for those who aspire to museum careers, and a growing bibliography of books and articles on museum philosophy and practice. With this book, yet another element of a profession is fitted into place: that of the self-awareness that comes from contemplating where we are and how we got to be that way.

No one, to my knowledge, is better equipped to provide us with a historical perspective of the museum profession than Edward P. Alexander. A trained historian with a doctorate from Columbia University, he made an early career commitment to the work of historical agencies and increasingly focused his interests on the museum field. He was director of the New York State Historical Association at the time that institution moved from Ticonderoga to Cooperstown and began its major commitment to the museum field. Then followed the directorship of the State Historical Society of Wisconsin. From 1946 to 1972, as director of the interpretation program of Colonial Williamsburg, he was the acknowledged leader in the development of outdoor museum interpretation as we know it today. Following his retirement at Colonial Williamsburg, and until I was privileged to succeed him in 1978, he established and directed the Museum Studies program of the University of Delaware, passing on to a new generation of students a lifetime of work and study in the museum field.

Dr. Alexander has also been one of the leaders in creating the museum profession. A founder and second president of the American Association for State and Local History, he was also author of its first technical publication, a slender book titled *What Should Our Historical Society Do?*, and he played a role in the founding of the magazine *American Heritage*. He is a past president and council member of the American Association of Museums, which he has also served in key committee roles. His other contributions to the field are too numerous to list here, but one deserving special mention and of which he is especially proud is the Williamsburg Seminar for Historical Administrators, which for two decades has helped train young people who have played important roles in the emergence of the museum profession.

This is an especially important book, because it reflects the analytical skills of the trained historian, the insights of an experienced leader of the profession, and the dedication of a teacher who wishes us to learn and to grow. The result is a pioneering effort that is informative, wise, and useful. Add to those virtues the fact that it is also highly readable, and you have a book that becomes "must" reading, not only for museum professionals, but for everyone who is interested in the museum world.

It would be fitting to remark how appropriate it is to have this book appear at the conclusion of a long and distinguished career; but that would be untrue, because Ed Alexander doesn't think about conclusions, only about forward steps. By careful scheduling, he will have completed the index in time to have this volume on the press while he is on an around-the-world tour. Exploring new places and meeting new people with his wife Alice, he will characteristically be visiting and photographing every museum he can find along the way and taking notes for yet another book or article that will help the rest of us to advance the profession he has helped to create and continues to serve so well.

WILLIAM T. ALDERSON

Newark, Delaware
July 4, 1978

Museums in Motion

1

What Is a Museum?

Charles Willson Peale, the artist, in his Philadelphia museum, 1822

Museums in the United States are growing at an almost frightening rate. If we count the smallest ones with only one person on the staff and he or she without professional training, about five thousand of them exist today, and recently a new one has appeared every 3.3 days. People are crowding into them in droves, and the annual visits made to museums are now estimated at 600 million, give or take 100 million.[1]

Museum Definitions: Friendly and Unfriendly

A museum is a complex institution, and defining it is not easy. Whether one likes or dislikes museums will influence one's definition. Douglas Allan, late director of the Royal Scottish Museum in Edinburgh, said that "a museum in its simplest form consists of a building to house collections of objects for inspection, study and enjoyment."[2] Except for the confining of the museum to a single building, perhaps most of us would agree with that generalization.

The American Association of Museums, in developing a nationwide museum accreditation program, has defined a museum as "an organized and permanent non-profit institution, essentially educational or aesthetic in purpose, with professional staff, which owns and utilizes tangible objects, cares for them, and exhibits them to the public on some regular schedule."[3] That definition has met some objection from art centers, neighborhood museums, science centers, and planetariums that have little or no collection, and the association is beginning to develop special definitions for some of these categories. Those who emphasize the research function of the museum would like to see research mentioned in the definition.

Thomas P. V. Hoving, former director of the Metropolitan Museum of Art, declares that the museum possesses "a great potential, not only as a stabilizing, regenerative force in modern society, but as a crusading force for quality and excellence."[4] Dillon Ripley, secretary of the Smithsonian Institution, which operates the huge national museum megalopolis in Washington, thinks that "a museum can be a *powerhouse*," though only if "museum people and the public get away from the 'attic' mentality."[5]

A lively German writer describes an art museum as a place "where every separate object kills every other and all of them together the visitor," and some critics would do away with museums altogether. Filippo Tommaso Marinetti, a founder of Italian Futurism, in 1908 urged artists to start afresh and ignore all tradition. He wished to destroy museums (and libraries also) and welcomed "the kindly incendiaries with the carbon fingers!" He went on to say:

> Museums, cemeteries! . . . Identical truly in the sinister promiscuousness of so many objects unknown to each other. Public dormitories, where one is forever slumbering beside hated and unknown beings. Reciprocal ferocity of painters and sculptors murdering each other with blows of form and color in the same museum.[6]

Today, unless museums reform themselves, some militant minority groups also advocate their destruction. June Jordan, a black poet, not long ago electrified a museum seminar in Brooklyn when she said:

> Take me into the museum and show me myself, show me my people, show me soul America. If you cannot show me myself, if you cannot teach my people what they need to know—and they need to know the truth, and they need to know that nothing is more important than human life—if you cannot show and teach these things, then why shouldn't I attack the temples of America and blow them up? The people who hold the power, and the people who count pennies, and the people who hold the keys better start thinking it all over again.[7]

Perhaps this is attempt enough at definition, for the moment, and we should leave the subject while enjoying the quip of an anonymous Englishman who considers the museum "a depository of curiosities that more often than not includes the director."

Ancient and Medieval Prototypes

The Latin word *museum* (Greek: *mouseion*) has had a variety of meanings through the centuries. In classical times it signified a temple dedicated to the Muses, those nine sprightly and pleasantly amoral young goddesses who watched over the welfare of the epic, music, love poetry, oratory, history, tragedy, comedy, the dance, and astronomy. The most famous museum of that era was founded at Alexandria about the third century B.C. by Ptolemy Soter ("Preserver") and was destroyed during various civil disturbances in the third century A.D. The Mouseion of Alexandria had some objects, including statues of thinkers, astronomical and surgical instruments, elephant trunks and animal hides, and a botanical and zoological park, but it was chiefly a university or philosophical academy—a kind of institute of advanced study with many prominent scholars in residence and supported by the state. The museum and the great international library of papyrus rolls and other writings collected by Alexander the Great were housed in the royal quarter of the city known as the Bruchium. Euclid headed the mathematics faculty and wrote his *Elements of Geometry* there. Archimedes, Appolonius of Perga, and Eratosthenes were only a few of the noted scientists and scholars who lived in the king's household and made use of library, lecture halls, covered walks, refectory, laboratories for dissection and scientific studies, and botanical and zoological gardens.[8] Some modern students of the museum movement, who emphasize its research function and prefer to define the museum as a community of scholars, look back on the Alexandria institution with real affection and nostalgia.

Though the Greeks and Romans thought of the museum in different terms from those we use today, the ancient world did possess public collections of objects valued for their aesthetic, historic, religious, or magical importance. The Greek temples had hoards of votive offerings of gold, silver, and bronze objects, statues and statuettes, paintings, and even bullion that could be expended in case of public emergency. The paintings were on planks (Greek: *pinas*), and thus a collection of them was called *pinakotheke*. In the fifth century the Acropolis at Athens had such paintings in the Prophylae, placed above a marble dado, lighted by two windows from the south, and protected individually by shutters. The Romans displayed paintings and sculpture, often the booty of their conquests, in forums, public gardens, temples, theaters, and baths. Roman generals, statesmen, and wealthy patricians often appropriated such objects for their country homes. The emperor Hadrian in the second century at his villa near Tibur (today Tivoli) reconstructed some of the landmarks he had seen in his travels through the empire, for example, the Lyceum and Academy of Athens, the Vale of Temple in Thessaly, and the Canopus of the Egyptian delta. In a sense he created an open-air or outdoor museum.[9]

The museum idea was barely kept alive in western Europe during the Middle Ages. Churches, cathedrals, and monasteries venerated alleged relics of the Virgin, Christ, the apostles, and the saints and embellished them with gold, silver, and jewels, manuscripts in sumptuous metal bindings, and rich oriental fabrics. The Crusades brought back fabulous art objects to add to these treasuries or to the palace collections of princes and nobles, thus illustrating what the late Francis Taylor wittily called the "magpiety" of mankind.[10] In Islam, China, and Japan similar accumulations were made, and the Shōsō-in (eighth century) at Todaiji Monastery at Nara near Kyoto is probably the oldest museum in the world.[11]

From Private Collection to Public Museum

"The modern museum," says J. Mordaunt Crook, in his architectural study of the British Museum, "is a product of Renaissance humanism, eighteenth-century enlightenment and nineteenth-century democracy." The humanist, with keen interest in the classical past and the world about him, began to throw off the reins of superstition and take halting steps toward a scientific method. Two new words appeared in the sixteenth century to express the museum concept. The gallery (Italian: *galleria*), a long grand hall lighted from the side, came to signify an exhibition area for pictures and sculpture. The cabinet (Italian: *gabinetto*) was usually a square-shaped room filled with stuffed animals, botanical rarities, small works of art such as medallions or statuettes, artifacts, and curios; the Germans called it *Wunderkammer*. Both types of collections rarely were open to the public and remained the playthings of princes, popes, and plutocrats.[12]

The ancient world had had its great gardens, and medieval monasteries cultivated and cherished plants and flowers, but true botanical gardens now began to appear at the universities—Pisa (1543), Padua (1545), Bologna (1567), Leiden (1587), Heidelberg and Montpellier (1593), and Oxford (1620). Scholarly botanists used them for scientific plant study; physicians, for testing remedies. Herbalists, barber surgeons, apothecaries, and physicians also established physic gardens as sources for medicinal materials, for example, at Holburn and Chelsea in London.[13]

The museum began to go public in the late seventeenth century. Basel opened the first university museum in 1671, and the Ashmolean Museum appeared at Oxford a dozen years later. The eighteenth century concerned itself with discovering the basic natural laws that formed a framework for the universe and humanity, and intellectuals of the day wished to preserve in museums natural specimens as well as human artistic and scientific creations. Supposedly they would help educate humankind and abet its steady progress toward perfection. The Vatican established several museums about 1750, and the British Museum was formed in 1753 when Parliament purchased Sir Hans Sloane's great collection devoted chiefly to natural science. In 1793 France opened the Palace of the Louvre as the Museum of the Republic. Napoleon confiscated art objects by conquest and devised a grand plan for a unified French museum system as well as subsidiary museums elsewhere. The scheme collapsed with his defeat, but his conception of a museum as an instrument of national glory continued to stir the imagination of Europeans.[14]

Museum Functions

Thus far, the museum movement had been intensely personal and haphazard in plan. The entire emphasis had been upon collection of the beautiful and curious. The objects gathered were chiefly works of art, historical rarities, or scientific specimens and equipment; some objects were animate, and the botanical garden, arboretum, menagerie, and aquarium were essentially museums. Collecting seems to be instinctive for many human beings. It may be based upon the desire for physical security (today collections often are considered good investments), social distinction (Thorstein Veblen would call it "conspicuous consumption"), the pursuit of knowledge and connoisseurship (genuine love for objects and desire to find out everything about them), and a wish to achieve a kind of immortality, as witness the great number of named collections in museums. Collectors also sometimes display neurotic symptoms that may result in obsession or a kind of gambling fervor.

Collectors traditionally have turned their hoards over to museums, and museums have often caught the raging collecting fever. Art museums have spent fortunes for paintings or objects while paying inadequate staff salaries and neglecting such everyday running expenses as air conditioning. Conservative museum directors sometimes consider collection far and away the most important museum function. One museum authority even suggests that it is the sole reason for museums and that exhibition, education, culture, and the social good are only rationalizations and window dressing used to justify the basic collecting passion.[15]

Closely connected with collection was the function of conservation. Collectors have always taken care of their hoards, oftentimes with miserly devotion. The techniques of conservation were at first little understood, and nearly all the panel paintings of antiquity have disappeared. The Greeks made crude attempts to preserve votive shields by coating them with pitch to prevent rust, and they placed vats of oil at the feet of Phidias's *Athena Parthenos* to reduce excessive dryness. By the sixteenth century, paintings were being cleaned and revarnished, but not until nearly 1750 was the rebacking process perfected that could transfer the layer of paint from its original wall, panel, or canvas to a new surface.[16]

As long as a collection was private, it could be kept under lock and key and relatively safe. When the public was admitted to the museum, however, precautions had to be taken against theft or handling, and the Industrial Revolution brought high-intensity lighting, central heating, air pollution, and other unfavorable conditions that could speed the deterioration of collections. Yet the revolution also brought scientific study and knowledge of the composition, conservation, and restoration of objects. Good housekeeping methods, proper control of lighting and relative humidity, and ingenious repair and rehabilitation procedures in the last fifty years have revolutionized the preservation of museum objects and added to museum staffs skilled conservators trained in physics and chemistry.[17]

Research was still another museum function. In a sense it could be viewed as an extension of collecting, for research thoroughly examined the objects collected in order that they could be accurately catalogued. In natural history museums, botanical gardens, zoos, and aquariums, this study resulted in important taxonomic contributions to biological studies. In all museums, in-house, programmatic research often led to additions to the collection, sometimes obtained through field expeditions and archaeological excavations. The study of art history and architectural history also advanced through the research of museum curators, and, though historians have been slower to study objects, cultural and social history is more popular today and only a step removed from the ethnological studies so zealously pursued by museums of anthropology and archaeology.[18]

Once the museum admitted the public, its exhibition function became predominant. Collecting, conservation, and research were used chiefly to secure excellent exhibitions. At first the displays were arranged to benefit the aesthete, the scholar, the collector, and the craftsman, a knowledgeable audience satisfied with a minimum of labels and interpretation. The collection usually was arranged either aesthetically or according to the principle of technical classification in chronological or stylistic order—a kind of visible storage with crowded walls of paintings or heavy glass cases crammed with ceramics, textiles, metalware, or natural history specimens. Museums were housed in palatial or templelike structures that made the man on the street feel uncomfortable and discouraged his attendance.[19]

In the nineteenth century, however, the exhibition function began to change. German and Swiss museum directors experimented with culture history arrangement—placing objects in period rooms or halls that gave the visitor the feeling of walking through different stages of national history.[20] Artur Hazelius established Nordiska Museet at Stockholm in 1873, devoted to the everyday life of the Scandinavian folk, and in 1891 he opened Skansen, the first true outdoor museum, on a seventy-five-acre tract overlooking Stockholm harbor. There he moved buildings chiefly of vernacular architecture, provided them with garden settings and interior furnishings, and employed costumed craftsmen, musicians, dancers, and interpreters to bring the whole folk village to life. No longer was the common man overawed by palace or temple; now the museum and the picnic could be combined and the whole family might share in enjoyment of the national heritage.[21] The new approach fitted well the increasing democratization of modern life, and the series of world's fairs that began with London's Crystal Palace in 1851 contributed ever more spacious and dramatic systems of exhibition.[22]

American Museums

Museums developed slowly in the United States. The Charleston Museum, founded in 1773, collected natural history materials in leisurely fashion.[23] Charles Willson Peale was the first great American museum director. Peale's Museum in Philadelphia began in his home, moved to the Philosophical Hall of the American Philosophical Society in 1794 and on to Independence Hall, and had branches in Baltimore and New York. He mounted specimens of animals, birds, and insects with realistic backgrounds and displayed portraits of nearly three hundred Founding Fathers, painted chiefly by himself or members of his family.[24] The Smithsonian Institution, started in 1846 with the Englishman James Smithson's bequest to the United States "for the increase and diffusion of knowledge," for a time was loath to accept collections and remained chiefly a research institution of pure science. When George Brown Goode, a talented museum man, joined the Smithsonian in 1873, it began to become a great national museum devoted to science, the humanities, and the arts. Today it has more than 55 million specimens of natural history and ethnology alone.[25] The founding in about 1870 of three great museums—the American Museum of Natural History and the Metropolitan Museum of Art in New York and the Museum of Fine Arts in Boston—marked the entry of the United States into the museum mainstream.[26]

The advent of the automobile enabled the historic house museum to flourish by attracting tourists. (The first American house museum had been established at Washington's Headquarters in Newburgh, New York, 1850, soon followed by Washington's plantation home of Mount Vernon in Virginia.) Museums also sprang up in the national parks, and Colonial Williamsburg in 1926 was the first of a host of preservation projects and outdoor museums that drew millions of visitors who usually traveled in the family car.[27]

By 1900 American museums were becoming centers of education and public enlightenment. This development was natural in a country that prided itself on its democratic ideals and placed deep faith in public education both as a political necessity and as a means of attaining technological excellence. George Brown Goode went so far as to declare that "An efficient educational museum may be described as a collection of instructive labels, each illustrated by a well-selected specimen." Benjamin Ives Gilman, secretary of the Museum of Fine Arts in Boston, considered this conception proper for science museums, but not for art museums. He thought "A museum of science . . . in essence a school; a museum of art in essence a temple." Works of art communicated directly with their beholders and needed little labeling; art museums were "not didactic but aesthetic in primary purpose."

But Gilman wanted art museums to have interpreters to help their visitors see the beauty of their collections. Thus in 1907 the Boston museum appointed a docent to its staff. Gilman dreamed up this new title that avoided any reference to "education"; he explained that "a museum performs its complete office as it is at once *gardant, monstrant,* and *docent.*" David McCord made fun of the word in an amusing quatrain that runs

> The decent docent doesn't doze:
> He teaches standing on his toes.
> His student dassn't doze—and does,
> And that's what teaching is and was.[28]

Still, the American Museum of Natural History, the Metropolitan Museum, and even the British Museum appointed such guides.[29]

Education or Interpretation

Since then, American museums have continued their leadership in educational programs. They frequently refer to the kind of education they provide as interpretation, that is, teaching through the use of original objects. Interpretation relies heavily on sensory perception—sight, hearing, smell, taste, touch, and the kinetic muscle sense—to enable the museum-goer emotionally to experience objects. This interpretation complements the rational process of learning through words and verbalization. American museums developed close relationships with the schools, welcoming thousands of students with their teachers and in return sending traveling exhibits and museum staff to the classroom. Museum clubs for children appeared, and also children's or youth museums. Nearly every museum authority from abroad who comes to visit American museums is deeply impressed by their devotion to education, just as American museum professionals comment on the research and scholarship they encounter in European curators. Still, the Victoria and Albert Museum in London was a European leader in using the museum as an educational force for both craftsmen and the general public, and museum education programs are thriving in many parts of Europe today, including the countries of the Communist bloc.

Many American museums in the past few decades have transformed themselves into cultural centers with music, theater, motion pictures, the dance, and other performing arts programs. State museum organizations send concerts, plays, dance groups, and lecturers on circuit, as well as traveling exhibits, sometimes contained in a "museumobile."[30]

The emphasis given educational functions by museums also had social implications. Some museums tried to reach all parts of their audience and to use their collection, research, exhibition, and interpretive functions for the benefit of the entire community. John Cotton Dana, the ingenious, innovative founder of the Newark (New Jersey) Museum in 1909, expressed his social philosophy thus:

> A *good* museum attracts, entertains, arouses curiosity, leads to questioning and thus promotes learning. It is an educational institution that is set up and kept in motion—that it may help the members of the community to become happier, wiser, and more effective human beings. Much can be done toward a realization of these objectives—with simple things—objects of nature and daily life—as well as with objects of great beauty. A museum should also reflect our industries—be stimulating and helpful to our workers and promote interest in the products of our own time. The Museum can help people only if they use it; they will use it only if they know about it and only if attention is given to the interpretation of its possessions in terms they, the people, will understand.[31]

As a result of the efforts of Dana and his successors, the Newark Museum managed to reach nearly all parts of the community, including the poor and minority groups. Not only did it build a collection of American and world art of high excellence, but it staged special exhibitions relevant to minority groups and timely for community interest. Titles of some of the subjects were: Modern Pictorial Photography; German Applied Arts; New Jersey Clay Products; Primitive African Art; Inexpensive Articles of Good Design; History of Newark; Aviation: A Newark Industry; The Human Body: How It Works; Newark of the Future; What Makes Music; Our Town; and Satellite Science. This broad, humanistic approach kept the museum close to the community and preserved its influence, even as many upper-middle-class citizens moved to suburbs, and Newark became a black city with numerous inner-city problems.

Museums like that of Newark largely avoided the criticism that they appealed only to the educated few and collected objects valued by wealthy leaders, that the immigrants, blacks, and other deprived minorities as well as the poor had been ignored, their cultural contributions and needs forgotten. Such discontent recently has led to the establishment of neighborhood museums in several slum-ridden inner cities. They are community centers that carry on varied programs that often employ museum techniques. The neighborhood museum is organized democratically and open to everyone. It conducts classes in painting, sculpture, and the crafts; presents African dances or varied musical and dramatic groups; and strives to improve the social welfare of the neighborhood. In many cases it has no collection, though it frequently borrows objects from museums. It is interested chiefly in people, not objects, and its critics say it is more of a settlement house than it is a museum.[32]

Pluralistic Museums

This rapid sketch of museum development through the ages underlines the flexible nature of the modern museum. The late Albert Ten Eyck Gardner, a curator of the Metropolitan Museum, summed up the situation well when he wrote:

> One reason that this Museum—like any major American Museum—is so complex is that its basic "personality," if it can be called that, is derived from various other, older social organizations. It is in fact a modern hybrid, bred with mingled characteristics of the cathedral, the royal palace, the theater, the school, the library, and according to some critics, the department store. As the emphasis of interest or activity shifts, the character of the organization changes. Thus when the museum serves as a place of entertainment it takes on the dramatic quality of the theater, when it is used for scholarly purposes it can become an ivory tower, when its educational activities are stressed it becomes a school. For the scientist or professor it may seem to be merely a series of specimens illustrating a seductive theory, or a library of artifacts filed in chronological order. In the family of social institutions invented by man, the place of the museum is not rigidly fixed. It is pliant and can develop in many directions, or sometimes move simultaneously in several directions.[33]

Thus we may think of the museum as collection, the museum as conservation, the museum as research, the museum as exhibition, the museum as interpretation, the museum as cultural center, and the museum as social instrument. Museum objects, so real and so convincing, constitute an important part of the human heritage and give their beholders a feeling of continuity and cultural pride. The priorities assigned to the different museum functions are important in establishing the essence of any museum, and its board of trustees, director, curators, educational staff, conservators, designers, and other specialists should all ponder its basic purposes, as well as try to find ever more effective ways of achieving them.

Obviously, the objects themselves are the heart of a museum, and their collection according to a logical over-all plan is of great importance. They also deserve the best kind of preservation and conservation that can be given them, for they constitute a precious heritage to be passed on intact to future generations. Of equal moment is the research that finds out everything possible about the discovery or creation and the provenance of each object, as well as its contributions to human knowledge. Thus the three traditional museum objectives—collection, conservation, and research—can be amply justified.

But of great significance also are the ways that objects can be used to bring understanding and appreciation to contemporary life, for, as Thomas Jefferson so cogently reminded us, "The earth belongs always to the living generation." Thus exhibition, education or interpretation, conveyance of culture, and contribution to community or social welfare are all worthy aims for the museum. The good museum will be conscious of all these purposes—traditional and educational—and devise such programs and activities as its collections, staff, and resources will allow it to pursue with excellence.

As an encouraging note, let us cite the opinion of Germain Bazin, a chief curator of the Louvre, who defines the American museum as the university of the common man. He says:

> Perhaps the most significant contribution America has made to the concept of the museum is in the field of education. It is common practice for a museum to offer lectures and concerts, show films, circulate exhibitions, publish important works of art. The museum has metamorphosed into a university for the general public—an institution of learning and enjoyment for all men. The concept has come full circle. The museum of the future will more and more resemble the academy of learning the mouseion connoted for the Greeks.[34]

2

The Art Museum

Napoleon and Marie Louise of Austria at the Louvre, 1810

Love of beauty is a basic human trait that goes back to man's earliest days on earth. The primitive Ice Age artists who created the vigorous bison and bulls, fleet horses, graceful deer, and other animals of the Lascaux or Altamira caves may have been appealing to supernatural powers to grant them good hunting and fertility or observing some since-lost traditional rites, but at the same time they took delight in combining line and color so as to please the human eye. Thus, it was natural that humankind collect and treasure paintings, sculptures, and other art objects. The ancient civilizations, whether Middle Eastern, Oriental, African, pre-Columbian American, Greek, or Roman, placed their finest productions in temple or palace treasuries. Even during the Dark Ages in western Europe, the artistic tradition was kept alive, chiefly in cathedrals, castles, and monasteries.

Collectors and Patrons

The collector was the force that made the art museum possible. Usually a prince, nobleman, high clergyman, rich merchant, or banker, he purchased or commissioned paintings, sculptures, and other beautiful and useful objects. As his collection grew, connoisseurship became his passion, and he added or discarded pieces, ever seeking the highest quality.

Jean de France, duc de Berry and brother of the French king Charles V, was a great medieval collector. At his death in 1416, he possessed a fine library, some of its bindings adorned with jewels and precious stones; handsomely illuminated manuscripts; antique gold and silver coins; cameos and intaglios; rich embroideries and fabrics; sculptures, panel paintings, and miniatures. Still he could not resist curiosities, so that he had a menagerie and a cabinet that contained ostrich eggs, shells, polar bear skins, and reputed antidotes against poison, such as bezoars–the concretions formed in the stomachs of wild goats—and unicorn horns (actually narwhal tusks).[1]

The coming of the Renaissance made Italy the center of the art world. The Medici in Florence were shrewd businessmen and bankers who for two centuries ruled city and state, erected handsome buildings, established a great library, and accumulated fabulous hoards of art objects. They tried to acquire the finest products of the Greek and Roman past, and sculptures and other antiquities, whether found above or below ground, henceforth became important collectors' items. The Medici (Riccardi) Palace in the fifteenth century was in a sense a private museum.[2] The other Italian states competed with Florence in collecting art, and the popes gradually made Rome pre-eminent. It was a virtual museum city, and soon archaeologists were unearthing its buried treasures. Sixtus IV in 1471 established a Capitoline Museum to house ancient statuary; he also forbade the exportation of antiquities from the city. Julius II obtained many rarities, including the *Apollo Belvedere* and *Laocoön*. Leo X filled the Cortile Garden near the Vatican with statues and in 1515 made Raphael his superintendent of antiquities. A dozen years later, Rome fell to a Lutheran army, and for a time leadership in art collecting moved elsewhere.[3]

Perhaps the most renowned collector of the first half of the seventeenth century was Charles I of England. As Prince of Wales, he had visited the Spanish court and sat for Velásquez. About 1627 he made an astonishing coup by purchasing for some £80,000 the collection that the Gonzaga family had accumulated at Mantua in more than a century. On the advice of Rubens, he bought Raphael's seven original cartoons for *The Acts of the Apostles* tapestries. At its height, Charles's collection contained 1,387 pictures and 399 sculptures, with works by Raphael, Correggio, Tintoretto, Titian, Leonardo, and many other Italian, German, and Flemish masters. He was also a patron of Rubens and Van Dyck. As the Reverend Mr. William Gilpin justly said: "Charles was a scholar, a man of taste, a gentleman and a Christian; he was everything but a king. The art of reigning was the only art of which he was ignorant." Two of Charles's friends and associates were also collectors—discerning Thomas Howard, earl of Arundel, and flamboyant George Francis Villiers, duke of Buckingham. But all their holdings were largely dissipated when Buckingham was assassinated, Arundel exiled to the continent, and Charles beheaded. The Puritan Parliament in the 1650s, by private sale and public auction, disposed of most of Charles's choice treasures, and many of them made their way into the possession of the king of France.[4]

The French royal art collection began to grow when the Queen Mother Marie de Medici called Rubens to Paris in 1622 to depict the most glorious scenes from her life in twenty-one great pictures. Two French prime ministers were passionate lovers of art and contended that a great collection was a valuable symbol of royal authority. Cardinal Richelieu not only helped his king acquire Italian and French art, but also constructed in Paris the Palais Cardinal (today the Palais Royal) to house his own jewels and religious plate, 500 paintings, 50 statues, bronzes, historical tapestries, textiles, furniture, and Chinese lacquers and ceramics. He left the palace and collection to the king. Richelieu's secretary and successor, Cardinal Mazarin, was a knowing connoisseur, but had some miserly attributes; he used to let his jewels flow through his hands. He feared that rival collector, Queen Christina of Sweden, and begged his business manager, Jean Baptiste Colbert, to "keep that crazy woman out of my cabinets . . . for one could so easily take some of my small paintings." When near death, Mazarin paced about his collection in his nightshirt, grieving: "I must leave all this. What trouble I had to acquire these things! I'll never see them again where I'm going." He left 546 paintings, the cream of which Louis XIV purchased. The Cologne banker Everhard Jabach, sole supplier of buff leather to royal armies, had a passion for drawings, but, during a financial crisis, sold the king 101 paintings and 5,542 drawings. Colbert himself, a skillful administrator, deserves great credit for building the royal art collection.[5]

The Hapsburgs, as Holy Roman Emperors, could draw on the German and Italian states, Spain, and the Low Countries. Rudolph II, one of the greatest connoisseurs of his day, had a magnificent collection in his Hradcany Castle in Prague. This mentally-ill emperor hid his paintings from public view. During the Thirty Years War, Gustavus Adolphus of Sweden, emulating the Roman conquerors and foreshadowing Napoleon, captured Prague and removed many of Rudolph's treasures to Stockholm. Gustavus's daughter, Queen Christina, in 1654 renounced her throne and took most of the finest Hapsburg paintings with her when she embraced Catholicism and settled in Rome. In Spain, the Hapsburgs acquired Italian, German, Flemish, and Spanish paintings for their palaces at the Prado, Escorial, and Alcazar. Charles V and Philip II had Titian as their court painter and art adviser, and Philip IV, Rubens and Velásquez. Archduke Leopold-Wilhelm at Brussels built an admirable collection of paintings (which he later took to Vienna) with David Teniers the younger as keeper and adviser.[6]

During the eighteenth century, the tide of collecting shifted to England. Her commercial empire brought the profits that enabled her nobility to build great country houses and allowed titled young Englishmen to take the Grand Tour to the continent and Italy. The stately homes of England fused the best of architecture, landscape design, paintings and sculpture, and rich furnishings into a unified, artistic style. London outstripped Amsterdam as an art market and threatened the supremacy of Paris. On the continent, Saint Petersburg joined the list of great art centers. Peter the Great acquired some art, including the solid gold jewelry found in prehistoric Siberian tombs, but Catherine the

Great was a compulsive collector, "a glutton," as she called herself. Represented at all important auctions and frequently buying collections en bloc, by 1785 she owned 2,658 paintings and, in order to house them, had begun building the Hermitage (1767) on the banks of the Neva in Saint Petersburg.[7]

Thus, during the fifteenth to eighteenth centuries, hundreds of devoted collectors gathered and preserved objects that today are found in the great art museums of the Western World. The flow of art objects from their creators through different ownerships to their present resting places has created many exciting chapters of art history.

The Earliest Museums

During the seventeenth and eighteenth centuries, private collections slowly developed into museums. Before that time, collectors had occasionally allowed visitors to see their treasures; the Medici, for example, did so at least as early as the sixteenth century. The arrangements usually were privately made and often required a large tip to a servant.[8] In Rome in 1773 Pope Clement XIV opened the Pio-Clementine Museum; it contained the Vatican collection largely as we know it today.[9] The famed Farnese collection accumulated by Cardinal Farnese (later Pope Paul III) was left to Charles of Bourbon, king of the Two Sicilies, in 1735 and formed the core of the National Museum in Naples; that museum also received much rich material excavated at Herculaneum and Pompeii.[10] The Uffizi Palace at Florence in 1743 secured the Medici collection of paintings under the will of Anna Maria Ludovica, the daughter of Cosimo III. By 1795 the Uffizi had become a true art gallery, with the paintings arranged by schools.[11]

The Hapsburg collection in Vienna under Emperor Charles VI in the 1720s had been given elaborate frames and ordered according to over-all symmetry and color, with individual paintings cut down or enlarged in size to conform to the arrangement. About 1776 the painter Rosa began to reinstall the collection in the Belevedere Palace. He called in Chrétien de Mechel from Basel, who restored the paintings to their original sizes in simple frames, arranged them chronologically according to schools, and produced a catalogue. In 1781 the public was admitted three times a week to view the collection.[12]

France was slow to show the royal holdings of pictures. Under Louis XIV, the gardens of Versailles were open to the public, and one could easily visit the palace and its paintings if equipped with a plumed hat and sword, which could be rented from the caretaker. Louis XV in 1750 exhibited 110 paintings and drawings in Paris at the Luxembourg Palace, to which the public was admitted twice a week. There was a constant agitation among the intellectuals of the Enlightenment to open a permanent picture gallery, and the Palace of the Louvre was usually suggested as the appropriate place. Diderot, in his *Encyclopédie* (1765), stated that the Louvre ought to rival the famed Mouseion of Alexandria.

Louis XVI in 1774 appointed Count d'Angiviller Director General of Public Buildings. D'Angiviller moved at once to prepare the royal collection for exhibition and eventually chose for this purpose the great gallery of the Louvre that paralleled the Seine. He had the paintings cleaned, repaired, and reframed, filled in gaps—especially of the Flemish and Dutch schools—and appointed the painter Hubert Robert keeper of the royal collection. The count created a commission of experts on museum problems. The commission prescribed overhead lighting and, for fire protection, that brick and iron be used wherever possible, as well as fire-resistant walls and a lightning conductor, an innovation popular in that day. But d'Angiviller was indecisive in carrying out the recommendations, and the gallery was not yet open when the French Revolution started.[13]

There were other scattered prototype museums. Basel probably had the first university art collection; in 1661 the city bought the Amerbach Cabinet that contained some excellent Holbeins; they were exhibited a decade later in the university library.[14] German collections were opened at Düsseldorf, Munich, Kassel, and Dresden about 1750.[15] The collection of the Tradescants became the first English museum, the Ashmolean, at Oxford University in its own building, 1683, but it was composed chiefly of natural history specimens with little art.[16] Sir Hans Sloane's collection, opened as the British Museum in 1759, contained some miniatures, drawings, and archaeological objects, but was devoted chiefly to natural history. The radical John Wilkes tried to join a National Gallery to the British Museum in 1777 with the Walpole Collection from Houghton Hall as a nucleus, but Parliament refused, and the collection went to Catherine the Great.[17]

Revolution and the Louvre

The Palace of the Louvre in Paris, opened to the public during the French Revolution, may be regarded as the first great national art museum. The cataclysm of revolution destroyed some art objects, which, of course, could be considered hated symbols of the aristocratic regime, but fortunately the leaders who overthrew the old order argued that the nation's art belonged to all the people of the new society created under the democratic ideals of liberty, equality, and brotherhood. The Louvre was to be the capstone of a system of museums to serve the common man and woman of the new Republic.

The National Museum, a "Monument Dedicated to the Love and Study of the Arts," was opened at the Louvre on August 10, 1793, the first anniversary of the fall of the monarchy. Its Grande Galerie exhibited 537 paintings on the walls and 184 art objects on tables in the middle of the hall. Three-fourths of them came from the royal palaces, most of the remainder from churches and religious orders, and a scattering from the emigrés. In the new *décade*, the ten-day period that had replaced the week, the museum reserved five days for artists and copyists, two for cleaning, and three for the general public. So popular were the public days that the crowds of visitors attracted swarms of enterprising prostitutes, and street lights had to be installed at the approaches.

The pictures were hung frame to frame from floor to ceiling by schools but within the schools according to the old miscellaneous principle; there were no labels, so that the museum was a confusing labyrinth for the untutored visitor. The hall was lighted by windows from two sides, and on bright days pictures were exposed to too much sunlight. Fortunately, Hubert Robert, former keeper of the royal collection, was respected in the new order and managed to maintain tolerable standards of housekeeping and conservation. The Louvre was in such bad structural condition that it had to be closed in May 1796, not to open fully again until July 14, 1801. The Grande Galerie was then more rationally arranged on a chronological principle; a few years later, marble columns and statues divided the long vista of the gallery, and overhead lighting was obtained.[18]

The victorious revolutionary armies brought art treasures to France. Many masterpieces were requisitioned from Antwerp, Brussels, and other cities when Belgium was overrun in 1794. The radical artist Luc Barbier, one of the requisitioning commissioners, melodramatically justified this pillage of "the immortal works left us by the brush of Rubens, Van Dyck and other founders of the Flemish school" because "it is in the bosom of free folk that the works of celebrated men should remain; the tears of slaves are unworthy of their glory."[19]

General Bonaparte's Italian campaign of 1796–1797 was even more successful in adding to the French national collections of the Louvre, the Bibliotheque Nationale, and the Jardin des Plantes. He took a commission of scholars with him—a mathematician, a chemist, a botanist, two painters, a sculptor, and an archaeologist—to appropriate "goods of artistic and scientific nature" that included books, paintings, scientific instruments, typefaces, wild animals, and natural curiosities from all over Italy. In July 1798 a triumphal procession brought the loot of the campaign to Paris, enormous chariots bearing the paintings in huge packing cases, labeled with large letters, and massive carts transporting statues decked with laurel wreaths, flowers, and flags. There were exotic animals in cages and camels led by their keepers. Military detachments, members of the Institut de France, museum administrators, art professors, and typesetters marched in the parade. The vehicles formed a circle on the Champs de Mars three lines deep around a monument to Liberty, amid the thundering cheers of the packed spectators. Among the choicest items were the famed four *Bronze Horses* from Saint Mark's Basilica in Venice; they were placed above the Arc de Triomphe of the Carousel in the Tuilleries Gardens. The Louvre received the *Apollo Belvedere, Laocoön, Dying Gaul,* Raphael's *Transfiguration,* and Correggio's *Saint Jerome.*[20]

One blessing may have arisen from this seizure of art by the French armies. Many of the paintings were in bad repair, not having been treated since their creation. A conservation workshop in the Louvre knew how to clean and restore paintings and understood the rebacking process that had been perfected in Italy and France about fifty years earlier. At any rate, the French authorities used conservation partially to justify their confiscation of the paintings.[21]

Napoleon and National Glory

Shortly before Napoleon decided to invade Egypt in 1798, he met Baron Dominique Vivant-Denon at a party. Denon was a charmer, a favorite of Madame de Pompadour. He had held diplomatic posts in Russia at the Court of Catherine the Great, in Switzerland, and at Naples. Napoleon and Denon became close friends, and Denon, though in his fifties, went on the Egyptian campaign. His scholarship helped Napoleon choose superb museum objects, including the Rosetta Stone that was afterwards captured on its way to France by Lord Nelson and sent to the British Museum. Denon also aroused general admiration by his reckless coolness under fire. In 1800 Napoleon visited the Louvre for the first time and soon insisted that Denon be placed in charge of the museums of France and of all artistic services. In 1803 the Louvre became the Musée Napoleon, a name it retained until the emperor's downfall.

Denon made a superb museum director. Endowed with brilliant imagination, personable address, and restless energy, he fought successfully to win appropriations for the Louvre and to make it the greatest picture gallery the world had ever seen. Painters and sculptors from all over Eurpoe flocked to view its holdings. Denon used the Salon Carré as a recent accessions room to show off the latest looted masterpieces. In one part of the Grande Galerie, he exhibited sixteen paintings by Raphael, grouped around the great *Transfiguration*. The Louvre also had more than four hundred statues, busts, and bas reliefs, and only Nelson's victory at Trafalgar kept Lord Elgin's Parthenon marbles from Denon's custody.

Always the accomplished courtier, Denon made the most of the requisitioned masterpieces; thus in 1803 he saved the unveiling of the *Venus de Medici* from Florence for Napoleon's birthday. Occasionally, he had trouble with his patron. In 1810 Napoleon gave him three weeks' notice that his marriage to Marie Louise of Austria was to take place in the Salon Carré and the wedding procession was to pass through the Grande Galerie before six thousand spectators. When Denon protested that *The Marriage at Cana* by Veronese was too large to move from the gallery, Napoleon suggested that he could burn it. Denon took some of the larger canvases off their stretchers and rolled them; he covered others with handsome cloths. The wedding was a memorable spectacle.[22]

Napoleon and Denon, between them, devised a comprehensive museum system for France and her conquered satellites. Denon always sought the greatest masterpieces for the Louvre, but Napoleon made the final decisions, based on political expediency. As early as 1800, he had agreed to place paintings in the provincial cities of France that then included Brussels, Mainz, and Geneva. Eventually twenty-two cities benefited from the distribution of 1,508 paintings. Several museums were planned for Italian cities, though only the Brera Gallery in Milan, opened in 1809, was successfully organized; it received confiscations from throughout northern Italy. Napoleon's raids in Germany and Austria produced booty that included 299 pictures from Kassel, 60 from Berlin and Potsdam, and 250 from the Belvedere Palace in Vienna.

Sometimes, reaction against French looting led to the establishment of museums. Thus, Louis Napoleon, king of Holland, founded the Koninklijk Museum (forerunner of the present Rijksmuseum) at Amsterdam in 1808. In Madrid, Joseph Bonaparte, king of Spain, worked with the artist Goya to keep the finest Spanish paintings from the clutches of Napoleon and Denon; later, in 1819, the collection was installed in the Prado and opened to the public. In 1813 Wellington captured paintings from the royal collection taken by Joseph on his flight from Spain. The duke offered to return them, but the Spanish government gave the 165 paintings to him. Today they repose in London as the Wellington Museum at Apsley House.[23]

But those who live by the sword and the requisition shall perish by the sword and the requisition. When Napoleon was finally defeated at Waterloo in 1815, the paintings and art objects he had seized began to flow back to their previous owners. Not all of them returned; Denon's conveniently poor memory of their location saved a few, and most of those taken from churches and monasteries remained. But in all, the French museums gave up 2,065 pictures and 130 sculptures, including, of course, the *Bronze Horses, Apollo Belvedere,* and *Laocoön*. With tears of frustration in their eyes, the French people saw many treasures leave the acknowledged art capital of the world. Never again would so many masterpieces of painting and sculpture be on view in a single institution. Napoleon indeed had made great art and the museum symbols of national glory, a concept that was to persist into the twentieth century of Hitler and Goering.[24]

Golden Age for Art Museums

The violent and democratizing changes in European life brought about by both political and industrial revolution were accompanied by a steady growth of public art museums, and the nineteenth century sometimes is considered the museum's golden age. Nearly every country in western Europe built a comprehensive collection of masterpiece art that extended from ancient times to the present. Usually a royal collection formed its nucleus, but the determined efforts of museum directors, sharpened by the development of the new science of archaeology and the systematic study of art history, greatly enlarged the scope and improved the exhibition methods of the museums.

In France the Louvre enjoyed rapid growth and soon filled the gaps in its galleries left by the return of the Napoleonic additions. In the international competition for archaeological discoveries, the Louvre got thousands of Greek vases and bronzes, the best Egyptian collection outside Cairo, and such striking individual masterpieces as the *Venus de Milo* and the *Nike* from Samothrace. Napoleon III completed the Louvre complex so as to provide badly needed exhibition, storage, and administrative space. He acquired a rich collection of paintings and art objects from the Marquis Campana in Rome, for a time shown as the Musée Napoleon III. Just before the fall of the empire in 1869, Dr. Louis La Caze of Paris left the Louvre the greatest gift it had ever received—802 paintings, of which he wished 302 distributed in the provinces. Public funds and private gifts—the organization called Friends of the Louvre was formed in 1897—continued to add to its comprehensive holdings.[25]

Great Britain did not establish its National Gallery in London until 1824. For forty years, efforts had been made to secure an art museum for the nation, and in the end the Royal Academy (1768) and the British Institution (1805) marshaled enough sentiment to carry the day. The National Gallery was unusual in that it did not grow from a royal collection. The fact that thirty-eight great pictures collected by the late John Julius Angerstein were up for sale triggered the establishment of the gallery; Sir George Beaumont, himself a collector of note, persuaded the prime minister, Lord Dover, to have the nation pay £57,000 for the Angerstein pictures. Soon, the present building of the National Gallery was under construction at Trafalgar Square, to be opened by Queen Victoria in 1838. The gallery admitted the public four days per week, but the rooms were often dark because no artificial light was provided; on two days, not more than fifty students were allowed to copy the pictures. The gallery also closed on Sundays and for six weeks each year for cleaning purposes. Until after World War I, the pictures were crowded together from floor to ceiling. An outstanding director of the gallery at mid-century was Charles Lock Eastlake, a painter and pioneer student of painting conservation. All in all, British collectors and artists generously supported the National Gallery, which may claim to represent most comprehensively the history of European painting.[26]

In Germany, the Hohenzollerns of Prussia backed the creation of one of the world's greatest museum centers in Berlin on a peninsula formed by the Spree and Kupfergraben rivers. This Museum Island, as it was called, contained an Alte Museum (1830) built around the collection of an eccentric English connoisseur, Edward Solly, who sold three thousand paintings to Frederick William III; a Neue Museum (1859) with Egyptian collection, antique ceramics, and national antiquities; a National Galerie (1876) for modern German art; the Kaiser Friederich Museum of Western Art (1904); and the Schloss Museum (1921), the royal Hohenzollern Castle turned into a Museum for the Decorative Arts. Most impressive of all was a group of monumental buildings (1907–1930) that contained the Pergamon Museum, with its Great Altar of Pergamon, one wing devoted to the Museum of German Art and another to the Near East Museum. Many of the buildings of the island complex were connected by covered footbridges. Dr. Wilhelm von Bode joined the staff of the museums in 1872 and served for fifty years, after 1905 as general director. A learned art historian with encyclopedic knowledge of the art market and great diplomatic and administrative talent, he raised the Berlin museums to the high levels attained by those of Paris and London.

The rise of Hitler brought increasing disaster to the Museum Island. Ludwig Justi, the long-respected director of the National Galerie, was dismissed, "degenerate" modern art was removed and in some cases destroyed, and many Jewish staff members were discharged. World War II entirely ruined the Neue Museum and Schloss Museum; other buildings were gutted by fire, and 1,353 paintings were lost. The partition of Berlin brought further trouble, for the Museum Island was situated in East Berlin. Many of its holdings had been stored in salt mines or other sanctuaries. Those captured by the Western armies went to West Germany, and thus a great many paintings once on the island are today housed in West Berlin's Museum Dahlem. The Russians took many of the collections with them for safekeeping but returned them in excellent condition to East Germany in 1958.

Justi came back to the Museum Island as director in 1948 and with his devoted staff worked hard to restore the museums to their former appearance. The Kaiser Wilhelm Museum was fittingly renamed the Bode Museum. Work on the Pergamon Museum, National Galerie, and Alte Museum was substantially completed. Once more the Museum Island is open to the public, with most of its greatest treasures restored and in place. They include the Facade of the Kassite Temple of Uruk (c. 1415 B.C.); the Processional Way, Ishtar Gate, and Old Palace Throne Room of Babylon (c. 580 B.C.); the Great Altar of Pergamon (180–160 B.C.); the Market Gate of Miletus (c. A.D. 165); the Facade of the Mshatta Desert Palace (743–744); and the Prayer Niche from the Maydan Mosque of Kashan (1226).[27]

Munich is virtually a museum city, for King Louis I of Bavaria planned to make it a second Rome. The Glyptothek (1830) contains the Aeginetan pediments from the Temple of Aphaia; the Alte Pinakothek (1836), a rich collection of old masters; and the Neue Pinakothek (1853), the Schack Gallery, and New State Gallery, more modern art. The Bavarian National Museum (1867) has historical paintings, decorative art, and period rooms, and the Residence, the former palace opened as a museum in 1920, possesses a rich treasury of exquisitely jeweled pieces. Dresden had a great picture gallery and other museum rarities that are still intact, though this East German city suffered the worst air raids of World War II.[28]

Catherine's huge collection in the Hermitage at Saint Petersburg (today Leningrad) was more properly housed in a great palace built by Czar Nicholas I in the 1840s. The Berlin museum director and art historian Gustav Waagen was called in to arrange the pictures and do a catalogue (1863). Visitors were allowed, but up until 1866, they needed to wear full dress, on the theory that they were visiting the czar and only incidentally the museum. The czars continued to collect great masterpieces, and the coming of the 1917 revolution gave the new Soviet Union control of rich art collections from throughout the old empire. Museums, historical monuments, and art treasures were nationalized. Some old masters were sold to raise much-needed funds for economic necessities, but the Hermitage remains one of the greatest art museums of the world, with Scythian goldwork; Greek vases obtained from sites on the northern Black Sea coast; Oriental, Egyptian, Babylonian, Assyrian, Near East, and Russian antiquities; and a comprehensive painting collection of high excellence.[29]

A specialized form of art museum collected and exhibited modern art, as, for example, the Luxembourg Palace (1818) in Paris, superseded by the National Museum of Modern Art (1937), recently moved to the new Centre Georges Pompidou, or Beaubourg; the Neue Pinakothek (1853) in Munich; the National Galerie (1876) in Berlin; and the National Gallery of British Art (1897) in London, now the Tate Gallery.[30] Another specialized museum was devoted to the decorative arts—architecture, furniture, metalwork, ceramics, glass, textiles, and the like. The Great Exhibition at South Kensington in London, the first true world's fair, in 1851 was enormously successful, and the profits (some £186,000) were used to acquire land for a group of museums in the South Kensington area. One of them finally evolved into the Victoria and Albert Museum in 1909. In France, a world's fair at Paris in 1855 inaugurated a similar interest in the decorative arts, and the Central Society of Decorative Arts established a museum in 1882, later moved to the Marsan Pavilion of the Louvre. Berlin and Vienna also had such museums.[31]

American Models

The art museum was slow to develop in the United States. Pierre Eugène du Simitière and Charles Willson Peale had portraits in their Philadelphia collections in the 1780s, but regarded them more as historical documents than as works of art. So also did the early historical societies, though the New-York Historical Society (1804) had secured the Luman Reed and Thomas J. Bryan collections of American paintings and European old masters by the 1860s. The society planned a museum of antiquities, science, and art, but failed to raise the necessary funds. The Pennsylvania Academy of the Fine Arts (1805) in Philadelphia not only conducted an art school and held annual exhibitions, but also acquired an outstanding collection of American paintings and sculpture. The Boston Athenaeum (1807), though essentially a library, collected paintings and sculptures that it later turned over to the newly established Museum of Fine Arts. In 1832 Yale built the pioneer American college gallery to house the historical paintings of Colonel John Trumbull. Perhaps the first true and continuing art museum in the country was the Wadsworth Atheneum (1842) at Hartford, Connecticut, which displayed about eighty works by Trumbull, Thomas Cole, and other Americans.[32]

The year 1870 saw a break-through for American art museums, with the establishment of the Metropolitan Museum of Art in New York and the Museum of Fine Arts in Boston. They were followed within the decade by the Corcoran Gallery of Art in Washington, the Pennsylvania (now Philadelphia) Museum of Art, and the Art Institute of Chicago. Other leading encyclopedic art collections in the United States today include the Brooklyn Museum (1893), Cleveland Museum of Art (1916), and National Gallery of Art (1937) in Washington.[33]

A closer examination of the Metropolitan and the Museum of Fine Arts will reveal the chief forces in the development of comprehensive American art museums. The purposes of the Metropolitan, clearly expressed in Joseph C. Choate's dedication speech of 1880, were to

> gather together a more or less complete collection of objects illustrative of the history of art in all its branches, from the earliest beginnings to the present time, which should serve not only for the instruction and entertainment of the people, but also show to the students and artisans of every branch of industry, in the high and acknowledged standards of form and color, what the past has accomplished for them to imitate and excel.[34]

The Metropolitan was greatly influenced by the South Kensington (today the Victoria and Albert) Museum in London, as also was the Museum of Fine Arts, one of whose founders wrote: "The designer needs a museum of art, as the man of letters needs a library, or the botanist a herbarium."[35] Both museums agreed that few masterpieces were available to them, and in the field of sculpture, they began to gather plaster casts of famed originals. A delay in the arrival by sea of fifty cases of casts and an amusing debate about the placement of fig leaves on nude statues accompanied the opening of the Museum of Fine Arts, and in 1883 the first large money bequest to the Metropolitan was earmarked for the purchase of architectural casts.[36]

The Metropolitan Museum and the American Museum of Natural History were responsible for a partnership arrangement between city government and private board of trustees that has been followed by nearly one hundred American museums, though not by the Museum of Fine Arts, which has refused until recently to accept public funds. The two New York museums in 1871 planned to erect a building together and secured the signatures of the owners of more than half of the real estate of the city on a petition asking the state legislature to authorize the city to tax itself $500,000 for this purpose. The two boards sent emissaries to visit William Marcy Tweed, the city's representative in Albany. Impressed by the standing of the petitioners, "Boss" Tweed had Peter Barr Sweeney, the city chamberlain, reputed to be the brains of the Tweed Ring, work out an important compromise under which the city agreed to erect and take title to the building (and later to maintain it), and the trustees would own and control the collections. As it turned out, the two museums built separate structures, but an important pattern of museum organization had been established.[37]

The Metropolitan and the Museum of Fine Arts have helped define what a comprehensive art museum should contain. General Louis P. di Cesnola, who became the first director of the Metropolitan in 1879, had been the United States consul on the island of Cyprus; he sold the Metropolitan two collections of classical antiquities he had excavated and also sold a smaller accumulation to the Boston museum. J. P. Morgan became president of the Metropolitan in 1904, and by the time of his death in 1913, the museum had acquired important Greek art, made numerous archaeological expeditions to Egypt, secured an outstanding collection of armor, and received the Benjamin Altman bequest of about two thousand masterpiece paintings and Chinese porcelains valued at $15 million. Morgan himself shocked the Metropolitan by failing to leave it his own collection, perhaps the greatest assembled in modern times, though his son eventually donated about 40 percent of its treasures.[38]

In 1924 the president of the Metropolitan, Robert W. de Forest, and Mrs. de Forest gave the museum its American Wing, which housed colonial and federal period rooms and a distinguished collection of decorative arts. The American Wing has had great influence upon both art and history museums, and this kind of collection reached new heights with the opening of the Henry Francis du Pont Winterthur Museum in Delaware in 1951. In 1938 the Metropolitan also added to its exhibits the Cloisters, on a lofty site in Fort Tryon Park facing the Hudson River. George Gray Barnard, the sculptor, had begun this collection of architectural elements and sculpture from medieval cloisters, and John D. Rockefeller, Jr., presented the park to the city and paid for erecting, furnishing, and endowing the Cloisters. During World War II a great collection of musical instruments, acquired as early as 1889, was rejuvenated and beautifully displayed at the Metropolitan; in 1941 a Junior Museum was established with its own exhibits and support facilities; and in 1946 the Metropolitan absorbed the ten-year-old Museum of Costume Art and installed it as the Costume Institute with sixteen thousand items dating from 1690. Recently, the Metropolitan has carried out a major expansion of its building with a greatly enlarged American Wing and new wings for the Robert Lehman Collection of three thousand items of paintings, tapestries, bronzes, and other objects; for Nelson A. Rockefeller's vast collection of primitive art; and for the Temple of Dendur from Egypt. The museum has been well described as "a sort of cultural coral reef, always growing and changing."[39]

The Museum of Fine Arts in Boston did not have the great wealthy patrons of the Metropolitan but, instead, had a host of devoted, well-to-do collectors who worked with knowledgeable curators to build a strong collection. The most remarkable of its holdings and perhaps the finest in the world is its Oriental art. Edward S. Morse and Ernest Fenollosa of Salem and Dr. William Sturgis Bigelow of Boston in the 1870s and '80s journeyed to Japan to collect ceramics, statuary, and paintings that eventually went to the museum, and Chinese, Korean, Indian, and other Near and Far Eastern art found an appreciative home there. The museum also acquired Egyptian materials, mainly through Harvard-Boston archaeological expeditions, and was for a time the leading purchaser of Greek, Roman, and Etruscan antiquities. In addition to a comprehensive collection of European and American painting, the museum's holdings of textiles, American decorative arts, and prints are of high quality. Its building on the Fenway, opened in 1908, was planned with great care and constituted a noble experiment in trying to separate the more popular display of outstanding masterpieces from study collections accessible to scholars.[40]

These recitals of American collecting could be multiplied manyfold, for by 1971–1972 there were 340 art museums in the United States. The combination of private beneficence, city maintenance, and federal tax laws that encouraged private support had produced some of the greatest art museums of the world. And not only encyclopedic art museums, but also three museums of modern art that have made New York City the center of today's art world. First came the Museum of Modern Art, familiarly known as MOMA (1929). Founded by Miss Lizzie Bliss, Mrs. John D. Rockefeller, Jr., and Mrs. Cornelius J. Sullivan, it hired a dynamic director, Alfred H. Barr, Jr. He sold New Yorkers on French postimpressionism (Cézanne, Seurat, Van Gogh, Gauguin, Picasso, and others) and on Bauhaus modernism, bringing together the visual arts, including architecture, industrial design, film, photography, graphics, and typography. At about the same time, Mrs. Gertrude Vanderbilt Whitney, assisted by the energetic and witty Mrs. Juliana Force, crowned their efforts to assist American militantly modern painters by establishing the Whitney Museum of American Art (1930). Still another aspect of modern art—this one glorifying the abstract art of Wassily Kandinsky and others—was served with the opening of the Solomon R. Guggenheim Museum (1939), financed by Guggenheim and directed by Hilla Rebay, baroness von Ehrenwiesen. These three museums were largely responsible for the enthusiasm of Americans for modern art and the rise of the New York School of Abstract Expressionism. They continue to give radical artists opportunities to show their work, though the difficulty of exhibiting their growing collections reminds one of Gertrude Stein's alleged remark that a museum can either be a museum or be modern, but it cannot be both.[41]

Educational Purpose

The charter or constitution of nearly every American art museum puts emphasis upon its educational aims—often specialized teaching for artists, craftsmen, and industrial designers but always general instruction for the public. In the 1870s the contemplation of art was sometimes considered a means of fighting vice and crime by providing "attractive entertainment of an innocent and improving character." Classes for artists and craftsmen and lecture series for the public were established at once, and comprehensive educational programs with emphasis upon co-operation with the public schools soon followed. Henry Watson Kent, appointed assistant secretary of the Metropolitan Museum in 1905, brought order and efficiency to its total operation, but was especially devoted to the educational program. Soon made supervisor of education, Kent organized gallery lectures, a lantern-slide collection, publications including a *Bulletin*, programs for visiting school groups, traveling exhibitions to schools, Saturday-morning story hours (sometimes with costumed clowns), and radio programs for handicapped children. Today the Metropolitan has not only a separate Junior Museum but a varied educational program that reaches numerous students and adult groups from preschool to postgraduate.[42]

The Museum of Fine Arts, in carrying out its aim "of offering instruction in the Fine Arts," promptly opened a School of Drawing and Painting in 1876, and then its secretary, Benjamin Ives Gilman, starting in 1906, established a lecture room, published a handbook, and appointed a docent who would take groups of ten persons on one-hour interpretive tours every Tuesday, Thursday, and Saturday morning. On Thursday afternoons curators and visiting scholars would hold conferences to discuss the collections, and storytelling sessions were provided for disadvantaged children.[43] Almost every American museum today offers a broad-based educational program, and an in-depth survey in 1971–1972 found that 92 percent of art museum directors rated as very important the provision of educational experiences for the public.[44]

Problems of the Art Museum

The art museum has had considerable difficulty in appearing relevant to the general public. In 1867 Honoré Daumier drew a caricature of a French working-class family gazing at an Egyptian frieze of gods with human torsos but heads of pigs, cocks, elephants, and storks; one of the family was remarking: "The Egyptians certainly weren't good-looking." A recent French study found that art museums were only appreciated by the more elevated classes of society, and that two-thirds of the ordinary visitors were confused, bored, and unable to recall the name of a single work or artist that had impressed them. On the other hand, recent surveys in New York City and upstate Rochester have found art museum audiences praising museums heartily and visiting them frequently. Still, museum boards of trustees today often are accused of elitism, and with museum support coming more from public funds or entrance fees, greater relevance and even decentralization of holdings is demanded for minority, ethnic, poor, and disadvantaged groups.[45]

The place of modern art in museum collections and modern artists in museum programs often presents a prickly problem. The Museum of Modern Art and the Whitney Museum were organized to collect contemporary art when the staid Metropolitan was reluctant to do so. In 1947 the three museums agreed to a loose designation of collecting fields, from which the Whitney withdrew in a year and the Modern after five years. The Metropolitan set up its own Department of Contemporary Art in 1967. The Cleveland Museum of Art (1916) purchased contemporary art from the beginning, especially from its May Show for Cleveland artists; despite public criticism of "art by anthropoid apes," "dirty and foul canvases," "degenerate art," and "meaningless emptiness," the museum always has exhibited abstract and other modern art. One director said, perhaps somewhat sadly, "There is nothing which says that a work of art is only something which we can recognize."[46]

The museum's pluralistic purposes also create difficulties. When an art museum needs to choose among the functions of collection, conservation, research, exhibition, and interpretation, and today perhaps also the performing arts, community services to disadvantaged and minority groups, and multimedia happenings, the less spectacular activities, especially conservation and research, may be neglected.

American art museums have developed differing and sometimes conflicting philosophies about their aims. Benjamin Ives Gilman of Boston insisted that art museums differ from science and history museums in that their collections exist to allow their viewers to experience beauty rather than to convey information. This aesthetic emphasis in a sense meant "art for art's sake," not education. John Cotton Dana of Newark had a very different idea—to emphasize art in the everyday activities of the community, to make immigrant and minority groups as well as factory workers proud of their culture and their products, to show how even wares sold in five- and ten-cent stores could be well designed; in short, to define the museum as an instrument for community betterment. Francis Henry Taylor of the Metropolitan added still another dimension to the argument, namely, that art objects are important and veracious documents of culture history. He held that items of lesser quality were as necessary for an art museum as outstanding creations. "Beautiful and important as it is, the masterpiece cannot stand alone. It is a prima donna which must have a supporting cast and chorus to speak authoritatively for the time and place of its creation." Taylor also joined Dana in urging museums to render more adequate service to the ordinary visitors, who had become bored and "had their bellyfull of prestige and pink Tennessee marble." Sherman E. Lee, director of the Cleveland Museum of Art, has decided that the museum has three functions—preservation, exhibition, and research and education—and that the greatest of these is preservation, "the basic need of the present *and of posterity*." One should notice, of course, that all of these writers with their differing points of view still pay allegiance to education as a basic museum purpose. Gilman, though insistent that art objects in themselves were aesthetic rather than educational, organized the first docents. Taylor moved the Metropolitan forward in providing broad educational offerings for many parts and all ages of its audience. Lee, though opposed to much gallery interpretation and to peripheral museum happenings, continues to build his museum's pioneering educational programs and has provided them with a beautifully designed and functional educational wing.[47]

The spread of art museums and art centers throughout the United

States has brought many practical operating problems. Usually communities and patrons have been more than willing to raise funds for impressive buildings, but securing worthwhile collections becomes ever more difficult as the prices of old masters and modern art zoom upward. It is also hard to obtain well-trained directors and curators to lead museums with undistinguished collections.[48]

Despite problems and the rapid rate of change, the art museum has come a long way since the Louvre opened its doors to the public. Great comprehensive collections have been gathered in many treasure houses in both Europe and the New World. Modern science has devised ingenious methods of conservation, and scholars, designers, and educators have used art objects to make visual beauty intelligible to a large audience. In fact, the public response to exhibitions and educational programs is so great as to bring huge crowds that almost swamp many museums. Clearly, the art museum has a respected place in modern society, and humankind still responds to the aesthetic and cultural appeal of art objects.

3

The Natural History Museum

The Museum of Ole Worm, Copenhagen, 1655

The early medieval and renaissance collectors gathered natural curiosities thought to have magical powers to promote healing, longevity, fertility, and sexual virility. During the sixteenth and seventeenth centuries, the collections showed signs of becoming research centers, since they provided important documents for the scientist—rocks and minerals, fossils and shells, anatomical and botanical specimens, and stuffed animals and fishes from all over the world. By the nineteenth century, the natural history museum had become a leading research resource for geologists, paleontologists, botanists, zoologists, anthropologists, and other scientists. And it enjoyed great popularity with the general public that sought to understand humanity's place in the universe and "the Wonderful World of Nature."

Collections of Natural Curiosities

Many of the holdings of the early museums seem strange indeed to the modern naturalist. The fabulous unicorn's horn, thought capable of foiling poisoners or assassins, was worth a fortune, though no such beast existed; horns of rhinoceros or other animals were used, as well as the sea unicorn (narwhal) or fossils. Giants' bones were found in many a collection, though they actually might be of mammoths, elephants, or fossil remains. Egyptian mummies were greatly prized, and mummy powder (sometimes a criminal's body treated with bitumen) was sold by apothecaries to staunch the flow of blood or heal bruises and fractures. Human skulls and human skin, the best grades supposed to come from unburied corpses, were used for medicinal cures, as were stag and elk antlers. Figured stones included fossils, thunderbolts (actually the axeheads of primitive man), and serpents' tongues (in reality fossil teeth of sharks). Barnacles were observed to have the shape of small geese and were thought to be born in decayed wood; barnacle geese became another medicinal source used by apothecaries.[1]

In the sixteenth and seventeenth centuries, an astonishingly large number of collections of curiosities was found in every western European country. Conrad Gesner, the Zurich physician sometimes called "the Father of Zoology," in about 1550 had one of the first museums devoted chiefly to natural history; his collection was combined with one belonging to Felix Platter, remnants of which are found today in the

Natural History Museum in Basel. Ulisse Aldrovandi had a large museum at Bologna that early in the seventeenth century was joined to one of Ferdinando Cospi and acquired by the City of Bologna.[2]

The seventeenth century saw technical improvements in handling zoological specimens. The use of spirits of wine made preservation in liquid possible; cheap flint glass enabled wet specimens to be viewed more easily; and wax or mercury could be injected into vascular systems so as to exhibit specimens dry. Ole Worm, physician, scientist, and founder of prehistoric archaeology, had a museum at Copenhagen, as did King Christian V. The Amsterdam collections of Bernhardus Paludanus, Frederick Ruysch, and Albert Seba found their way to the Imperial Palace in Saint Petersburg.[3]

Important centers of scientific research developed in Italy. At Bologna the Aldrovandi-Cospi collection was joined by the Instituto dele Scienze of the Conte de Luigi Ferdinando Marsigli. The Medici in Florence collected natural science specimens as well as art. Ferrante and Francesco Imperati had a well-known museum at Naples, while the Jesuit Athanasius Kircher, who considered Noah's Ark to have been the most complete natural history museum, was director of the Museo Kircheriano, still extant today in Rome.[4]

The collectors gave considerable thought to the classification and arrangement of their treaures. Caspar F. Neickel in his *Museographia,* printed at Leipzig in 1727, recommended six shelves around the room. Natural objects should go on one side with human anatomy, including skeletons and mummies, on the top shelf, and quadrupeds, fishes, and minerals below. Another wall was to hold man-made objects with ancient and modern productions separated. The short end of the room opposite the entrance and lighted by three windows contained cabinets for coins. Portraits of famous men occupied the space above the shelves. Ole Worm's Museum in Copenhagen used three continuous shelves and suspended from the ceiling or mounted on the walls large objects such as stuffed crocodiles, a polar bear, skeletons, arms and armor, and an Eskimo kayak. The Imperati museum in Naples presented a similar appearance, while an Egyptian mummy at the entrance lured the visitor into the Museo Kircheriano.[5]

The Ashmolean Museum

The first public natural history museum was established at Oxford University in 1683. Two remarkable gardeners, the John Tradescants, father and son, may be considered its founders. The elder Tradescant laid out gardens for several English noblemen and journeyed to Flanders, France, Russia, Algeria, and the Mediterranean as far east as Turkey to bring back trees and plants chosen for their beauty and rarity rather than their medicinal qualities. In 1626 he moved to South Lambeth, outside London; his house, known as "Tradescant's Ark," was filled with his renowned Cabinet of Rarities and surrounded by a fine garden.

In 1656 the younger Tradescant issued *Musaeum Tradescantium,* a catalogue of the collection that listed preserved birds, animals, fish, and insects; minerals and gems; fruits; carvings, turnings, and paintings; weapons; costumes; household implements; coins and medals; and beautiful and exotic plants, shrubs, and trees. The garden was especially strong in Virginia materials, many of them gathered by the son on three trips he made there. Typical rarities in the collection were "unicornu marinum" (narwhal); "dodar, from the Island Mauritius" (the famed, now-extinct dodo); "a cherry-stone, upon one side *S. Geo*: and the Dragon perfectly cut; and on the other side 88 Emperour's faces"; "*Pohaton*, King of *Virginia's* habit all embroidered with shells, or Roanoke"; "Henry the 8 his Stirrups, Haukes-hoods, Gloves"; and "*Anne* of *Bullens* Night-vayle embroidered with silver."

Elias Ashmole, smooth-talking lawyer, amateur scientist, and collector, had helped his friend Tradescant issue the catalogue. When John died in 1662, a sad story unfolded. He and his second wife Hester had signed a deed of gift for the collection to Ashmole in 1659, but Tradescant's will left the rarities to Hester during her lifetime and then to Oxford or Cambridge. Ashmole won a chancery suit to establish his ownership, though Hester could keep the collection for life. When she began to sell off items, Ashmole built a house next door; he also successfully sued to stop her circulating malicious libels about him. In 1678 the troubled Hester drowned herself, and the rarities passed to Ashmole.

Ashmole gave the collection to Oxford but required the university to put up a special museum building to house the twenty cartloads of the Tradescant accumulation, to which he added books and coins of his own. The museum was on the upper floor, a school of natural science below it presided over by Dr. Robert Plot, keeper of the museum and professor of chemistry, and a chemistry laboratory in the basement. The whole was called the Ashmolean Museum, though some thought it might better have been named for the Tradescants. The museum printed regulations on its use in Latin in 1714. Only one group was admitted at a time, and entrance fees were in proportion to the time spent on the guided tours, though groups received a discount. Unfortunately, the Tradescant dodo, in mouldy condition, was ordered removed and burnt in 1755, though the head and one foot were salvaged from the flames.

The old Ashmolean building (now the Museum of the History of Science) is still extant today beside the Sheldonian Theatre on Broad Street. Its contents have been scattered—the geological and physical collection to the Clarendon Building, the ethnographic specimens to the Pitt Rivers Museum, natural history material to the University Museum, and the books and manuscripts to the Bodleian Library. The new Ashmolean Museum of Art and Archaeology (1894) is a general collection of art, antiquities, and numismatics with a few items related to its predecessor, including portraits of the Tradescant family and of Ashmole, and the shell-embroidered mantle said to have belonged to Powhatan.[6]

The British Museum and Others

The British Museum, the first great national museum in the world, was founded by the House of Commons in 1753 as a combined national library and general museum that soon became especially strong in collections of antiquities, natural history, and ethnography. The man behind the museum part of the enterprise was Sir Hans Sloane, eminent physician and observant naturalist and scientist. Sloane began collecting during his medical studies in France and his sojourn of more than a year, from 1687 to 1689, in Jamaica as physician to its governor, the duke of Albemarle.[7]

Sloane as physician attended various members of the royal family, and he knew intimately the great men of his day—Isaac Newton, John Locke, John Ray, Samuel Pepys, and many others. He served as president of the Royal Society in succession to Newton and of the Royal College of Physicians. He was best known for his collection that was a kind of private museum housed in his home at the present Bloomsbury Place in London, expanding into a rented house next door, and in 1742 accompanying him in his retirement to a manor house he had purchased in Chelsea. Sloane's collection attracted many distinguished visitors—among others, Voltaire, Benjamin Franklin, Linnaeus, and Handel. The great composer angered Sloane by putting down a buttered muffin on one of his rare volumes.[8]

Wits and poets had fun with Sloane. One of them mocked him: "Was ever year unblest as this, he'll cry/It has not brought us one new butterfly." Another referred to "Dear Doctor" with his quaint "knick knackatory." James Salter, probably an old retainer of Sloane's, even set up a comic museum in his Don Saltero's Coffee-House in Chelsea. It contained an asbestos purse from North America that Franklin had sold Sloane but also such fakery as "the Queen of Sheba's Fan and Cordial Bottle" and "Pontius Pilate's Wife's Chambermaid's Sister's Hat." Salterno printed a satirical catalogue of his collection.[9]

At his death in 1753, Sloane's natural history collection was enormous—a herbarium of 334 large folio volumes of dried plants; 12,500 vegetable specimens; zoological objects; and stones, minerals, shells, and fossils—without doubt the finest in the world. Then there were 50,000 volumes, including 7,000 manuscripts; 23,000 coins and medals; classical, medieval, and oriental antiquities; drawings and paintings; ethnographic objects; and mathematical instruments. All together, there were more than 80,000 objects in addition to the herbarium. Sloane had spent large sums on arranging and cataloguing his collections that had cost him at least £100,000.[10]

In his will, Sir Hans stated that he had made the collection for "the manifestation of the glory of God, the confutation of atheism and its consequences, the use and improvement of physic and other arts and sciences, and benefit of mankind." He wished it to "remain together and not be separate" in the vicinity of London with its "great confluence of people." He offered the whole for £20,000 (to be paid to his two daughters), first, to the king, and if he refused, in turn to the Royal Society, to Oxford, to the Edinburgh College of Physicians, and to royal academies of science in Paris, Saint Petersburg, Berlin, and Madrid. If none of them took the collection, it was to be sold at auction.[11]

Parliament decided to meet Sloane's terms and arranged a lottery to raise £300,000— £200,000 for prizes; £30,000 for expenses; £20,000 to the Sloane family; £10,000 to the Harley family for 8,000 volumes of the Harleian Manuscripts also to be placed in the new museum; and £40,000 for a building. The British Museum opened in 1759 in Montagu House in Bloomsbury. No admission charge was made, but tickets were required that often took several weeks and at least two visits to obtain. Armed sentries guarded the entrance after the Gordon riots of 1780; children were not admitted; and tours were hurried, lasting no more than an hour. By 1810, however, "any person of decent appearance" was admitted without a ticket during restricted hours.[12]

At first there were three departments—Manuscripts, Medals, and Coins; Natural and Artificial Productions; and Printed Books, Maps, Globes, and Drawings. A fourth—Antiquities—was added in 1807 that contained such rarities as the Rosetta Stone, the Towneley collection of Greek and Roman sculptures, bronzes, and terra-cottas, and later, the

Portland Vase and the famed Elgin Marbles from the Parthenon. Both the library and the archaeological collections with outstanding Egyptian, Babylonian, and Assyrian rarities expanded enormously and remained together at Bloomsbury in the neo-Grecian building begun by Sir Robert Smirke in 1823 and expanded often since that day. The ethnographic collection, since named the Museum of Mankind, moved in 1970 to Burlington Gardens.[13]

Captain James Cook and other explorers contributed many specimens to the British Museum, and the Royal Society turned over its collection in 1781. Sir Joseph Banks in 1820 left it a herbarium, natural history library, and botanical collection. Between 1880 and 1883 the natural history collection was transferred to a twelve-acre site in Kensington; the institution (to become independent in 1963) was known as the British Museum (Natural History). Sir William Flower, its director from 1884 to 1898, divided the collections into a selected and meaningful exhibition series and a vastly larger reserve or study series.[14]

There were also several well-known private museums. Sir Ashton Lever began with a bird collection near Manchester, moved to London in 1775, and was knighted for his natural history museum. Though he charged one-half guinea admission, he could not make a go of it, and his collection was finally sold at auction in 1806. William Bullock was more successful. He formed a collection at Sheffield, moved to Liverpool, and then came to London in 1809. Two years later he had the Egyptian Hall built in Piccadilly with an appropriate facade. He was an innovator who, like P. T. Barnum, did much to popularize museums; he devised crude habitat groups and displayed Napoleon's coach captured after Waterloo, parrots brought back by Captain Cook, Laplanders and their reindeer from Norway, and a distinguished Mexican Exhibition that he had gathered on a trip there.[15]

Continental Natural History Museums

In 1626 a royal garden of medicinal herbs, the Jardin des Plantes, was formed in Paris and soon opened to the public. Georges-Louis LeClerc, comte du Buffon, its intendant from 1739 to 1788, used it in writing his thirty-six-volume *Histoire Naturelle*. During the French Revolution in 1793, the Muséum National d'Histoire Naturelle was established there. Twelve professional chairs attached to the museum were held, over the years, by the leading French naturalists—Jussien, Geoffroy Sainte-Hillaire, Lamarck, Cuvier, Chevreul, Milne-Edwards, Quatrefages, and Marcellus Boule. The museum, situated in the sixty-acre Jardin des

Plantes, today has botanical and zoological gardens as well as pavilions of anatomy and paleontology, mineralogy and geology, botany, and zoology. Its impressive library contains 500,000 volumes and 2,500 manuscripts. Though its staff is the largest of any natural history museum and its research program continues first rate, its galleries are arranged on the old principle of showing everything and some of them are dark, confused, and dirty. In 1939 the museum's important collections devoted to ethnography, physical anthropology, prehistory, archaeology, and folklore were combined as the Musée de l'Homme.[16]

The Naturhistoriches Museum in Vienna was founded in 1748, when Emperor Francis I purchased a collection of J. de Ballou of Florence. The museum is housed today in an Italianate building (1881), situated with a twin art museum in a handsome garden. Its collections cover mineralogy, petrography, geology, paleontology, zoology, and botany. Rarities include the finest meteorites in Europe and outstanding prehistory exhibits. It has transferred superb ethnographic materials, including feather ornaments of the Aztecs, to the Museum fur Volkerkunde (1876).[17]

The closest approximation to a natural history museum in Italy today is La Spécola, the zoological museum of the University of Florence. It goes back to the Medici, but was opened to the public by Grand Duke Peter Leopold in 1775. It contains wet specimens, live reptiles and amphibians, mollusks, skeletons, dried bird and mammal skins, mounted specimens, and dioramas. Most unusual of all are wax anatomical models—twenty-five lifelike reproductions of human bodies based on dissected cadavers and more than a thousand enlargements of particular structures such as man's internal ear. They were modeled between 1770 and 1840 in the museum laboratories. This collection may someday become the basis for an Italian national museum of natural history.[18]

American Beginnings

The first permanent museum in the American English colonies was started in 1773 when the Charleston Library Society decided "to collect materials for a full and accurate natural history of South Carolina." Gentlemen were asked to send natural productions—animal, vegetable, or mineral—with careful descriptions to be looked after by four curators. The society ordered an orrery from David Rittenhouse of Philadelphia and acquired a telescope, camera obscura, hydrostatic balance, and a pair of elegant globes. Early accessions included an Indian hatchet, Hawaiian woven helmet, cassava basket from Surinam, and parts of a skull and other bones of the fossilized Guadaloupe man. In 1850 the College of Charleston agreed to house the collection, and the Charleston Museum, incorporated in 1915 with its own board of trustees, has maintained unbroken its historical primacy.[19]

Pierre Eugène du Simitière, the Swiss painter of miniatures, preserved snakes and other natural history specimens in his Curio Cabinet or American Museum opened to the public at Philadelphia in 1782. Du Simitière may have been "the nation's earliest museologist," but far more important was Charles Willson Peale, also of Philadelphia.[20] An accomplished artist, ingenious craftsman, enthusiastic student of nature, and a kind of universal scholar, Peale acquired most of du Simitière's collection in 1784 to add to some mastodon bones, a preserved paddlefish from the Allegheny River, and paintings of Revolutionary heroes on display in his home.[21] In 1786 he announced that he was forming a museum there—"a Repository for Natural Curiosities" or "the Wonderful Works of Nature"—to be arranged according to Linnaean classification. Among other exhibits was a grotto showing snakes and reptiles in natural surroundings. By 1794 the museum had outgrown Peale's house and moved to the newly completed Philosophical Hall of the American Philosophical Society; in 1802 it acquired the Long Room and Tower of what is today Independence Hall, rent-free by unanimous action of the Pennsylvania Legislature. The Philadelphia Museum or Peale's American Museum was one of the leading attractions of the city and indeed of the eastern United States.[22]

Peale was an imaginative and skilled museum director. His enthusiasm and good nature brought many gifts, and the American Philosophical Society in 1801 financed his expedition to Ulster County, New York, to exhume the bones of three "mammoths" (actually mastodons). Peale originated a habitat arrangement with curved, tastefully painted backgrounds to exhibit birds and animals showing their customary environment. He developed his own methods of taxidermy and carved larger animals of wood in natural poses to receive the skins. He used arsenic (even though it made him ill) and bichloride of mercury to protect his mounted specimens from insects. The fangs of a rattlesnake were shown under a lens, and "insects too small to be examined with the naked eye" were "placed in microscopic wheels." He also housed living animals and reptiles in the yard at Independence Hall.[23]

Peale's interest in interpreting his "School of Nature" was equally great; he was one of the first to appeal to the general public as well as to the scholar. His sons—Rembrandt, Raphaelle, Titian, and Rubens—served as assistants in Philadelphia or established branches in Baltimore and New York. The Philadelphia and Baltimore museums developed pioneer systems of gas-lighting so as to stay open at night. In addition to a framed catalogue after the Linnaean system and an eight-page guidebook, there were lectures, magic-lantern shows, and demonstrations of chemistry and physics (including electricity). Peale considered music as "the harmony of sound" akin to "the greater, deeper harmony of nature"; thus he arranged evening concerts and in 1807 added a pipe organ with eight stops.[24]

Peale's museum, however, received increasingly heavy competition from catchpenny museums and shows devoted solely to entertainment. The city of Philadelphia also took over Independence Hall and charged Peale $1,200 annual rent. The result was that the museum began to sacrifice the "rational amusement" of its educational and scientific programs to become more entertaining. By 1820 it was featuring Signor Hellene, an Italian one-man band who played the Italian viola, Turkish cymbals, tenor drum, Pandean pipes, and Chinese bells. The Peale museums went downhill rapidly after the father's death in 1827, and the Baltimore and New York ones were soon bankrupt.[25]

With so many talents for museum administration and interpretation, why did Peale's museum fail to survive? The chief answer is that he neglected to give it a nonprofit institutional form. In 1792 he announced his plans for a National Museum with an advisory board of twenty-seven visitors or directors that included Jefferson, Madison, and Hamilton. The scheme was never carried out, however, probably because Peale and later his sons were unwilling to give up the impressive income the museum generated. In 1816, for example, it had gross receipts of $11,924, indicating total paid attendance of nearly 48,000, and expenses came to only about $2,000. The net income was substantial for that day.[26]

Phineas T. Barnum took over John Scudder's American Museum in New York late in 1841. This master showman was determined to make his fortune by amusing and even bamboozling the public. He never allowed scientific principles to stand in his way. By 1845 the Philadelphia Museum had failed, and Barnum eventually acquired much of its collection as well as holdings of the Baltimore and New York branches.[27] Barnum's American Museum, with more than 600,000, accessions, included "industrious fleas," three serpents fed their noonday meals in front of the crowds, two white whales swimming in tanks of salt water, a white elephant from Siam, two orangutans, a hippopotamus ("The Great Behemoth of the Scriptures"), grizzly bears, wolves, and buffalo. In addition there were a national portrait gallery, panoramas of the Holy Land, waxwork figures showing the horrors of intemperance, and an anatomical Venus (one shilling extra). Even more spectacular were General Tom Thumb and assorted midgets, giants, and bearded ladies; Barnum's traveling circus developed from this start.[28]

Despite the emphasis on entertainment and hokum, Barnum's American Museum had serious collections of shells, fish, animals, minerals, and geological specimens. When the museum was destroyed by fire in 1865, Barnum talked of building a great new national museum in New York open to the public without charge. Henry Ward Beecher, Horace Greeley, William Cullen Bryant, and other leading New Yorkers backed the plan and urged President Andrew Johnson to instruct American ministers and consuls to help collect specimens. Nothing much came of the effort, though Barnum, in union with the Van Amburgh Menagerie Company, set up a New American Museum, which also burned, in 1868. His interest in natural history and museums continued, however, and he made gifts of animal skeletons, hides, and other materials chiefly to the Smithsonian Institution, American Museum of Natural History, and Tufts College. His chief contributions to the museum movement, however, were on the popularization and entertainment side, where his promotional talent and sense of fun were most effective.[29]

Smithsonian Institution

James Smithson, illegitimate son of an English duke and keen student of chemistry and mineralogy, at his death left a contingent bequest to "the United States of America, to found at Washington, under the name of the Smithsonian Institution, an establishment for the increase and diffusion of knowledge among men." When his heir, a nephew, died unwed and childless, the contingent inheritance became a reality. In 1835, 110 bags of gold sovereigns worth $508,318.46 were shipped to the United States. Smithson had never visited there, and a somewhat startled Congress began to debate what to do with the unprecedented gift.

Proposals were made to use it for a national university, a large museum of natural science, an astronomical observatory, an agricultural experiment station, a normal school for training teachers of natural science, a school for orphan children, or an agricultural bureau to aid the farmers. John Quincy Adams, the grand old former president then serving selflessly in the House of Representatives, fought hard to keep the fund intact as an endowment for the promotion of science. In 1846 Congress created the Smithsonian Institution with a Board of Regents composed of the chief justice of the United States, the vice-president, three congressmen, three senators, and six private citizens. The dispute over the use of the money (the income then amounted to about $30,000 per year) was reflected in the provision that the board erect a building to house a museum with a study collection of scientific materials, a chemical laboratory, library, art gallery, and lecture rooms.[30]

The regents chose as their executive or secretary Joseph Henry, probably the leading American scientist of the day, who had done distinguished research in electromagnetism and discovered the principle of the telegraph. Henry thought the increase of knowledge more important than its diffusion; there were "thousands of institutions actively engaged in the diffusion of knowledge in our country," he wrote, "but not a single one which gives direct support to its increase. Knowledge can only be increased by original research, which requires patient thought and laborious and often expensive experiments."[31]

Henry passionately argued the merits of pure science and resisted as much as he dared putting Smithsonian income into erecting a large building, acquiring a library, establishing a museum and art gallery, and offering a series of public lectures. He set up a system of meteorological observations throughout the country that became the United States Weather Bureau; cautiously backed Smithsonian participation in exploring expeditions to the western states, Alaska, and elsewhere; inaugurated an international exchange of scientific publications; and began to publish the *Smithsonian Contributions to Knowledge*. He managed to defeat efforts to make the Smithsonian a general copyright library, firing the librarian and transferring the accumulated books to the Library of Congress. He placed the Smithsonian art holdings on permanent loan with the Corcoran Gallery of Art.[32]

Henry could not, however, stop the growth of a natural history museum. Spencer Fullerton Baird, a first-rate biologist who became Henry's assistant secretary in 1850, was too clever and too patient for him. Baird thought a United States National Museum would both increase public knowledge of flora and fauna and provide scholars with comparative materials for biological research. Pressure for such a museum came from the exploration of natural resources in the western United States and from Smithsonian participation in international expositions. Both activities brought a stream of specimens and artifacts to Washington.[33]

Baird employed a promising young icthyologist, George Brown Goode, to arrange Smithsonian and United States Fish Commission exhibits for the Philadelphia Centennial Exposition of 1876. Goode became the leading American museum professional of his day and in his short career (he died in 1896 at age forty-five) placed Smithsonian museum activities on a sound scientific basis. He brought back forty-two freight carloads of specimens and objects from Philadelphia, and after Baird succeeded Henry as secretary, Congress established the United States National Museum in 1879 and provided it with a new home, the present red-brick Arts and Industries Building. Goode argued that they were creating a museum of record to preserve material foundations of scientific knowledge, a museum of research to further scientific inquiry, and an educational museum to illustrate "every kind of material object and every manifestation of human thought and activity." In other words, Goode was determined to collect not only natural history specimens but also art, historical, and technological objects. The centennial haul included sculpture and graphics, machinery, and decorative arts materials of wood, metal, ceramics, glass, and leather.[34]

Since then the Smithsonian has grown enormously and today contains more than sixty-five million objects, about 80 percent of them in the National Museum of Natural History. It has been housed in its own building since 1911 and has sections devoted to anthropology (including what was once the famed Bureau of American Ethnology), botany, entomology, invertebrate and vertebrate zoology, mineral sciences, and paleobiology. One wing contains the three million dried plants of the National Herbarium. The museum has for more than a century led the world in the study, classification, and publication of descriptions of new forms of animals, plants, and fossils. Its huge collections of specimens from all over the globe have permitted systematists to conduct outstanding taxonomic research.[35]

The Smithsonian museums have gradually overcome the crowded, poorly organized conditions that made them known as "the Nation's Attic." The National Museum of History and Technology moved into its new building in 1964, as did the National Air and Space Museum in 1976. Then there are the National Zoological Park (1887); the Freer Gallery of Art (1906); the National Collection of Fine Arts (1846) and National Portrait Gallery (1962) sharing the former Patent Office Building since 1968; the Joseph H. Hirshhorn Museum and Sculpture Garden (1966); and several smaller specialized art museums. Nominal bureaus of the Smithsonian, but with their own boards and financing, are the National Gallery of Art (1937) and the John F. Kennedy Center for the Performing Arts (1958).[36]

Today the Smithsonian Institution is a complex mixture of scientific and museum programs. Though not entirely an agency of the national government, it receives more than $130 million per year of federal funds, while its private endowment of some $23 million yields only about one million annually. The Smithsonian regards itself as "an independent establishment devoted to public education, basic research, and national service in science, the humanities, and the arts."[37] Dichotomies such as Smithson's "increase and diffusion of knowledge" or Henry's pure science and Baird's taxonomic research still exist, but Congress has been willing to support their different approaches. And the National Museum of Natural History remains a world leader in its field.

American Museum of Natural History

Albert S. Bickmore had studied with Louis Agassiz, founder of the Museum of Comparative Zoology at Harvard, and was determined that New York City should have a museum of natural history second to none, "affording amusement and instruction to the public" and "teaching our youth to appreciate the wonderful works of the Creator." Bickmore's enthusiasm enlisted the aid of the financial titans of the city, including William E. Dodge, Jr., Theodore Roosevelt (father of "T. R."), Benjamin A. Field, Robert Colgate, and, later, J. P. Morgan. The state of New York chartered the American Museum of Natural History on April 9, 1869. Bickmore resigned his teaching post at Madison (today Colgate) University to become superintendent of the new institution, which the Commissioners of Central Park provided with quarters and exhibit cases on the upper floors of the Arsenal Building in the park.[38]

As we have already seen, the American Museum joined with the Metropolitan Museum of Art in 1871 to enlist the assistance of "Boss" Tweed in securing a compromise arrangement under which New York City provided museum buildings and paid for maintenance and guards, while the boards of trustees furnished collections and the curatorial and educational staffs. President Ulysses S. Grant in 1874 laid the cornerstone of the American Museum's new building on Central Park West, which President Rutherford B. Hayes dedicated three years later. On that occasion, Professor Othniel C. Marsh, of the Peabody Museum at Yale, made a singularly accurate prophecy. "These vast collections," he said, "will spread the elements of Natural Science among the people of New York and the surrounding region, but the quiet workers in the attic, who pursue Science for its own sake, will bring the museum renown throughout the world."[39]

Professor Bickmore continued an excellent money raiser but resigned as superintendent in 1884 to become curator of a new department of public instruction, for a time paid for by the state of New York. He offered schoolteachers a special course in natural history, devised high-quality lantern slides (known as "Bickmore slides"), and soon had reached more than one million persons with his public lectures.[40]

Morris K. Jesup, multimillionaire banker, became president of the museum in 1881. He was actually what today would be called the director—a working administrator who concerned himself with the smallest operating decisions. Though no scientist, Jesup attracted wealthy men to support the museum, appointed scholarly curators, personally financed museum expeditions and helped send Robert E. Peary to the North Pole, and supported Frank M. Chapman in developing his bird-habitat groups. Jesup liked to see young people in the museum, which he considered a most effective agency "for furnishing education, innocent amusement, and instruction to the people." He and his widow left the museum more than $6 million, a sum that has grown to constitute one-fifth of its total present endowment.[41]

Jesup was followed in the presidency in 1908 by Dr. Henry Fairfield Osborn, who, under a joint appointment since 1891, had been in charge of paleontology at the museum and of biology at Columbia University. Osborn sensed the public appeal of large fossils, especially dinosaurs. When museum expeditions to the West brought back dinosaur bones, he had the huge skeletons articulated and placed on display. Many scientists considered this innovation radical and vulgar showmanship and insisted that the bones ought to be sorted into drawers and reserved for scientific study. Osborn got Carl E. Akeley, brilliant taxidermist, sculptor, explorer, and inventor, to obtain specimens from which a Hall of African Mammals developed with twenty-eight habitat groups placed around eight mounted elephants. Roy Chapman Andrews was dispatched on a series of explorations of the Gobi Desert in Mongolia and in 1923 brought back dinosaur eggs.

Osborn could be dictatorial and rude; he gave Dr. Hermon C. Bumpus, the museum's first director appointed to relieve Jesup of details, an unsolicited six-month leave of absence and kept each succeeding director under his control. Still, he developed a well-balanced program to increase knowledge through exploration and scientific laboratory work and initiated dramatic exhibition techniques that attracted a large popular audience including numerous school groups. Publications were of great importance, both the numerous series of scientific reports and the popular, copiously illustrated *Natural History* magazine. Continuous reaction took place between patrons contributing financial backing and a quality program that attracted new patrons. The Smithsonian museums often contrasted governmental penury with this private generosity.[42]

After Osborn's retirement in 1932, the museum secured less flamboyant but more professional administration. Its departments were devoted to astronomy, minerals and gems, paleontology, forestry and conservation, living invertebrates, insects, living fishes, living reptiles, living birds, living mammals, and man and his origins. The museum continued to attract strong financial support from the wealthy and installed the much-appreciated Hayden Planetarium. The team of curators and designers provided ever more authentic and telling exhibits, and school programs broadened in their appeal. Still, the museum's chief function remained research; its 23 million specimens were under study by a large staff of scientists, while its expeditions constantly brought in more materials.[43]

The late Margaret Mead, the museum's well-known anthropologist, thought that the museum existed for the children and ideally should be planned for twelve-year-olds. But she valued its research function also when she said:

> The Museum is an old-fashioned institution, though up-to-date in relation to the media. Nobody is here just to make money. . . . Most of the curators could get better paying jobs elsewhere, and some of them have, but the ethos is so good that not many are tempted. The Museum gives you great intellectual independence.[44]

Field Museum of Natural History

A third great American natural history museum was the result of another world's fair—the World's Columbian Exposition of 1893 in Chicago. Frederick Ward Putnam, curator of the Peabody Museum at Harvard, in 1891 was appointed to head the department of anthropology for the exposition, and he urged that the collections to be shown there become a permanent museum. For two years Putnam and his assistants carried out excavation, collecting, and research from Greenland to Tierra del Fuego that brought anthropological and ethnographic materials to the exposition. Putnam also secured a great collection of minerals, skeletons, mastodon bones, and mounted mammals and birds from Ward's Natural Science Establishment of Rochester, New York. When Marshall Field, the merchant prince, was asked to give money for the proposed museum, he said: "I don't know anything about a museum and I don't care to know anything about a museum. I'm not going to give you a million dollars." But Edward E. Ayer, an incorporator and the first president, convinced Field that his gift would bring him a kind of immortality, so that he changed his mind and gave $1 million; other wealthy patrons contributed nearly $500,000. The articles of incorporation of 1893 defined the museum's purpose as "the accumulation and dissemination of knowledge, and the preservation and exhibition of objects illustrating Art, Archaeology, Science and History." Putnam secretly hoped to become the director, but was passed over in favor of Dr. Frederick J. V. Skiff, who had been chief of the exposition's department of mines and mining.[45]

The new museum, opened in 1894 in the Palace of Fine Arts building of the exposition in Jackson Park, has been generously supported by the elite of Chicago, and the Park District pays maintenance and security expenses through taxation. Marshall Field eventually gave the museum $9 million; his nephew Stanley Field was its president for fifty-six years and contributed $2 million; and his grandson Marshall Field III bestowed another $9 million. Such backing enabled the museum to move into a mammoth white marble building in Grant Park along the lakeshore in 1921.

The museum has four main departments—anthropology, botany, geology, and zoology—and issues scholarly research publications known as *Fieldiana* in each area. Its scientific expeditions were outstanding and numerous; in 1929, for example, seventeen expeditions included Eastern Asia (with Theodore Roosevelt, Jr., and Kermit Roosevelt), the Pacific (on Cornelius Crane's yacht, the *Elyria*), West Africa, the South Pacific, the Amazon, Mesopotamia (the Field Museum-Oxford University Expedition to Kish), Abyssinia, the Arctic, British Honduras, and the Bahamas.

Many of the museum's exhibits are world-famous, as, for example, Malvina Hoffman's life-size bronze sculptures showing the races of mankind; the Hall of Indian America before Columbus; the fossil vertebrates with a seventy-two-foot brontosaurus skeleton; and a coal-age forest of 240 million years ago. The museum co-operated closely with the American Museum of Natural History, both on expeditions and in developing exhibitions. Carl E. Akeley, chief taxidermist at Chicago for fourteen years, had African halls named in his honor at the two institutions, and Charles R. Knight did many paintings for both. The museum's work with the schools has been outstanding. Norman W. Harris in 1911 gave $250,000 to establish a public school extension service that was soon distributing 1,000 traveling exhibits to 600 schools and reaching 500,000 students. The James Nelson and Anna Louise Raymond Foundation in 1925 financed public school and children's lectures; today 400,000 schoolchildren visit the museum each year in organized groups.

Attractive exhibits and good school programs have resulted in attendance of more than a million yearly since 1926, and the museum has continued its far-flung collection policies and its scholarly research. Its holdings contain approximately 10 million specimens and it has 21,000 members. One of its mottoes truly states that "A living museum is never finished."[46]

Problems of the Natural History Museum

When the early natural history museums were established, they were centers of scientific work. Their expeditions added to human knowledge of the natural world and brought in vast collections of specimens. Their staffs described and classified these ever-increasing materials, and Darwin's theory of evolution provided a rational framework to explain the whole. The research scientists who were key members of the museum staffs could transfer easily to a scientific institute or a university.

Today, however, the study of nature and life has moved in many directions. Paleontologists, with their basic interest in fossils and geologic eras, and physical anthropologists need museum collections, and so do biologists specializing in taxonomy or systematics and comparative anatomy. Most biologists, however, work mainly with living organisms in studying animal physiology and behavior, animal and plant ecology, genetics, microbiology, and other aspects of life. The same is true for students of cultural anthropology. These scientists have greater need for field studies and laboratories than for museum collections and are tending to work for scientific agencies or universities.

A large museum with sophisticated, complex exhibits and other forms of interpretation often needs research scientists; in a sense this situation resembles the graduate teaching university in which creative scholarship benefits from both fruitful research and inspiring teaching. Still, the systematists serve another part of such a museum—the study collections numbering millions of specimens. Occasional proposals have been made to turn the study collections and their researchers over to a university and keep the exhibits and other interpretive functions for the museum, bringing in occasional research from the outside to develop new exhibitions. The idea of separation sometimes has been supported by those who decry the classes of lively schoolchildren who overrun the museum; the resulting noise and confusion tend to daunt scholarly research and even discourage individual adult visitation.

The natural history museum, however, occupies a unique place in the cultural world. Naturalists are often generalists who examine plants and animals as wholes or entities living in the complex environments of the natural world. These scientists can help solve modern-day problems of population control and environmental quality—ecological problems of the highest social and economic importance to all humankind. Thus, the large natural history museum has increased contributions to make, and its research is as vital and valuable as its educational exhibits. A wise administration will further both functions and see that they support each other.[47]

Anthropological Museums

A word should be said here about the placement of collections of anthropology, archaeology, and ethnology in museums. Sometimes encyclopedic museums such as the British Museum, the Louvre, the state museums of West and East Berlin, the Metropolitan Museum of Art, and the Museum of Fine Arts, Boston, possess important antiquities and ethnological materials. Many natural history museums contain such objects, as, for example, the three American ones we have just discussed.[48] Other museums are devoted primarily to the anthropological field. Outstanding among them are the National Museum of Ethnology in Leiden, the Musée de l'Homme in Paris, the University Museum of the University of Pennsylvania in Philadelphia, and the National Museum of Anthropology in Mexico City.

The Leiden museum was founded in 1837 by Dr. F. B. von Siebold, who had lived in Japan and gathered an ethnographic collection of some five thousand objects. The museum suffered for a century because of inadequate housing, but slowly accumulated an important collection of materials from outside the European and classic regions. Transfers from the Royal Cabinet of Rarities, the International Colonial Exhibition held at Amsterdam in 1883, and the National Museum of Antiquities greatly strengthened the museum's holdings. In 1939 it was able to expand its exhibits as a result of acquiring the former building of the University Hospital. Its chief strengths lie in materials from Japan (such as five bronze Buddhas shown dramatically in a dimly lighted room), China, Indonesia, Oceania, India, the Near East, Africa (including Benin bronze heads), America (Peruvian pottery and the Mayan so-called Leiden plate), Java, Tibet, and Siberia. The museum has always conducted excellent scientific research, and since World War II has had special exhibits and school programs that include concerts of Javanese music on the gamelan and creative dramatics or role-playing.[49]

The Musée de l'Homme in Paris is an offshoot from the Muséum

National d'Histoire Naturelle. Paul Rivet coined the name for the new museum; he believed that "humanity is an indivisible whole, in space and in time," and that scholarship should break down the barriers of political geography and synthesize the artificial classifications of physical anthropology, prehistory, archaeology, ethnology, folklore, sociology, and philology.[50] The Musée de l'Homme opened in 1939 in the Palais de Chailot that had been built for the world's fair of 1937. The museum has been innovative in its exhibits, using sound ethnography and aesthetic display but subordinating them to the exposition of anthropological theory. It seeks to illustrate the function of the objects against the total background of the culture but sometimes produces somewhat lengthy and intellectualized labels.[51]

The University Museum in Philadelphia, founded in 1889, was the first American institution to excavate in biblical lands, and its basic tradition is "to dig and to find out." As a result of numerous expeditions (for example, eighteen to fourteen countries in 1966; its quarterly bulletin is appropriately named *Expedition*), it has built a superb archaeological and ethnological collection that covers Mesopotamia, Egypt, the Mediterranean, China, Africa, Oceania, Australia, and North, Middle, and South America. The museum serves as a training center for graduate students in anthropology and also conducts a popular statewide program making skillful use of television and radio. Especially effective is its introductory exhibit, "Hall of Man," which states some of the basic conclusions of general anthropology with emphasis on the theory of evolution.[52]

One of the greatest museums of the world is the National Museum of Anthropology in Mexico City, opened at Chapultepec Park in 1964, an architectural triumph reminiscent of the ancient Mayan Governor's Palace in Uxmal with an imposing interior patio and pool dominated by a vast umbrella fountain from which falls a curtain of water. The building is set in a handsome park, and from the interior visitors can see gardens and exciting outdoor exhibits that they may inspect, such as a colossal Olmec stone head from LaVenta or the reconstructed Mayan temple of Hochob. Near the entrance is an imposing twenty-three-foot-high ancient statue of the rain god Tlaloc that weighs 168 tons.

The museum has two floors of display rooms, the first devoted to anthropology and archaeology. In the Aztec Room, for example, are Coatlicue ("Goddess of the Serpent Skirt"), the Sun Stone ("Aztec Calendar"), twelve feet in diameter, and the Stone of Tizoc. These three huge monoliths, found in Mexico City about 1790, inspired official collection of antiquities. In addition to original artifacts, the museum has ingenious and artistic displays, such as the spectacular diorama of the Market of Tlatelolco with hundreds of authentically modeled miniature figures in an area measuring thirty by twelve feet. The second floor of the museum is devoted to ethnology with buildings, furnishings, tools, and costumes of the different cultures of Mexico as they exist today. Not only did the anthropologists, archaeologists, architects, and artists co-operate in the creation of this museum, but also the humble skilled craftsmen from the different cultures who came to build the ethnographic displays—until they were complete, actually living in the museum. The result of all this scientific, artistic, and practical effort is a museum of breath-taking beauty that also serves as a scientific anthropological center for all Mexico.[53]

4

The Museum of Science and Technology

Water Purification Unit, Ontario Science Centre, Toronto

Artificial curiosities in the early collections included a broad spectrum of practical and scientific technology—tools and utensils; locks and keys; lighting devices; clocks and watches; arms, armor, and apparatus of warfare; musical instruments; globes, astrolabes, and navigational devices; machines, automatons, engines, and mechanical models; telescopes, microscopes, and other optical apparatus; magnetic and electrical equipment; and scientific or philosophical apparatus and instruments devoted to mathematics, medicine, astronomy, chemistry, and physics. With the coming of the Industrial Revolution in the eighteenth century and the advent of the world's fair in the nineteenth, increased recognition came to the products of man's inventive mind, and the museum of science and technology arose. To keep up with the dizzy pace of technology, the museum has become chiefly a science center, but its popularity is unmatched.

Collections of Artificial Curiosities

The medieval and renaissance collectors usually owned abundant artificial curiosities. Jean de France, duc de Berry, had clocks, mechanisms, and scientific apparatus. Emperor Rudolph II brought to Prague great instrument makers like Erasmus Habermel and Tycho Brahe, as well as the distinguished mathematician Johannes Kepler. Landgrave Wilhelm IV at Kassel collected instruments and studied mathematics and asronomy, while August I in Dresden used his collection to form a scientific research center in the famed Green Vaults of his palace.[1]

Most of the seventeenth-century Italian scientific centers mentioned in the last chapter had artificial as well as natural curiosities—Aldrovandi, Cospi, and Marsigli at Bologna; the Medici brothers, Grand Duke Ferdinand II and Leopold, with their Academia del Cimento (of the Experiment) in Florence; Ludovico and Manfredo Settala, father and son, in Milan; and the Jesuit Kircher in Rome.[2] So did Ole Worm and Christian V in Denmark and the Tradescants and the Royal Society (1662) in London. The Society for the Encouragement of Arts, Manufactures, and Commerce (now the Royal Society of Arts), founded in 1754, eventually placed its collection of models in the Science Museum. The Teyler Stichting (Foundation) established at Haarlem in 1778 had the chemist and electrical experimenter Martin van Marum as its first director and still contains his great electrostatic machine of 1784.[3]

Conservatoire National des Arts et Métiers

In the seventeenth century René Descartes suggested that the French government collect models of inventions for the instruction of artisans, but it was not until 1794 that the revolutionary National Assembly established the Conservatoire National des Arts et Métiers. This public depository of machines, inventions, models, tools, drawings, descriptions, and books on the applied arts and trades was housed in the buildings of the old Priory of Saint-Martin-des-Champs in Paris. The construction and use of tools and machines was to be explained there so as to advance the practical arts and trades and encourage industrial development.

The machines and models collected by the great engineer and inventor Jacques Vaucanson and by the Académie Royale des Sciences (1666) were the core of the collection that grew rapidly during the last half of the nineteenth century and received much material from the various universal exhibitions. The chief divisions of the collection were physics, electrical industries, geometry, weights and measures, mechanics and machines, transportation, chemical industries, mining and metallurgy, graphic arts, textile arts, arts of construction, and agriculture, and later industrial accident prevention and industrial hygiene. As early as 1819 the Conservatoire hired professors to give courses on applying science to arts and industries that in one year in the 1860s enrolled 177,000 persons. About 1900, laboratories were established to test scientific apparatus, building materials, machines, and vegetable substances. The Conservatoire also published a six-volume catalogue of its holdings, between 1905 and 1910.

For a time despite its great collection the Conservatoire was a barren and forbidding storehouse without sound principles of collection or appealing methods of presentation. About 1849 some experiments and machines were operated by reservoirs of water in the tower of the former priory, but by the early twentieth century only a few models were electrified, and the lighting was so poor that many objects could not be seen. Recently, however, the collection is being rearranged on modern principles as the Musée National des Techniques and features early aircraft, including the first helicopter, old automobiles, the origins of photography, motion pictures, radio and television, radar and the laser, and much other modern technology. These popular displays complement the older rarities such as the ornamental turning lathes Peter the Great presented to the Académie des Sciences, materials on the evolution of the Jacquard loom, apparatus from Lavoisier's laboratory, or Daguerre's early equipment.[4]

More of a science center than a museum is another institution of technology in Paris, the Palais de la Découverte in the Grand Palais. Built for the International Exposition of 1937 and attached to the University of Paris, the Palais contains relatively few original objects but uses ingenious mock-ups, some of them automated, as well as photographs, art work, and demonstrators to teach the principles of pure science and scientific research as applied to the fields of mathematics, astronomy, physics, chemistry, biology, and medicine. Designed chiefly for young students, its exhibits include a planetarium, an IBM computer, a 300,000-volt electrostatic machine, and a hall of space exploration. The French Ministry of Education has approved in principle placing the National Musée des Techniques and the Palais de la Découverte in the same building in a suburb of Paris as part of the new Faculty of Science.[5]

The Science Museum, London

British manufacturers and businessmen were concerned to see that workingmen received practical technical education so as to produce more and better goods. Mechanics' institutes and government schools of design were established in the 1820s and '30s, and sporadic trade exhibitions were held to show how art and science could be applied to industrial products. The Royal Society of Arts held several such exhibits, imitating those started in France. Henry Cole, versatile artist, musician, literateur, and civil servant, became convinced that the society should sponsor an international exhibition so as to compare the industrial progress of many nations. Prince Albert, consort of Queen Victoria and president of the society, eagerly embraced the idea, and his support was chiefly responsible for bringing into actuality the Great Exhibition of the Industry of All Nations at London in 1851.

A plan for a conventional brick exhibition building with a monstrous dome was eventually rejected, and Joseph Paxton, landscape architect and conservatory builder, drew an imaginative design that used modular construction of cast-iron beams and glass panes. The building—1851 (the date of the year) feet long and some 450 feet broad—enclosed eighteen acres that included several large trees and was erected in the incredibly short space of twenty-three weeks. Queen Victoria wrote, "Truly it was astonishing, a fairy scene," and everyone began to call the magical soaring structure the "Crystal Palace."

The exposition was an enormous success. Queen Victoria and Prince Albert attended three times a week, and in 120 days it attracted more than six million visitors. When it closed in October, unlike most later world's fairs, it had a surplus— £186,000. The exhibition had beneficial effects on British industrial design and international trade and inspired a series of world's fairs including a New York Crystal Palace (1853) and the Philadelphia Centennial Exhibition (1876). Many of these expositions influenced the museum movement; their collections and, in some instances, their buildings were used to start museums.[6]

The royal commissioners, at the urging of Prince Albert, invested the earnings of the Great Exhibition in South Kensington real estate that adjoined the exposition site and eventually helped build a museum complex there. In 1857 the South Kensington Museum of Science and Art was opened; it contained much material from the Crystal Palace. Bennet Woodcroft, patent commissioner, who gathered mechanical models in the Patent Office Museum, brought the collection to South Kensington, but because of a quarrel with Cole, then the secretary of the South Kensington Museum, placed it, not in the main structure but instead in two unsightly iron buildings known as the Brompton Boilers. Woodcroft preserved important historic equipment including a Necomen type of atmospheric engine (1791); the Boulton and Watt rotative beam engine (1788); Arkwright's cotton-spinning machine (1769); Symington's marine engine (1788); and the locomotives *Puffing Billy* (1813) and Stephenson's *Rocket* (1829). The collection eventually went to the South Kensington Museum, but in 1909, when the building for the Victoria and Albert Museum was completed, the Science Museum became independent and moved into temporary buildings across Exhibition Road.

For long without an adequate building and hampered by two world wars, the Science Museum slowly developed into one of the greatest museums of science and technology. It collects important historical material for permanent retention as well as current examples of technology on a selective, changing basis. The museum offers lectures, demonstrations, and films, and its imaginative special exhibits (about three yearly) have treated topics of contemporary research interest, such as glass technology, noise abatement (1935), smoke abatement (1936), X-rays, television, and atomic energy. The National Physical Laboratory and other scientific institutions as well as industry have helped with these shows. The museum also has an excellent Children's Gallery (children make up 25 to 30 percent of its total attendance) with participatory exhibits, and it sends traveling exhibits to museums and other educational institutions throughout the United Kingdom. Its attendance of nearly 3,400,000 yearly exceeds that of any other museum in Britain.[7]

The Deutsches Museum, Munich

The French and British had established the first technical museums, but Germans devised an even more striking and influential one. Oskar von Miller, an outstanding engineer largely responsible for the Bavarian grid electrical system including the Walchensee Hydraulic Power Station (1911), was the founder of the Deutsches Museum von Meisterwerken der Naturwissenschaft und Technic (of Outstanding Achievements in Natural Science and Technology). As a young man in 1879, von Miller visited the Conservatoire in Paris and the Patent Office Museum in South Kensington. He returned home determined to set up such a museum in Munich, a decision strengthened by attendance at the 1881 International Electrical Exposition in Paris.

Von Miller, a man of massive frame and boundless drive, in 1903 presented a plan for a museum to illustrate the development of natural science and technology and the vivid influence of invention and mechanical progress on society. It was endorsed enthusiastically by leading industrialists and scientists, engineering and scientific organizations, the National and Bavarian governments, and the city of Munich. The museum was housed for many years in an old building of the Bavarian National Museum and expanded into a disused infantry barracks, but in 1911 the city gave it an island, formerly used as a coal dump, in River Isar. The city, Bavarian state, and German empire contributed millions of marks for construction. Industries furnished building materials free or at cost, organizations of workers donated labor, and the German railroads contributed transport; von Miller enjoyed his reputation as "the biggest highwayman and sturdiest beggar in Christendom." By 1913 the reinforced concrete structures were complete, but war delayed moving the collections, and the new museum island did not open its 250,000 square feet of displays to the public until May 6, 1925, the seventieth birthday of its founder.

The Deutsches Museum introduced many innovations in its effort to make science and technology understandable for the general public. At the entrance was a Science Hall of Fame with likenesses of Germans such as Leibnitz, Siemens, Krupp, and Kepler, as well as world scientists and inventors from Arkwright and Stephenson to Thomas Edison. Full-scale original or reproduced equipment was on display—for example, replicas of the *Puffing Billy* and *Rocket* locomotives in the Science Museum, the first Siemens electric locomotive (1899), early automobiles by Benz (1885) and Daimler (1886), and Edison's electric-lighting apparatus (1879). Many ingenious scale models could be animated by the individual visitor with push buttons or cranks. The principles of physics and chemistry were demonstrated, and a dramatic electrical surge generator (1,300,000 volts) produced lightning flashes two meters long. The first Zeiss planetarium was installed, as well as realistic mines for coal, iron, and salt with full-sized shafts, drifts, and galleries. The museum used period settings, such as an alchemist's laboratory and Galileo's study, as well as dioramas that included a glassblower's workshop and a high-tension power plant.

The Deutsches Museum retained the traditional chronological presentation of objects of historical interest but pioneered in offering ingenious and exciting exhibits and demonstrations of the scientific laws of nature and their application through contemporary technology. It encouraged technological research with a fine scientific library of 300,000 volumes, but its chief purpose was informal education for the masses. A well-equipped auditorium accommodated two thousand persons at public lectures. Its present yearly attendance is one million, three-fourths of which consists of elementary and secondary school students.[8]

The influence of the Deutsches Museum has been pervasive and extensive. Its display techniques for modern technology emphasized how science works today, and most smaller technical museums have concentrated on this aspect, largely giving up the goal of exhibiting historical development. The Conservatoire des Arts et Métiers, originally arranged on the traditional historical principle, has been reorganizing its displays, and the Palais de la Découverte has almost entirely omitted historical exhibits. The Science Museum in London still uses both approaches, but its temporary and traveling exhibits emphasize modern technology. The Technical Museum of Vienna used materials accumulated during the International Exposition held there in 1873 and the Jubilee of Emperor Franz Joseph in 1908. It was greatly influenced by the Deutsches Museum and when it finally opened, in 1918, used many of von Miller's vivifying exhibition techniques. Though possessed of an excellent collection, it has not lately had the financial support it deserves. The privately financed Tekniska Museet of Stockholm (1936) followed Deutsches Museum practices, as did other museums as far away as Australia, Japan, Singapore, and, of course, North America.[9]

The Smithsonian Institution's Technology Museums

The Philadelphia Centennial Exposition of 1876 was a six-month extravaganza paying tribute to the hundredth anniversary of the Declaration of Independence. Five huge main buildings devoted to industrial exhibits, machinery, agriculture, horticulture, and art, together with 250 smaller structures, were scattered through 233 acres of the broad reaches of Fairmount Park. There were some 30,000 exhibitors, including those from forty-one foreign governments. Machinery Hall was especially impressive with its great, seven-ton Corliss Engine started up by President Grant and Dom Pedro II, emperor of Brazil, and furnishing power to fourteen acres of clattering machinery that included printing presses, typecasting machines, envelope makers, and pin-forming machines amid huge Krupp cannons, car wheels, water pumps, boats, and locomotives. One enthusiastic reporter wrote: "Surely here, and not in literature, science, or art, is the true evidence of man's creative power; here is Prometheus Unbound." Federal, state, and city funds underwrote the cost of the fair to supplement concession fees and admission revenue from more than eight million visitors.[10]

Many foreign and state governments donated their centennial exhibits to the Smithsonian, and this flood of materials led to the erection of a new red-brick National Museum Building (today the Arts and Industries Building) completed in 1881. Its seventeen halls contained a conglomeration of pottery, textiles, costumes, historical objects, minerals, metals, furs, woods, fibers, and natural history specimens. George Brown Goode, assistant secretary of the Smithsonian, established a Department of Art and Industries to include historical, natural history, and technological objects, but after his death in 1896, it languished. Soon, a growing, crowded jumble of costumes, medals and coins, military paraphernalia, locomotives and automobiles, and stuffed animals constituted the museum.

Since that day, order has slowly been brought from chaos. In 1911 a new building across the Mall housed the National Museum of Natural History. The Smithsonian regents in 1924 appealed to Congress unsuccessfully for a "Museum of Engineering and Industry." At last, in 1955, Leonard Carmichael, the Institution's seventh secretary, persuaded Congress to appropriate funds for a new National Museum of History and Technology that opened in 1964 under the direction of Frank A. Taylor. The famed Wright Brothers *Flyer* (1903), Langley's *Aerodrome Six*, Charles Lindbergh's *Spirit of St. Louis*, Dr. Robert Goddard's first successful rocket, Alan Shepherd's Mercury capsule, and numerous other examples of air and space equipment were left in the Arts and Industries Building or in a temporary structure until the gigantic new Air and Space Museum on the Mall could be completed in 1976.

A single amusing story will illustrate the difficulties that sometimes attended the accumulation of the air and space materials. Samuel P. Langley, the third secretary of the Smithsonian, experimented with heavier-than-air machines, but in December 1903 his piloted *Aerodrome Six* failed to take off when catapulted over the Potomac. Nine days later the Wright Brothers, Orville and Wilbur, made their successful flight at Kitty Hawk in North Carolina. Secretary Charles D. Walcott, Langley's successor at the Smithsonian, asserted that the *Aerodrome Six* had made the first successful flight. This claim so angered Orville Wright, the surviving brother, that in 1928 he deposited the Kitty Hawk *Flyer* in the Science Museum, London. The Smithsonian finally made apologies satisfactory to Wright, and the *Flyer* came to the Smithsonian in 1948, to be placed on display on December 17, the forty-fifth anniversary of its first flight.

At the Museum of History and Technology, the chief science and technical displays include military ordnance, graphic arts, photography, musical instruments, farm machinery, road vehicles, American merchant shipping, railroads (with the 12½-ton *Pioneer* locomotive (1851) standing beside the 280-ton Southern Railway's *1401*), bridges and tunnels, heavy machinery, electricity, tools, timekeepers, record players, typewriters, locks, physical sciences, medical sciences, manufactures, textiles, petroleum, nuclear energy, coal, and iron and steel. Full-scale original objects, meticulously built scale models, period rooms and shops, visitor-activated demonstrations, and motion pictures are used in interpreting these subjects.[11]

The technological exhibits of the Museum of History and Technology and of the Air and Space Museum rank with the Musée National des Techniques-Palais de la Découverte of Paris, the Science Museum of London, and the Deutsches Museum of Munich in combining the history of science and technology with the analysis of ways in which they are applied to contemporary life. Most other modern science centers today emphasize the interpretation of applied science and do not attempt historical treatment. Thus the Smithsonian has the opportunity to develop as one of the unique technical museums of the world.

The Museum of Science and Industry, Chicago

Julius Rosenwald, head of Sears, Roebuck and Company in Chicago, took his family to Munich in 1911. His eight-year-old son William was fascinated with the Deutsches Museum in the old Bavarian National Museum there; by pushing buttons or working levers, he could do all sorts of exciting things—see the bones in his hand on an X-ray screen, generate static electricity, or make the wheels of a gigantic locomotive spin. Rosenwald, who met the enthusiastic Dr. von Miller and continued visiting him through the years, in 1921 told the Chicago Commercial Club "that Chicago should have . . . a great Industrial Museum or Exhibition" with "machinery and working models illustrative of as many as possible of the mechanical processes of production and manufacture."[12] By 1926 the museum was incorporated, Rosenwald had given it $3 million, and the Chicago South Park Board had earmarked $3.5 million of a bond issue to renovate for its use the crumbling Palace of Fine Arts, a building left from the Columbian Exposition of 1893 and once used by the Field Museum of Natural History.

Rosenwald ultimately gave the Museum nearly $7 million, though at his death in 1932 its exhibits were far from finished, and the Great Depression had cut markedly into its endowment income. In June 1933, during the Chicago centennial world's fair, "A Century of Progress," the museum managed to open partially. It featured a simulated coal mine with operating mine cage elevator, shaft, pump room, mine train, working face of a coal seam, and various cutting equipment. By 1940, however, the financial situation was desperate with $400,000 yearly expenditures and only $85,000 income, mainly from Sears, Roebuck dividends. Then the museum board elected as its president Major Lenox R. Lohr, who had successfully managed "A Century of Progress" for two summers and had since been serving as president of the National Broadcasting Company.

Major Lohr combined the qualities of the hard-driving, tough businessman and the imaginative promoter. He at once fired half the museum curators with their supporting staff and made the director resign. He did everything he could to build attendance, which in 1939 was about 470,000. If it could reach a million and more, he thought, industry would be attracted to design and install significant technological displays. He set about making the museum bright, colorful, and comfortable for visitors; a favorite saying of his was: "A woman can be beautiful and gay, and still be dignified and virtuous."[13] He thought 90 percent of the exhibits should be devoted to the present, only 10 percent to the past, and that 10 percent of the total should change each year. In exchange for a company's planning and erecting an exhibit, the museum would guarantee to show it for at least five years, would charge the company a fixed yearly fee that would reimburse the museum for operating, maintaining, and demonstrating it, and would give the company credit with an appropriate and discreet label. The museum would have full control of the exhibit to see that it met its standards of truthfulness, clarity, and educational purpose.

This was, essentially, a world's-fair approach to the technical museum and required no curators, but much imaginative showmanship and excellent public relations and promotion. Thus Major Lohr and his director, Daniel M. MacMaster, in 1948 continued operating the museum while also directing the Chicago Railroad Fair that attracted 2.5 million visitors. Exciting exhibits at the museum included the coal mine, Hall of Communications of the Bell Telephone System, an International Harvester "Harvester Farm" complete with livestock including baby chicks hatching from an incubator, a "Motorama" exhibit by General Motors, the German submarine *U505* captured by the Navy in 1944 off French West Africa (with motion pictures of its seizure), and dozens of other glamorous technical exhibits. In addition, Major Lohr occasionally included highly popular displays from outside the technical field, such as "Christmas Around the World," "Yesterday's Main Street," and Colleen Moore's famed "Fairy Castle" dollhouse. So contemporary was the emphasis that occasional violent controversy was stirred. Thus in 1968 an exhibit allowed visitors to take a simulated Huey helicopter flight in Vietnam, "firing" a machine gun at shacks in a hostile village compound that would light up when direct "hits" were scored. Peace demonstrators staged a sit-in that made the museum shut down the exhibit.

At Lohr's death in 1968, MacMaster succeeded him as president. Clearly, the museum was a tremendous success with the public, exceeding a million attendance in 1942 and now reaching 3.2 million. The museum's emphasis is strongly upon education, and it conducts tours and gives scientific demonstrations. Among the experimental programs it offers to the 400,000 schoolchildren in classes that visit it annually are plays about Galileo, Thomas Edison, and Daniel Hale Williams, a black surgeon; a multimedia show on "Working for a Better Environment"; a children's science book fair; and a science-oriented exhibit for preschool children. The exhibits themselves are financed by leading industries, and fees from displays, tax support from Chicago, income from an $11 million endowment, and admission fees from special features such as the coal mine and submarine have supplied generous operating funds of more than $5 million yearly.[14]

Other Noteworthy Technical Museums

Henry Ford, about 1940, began to accumulate vast stores of cultural and industrial Americana, including historic American buildings. He arranged his collections at Dearborn, Michigan, into two sections—an outdoor or open-air historical village similar to the Scandinavian folk museums, and an indoor museum extending behind a reproduction of Philadelphia's Independence Hall, Carpenter's Hall, and Old City Hall. In 1929 Thomas Alva Edison, Ford's close friend and idol, came to Dearborn with President Herbert Hoover and other notables to open Greenfield Village and Edison Institute (today Henry Ford Museum).

Ford wished to show "the history of our people as written into things their hands made and used," and he argued that "a piece of machinery, or anything that is made is like a book, if you can read it."[15] Though his museums contained many historical, architectural, and decorative arts materials, they were especially rich in important American and British items of industrial development. Greenfield Village included craft and early machine shops, as well as the cycle shop of the Wright brothers, three Edison laboratories in the Menlo Park compound, and birthplaces or other buildings connected with the Wrights, Edison, Luther Burbank, Charles Steinmetz, and Ford himself. The main museum today contains a Street of Early American Craft Shops with twenty-two examples.

Most important of all in showing technological development was the Mechnical Arts Hall, an eight-acre teakwood expanse with serried rows of machines and apparatus devoted to agriculture, domestic arts, lighting, power, machinery, communications, and transportation. Ford was well acquainted with the London and Munich technical museums, and the power and machinery sections are especially strong. All objects are full scale, most of them original, but with a few reproductions. The vast hodgepodge of largely uninterpreted artifacts today may give the ordinary visitor visual and intellectual indigestion, but much of value is being preserved that may eventually be better presented and studied. A great opportunity exists to meld the industrial components of Greenfield Village and Henry Ford Museum into a stunning, animated exhibition series that, perhaps, could end in the present with a tour of the River Rouge Plant of the Ford Motor Company.[16]

The Science Museum and Planetarium of the Franklin Institute in Philadelphia somewhat resembles the Chicago Museum of Science and Industry. The Franklin Institute was founded in 1824 as a mechanics' institute to dispense information on the useful arts. It held important industrial exhibitions and awarded prizes, conducted classes and lectures, accumulated a library and a small technological museum with models and natural history specimens, and published a journal. In 1918 it began to develop laboratories, where scientists carry on chemical, biological, physics, and space research. The Franklin Institute opened its Fels Planetarium in 1933 and a year later its Science Museum. Many of its exhibits of the physical sciences and allied technology are visitor-operated, and it holds demonstrations, workshops, seminars for gifted students, and courses for adults and teachers. The museum works closely with the Philadelphia School District in innovative programs that recently have involved sixth-graders from paired schools of varied racial and socioeconomic backgrounds, science-enrichment classes for fifth- and sixth-graders, and the Parkway "School Without Walls" for high school students that uses also the Philadelphia Museum of Art, Academy of Natural Sciences, Free Library, and other cultural organizations. Thus the Science Museum and Planetarium concentrate on explaining contemporary technology to a broad and varied popular audience.[17]

The Ontario Science Centre opened at Toronto in 1969 is an unusual architectural complex of three extremely innovative buildings. Though it has a few historical technological exhibits, its director declared its purpose was "to take science out of the laboratory and put it where casual browsers could observe and experience some of its challenge for themselves."[18] The center, sometimes described as a push-button Science Adventureland, treats not only physical science and technology, but also natural history, medicine, music, and the theater, and operates an arboretum and an aquarium. It enjoys an annual attendance exceeding 1.2 million and can accommodate 3,000 schoolchildren and 50 school buses per day.[19]

In addition to general centers of science and technology, there are many museums closely related to a single industry or company. European examples include the Stora Kopparbergwerks Museum at Falun, Sweden (this copper company going back to the eleventh century, with a museum open to the public since 1922); the Pilkington Glass Museum at St. Helens, United Kingdom (1964), and the Philips Evoluon at Eindhoven, Netherlands (1967). The last is a broad-based technical museum that the Philips Company erected at its headquarters at a cost of $8 million, the amount accumulated when the company did not exhibit at three world's fairs. Two similar high-grade American technical museums are the Corning Glass Center (1951) at Corning, New York, and the Hagley Museum (1952) at Wilmington, Delaware, broader than but closely connected with Du Pont Company history.[20]

Problems of the Museum of Science and Technology

The short histories of some of the leading technical museums just outlined make clear an underlying difficulty in this area. The tendency everywhere today is to begin with present machines and technological processes and to show how they operate and the scientific principles on which they are based without paying much attention to their historical development, to say nothing of the society that produced them. Only a few of the oldest, largest, and best-supported museums collect historical industrial objects. Most science centers put more emphasis on mock-ups, models, graphs, and multimedia devices. This approach of "presentism" often leads the museum to drop all attempts at study and research; if industry is called upon to design and build the exhibits, curators may be entirely dispensed with, so that impartial and scientific study disappears, and emphasis is placed on the idea that progress automatically follows technology and on glossy, soft-sell advertising for industry.

Industrialization and the machine have, of course, brought much progress; a large portion of humankind no longer works from sunup to sundown to obtain the bare necessities of life. But industrialization also creates problems—harm to the environment and ecology, neglect of social, cultural, and humanistic values, depletion of resources, and even threats of human extinction. Thus progress needs to be considered critically—from a holistic social and humanitarian point of view. As for glossiness, there can be no doubt that most museums of science and technology glorify machines. Displayed in pristine condition, elegantly painted or polished, they can make the observer forget the noise, dirt, danger, and frustration of machine-tending. Mines, whether coal, iron, or salt, are a favorite museum display but only infrequently is there even a hint of the dirt, the damp, the smell, the low headroom, or the crippling and destructive accidents that sometimes occur.

Machinery also ought to be operated to be meaningful. It should not be shown in sculptured repose but in full, often clattering, action. This kind of operation is difficult to obtain, and few museums can command the imagination, ingenuity, and manual dexterity it requires. Problems also arise in providing adequate safety devices for both the public and the machine operators. These, then, are some of the underlying problems of the technical museum—problems not solved by the usual push buttons, cranks, or multimedia gimmicks. Yet attendance figures show that technical museums outdraw all the others; the public possesses lively curiosity and real desire to understand science and technology. On this base, powerful educational institutions can build.[21]

5

The History Museum

Costumed interpreter at dry stone sink, Old Sturbridge Village, Sturbridge, Massachusetts

Since classical days, humankind has taken some interest in the past and gradually has learned to separate myth from actual happening. The history museum, however, has been slow to develop, probably because historians, preoccupied with their exploration of written evidence, have taken little interest in objects and have left them to the attention of antiquarians. Today, history museums are collecting and preserving three-dimensional objects of the past and using them to convey historical perspective and inspiration as well as a sense of what it was like to live in other ages. These objects supplement literary and oral records and thus are revealing documents for the historian, if he will only learn to use them.

Museum Jovianum

The history museum developed more recently than those devoted to art and science. It was, at first, a spin-off from the art collection. Paolo Giovio, bishop, humanist, and scholar, was the best-known of the early collectors of likenesses of famous men. At his residence in Como about 1520, he began to assemble 280 portraits in four categories—deceased poets and scholars, living poets and scholars, artists, and political leaders, including military commanders, statesmen, popes, and monarchs. The living members of this cult of glory were represented by portraits painted from life (Hernando Cortez, for example, hastened to send Giovio his likeness), but the others by busts one and one half feet high painted on canvas and based upon what sources Giovio could find. The Museum Jovianum (Giovio revived and brought into general use the word *museum*) was considered one of the marvels of the age, and when Giovio died, Cosimo de Medici sent Christofano dell' Altissimo to Como to make copies of its portraits for the Medici collection in Florence. Even more important in keeping alive the idea of this type of historical collection were the books of engravings of the portraits that appeared in Florence (1551), Paris (1552), and Basel (1557).[1]

This kind of history museum became enormously popular with noble and wealthy collectors in the sixteenth and seventeenth centuries. Catherine de Medici, wife of the French Dauphin (later Henri II), in her Paris residence had 551 portrait drawings, many of them set in paneled walls. Her Enamel Cabinet paired 32 portraits with 32 Limoges enamels, and her Mirror Cabinet contained another 83 portraits mounted with 119 Venetian looking glasses.[2] Paul Ardier, lawyer and secretary of defense, filled a long gallery of his Chateau de Beauregard in the Loire Valley with 363 portraits disposed by reigns around each king of France; his collection can still be viewed in the chateau today. Bussy-Rabutin, soldier and philanderer, exiled to his chateau in Burgundy, developed a museum of historical portraits that included a rotunda exhibiting likenesses of the beautiful women of court; the collector boasted that he had slept with most of them. The Gonzagas had a special room, about 1600, containing likenesses of "the most beautiful women in the world," and Catherine the Great later bought such a "Cabinet of Muses and Graces" for her Peterhof palace.[3]

The concept of the Museum Jovianum may have appealed to antiquarians, but rows of portraits, often uniform in size, did not constitute an exciting exhibition technique. Nevertheless, it had American versions. Du Simitière's small museum at Philadelphia in 1782 exhibited many of his drawings of Revolutionary military leaders and statesmen; some of his works were engraved and published in French, Spanish, and English editions. Peale's Philadelphia Museum displayed 269 portraits and paintings, most of them by Peale and his family and of Revolutionary leaders and Founding Fathers. From 1817 until his death in 1834, John H. I. Browere sought unsuccessfully to establish a National Gallery by modeling busts of famous Americans, most of their faces delineated from life masks made by a secret process of applying thin coats of quick-drying grout to the greased subject. Hamilton, Jefferson, Lafayette, John and John Quincy Adams, James and Dolley Madison, Monroe, Van Buren, and Clay are some of the 23 busts or masks that have survived, most of them at the New York State Historical Association in Cooperstown. The early American historical societies also collected portraits, and as late as the 1850s Lyman Copeland Draper of the State Historical Society of Wisconsin was forming a frontier historical art gallery composed chiefly of portraits of pioneers and Indians; he thought "the noblest aim of Art . . . the illustration or perpetuation of great events in history." Many of the Peale portraits, together with others of the signers of the Declaration of Independence, are shown today by the National Park Service in the old Second Bank of the United States in Philadelphia, while the National Portrait Gallery (1962) of the Smithsonian Institution in Washington is fast becoming a great American Museum Jovianum.[4]

Battle Galleries

As the nationalistic spirit burgeoned in Europe, the history museum began to contain other materials. About 1630, Philip IV of Spain commissioned Rubens to decorate a reception room in his palace, El Retiro, near Madrid, with wall paintings showing twelve great Spanish victories.[5] Napoleon had similar ambitions, but it remained for Louis-Philippe, the Citizen King, to establish the Historical Museum at Versailles in 1837. It had something to inspire every Frenchman. The Gallery of Battles, four hundred feet long, held thirty-three huge paintings that depicted many of Napoleon's victories. The Hall of 1830 glorified the peasants who constructed barricades during that uprising, while the Hall of Crusades complimented the old aristocracy. Later, gigantic paintings were added on the conquest of Algeria, the Crimean and Italian campaigns, and the Franco-Prussian War. The museum consciously sought to instill a love for glory in young Frenchmen; this patriotism perhaps paid off in 1914. Vienna's Museum of National Glories, established in 1850 in reaction against the 1848 uprising, had a Salon of Honor with fifty-six statues of famous Austrians. Rebuilt after World War II, it contains military equipment and recalls the great wars waged by Austria through the ages.[6] Many other museums in eastern Europe today have sections devoted to military history and the glories of communist uprisings with paintings, enlarged photographs, and newspaper clippings.

The idea of the museum of national glory has not been widely adopted in the United States. The four large murals of Confederate heroes and battle scenes by the French painter, Charles Hoffbauer, in Battle Abbey of the Virginia Historical Society, Richmond, constitute a minor exception.[7] Gutzon Borglum's gigantic sculptural group of Lee and other Confederate generals at Stone Mountain, Georgia, is somewhat similar in concept.

This kind of museum has several weaknesses. Battle paintings are seldom accurate in their details and certainly romanticize warfare. They also take up an inordinate amount of space and constitute a static display. The odor of propaganda clings to them always; whether overlarge and overbright as paintings or monotonous and flat as photographs, documents, and newspaper extracts, they often lack human interest.

Panorama Craze

A specialized form of the history museum employed the panorama or cyclorama—a huge circular painting of a battle or other extensive scene with the observer placed at the center and, sometimes, three-dimensional objects in the foreground. The painting often was housed in a rotunda and lighted from above. Robert Barker, a young Edinburgh painter in prison for debt, conceived the idea of the panorama and at London in 1792 exhibited one, of the English fleet anchored between Portsmouth and the Isle of Wight. A panorama craze developed in both Europe and America. In 1823 Louis J. M. Daguerre and Charles Marie Bouton invented the diorama (not our present-day miniature modeled group); by painting on translucent gauze and using moving lights, they could give an impression of movement and changing scenes. No more spectacular panorama ever existed than Colonel Jean-Charles Langlois's *Battle of Navarino,* shown in the Champs Elysées Rotunda in 1830. One entered between-decks of a fighting ship and came out on the poop deck to view the conflict. Wax representations of maimed and dying sailors and realistic sound supplied by hidden men heightened the effect. Cadets entering the Naval Academy of Brest, when taken to see the panorama, were considered to have experienced what it was like to be aboard a warship during battle.[8]

The true panorama reached New York in 1797 with a complete view of London 20 feet high and nearly 130 feet in circumference. Yet as early as 1784 Charles Willson Peale had shown in his Philadelphia residence a primitive type of small moving pictures entitled "Perspective Views with Changeable Effects; or, Nature Delineated and in Motion." An assistant with screens and lights made the scenes appear to move, and they were accompanied by sound effects. The system had been invented by Philippe de Loutherbourg in London in 1781, and Peale spent eighteen months perfecting a two-hour program that included portrayals of Walnut Street at dawn and at nightfall; a view of hell itself, its evil mood enhanced by appropriate music; and the naval battle between *Le Bonhomme Richard* and *Serapis*. Peale charged one shilling, or twenty-five cents, for his moving pictures, and during the summer of 1787 the delegates to the Constitutional Convention were amazed and entertained by the show. American artists continued to experiment with such art forms for nearly a century. In 1849 Henry Lewis completed a panorama of the Mississippi River from Saint Paul to New Orleans; it was 1,975 feet long and unrolled from one creaking upright spool to another amid the spiel of an interpreter and musical accompaniment. Two panoramas of the 1880s are still to be seen in the United States today—*Pickett's Charge*, by the Frenchman Philippoteaux at Gettysburg National Historical Park, and the *Battle of Atlanta,* painted by German artists in Milwaukee, at the Cyclorama in Atlanta.[9]

Historic Preservation

The French Revolution not only opened the Louvre and the Muséum National d'Histoire Naturelle as museums for the people, but also in 1795 created a Muséum des Monuments Français in the Convent of the Petits Augustins. The painter Alexander Lenoir, its founder and director, placed there many architectural and sculptural elements from confiscated churches and palaces. Separate rooms were devoted to each century, beginning with the thirteenth, and an "Elysian Field" had tombs recalling great men such as Descartes, Molière, and La Fontaine. For Héloise and Abelard, there was a romantic monument. The historian Jules Michelet decried the museum's dissolution in 1816 and said: "It was there and no other place that I felt a keen intuition of history."[10]

The attempt to use historical structures as a means of stimulating national pride and giving psychological stability to a government in power also expressed itself in the field of historic preservation. Louis-Philippe and his historian Minister of Interior Guizot established the service of Monuments Historiques in 1830. Brilliantly led by Prosper Mérimée, man of letters and later author of *Colomba* and *Carmen*, and by the architect Viollet-le-Duc, the French government began to inventory historic monuments and to classify them. Buildings of historic or aesthetic importance, even when privately owned, were placed under government protection to prevent their destruction and to control any exterior modification. Viollet-le-Duc also developed the concept and techniques of restoration; though sometimes he has been criticized for overrestoring and going beyond the bounds of strict historical authenticity, he saved hundreds of precious chateaux, churches, and other monuments.

These survivals of the past often became virtual history museums. Thus, when Henry James visited Carcassonne, the ancient fortified town near the Spanish border, about 1880, he could walk around the great double wall, its gray towers contrasting with the green grass of the filled-in moat, and imagine its busy life under the Romans, Visigoths, and medieval French. A lively little custodian led a small group that included James about the old Cité. For an hour, they passed along battlements, ascended and descended towers, crowded under arches, lowered themselves into dungeons, and "halted in all sorts of tight places while the purpose of something or other was described." The custodian also sold James a guidebook written by Viollet-le-Duc himself, as well as a set of post cards.[11]

Open-Air or Outdoor Museums

The historic preservation movement in France expressed that nation's respect for its heritage of ancient buildings. In the last quarter of the nineteenth century, while that feeling was at its flood, to the north the Scandinavians developed another form of cultural self-esteem. As a result, they gave the world a new kind of museum devoted to folk culture, ethnography, and social history. Artur Hazelius of Stockholm was father of the idea.

Hazelius was distressed to see the Industrial Revolution threaten the pleasant, coherent, and distinctive ways of living found in the different regions of Sweden and, indeed, all Scandinavia. He determined to collect and preserve the furniture, furnishings, implements, costumes, and paintings of the old days. In 1873 he opened in Stockholm his Museum of Scandinavian Folklore (later called Nordiska Museet). As his collection grew, he was offered entire buildings and other materials too bulky to show indoors. The result was that he acquired seventy-five acres on a rocky bluff at an old fortification (Skansen) overlooking Stockholm Harbor and started an open-air or outdoor museum there in 1891.

A few attempts at outdoor museums with a strong ethnographic flavor preceded Hazelius's Skansen. The Paris World's Fair of 1889 had shown members of twelve African tribes, as well as Javanese, Tonkinese, Chinese, and Japanese living in native houses, wearing native costumes, eating native food, practicing native arts and rites, and playing native music. (The World Exhibition of 1958 at Brussels had Congolese living in a typical village, but the spectators threw peanuts and bananas at them so that they returned home in disgust.) A Colonial Exhibition at Amsterdam in 1883 displayed an Indonesian *Kampong*, and, two years later, this outdoor village was given to the Rijksmuseum voor Volkenkunde at Leiden, where it attracted large crowds before damage from the harsh winters led to its closing in 1891.

Skansen's framework was its old buildings moved from various parts of Scandinavia—today, some 120 structures dating from medieval times to the twentieth century that include farm houses, a manor house, barns, outbuildings, cottages, shops, a church, and craftsmen's workshops. Hazelius and his successors added attractive gardens and typical farm crops to set off the buildings, as well as authentic furniture and furnishings for the interiors. Guides in the costumes of another day interpreted the culture, traditions, and life of the former inhabitants. Wherever possible, historically correct or appropriate modern activity went on. Divine services and numerous weddings used the eighteenth-century wooden church from Seglora. Musicians played and sang the old melodies, and folk dancers traced ancient steps with vigor. Glassblowers and other craftsmen made traditional products by hand; animals, domestic and exotic, enlivened the park; orchestras and the best musicians of Europe performed in an outdoor auditorium; an excellent theater presented Shakespeare, Selma Lagerlöf's comedies, and other favorite plays; and restaurants and bars served period food and catered to every taste. To this living museum now come more than two million visitors each year.

Hazelius was trying to use the idea of heritage and understanding of the past as a steadying influence in the face of the violent changes of modern life. He offered a new approach in museum exhibition, for he wished "to place the historical objects in their functional context . . . against the background of their entire cultural environment." He re-created the life of older periods, stimulating the sensory perceptions of the visitors and giving them a memorable experience. As they walked about the carefully restored environment of another day, their thoughts and emotions helped bring the place to life. "Hazelius's achievement," says Iorwerth C. Peate, sometime director of the Welsh Folk Museum, "was that of taking a sudden leap in museum technique and so transforming the museum from a curiosity shop into a home of national inspiration."

Hazelius's museum idea inspired other Scandinavian versions. Bernhard Olsen, former director of the Tivoli amusement park in Copenhagen, saw Hazelius's period tableaux in 1878 at the world's fair in Paris. He organized folk collections that became part of the Danish National Museum and in 1901 opened Frilandsmuseet that now has more than thirty-eight farmhouses, barns, cottages, craft shops, and wind and water mills situated in a lush ninety-acre rural park about eight miles from Copenhagen. Dr. Anders Sandvig, a dentist of Lillehammer in Norway, was so indignant at seeing five wagonloads of furniture and furnishings of the region on their way to Hazelius in Stockholm that he began collecting folk materials. They were finally placed in 1904 at Maihaugen (May Hill), where the Norwegian National Day was observed every May 17. Lillehammer's Sandvig Collection at Maihaugen is one of the loveliest outdoor museums clustered about five lakes and including a tiny log cabin (about 1440), the Garmo Stave Church (begun in the early twelfth century), an eighteenth-century farm estate, *Seters* or summer farm buildings from the mountains, and some fifty workshops. Dr. Hans Aal founded the Norsk Folkemuseum at Oslo, which in 1902 moved to Bygdoy, a peninsula extending into Oslo Harbor. Its Stave Church from

Gol dates from 1200. Peter Holm, a charismatic schoolteacher, established *Den Gamle By* (the Old Town) at Aarhus in Jutland in northern Denmark in 1909. Its emphasis is on the folk life of a town instead of a peasant community.

The outdoor museum has since spread around the world, and its influence seems to be constantly increasing. Some scholars regard it chiefly as a folk museum or ethnographic park, but separating folklore and ethnography from social history is a difficult task. Most American outdoor museums consider themselves history museums and try to include political, economic, and social history in their offerings. Everyone agrees that the outdoor museum was "more than a new idea of museum arrangement," more than combining the pleasant atmosphere of the picnic with the serious museum visit. Its most important contribution "was the conception that the greatness of a country, the strength of its industries, the beauty of its art, have firm roots in that country's own history."[12]

Culture History Arrangement

Still another ancestor of the history museum was the museum of industrial or decorative arts. After the Great Exhibition of 1851 in London, the South Kensington Museum was founded with industrial and decorative art from the Crystal Palace. Its exhibits were organized under the technical classification system, by which ceramics, glassware, metalwork, enamels, and the like were placed together, often in separate rooms, arranged chronologically or by patterns. Nearly everything was on display (today we call this system "visible storage"). This kind of exhibit may have satisfied scholars intent upon examining large numbers of examples and craftsmen looking for sources of inspiration for their own work, but crowded paintings on walls and heavy glass cases crammed with objects bored and repelled the general public.

A group of German museum curators conceived a new arrangement for such material. The Germanisches Museum at Nuremberg in 1856 purchased an old Carthusian monastery and installed there six original rooms ranging from one of a Tyrolean peasant (fifteenth century) to those of Nuremberg patricians (seventeenth century). By 1888 the museum had many such rooms following this culture history arrangement, so that one could imagine that he was walking through several centuries of German history. At the turn of the century, the Swiss Landesmuseum in Zurich was showing sixty-two such rooms, and the Bavarian Museum in Munich, seventy-six period galleries and rooms.

The culture-history arrangement placed too heavy a burden on museum collections, which could not furnish all the materials needed and thus sometimes resorted to conjectural reproductions. Historical period rooms were excellent in providing a unity of vision and arranging hundreds of objects in a functional, easily understood whole; on the other hand, they did not allow small individual pieces to be inspected closely and compared easily. The best arrangement, museum curators agree today, is to have some period rooms, some exhibits with a suggestive historical background, and still others with objects arranged chronologically or stylistically in separate groups or cases so that they may be examined minutely.[13]

American Historical Societies

The historical society has been a staunch backer of the history museum in the United States. The founders of the first societies—Massachusetts Historical Society (1791) at Boston, New-York Historical Society (1804), and American Antiquarian Society (1812) at Worcester—were driven by zeal for learning and love of country. As true disciples of the Enlightenment, they had unlimited faith in the power of knowledge and reason. They also were determined to preserve the, to them, thrilling story of their defeat of the powerful British empire and to point out the factors that caused the American genius for self-government to flower.

With their broad aspirations and enthusiastic energy, the early historical societies often embarked upon programs too ambitious and too widely dispersed. Thus the New-York Historical Society collected animal, vegetable, and mineral specimens; productions of "the American Continent and the adjacent Islands"; coins and medals; European old-master paintings; artifacts of the Plains and South American Indians; Nineveh sculptures; Egyptian rarities, including three large mummies of the sacred bull Apis; as well as documents, paintings, and objects of New York origin and interest. Eventually, the society narrowed its field of collection to New York and began to dispose of much of the extraneous material.

By 1876, the centennial of American independence, seventy-eight historical societies were counted in the country, about half of them with museums. Today there are some five thousand societies with the same ratio of museums. Some of the earliest societies, for example, Massachusetts and the American Antiquarian, had limited membership; still, the general trend has been to admit anyone with the proper interest and willingness to pay dues. The earliest societies were all entirely private in finance and control, but starting in the 1850s Wisconsin and others in the Midwest received state appropriations. Their ideal has become to serve everyone in the state, and programs have broadened; the imaginative efforts of Reuben Gold Thwaites of the State Historical Society of Wisconsin to reach both learned and popular audiences well illustrate this development. Many societies no longer limit themselves to the scholarly activities of library, research, and publication; instead they now also promote museums, the marking of historic sites, historic preservation, school tours and clubs, and a host of other programs appealing to all ages. Their central indoor museums often have expanded to include a chain of historic houses, preservation projects, and outdoor museums. As part of its central function, the historical society sometimes institutes educational, cultural, and ethnic outreach programs similar to those carried on directly by art or science museums, and state historical societies have often helped promote and assist local historical societies in counties and municipalities.

The organization of all this activity was not always done by a historical society. Sometimes a government department or commission was in control; in other instances, history museums were privately organized without the historical society form. A few examples of high-grade American history museums in this general category would include the National Museum of History and Technology, part of the Smithsonian Institution in Washington; the Museum of the City of New York; the Pennsylvania Historical and Museum Commission; the Detroit Historical Museum; the North Carolina Division of Archives and History; and the Museum of New Mexico.[14]

Historic Houses

Americans developed their own distinctive version of historic preservation while Europeans were restoring their churches and castles or gathering vernacular architecture and folk objects into outdoor museums. The historic house museum, in the opinion of its founders, was a way to teach love of country. The committee seeking to save the Hasbrouck House, Washington's headquarters in Newburgh, New York, argued that no traveler in the area would

> hesitate to make a pilgrimage to this beautiful spot, associated as it is with so many delightful reminiscences of our early history. And if he have an American heart in his bosom, he will feel himself to be a better man; his patriotism will kindle with deeper emotion; his aspirations for his country's good will ascend from a more devout mind, for having visited "Head-Quarters of Washington."

The State of New York bought the house for about $10,000 in 1850, agreed to maintain and operate it, and appointed the Newburgh Village Board of Trustees custodian "to keep it as it was during General Washington's occupancy."[15] This was the first historic house museum opened in the United States, but another one much better known was Mount Vernon, Washington's plantation in Virginia. It is a monument to the first outstanding American historic preservationist, Ann Pamela Cunningham of South Carolina.

Various proposals had been made for Mount Vernon—that it serve as a summer residence for the president, that it be an old soldiers' home, a model farm, or an agricultural college. Private speculators suggested converting the mansion into a resort hotel or using the estate as a factory site. Neither the federal government nor the commonwealth of Virginia would agree to acquire it, but Miss Cunningham determined to "save American honor from a blot in the eyes of the gazing world" and to establish a shrine where "the mothers of the land and their innocent children might make their offering in the cause of greatness, goodness, and prosperity of their country." She had found her life work and soon showed herself a shrewd planner, promoter, and organizer. The commonwealth of Virginia in 1856 chartered the Mount Vernon Ladies' Association of the Union. Miss Cunningham, as regent, chose prominent, energetic vice-regents from some thirty states and outlined a varied assortment of imaginative money-making schemes. The Ladies' Association raised $200,000 to buy the plantation and began preservation work on the mansion on February 22, 1860. Extravagant schemes were suggested, such as taking the house down piece by piece and replacing it with a marble-faced replica, but Miss Cunningham with good common sense declared that the Ladies' Association would "preserve with sacred reverence" Washington's house and grounds "in the state he left them."

Mount Vernon illustrated American reliance on private voluntary organizations. Amateur efforts could count, especially when led by clever, energetic women. The Ladies' Association as an early example of effective organization helped advance the cause of women's rights. Mount Vernon inspired many imitators. General Andrew Jackson's Hermitage near Nashville, Tennessee, George Mason's Gunston Hall and the Lees' Stratford in Virginia, and Valley Forge in Pennsylvania are only a few of them. The fashion was for historic-house projects to refer to themselves as "second only to Mount Vernon."[16]

Another great contribution to saving historic houses was made by William Sumner Appleton through the Society for the Preservation of New England Antiquities, which he organized at Boston in 1910.

Appleton had a much broader concept of historic preservation than the women who worked at Mount Vernon and on other early projects. To them, historical and patriotic purposes were dominant, and they regarded historic houses as shrines. They thought it best to develop the houses as museums devoted to great personalities and important historical events. Appleton, on the other hand, played up the architectural or aesthetic worth of historic houses. He wished to save them as useful documents of the past, and he saw clearly that many valuable houses would be lost if only those connected with great leaders and significant historical events were preserved. He also realized that not every historic house was suitable for, or could be supported as, a museum.

Thus Appleton's society tried to save houses by continuing them as residences or by finding some suitable adaptive use (as offices, antique shops, community centers, tearooms, and the like) that would not harm their fabric and would prolong their life. This approach emphasized the mellow and pleasing aura of an old building for modern living. It also had the practical advantage of keeping the house on the tax roll. Sumner Appleton was so enthusiastic, inspiring, and ingenious that, at his death in 1947, his society possessed fifty-one historic structures scattered throughout New England outside of Vermont. Since then, the Society for the Preservation of New England Antiquities has continued its leadership in the preservation field.[17]

The National Park Service, created in 1916 in the U.S. Department of the Interior, brought the federal government fully into the history museum and historic preservation movement with the Historic Sites Act of 1935. It declared it "a national policy to preserve for historic use historic sites, buildings, and objects of national significance for the inspiration and benefit of the people of the United States." This policy was greatly expanded by the Historic Preservation Act of 1966, which established the National Register of Historic Places, created the Advisory Council on Historic Places to protect registered landmarks, and authorized the Park Service to administer a matching grants-in-aid program. (These activities were transferred in 1978 to a newly created bureau, Heritage Conservation and Recreation Service, in the Department of the Interior). The Park Service has also developed trailside museums and visitor centers for its numerous archaeological and historical properties. A central co-ordinating but nongovernmental preservation agency appeared in 1949 in the National Trust for Historic Preservation, which operates a few properties of its own but advises and assists numerous member organizations.

Today there are about two thousand historic house museums in the

United States, and new ones open every year. One reason for this expansion has been the increased interest Americans are taking in their early history. In an era of rapid technological change, threatening atomic annihilation, and deteriorating economic prosperity, thoughtful citizens seek reassurance that the American system of government is well conceived and sturdy enough to survive. Emphasis on a common national background has important psychological values. Then, practical sociological/economic developments—the automobile and increased leisure—are other reasons for historic house museum proliferation. At the same time, leaders of the historic preservation movement agree that its great future growth lies not in the museum field, but in historic districts—areas of residential and adaptive uses in our cities. The first of these districts developed in Charleston and New Orleans in the 1930s, and there are about thirteen hundred of them in existence today. Though the districts usually designate some buildings as museums, the emphasis is on using the architectural past as a pleasant, inspiring background for modern living.[18]

American Outdoor Museums

Colonial Williamsburg, the preserved and restored capital of eighteenth-century Virginia, is probably the best-known outdoor museum in the United States. As a history museum, it is an expansion of the historic-house concept to include the major part of a colonial city, some 175 acres and about 30 buildings with carefully furnished interiors open to the visiting public. As a living historic district, it also has about 100 properties occupied by residents of Williamsburg or rented to tourists.

Colonial Williamsburg was founded in 1926, when John D. Rockefeller, Jr., decided to finance the dream of the Reverend W. A. R. Goodwin, rector of Bruton Parish Church, to bring the colonial capital back to life. The town plan was virtually intact, and some eighty-five original buildings still stood. They were provided with authentic outbuildings; gardens based on American and English precedents were developed; and some important buildings were reconstructed when enough evidence was available. Historical, architectural, archaeological, and curatorial researchers worked together to obtain a high degree of authenticity. As the project matured, careful attention was given to its education program or interpretation. Well-trained, costumed guides, working craftsmen, life on the scene (carriages, oxcarts, and livestock), period dining, military drills, music, dancing, plays, fireworks, and many other activities appealed to the visitor and encouraged his participation, while a varied list of publications and audiovisual productions as well as reproduced furniture and furnishings spread the Williamsburg story outside the restored city. Special attention was given to school groups, with emphasis placed on using the historical environment with the new inquiry method of teaching history. A forum series employed the Williamsburg background for in-depth study of furniture and furnishings, gardens, principles of government, and other areas.

The idea of making use of a preservation project as an outdoor museum has become popular in the United States. Historic Deerfield in Massachusetts preserves a typical New England village; Old Salem in North Carolina restores an early Moravian community; Spring Mill Village in Indiana recreates a Midwest frontier settlement; and Columbia, California, shows a typical mining town. These are only a few examples of this kind of museum.[19]

The first large American outdoor museum organized on the Scandinavian model and moving historical structures to a central location was Greenfield Village at Dearborn, Michigan, dedicated by Henry Ford in 1929. Ford thought that historians emphasized politics and wars too much, and he was sometimes contemptuous of book learning, big ideas, and windy generalizations. His anti-intellectual attitude led him to assert: "Most history is more or less bunk." Still, he was interested in his own kind of history, and he said about Greenfield Village:

> When we are through, we shall have reproduced American life as lived; and that, I think, is the best way to preserve at least a part of our history and tradition. For by looking at things people used and that show the way they lived, a better and truer impression can be gained than could be had in a month of reading.

In 1922 the Ford tractor factory buildings covering three acres in Dearborn became vacant, and Ford had a repository for his almost compulsive collecting. Sometimes he bought entire antique shops; a noted collection of carriages and automobiles he purchased was transported in fifty freight cars; and one of his engineers in the Ford plant in Manchester, England, shipped him "huge steam engines weighing hundreds of tons and delicate porcelains requiring most careful handling." Ford called his collection "my Smithsonian Institute," and the *New York Times* considered it "the greatest collection of antiques ever acquired by one man."

By 1936 the village contained more than fifty buildings that included a traditional New England green with church, town hall, courthouse, post office, and general store; the Scotch Settlement schoolhouse Ford attended as a boy; the Plymouth, Michigan, carding mill to which Ford's father took wool; Noah Webster's house; William Holmes McGuffey's Pennsylvania log-cabin birthplace; a 500-ton stone Cotswold Cottage; and the Sir John Bennet jewelry shop from Cheapside, London, with its clock graced by statues of Gog and Magog. This partial listing makes clear the weakness of Ford's conception—its lack of coherence and of a clear central idea. He also distrusted museum professionals and took pleasure in making all decisions himself. The indoor Henry Ford Museum and Greenfield Village nevertheless remain an important and valuable collection that slowly takes more meaningful form.

Many outdoor museums of this general type have developed since World War II, including Old Sturbridge Village in Massachusetts, Mystic Seaport in Connecticut, Farmers Museum at Cooperstown, New York, Shelburne Museum in Vermont, Upper Canada Village in Morrisburg, Ontario, and Stonefield and Old World Wisconsin in Wisconsin. It should be pointed out, however, that the best of these projects work hard to define a clear concept of purpose and do painstaking historical research to recreate an authentic, historically justifiable community. This scholarly approach makes the outdoor museum much more useful for teaching social history and advances it several steps beyond the idea of moving disparate old buildings into a pleasant parklike setting.[20]

The historic houses and outdoor museums of the United States constitute a three-dimensional panorama that traces American history from its earliest colonial settlements to its modern industrial civilization. Although the relative youth of the United States must be taken into consideration, the fact remains that this country has more of its three-dimensional history left than any of the older nations. It is possible today to experience buildings and other remainders of every period of our history, though it would take more than one lifetime to visit all these historical places.

Problems of the History Museum

This rapid survey should have made clear the lack of definition that characterizes this type of museum. The basic problem, as Loris S. Russell says, is that

> History is a record of events. It is a stream, a sequence, a continuum. The museum, in contrast, is concerned with things. It is basically static. The totem pole is the end product of many hours of work but tells us little of the work itself.

Georges-Henri Rivière and several other European museum scholars have remarked that history museums too often still follow the conventional anecdotal, great-men, great-events approach to history instead of considering economic, social, and cultural factors. Rivière and Jean-Yves Veillard have set up a model history museum in the Musée de Bretagne in Rennes; they have outlined a general historical framework and themes for the history of that region from geological times to the present. They have called in historians, ethnographers, geologists, geographers, economists, and linguists (as many as twenty outside experts) to assist the museum staff and designers. The working groups criticized the themes and agreed on contents of each one; the historical materials at hand were not allowed to determine them. The experts thought that many museums give too much attention to high-style costumes and furniture, simply because they survive. The planners at Rennes also insisted that the history museum must consider the present, must "foster the dynamic assimilation of knowledge in order the better to challenge the values of the contemporary world." Their theories provide some sound guidance, but the resulting displays are still often static and fragmentary. Placing a Roman milestone and an ancient horseshoe together does little to explain transportation in the Gallo-Roman period; the long labels, manuscripts, maps, and art work used to supplement such scanty objects are still better suited to books than to museums.

The conflict between fluid history and static museum objects helps account for the popularity of the outdoor history museum. It appeals to the visitor's sensory perception and thus gives hints of what it was like to live in another age. Some outdoor museums, however, treat so limited an area and time period that they transmit little sense of development, though the visitors glimpse some continuity in comparing the material culture of another age with that which they experience today. Most outdoor museums also are too neat and clean, and do not pay enough attention to the darker side of human existence—to poverty, disease, ignorance, or slavery. Museum objects may be ill-suited to explain these deficiencies of the past, but oral presentations, books, or audiovisual devices can provide supplementary means for interpretation.

How can historical buildings, furnishings, settings, and isolated objects—frozen bits of history, as it were—convey understanding of a dynamic, continuous flow of human experience? This is the basic problem to which history museums should address themselves; their staffs should give the highest priority to finding solutions. The opinion expressed in 1888 by George Brown Goode, pioneer museum scholar at the Smithsonian, is still pertinent today: "What the limitations of history museums are to be is impossible at present to predict. In museum administration, experience is the only safe guide. . . . In the history museum most of this experimental administration still remains to be performed."[21]

6

Botanical Gardens and Zoos

The Palm House, built in 1848, Royal Botanic Gardens, Kew

Panorama of Carl Hagenbeck's Moated Zoo, Hamburg, 1907

Botanical gardens, arboretums, zoos, and aquariums fit into the definition of a museum adopted by the American Association of Museums. They are organized, permanent, and nonprofit in form, essentially educational or aesthetic in purpose, have a professional staff, and own, utilize, and conserve tangible objects that they exhibit to the public on some regular schedule. The only difference between them and an ordinary museum is that their objects are alive. The botanical garden is a collection of labeled plants, the primary purpose of which is the advancement and diffusion of botanical knowledge. The garden studies taxonomy, the system of classification and nomenclature of plants, and experimental botany that deals with their anatomy, cytology, and metabolism. An arboretum is virtually the same as a botanical garden except that it specializes in woody plants. Similarly, a zoological garden (usually shortened to "zoo") or aquarium contains a collection of labeled animals to be protected and studied while incidentally providing enlightenment and enjoyment for the public. Animal physiology and psychology are the chief subjects for zoo research.

The First Botanical Gardens

Humankind has for long enjoyed and appreciated the aesthetic, medicinal, and economic uses of plants and has mixed these purposes for organizing a garden with the purely scientific and botanical ones. While the gardens of the ancients, of the semimythical Emperor Shen Nung (2800 B.C.), of the King of Thebes or of Thutmose III at the Temple of Karnak in Egypt (both about 1500 B.C.), and of Aristotle in Athens or the Mouseion at Alexandria (4th century B.C.) may not have been true botanical gardens, yet they contained exotic plants, both beautiful and useful. Similarly the gardens of herbs and simples of the early monasteries such as Saint Gall (9th century) or even the Holburn Physic Garden at London (1575) had many botanical features, and the Mexican gardens of Istapalan and Chalco encountered by Cortez and his followers were closer to true botanical gardens, for the Aztecs had made considerable study of medical botany.[1]

There is a long-standing dispute over whether the first European botanic garden was situated in Padua or Pisa. The senate of the Venetian Republic ordered the garden at Padua in May 1545, and its original layout remains largely intact. Its rectangular plan shows elegance and taste, with a central circle eighty meters in diameter and beds arranged geometrically inside. Francesco Bonafede was its founder, Giovanni Moroni drew the plan, and Luigi Squalerno (commonly called Anguillara) was its first prefect. It was attached to the University of Padua, which had had a Chair of Simples since 1533, and in 1591 it issued the first garden catalogue. The English botanist John Ray reported on his visit to Padua in 1644: "Here is a publick Physick garden, well stored with simples but more noted for its prefects, men eminent for their skill in Botanics." Goethe visited the garden before 1790 and especially admired a palm planted in 1585; "Goethe's Palm" still flourishes today in its unique greenhouse.[2]

The Pisa garden may have been in existence in July 1545, but was moved to a new site in 1562. It was founded by Lucca Ghini, and its second prefect, Andrea Cesalpino, was also a famed botanist. Its arrangement was geometric with separate sections for bulbs and poisonous, prickly, odoriferous, and marsh plants. The prefect gave lectures on simples and actual demonstrations on living plant specimens in the garden. It was attached to the University of Pisa.[3]

Another famed early botanic garden was established at Leiden in 1587. The university there decided that a botanical, rather than an apothecary, garden was better suited for the development of its medical faculty and persuaded the great botanist Charles de l'Ecluse (Carolus Clusius) to become its second prefect, 1593–1609. The Leiden garden had a succession of able directors, including Hermann Boerhaave, 1709–1730, with whom Linnaeus studied. In 1740 the garden was open every day (even on Sundays), though a small fee was charged and "Couples openly in love are on no account admitted." By this time, also, botanical gardens were growing as many plants as possible; when Boerhaave took over there were only 3,700 species, but within a few years he could count 5,846.[4]

Other sixteenth-century gardens were established at Zurich, Bologna, Leipzig, Montpellier, Paris, and Heidelberg, and by 1700 there were twenty such gardens in Europe, usually connected with universities. Interest in close observation and taxonomy caused scientific botany to thrive as an adjunct to the medical schools in the universities at a time when the development of other sciences there was being hampered by medieval tradition. The Oxford Botanic Garden (1621) boasted a "Nursery of Simples" and "a Professor of Botanicey"; its conservatory was heated by a four-wheel fire-basket of burning charcoal hauled back and forth by a gardener. Dr. Robert Morison, professor of botany, in 1670 took his class in the Medical School "to the Physic Garden where he read in the middle of it (with a table before him) on herbs and plants for five weeks space, not without a considerable Auditory." At Montpellier in 1773 a professor taught anatomy at the university in the winter and botany at the garden in the summer.[5]

The private garden of the Tradescants was contemporary with Oxford, and the Chelsea Physic Garden was founded at London in 1673 by the Society of Apothecaries. Sir Hans Sloane purchased a site for it in 1722 on condition that it present fifty well-dried and preserved specimens of distinct plants to the Royal Society each year until two thousand had been given. Philip Miller, whom Linnaeus called "the Prince of Gardeners" and whose *Gardeners Dictionary* (1731) soon ran through eight editions, was head gardener at Chelsea in 1723, and he trained William Aiton, first gardener of Kew, and Dr. Nathaniel Bagshaw Ward, the physician who, about 1833, invented the Wardian case, a small portable greenhouse that made possible the successful transportation of plants. By Miller's day, botanical gardens were found throughout western Europe, including one on the Apothecary Island in Saint Petersburg (1714).[6]

The Royal Botanic Gardens at Kew

In the 1750s Augusta Saxe-Gotha, dowager princess of Wales, began to develop her nine acres in Kew House west of London as a botanical garden. They had been laid out by William Kent, the landscape architect. She was assisted in this work by Lord Bute (John Stuart, third earl of Bute), a keen and knowledgeable botanist, though American colonists later disliked him as prime minister. The dowager princess commissioned Sir William Chambers, the distinguished architect, to embellish the grounds with various fanciful structures. Of these, the Alhambra, Mosque, and Gothic Cathedral have disappeared, but the Pagoda (1761–1762), Ruined Arch (1759), Orangery (1760), and several smaller temples remain. The garden was arranged scientifically under the Linnaean system and had a physic garden section. In 1759 William Aiton, upon Philip Miller's recommendation, became its head.[7] Augusta's son, George III, also unfavorably known to Americans, in 1772 inherited Kew and joined to it his Richmond Lodge garden; thus, the name, "the Royal Botanic Gardens of Kew." The king loved Kew and enjoyed playing the role of "Farmer George" there. He retained Aiton as "His Majesty's Principal Gardener of Kew" and also employed Lancelot ("Capability") Brown to landscape the gardens.[8]

The king's chief botanical adviser, however, was Sir Joseph Banks, just home from a round-the-world trip with Captain Cook on the *Endeavour*. Banks determined to make the little botanic garden a place where plants from every country could be seen and "a great exchange house of the Empire, where possibilities of acclimatising plants could be tested." He sent out collectors to South Africa, the West Indies, North America, Australia, Timor, India, China, Brazil and elsewhere in South America, New Zealand, and the Congo. By the time the king and Sir Joseph died in 1820, some seven thousand new plants had come to Kew from overseas.[9]

Meanwhile, William Townsend Aiton had succeeded his father upon the elder Aiton's death in 1793 and did not retire until 1845, at age eighty. After the passing of George III and Banks, the Royal Gardens deteriorated, but an investigative committee report caused Parliament in 1840 to transfer them from the personal property of the Crown to the Commissioners of Woods and Forests. Thus, Kew became a national institution, and in 1841 Sir William Jackson Hooker was named its first director. Sir William had served for twenty years as regius professor of botany at Glasgow University and developed a small botanical garden there in exemplary fashion. Not only was he a magnetic teacher and a leading scholar, but also a tall, slim six-footer of tremendous energy who could walk sixty miles in a day. In five years he expanded the 15 acres of the gardens he took over to 250 acres. With the help of Decimus Burton, architect, and Richard Turner, engineer, he built the graceful and airy Great Palm House—363 feet long and 62 feet high, with 45,000 square feet of glass, the largest planthouse in the world. In 1848 he started a Museum of Economic Botany to exhibit plants useful for commerce, industry, and medicine.

Kew became the great center for botanical exchange. Plant exploration resumed, and Sir William's son, Dr. Joseph Dalton Hooker, after going with Ross to the South Pole from 1848 to 1850, explored the Himalayas in India, Sikkim, Tibet, and Nepal and sent back many exotic plants, including beautiful rhododendrons. Cinchona plants (from which quinine is derived) came to Kew from Peru, to be grown and sent to India. Cork oaks from Portugal were developed for South Australia, tobacco for Natal, and China tea for Assam. Coffee, allspice, cinnamon, mango, tamarind, cotton, ginger, and indigo went around the world in Wardian cases from the nurseries and forcing houses of Kew.[10]

In 1855 Dr. Joseph Dalton Hooker became assistant director at Kew and ten years later, on the death of his father, director. He continued the plant exploration and exchange; in 1876 Henry A. Wickham sent para rubber plants from the Amazon to Kew, where they were grown and forwarded to India and Malaya. Joseph Hooker greatly improved the research facilities. The Herbarium begun in 1853 was much enlarged when Parliament purchased his father's collection in 1866; today Kew has the largest herbarium in the world, with some six million dried specimens. The library counts 55,000 bound volumes in addition to numerous separates, maps, and manuscripts. In 1876 the Jodrell Laboratory was set up to study the structure and physiology of plants. Dr. Hooker had a nasty clash with one Ayrton, first commissioner of works in Gladstone's cabinet. Ayrton used every insult to try to make Hooker resign, but the scientific world stood by him. Ayrton was defeated twice for re-election to Parliament, and Hooker was elected president of the Royal Society and knighted by Queen Victoria.[11]

Kew also began to be known in this period as a nursery for botanists and gardeners. As early as 1860 lectures were given to foremen and gardeners, and more recently a one- or two-year student-gardener internship developed. In the 1950s a census of 277 former student gardeners found them working in public parks and gardens in Britain and 47 different foreign countries.[12]

Sir Joseph retired as director of Kew in 1885, to be followed by his son-in-law, William Turner Thistleton Dyer, who had become assistant director in 1875. Thistleton Dyer was especially interested in economic botany; for example, he helped introduce rubber into Ceylon and Malaya and cacao into Ceylon. He remained director until 1905. Thus Kew enjoyed remarkable longevity of service from its administrators—eighty-six years for the two Aitons and sixty-five years for the two Hookers and Thistleton Dyer. Since then, through two world wars and numerous crises, Kew has maintained its place as the leading botanical garden of the world. In 1965 it leased from the National Trust the great Wakehurst garden at Ardingly in Sussex—five hundred acres with fertile soil, abundant rainfall, long periods of sunshine, mild climate, and beautiful topography.[13]

Other European Botanical Gardens

The Royal Botanic Garden at Edinburgh is another important British horticultural institution. The fourth garden in that city since 1670, it moved to its present site (now fifty acres) in 1820. Again, the family succession was important. William McNab, the principal gardener, was followed by his son James, a true landscape artist who also helped Edinburgh University develop an outstanding school of landscape gardening. John Hutton Balfour and his son Isaac Bailey were both regius keepers, and the son shifted the research focus to investigating the function and structure of living plants. George Forrest, of the garden's herbarium, made seven plant-exploring trips to China and brought back many of the rhododendrons for which the Royal Botanic is famous. Its rock garden, rose garden, arboretum, herbaceous borders, and greenhouses are all outstanding.[14]

The Jardin des Plantes in Paris (1635), closely associated with the Muséum National d'Histoire Naturelle, has been famed for its great botanists but not strongly interested in either ornamental horticulture or economic botany.[15] Vienna has two botanical gardens that go back to the eighteenth century—the Belvedere, with the oldest Alpine collection in Europe, and Schönbrunn, with an elaborate set of greenhouses, not so important botanically, but demonstrating that a garden can survive economically by growing beautiful plants for commercial sale.[16] The Berlin Botanical Garden (today the Berlin-Dahlem Botanical Museum) was founded by Carl Ludwig Willdenow in 1801, who also taught at the University of Berlin and had Alexander von Humboldt as a student. Heinrich Friedrich Link fused the botanical garden, royal herbarium, and library into a single powerful institution that placed scientific botany first but never forgot to attract and educate the general public with ingenious and exciting exhibits.[17]

Uppsala University in Sweden has a botanical garden that goes back to the early eighteenth century. Its students stood in the center of a geometric plan looking toward the circumference of a circle; the labels faced out so that only the professor could see them. The university also properly maintains the little garden in which Linnaeus worked when he moved from Lund to Uppsala in 1728.[18] The first Russian botanical garden (1714) was in Saint Petersburg (now Leningrad), and with the National Herbarium is today part of the Komarov Botanical Institute. Moscow has the Principal Botanic Garden of the USSR Academy of Science; it contains more than 900 acres and conducts a vast plant survey and collection activity for the whole Soviet Union, which possesses 150 botanical gardens, more than any other nation. Their first aim is crop improvement and economic botany, and some of the best gardens are at Minsk, Kiev, Yalta, and Tashkent.[19]

Economic Botanical Garden Expansion

The British Empire was largely responsible for a worldwide expansion of botanical gardens, chiefly founded to provide new crops and economic resources for its colonies. Its first tropical garden was at Pamplemousse in Mauritius (1735), which introduced nutmeg, pepper, cinnamon, and other spices from the East Indies and improved the production of sugar cane. Gardens were also established in the West Indies at Saint Vincent (1764), Jamaica (1774), and Trinidad (1819).[20]

What today is the Indian Botanic Garden at Calcutta was started by Robert Kyd in 1787 as a garden of acclimatization for food and spice plants, teak trees, and the like. Six years later, Dr. William Roxburgh, a distinguished botanist, became its superintendent and transformed it into a true botanical garden. In 1861 Superintendent Thomas Anderson introduced cinchona for the production of quinine, for which he established a commercial plantation in Sikkim. After two disastrous tornadoes, Sir George King in 1871 rebuilt the garden in its present form. Its great banyan tree may be the largest plant living—about two hundred years old, one hundred feet high, one-fourth mile long, and with a canopy covering four acres.[21]

The botanic garden in Ceylon was started on Slave Island in 1812 by William Kerr, its chief gardener, and moved to its present location at Peradeniya ten years later by Alexander Moon. Its most famous superintendent was Henry George Kendrick Thwaites. In 1860 he established a satellite garden high in the mountains at Hakgala for the successful growing of cinchona and later at Henaratogoda for rubber. He fought a parasite disease attacking coffee plantations, developed the tea brought from China to Peradeniya in 1828, failed to establish cotton, but secured good results with cacao, coca (from which comes cocaine), camphor, nutmeg, clove, vanilla, croton, oil palm, mahogany, and eucalyptus.[22] Two beautiful botanical gardens are situated at Bogor in Java and at Singapore. Bogor (1817), developed by the Dutch, has two hundred acres with six thousand species of trees and shrubs and five thousand species of lesser flowering plants as well as a mountain garden of five thousand acres at Tjibodas. Singapore (1822) was especially important under Henry Nicholas Ridley after 1888 in developing rubber plants brought from Brazil via Kew. Australia has two botanical gardens with especially handsome sites at Sydney (1816) and Melbourne (1854).[23]

The South African National Botanical Garden at Kirstenbosch, a few miles from Cape Town, is descended from the Company's Garden or Town Garden (1750) and the Botanic Garden of Cape Town (1848). Cecil Rhodes bought four hundred acres at Kirstenbosch and left it to the state. Harold Welch Pearson in 1911 organized the wild site filled with Cape Province plants in the lee of Table Mountain into a botanical garden and served as its first director.[24]

The Botanic Garden in Rio de Janeiro was founded largely for economic reasons. In 1808 Prince Regent John VI of Portugal bought an old sugar mill property to acclimatize useful plants from the East Indies. That same year Luiz de Abreu, a Portuguese naturalist, was captured by the French and interned in the West Indies on Ile de France, which had an acclimatization garden, Jardin Gabrielle. De Abreu escaped to Brazil, carrying seeds and roots that he planted in the royal garden. At his urging, Asiatic plants including tea and superior sugar cane were imported. Frei do Sacramento and Joao Barbosa Rodriguez were two of the garden's great directors. The garden contains marvelous avenues of royal palms two hundred feet high, descended from the seed smuggled from Jardin Gabrielle by de Abreu.[25]

American Botanical Gardens

During the colonial period, John Bartram, plantsman and plant explorer, collected native species at his farm near Philadelphia as early as 1728, and his son William continued this somewhat less than a botanical garden. John Bartram's cousin, Humphrey Marshall, in 1773 established a similar garden at West Bradford in Chester County near Philadelphia. Robert and William Prince started a nursery at Flushing, Long Island, in 1737, and four generations of their family continued the business until 1867; for a time they called part of it the Linnaean Botanic Garden. A most important early venture was the Elgin Botanic Garden of 1801 that occupied twenty acres in New York City on the present site of Rockefeller Center. Its founder was Dr. David Hosack, prominent physician and professor of botany and materia medica at Columbia College, who considered the garden a valuable adjunct to his teaching. By 1811, however, he was compelled to sell to the state of New York, which eventually turned the property over to Columbia College. It allowed the garden to deteriorate and disappear.[26]

Today there are about a hundred botanical gardens in the United States. The oldest is the Missouri Botanical Garden of seventy-five acres, organized at Saint Louis in 1859. Henry Shaw, a native Englishman, came to Saint Louis in 1819 and made a fortune in merchandising. Dr. George Engelmann, a German immigrant physician and botanist, urged Shaw to transform his estate into a botanical garden, and Asa Gray of Harvard and Joseph Hooker, later director at Kew, supported that idea. Dr. Engelmann refused the directorship of the garden because it was too far out of town (now about twenty minutes from center city) and Shaw, from 1859 to 1889, served as director of what is often still called "Shaw's Garden."

The Missouri Botanical Garden has a fine herbarium (including the

Bernhardi collection of more than two million specimens), a library, an orangery (the Linnaean House) built in 1850, conservatories for American and South African desert plants, two rose gardens, outstanding collections of the flora of Panama and of water lilies (developed by George H. Pring), and good arrangements with local colleges and universities for training gardeners. Perhaps its most spectacular feature is the Climatron, a Buckminster Fuller geodesic dome, built in 1960, 80 feet high and 175 feet in diameter. The Climatron controls air and humidity so as to provide different climatic environments for the plants grown there.[27]

The Arnold Arboretum of 265 acres, situated at Jamaica Plain, just outside Boston, contains the greatest collection of woody plants in the United States. James Arnold left Harvard University money to establish the arboretum in 1872, and Charles Sprague Sargent, brother of the artist John Singer Sargent, served as its director for fifty-four years, from 1873 to 1927. He was a remarkable botanical administrator who carried out well his charge to grow "all the trees, shrubs, and herbaceous plants, either indigenous or exotic, which can be raised in the open air" at that location. Sargent and Frederick Law Olmsted, the distinguished landscape architect, persuaded the city of Boston to include the arboretum in its park plan and to construct driveways and help with its maintenance. It was planted according to Olmsted's plan in 1885 and soon acquired a fine herbarium and library.

Sargent's greatest contribution to the arboretum was the collection of exotic plants from all over the world. He persuaded Ernest Henry ("Chinese") Wilson to go to China for the arboretum, 1907-1909, and Wilson brought back 2,262 packages of seed, 1,473 kinds of living plants and cuttings, 30,000 herbarium specimens of 2,500 species, and 720 photographic plates. On later trips Wilson visited Japan, Formosa, Korea, Australia, New Zealand, Tasmania, India, Kenya, Rhodesia, and South Africa. Joseph Roch, the Viennese plant explorer, also went to China and Tibet for the arboretum. All together, Sargent added more than 3,000 exotic species to the collections.[28]

The New York Botanical Garden in the Bronx is the country's largest, with two thousand acres (including its Cary Arboretum at Millbrook), an annual budget of $5 million, and a staff of 350, with 40 research scientists. It was founded in 1891 and is strongly research oriented with a magnificent library and numerous publications. It does advanced scientific work in fields that include fungi, mosses, algae, plant ecology, geography, plant nutrition, microbiology, physiology and pathology of fungi, and diseases and pests of ornamental plants.[29]

The Huntington Botanical Gardens in San Marino, California, were established in 1906, when Henry E. Huntington, the railroad magnate, acquired an estate there and decided to develop a library and art gallery with encircling gardens. William Hertrich, Austrian-trained botanist, was superintendent of the 207 acres. It contains camellias and wildflowers; gardens featuring sculpture, palms, roses, herbs, and Shakespearean and Japanese themes; and an unrivalled desert garden made by Hertrich of ten acres and 25,000 plants.[30]

The Brooklyn Botanic Garden, founded in 1910, is a small oasis (fifty acres) in a busy city and is devoted to teaching botany, horticulture, and nature conservation. It is supported partially by a nonprofit society with enthusiastic dues-paying members and partially by the city of New York. It has three Japanese gardens and two for roses; boulder, herb, local flora, children's, and small model gardens; a Fragrance Garden for the blind, with Braille labels; and a superb collection of bonsai. The Botanic Garden started as an empty field but was cleverly planned by Frederick Law Olmsted and Calvert Vaux. Dr. C. Stuart Gager, its first director, was determined to bring plants and people together, and it is in the educational area that the garden has excelled. The ideal has been public participation— to learn by growing.

About five thousand adults enroll in varied short courses each year and use working greenhouses. New York City teachers take in-service courses. Especially effective has been the work with young people— always on a volunteer basis, with Saturday morning classes in a working greenhouse in winter or in the two hundred plots of the Children's Gardens in summer. Making cuttings, potting small plants, sowing seeds, and transplanting seedlings have provided participatory interpretation. In the spring two young gardeners are given an eighty-by-ten-foot vegetable plot to plant, tend, and harvest as partners.[31]

Longwood Gardens at Kennett Square, Pennsylvania, contain plants chosen for beauty and display and thus do not constitute a true botanical garden. The gardens cover a thousand acres and include an arboretum established about 1800 by Joshua and Samuel Peirce. In 1906 Pierre S. du Pont, prominent industrialist of the Du Pont Company and General Motors, bought the tract to save the arboretum from destruction, and in 1921 he established the gardens as a permanent public institution. He conceived of Longwood as a cultural center devoted primarily to horticulture but also to architecture, music, and drama. Thus Longwood has gardens, conservatories, perhaps the most spectacular fountains in the world, a singing-chimes tower, a pipe organ, and an open-air theater.

The outdoor gardens include the unstudied plantings of the old arboretum and varied wildflowers. A more formal arrangement is usually followed with rock, topiary, rose, and water lily sections. Especially evident is the influence of the Italian Villa d'Este and Villa Gamberaia and the French Versailles and Fontainebleau. Most dramatic of all are the fountains—some twenty-two separate displays that sparkle during the day are enhanced at night by lights and colors that make them "liquid fireworks." The conservatories cover about four acres and vary from desert to tropical rain forest; the favorite plants of the public include roses, azaleas, orchids, waterlilies, and acacias. Special displays are installed seasonally—lilies at Easter, azaleas and rhododendrons in the spring, chrysanthemums in the fall, and poinsettias at Christmas.

Longwood has supported many activities of value to American horticulture. It has co-operated with the United States Department of Agriculture in sending plant explorers to the far reaches of the world, and it has backed the American Horticultural Society's project to computerize all plant species in American botanical gardens.[32]

The Fairchild Tropical Garden on the outskirts of Miami, Florida, occupies eighty-three acres and was founded in 1935 by Col. Robert A. Montgomery, a former resident of Connecticut. It was named to honor Dr. David Fairchild, who, as head of the Plant Introduction Bureau of the United States Department of Agriculture, had brought many tropical plants to Florida. Fifty-eight acres of the garden are maintained by Dade County, and the remaining twenty-five acres by the Fairchild Tropical Garden Association, which has planted and maintains a palmentum, the best and largest in the world, with more than five hundred species. The garden also possesses outstanding collections of cycads, bromeliads, and philodendrons; conducts important scientific research; and has a varied educational program for adults and schoolchildren.[33]

Problems of the Botanical Garden

Botanical gardens in the past have been much like art museums, in that the beauty of their collections has attracted an audience sensitive to aesthetic appeals—in this case, color, texture, design, perfume, and natural growth. Professional botanists, nurserymen, and keen amateur gardeners have come to the gardens to study plants and ways to grow them. Women's garden clubs (often the most elite of organizations) have also patronized the gardens. Too seldom have they devoted their resources to inculcating in the general public an understanding of plants and their uses. Sometimes the burgeoning of racial and ethnic groups in the inner cities and the flight of the well-to-do to the suburbs have left a botanical garden like a beached whale on a barren and unfriendly shore.

An obvious solution for this situation is for the garden to develop broad and dynamic educational and interpretive programs such as that of the Brooklyn Botanic Garden. The gardens can also obtain increased relevance by promoting community gardens, establishing a widespread garden information service, designing planting and maintenance procedures for parks, roadsides, and urban renewal projects, and training and employing high school dropouts and handicapped persons. The botanical garden has a chance to join the crusade for a better environment and ecology so needed in modern life, as well as the opportunity to apply its plant research to such problems as the detection and lessening of air pollution.

Another evil of the botanical world is the number of plant species that are becoming extinct—for example, many varieties of the bean or the tomato. Often such species may prove valuable for their resistance to disease or for other qualities. While the preferred solution may be to preserve native plants in parklike natural environments, still the botanical garden or the agricultural experiment station may serve as a species bank.[34]

From Menageries to Zoos

Humankind has always been interested in the other animals of the world as sources of food and clothing, as companions or pets, and as strange and curious phenomena. The domestication of animals goes back many milleniums, perhaps fifty thousand years for the dog. Queen Hatshepsut of Egypt in the fifteenth century B.C. had an extensive palace menagerie that she stocked with monkeys, leopards, birds, wild cattle, and a giraffe; she sent an animal-collecting expedition through the Red Sea to what is today Somalia. The Assyrians fancied leopards and lions by 1,000 B.C., and King Solomon maintained herds of cattle, sheep, deer, and horses, as well as flocks of fowl; he traded with King Hiram of Tyre to obtain apes and peacocks or parrots. About that time, Emperor Wen Wang established a zoological garden in China.

After 700 B.C. the Greeks were setting up menageries, and Aristotle described three hundred separate species in his *History of Animals* (fourth century B.C.). The Mouseion at Alexandria possessed animals, and the Romans had aviaries and menageries, some of the latter with bulls, elephants, rhinoceroses, hippopotamuses, lions, bears, leopards, tigers, and crocodiles to be used in gladiatorial combats. Charlemagne had three small zoos in the eighth century, Henry III in 1230 had a menagerie in the Tower of London, Marco Polo saw Kublai Khan's great animal collection in the fourteenth century, and Cortez visited Montezuma's zoo at Mexico in 1519.

Holy Roman Emperor Francis I established the first great modern zoo at Schönbrunn in Vienna in 1752, with a rococo pavilion where his wife Maria Theresa could breakfast while watching the animals. He sent collectors to America, and his son opened the zoo to the public in 1765. Other zoos were started at Madrid and at the Jardin des Plantes in Paris during the eighteenth century; the latter received animals from the Menagerie du Parc founded by Louis XIV at Versailles.

Sir Thomas Stamford Raffles, an English administrator who founded Singapore, was an animal lover and an admirer of the Jardin des Plantes zoo. He began the Zoological Society of London in 1826. Its royal charter called for the "advancement of zoology and animal physiology, and the introduction of new and curious subjects of the animal kingdom." The zoo, situated at one end of Regent's Park, opened to the public in 1828 with two llamas, a leopard, kangaroos, Russian bear, emus, cranes, and other birds in suitable dens, aviaries, and paddocks. This zoo, with 1,351 species and 6,611 specimens, has continued to be one of the world's greatest with excellent research as well as good showmanship. In 1931 it opened a five-hundred-acre branch thirty miles from London at Whipsnade, in Dunstable, Bedfordshire, the first wild-animal park in the world, that displays and breeds large groups of animals. Other outstanding European zoos are found in Antwerp, Amsterdam, East and West Berlin, Munich, Frankfurt, Cologne, and Zurich.[35]

A revolution in zoo construction took place between 1902 and 1907, when Carl Hagenbeck, an animal dealer, set up his own zoo in Stellingen, a suburb of Hamburg. Beginning with a flat plain, Hagenbeck built an artificial, mountainouslike terrain with carefully constructed moats to contain the animals and with none of the customary cages and iron bars. This open-enclosure zoo was the prototype of the present spacious wild-animal parks that leading zoos in the world are beginning to acquire to supplement their city-restricted activities and show wildlife in a proper environment while strengthening their research and breeding functions. Hagenbeck's invention also made possible the safari zoo, the modern drive-through wild-animal domain that is often connected with an amusement park. Not only was Hagenbeck an innovator in zoos, but he also loved the animals he collected and developed techniques for training them by gentle methods using simple rewards of food tidbits instead of torture of whips and red-hot irons. For a time Hagenbeck exhibited primitive human beings—Laplanders, Nubians, Eskimos, and other "wild men," ending in 1884 with a Senegalese Show caravan that contained sixty-seven human beings, twenty-five elephants, and many cattle. In 1887 Hagenbeck's famed circus opened in Hamburg.[36] William Temple Hornaday, director of the New York Zoological Society, remarked in 1920:

> The zoological garden directors of all Germany were industriously engaged in boycotting Mr. Hagenbeck . . . [who] has had the temerity to build . . . a private zoological garden so spectacular and attractive that it made the old Hamburg Zoo look obsolete and uninteresting.[37]

Some Leading American Zoos

The Philadelphia Zoological Garden (1854) is the oldest chartered zoo in the United States, though the tiny Central Park Menagerie in New York was the first actually to exhibit animals. Other prominent mainstream zoos are found in Chicago's Lincoln Park (1868), the National in Washington (1889), Milwaukee County (1892), New York's Bronx (1895), Saint Louis (1913), San Diego (1916), Fort Worth (1923), Detroit (1928), and Brookfield near Chicago (1934). The Arizona-Sonora Desert Museum at Tucson (1952) specializes in animals of the American desert and for its size is one of the best zoos in the country.[38] A brief history of the Bronx and San Diego zoos will bring out some of the chief developments and problems of the field.

The New York Zoological Society, formed in 1895, adopted a plan radical for its day. Instead of showing native and foreign animals in cramped pens and paddocks, it tried to place them in free range in large enclosures and natural surroundings. Hornaday, the first director, was a strong and energetic leader who served for more than thirty years until his retirement at age seventy-two in 1926. He chose a site in the southern Bronx covering 252 acres. New York City purchased the land, constructed roads and buildings, and provided maintenance and keepers, while the society paid for animals and the curatorial and educational staff.

Hornaday frequently had considerable difficulty with his board of trustees, especially Henry Fairfield Osborn of Columbia University and the American Museum of Natural History, chairman of the executive committee, and Madison Grant, the secretary. The public resented Hornaday's banning cameras so that the society could profit from the sale of photographs, but the restriction was not lifted until after his retirement. Hornaday also disliked the term *Bronx Zoo*, though it came into general use. He refused to employ the Hagenbeck system of moats, because he did not want to keep the public sixty or seventy feet away from the animals. In 1906 Ota Bengh, a pygmy from the Congo, was employed or "exhibited" in the Primate House at the zoo for a time, but Negro ministers protested and Hornaday removed him. After David Garnett's novel, *A Man in the Zoo*, appeared in 1924, one John Cromatie offered to be displayed between an orangutan and a chimpanzee for educational purposes, but Hornaday refused, no doubt remembering the pygmy.

Hornaday thought a zoo existed mainly "to collect and exhibit fine and rare animals" and to enable "the greatest possible number of people to see them with comfort and satisfaction." All other purposes were distinctly secondary, such as "breeding of wild animals" and the "systematic study of them." The Zoological Society took over the Aquarium at Castle Clinton on the Battery in 1902 and operated it there until 1941; it reopened at Coney Island in 1957.

Dr. W. Reid Blair succeeded Hornaday in 1926 and at once began experimenting with barless, moated parks, built a separate Ape House, and improved the educational program. A real change of direction came in 1940 when Fairfield Osborn, son of Henry Fairfield Osborn, became president of the board. He believed that a zoo's chief function was protection of animals as part of the whole environment—forests, soils, waters, and wild life. He saw that the society took a leading role in the Conservation Foundation (1948), Institute for Research in Animal Behavior (1965), and Osborn Laboratories of Marine Science at the Aquarium (1967). John Tee-Van was director from 1956 to 1962, and William G. Conway succeeded him. The goal now was "to preserve the fast-vanishing wildlife of the world," for "zoos are actually refuges, perhaps the only safe refuges, for hard-pressed species."

With these changes of purpose went many experiments in better exhibition techniques—an African Plains, Lion Island, Children's Zoo, Farm-in-the-Zoo, Conservation Exhibit, World of Darkness (nocturnal animals), World of Birds, Man and Animal in Tropical Asia, and the Skyfari aerial tramway. In 1977 a new Wild Asia exhibit was opened with thirty-eight acres where 200 mammals and birds representing 15 Asian species are displayed in spacious vegetated areas; visitors view the animals from a silent electric monorail train. The zoo housed 710 species, with 3,077 specimens in 1974, and yearly attendance reached 2.5 million. The Bronx Zoo recently acquired Saint Katherine's Island, off the coast of Georgia, which it will use purely for conservation purposes to breed endangered species and establish a kind of gene pool for them. The installation, not open to the public, can be reached by an eleven-mile boat ride. Many zoos are acquiring such refuges, and the National and the Bronx are planning co-operative use of each other's breeding farms at Front Royal, Virginia, and Saint Katherine's Island.[39]

The San Diego Zoological Garden, founded in 1916, has become in a short time one of the leading mainstream zoos of the world. It began when a physician, Dr. Harry M. Wedgeforth, an enthusiastic animal lover, was outraged at the poor quality of the small menagerie shown at the Panama-California International Exposition at San Diego that year and determined to build the miscellaneous collection of monkeys, coyotes, and bears left by the exposition into a first-class zoo. Assisted by dynamic Mrs. Belle J. Benchley, at times virtually the zoo director, Dr. Harry wheedled, pushed, and promoted to secure private and ultimately city tax support for the project.

The zoo occupies 128 acres, with a series of canyons and almost perfect weather that have allowed it to develop an ideal moated system. It also has a superb collection of beautiful flowers, shrubs, and trees that makes it a veritable Garden of Eden. As early as 1926, the zoo began to develop a guided bus tour that permits visitors to see the animals roaming free in their moat-protected areas. The bus drivers are trained zoologists who point out the different animals and interpret them knowledgeably and with good humor.

In 1974 the zoo in the city (and its Wild Animal Park) contained 1,412 species with 5,406 specimens and attracted an annual visitation of 3,250,000. Some of its features are moving sidewalks over certain canyons; a superb walk-through aviary in one canyon; the Wedgeforth Bowl that seats 3,000 spectators for a sea-lion show; a properly scaled-down Children's Zoo where youngsters may encounter and fondle turtles, antelopes, baby leopards, and elephants; a Skyfari ride; a man-made waterfall in Cascade Canyon; and a koala bear feeding on the zoo's own eucalyptus trees.

The zoo officials had for long discussed developing a natural wild-animal park or preserve, where animals would be free to live according to natural behavior patterns, to reproduce their kind, and to be little disturbed by human intrusion on their territory. In 1972 at San Pasqual, thirty miles north of the downtown zoo, the San Diego Wild Animal Park was opened on an 1800-acre tract. A bus links the two sections of the San Diego Zoo, and a five-mile-long monorail, silent and unpolluting, winds through seven major preserve areas of the park perimeter, to allow zoo-goers to observe some of the 1,500 animals and birds as they eat, sleep, fight, or mate.

The buildings and landscape of the Wild Animal Park try to reproduce the African environment. Nairobi Village, to one side, is a pedestrian area with restaurant and visitor facilities as well as an elephant bath, a huge gorilla grotto, a free-flight, 220-foot-long aviary, a kraal or pen in which children may pet tame animals, and a performing animal show. A one-and-one-half-acre lagoon filled with flamingoes, pelicans, and exotic fowl has a Congo River fishing village astride a waterfall.

Plans are being made for a walkway that goes over but not into the preserves and for a cable-car system. The park also tries to conserve endangered species of African plants in the garden and forest environment; one project calls for a twenty-five-acre jungle greenbelt near the gorilla area behind Nairobi Village. A conservation/ecology orientation center seeks to enlist visitor support for the underlying purposes of the park, which has a phenomenal breeding record and offers new vistas for zoological research. It is San Diego's answer to the commercial drive-through zoo.[40]

The Safari Zoo

The safari zoo is a commercial enterprise that allows a family in its own automobile to drive through an area in which wild animals and birds are roaming free. The car may encounter a lion "eyeball to eyeball," or a herd of curious camels may sniff it. The idea began in 1966, when Lord Bath invited the English public to gaze at the lions of Longleat from inside their cars on his Longleat estate in Wiltshire. A year later, Lion Country Safari opened near West Palm Beach, Florida, on 640 acres enclosed by moats and steel fencing. Prides of lions, herds of zebras, giraffes, ostriches, and other animals apparently grazed freely, and visitors could drive among them in their own cars (with windows closed) or in air-conditioned buses or rented cars. Outside the fenced area were a snake pit, children's zoo (with lion nursery), chimpanzee islands, exotic shorebirds, pygmy hippopotamuses, and sea lions. The project stressed recreation, conservation, education, and zoological research (through outside universities). It asserted that animals were as free there as wild populations, except that the predator-prey interactions were missing.

These privately-owned wild animal parks have proved enormously popular and are spreading rapidly. Jungle Habitat, Great Adventure, Wild Animal Kingdom, World Wildlife Safari, Wild Animal World, and World of Animals are only a few of them. They offer a more natural way of showing wildlife, their breeding records are excellent, and visitors see the animals in an intimate way, not through binoculars, as at the San Diego park. On the other hand, the animals, while appearing free, are still confined by fences or moats; sometimes their environment is dirty and dusty, not at all like the plains or jungle of their normal habitat. The long lines of cars with their exhaust fumes are far from a natural environment; in essence, the observers have been caged as the animals formerly were. There is real danger to car occupants who foolishly lower their windows. Many of the drive-through zoos lack the trained personnel that understand and love animals.[41]

Zoo Problems

The early menageries and the public zoos frequently mistreated wild animals by confining them in small cages, keeping them from any social experience, and condemning them to a life of boredom. Zoos tried to be comprehensive and to include as many species as possible, no matter how small their financial and staff resources. Animals were often exposed to unwise feeding by the public, and their health was not properly looked after. Breeding too many animals often resulted in mistreatment of the surplus. Zoo animals sometimes were not properly protected day and night from the cruelty of inebriated or mentally-ill vandals. Many of these deficiencies persist today; thus public opinion has frequently turned against zoos, and organizations have been formed to do away with them entirely.

On the other hand, animals in the wild have been more and more threatened with extinction. Increasing human populations with agricultural and industrial needs have cut into wild animal preserves, and hunters and poachers have relentlessly killed animals for purposes of fashion or trophies. Today's well-run zoos with emphasis on animal health and protection have truly become the safest havens for wild beasts, the only sure way to avoid their total extinction. The zoos that are expanding into large wild-animal parks as in London, New York, Washington, and San Diego offer optimum environmental conditions for their animals; like some of the botanical gardens, they are serving as species banks.

Zoos today stress preservation, zoological research, and education as their chief purposes, though recreation and amusement, when properly administered, can accompany the basic aims. The safari or drive-through commercial zoos, though they emphasize recreation and may be overcommercial, have opportunities to forward the more serious purposes of wild-animal preservation and study.[42]

7

The Museum as Collection

Charles Towneley and his friends in the Park Street Gallery, Westminster, 1782

The first function of museums to appear historically was that of collection, and collection remains the predominant reason for many a museum's existence. Collecting is an instinctive drive for most human beings, as well as for various beasts, birds, and insects; dogs bury bones, ants store grain and bees honey, and some birds collect bright objects in their nests. Physical security for long has been an underlying purpose of collectors, and Lewis Mumford has perceptively observed that "Granary, bin, and cellar are village prototypes of library, archive, museum, and vault."[1] Collections still offer some physical security today; art objects, for example, often provide a hedge against inflation and, in time of war, may be portable and command a ready market. Collections also usually give their possessors social distinction—power, prestige, and status. Such distinction may ripen into a kind of immortality if the collector leaves his life's work to a museum, thus assuring "the survival on earth of the collector's name inscribed over a museum door."[2] The collector also may take joy in the chase, in running down clues and bargaining with owners or dealers. Collecting in a few instances has become a neurotic obsession, "a kind of gambling passion" that has driven its practitioners even to cheating and theft.

Collectors usually perform great services for museums and indeed for society as a whole. They preserve objects of artistic, historical, and scientific importance for the enlightenment and enjoyment of present and future generations. Collectors, too, may become knowledgeable about the stream of objects that passes through their hands, and their research may make them leading authorities in their field of collection.[3]

Why Museums Collect

Most museums collect because they believe that objects are important and evocative survivals of human civilization worthy of careful study and with powerful educational impact. Whether aesthetic, documentary, or scientific, objects tell much about the universe, nature, the human heritage, and the human condition. Museums thus carefully preserve their holdings so as to transmit important information to the present generation and posterity.

These basic generalizations hold true for all museums, but each type has special characteristics. Art museums may be said to concentrate on beauty, and their mission is often defined as the direct transmission of the artist's aesthetic understanding to the beholder through the picture or object. Some art museum directors are so devoted to the idea of direct aesthetic communication that they begrudge any interpretation of the object beyond the simplest one-line factual label placed as inconspicuously as possible, and they bar printed interpretation sheets or sound tapes from their galleries. Other directors are more interested in works of art as documents, whose creators had insight into, and gave a clear view of, the social conditions of their day; thus the object transmits historical information and understanding. Some art museums try to combine the two points of view by keeping their main galleries aesthetically pure with a minimum of interpretation and constructing a separate building or wing devoted to education with a great variety of interpretive devices.

Since World War II, however, the American art museum has undergone enormous changes. Public involvement has increased markedly, with numerous temporary exhibitions accompanied by lectures, films, demonstrations, and symposiums. Music, theater, dance, and film have invaded the museum. Programs for schoolchildren have multiplied. The museum has been urged to take its collections and staff to other centers—to conduct outreach programs in the inner city. Some of these developments may cause an institution to become more of an art center devoted to cultural activity than a museum concentrating on collection.[4]

The history museum treats artifacts or objects as social documents—often as important for the historian, argue the museum curators, as the library's printed books or manuscripts. These artifacts may have many forms; they may be associated with political events, military armament and equipment, industrial or technological machines and processes, or buildings, furnishings, and gardens. E. McClung Fleming asserts that decorative art objects can throw light on many different aspects of a culture. Furniture, textiles, ceramics, glass, and metals show the kinds of materials available to the craftsman and his manufacturing methods, the area trade in raw materials, the functional technology of the era, the standards of living of different classes and regions, and everyday life and social customs. From the designs, the historical heroes, events, landmarks, literary themes, and folklore emerge, as well as the taste of the era.[5] This material culture becomes especially vivid and impressive in period room, historic house, and historical village. The history museum collects the surviving objects of an age or ages and is especially interested in ethnography and social history. The museum of science and industry is similar to the history museum if it collects industrial paraphernalia of the past but more like the art center if its exhibits explain the processes of physical and biological science and present-day technology.

The natural science museum does a different kind of collecting in that it gathers specimens of geology, paleontology, and biology, and identifies and classifies them. This taxonomic kind of collecting has led to great advances of knowledge and is still important in the study of natural science. Botanical gardens and zoos are special museums in the natural history field with collections of living, rather than inanimate, specimens.[6]

How Museums Collect

Gifts and bequests are the most common kind of museum collections. Many, probably most, private collectors cannot bear to see dispersed the objects on which they have lavished so much attention and thought; thus they donate them to appropriate museums. Their generosity is often heightened by the desire to preserve their names as important donors and by the tax laws that make it worth their while. In Great Britain, heavy inheritance taxes often cause the executors of an estate to give paintings or objects to the nation in partial payment. In the United States, such materials may have greatly appreciated in value since a donor obtained them, and the going market value may be legitimately deducted from inheritance or income tax. Many smaller museums, rarely able to purchase objects, are almost totally dependent upon gifts and bequests. Dealers are sometimes important in this field, because they may have helped the private collector secure his objects and may counsel him on giving them where they will be best preserved and used.

Larger or wealthier museums also acquire objects by purchase from private sources, dealers, or at auction. Collections may be built steadily and comparatively inexpensively over a period of time by knowledgeable curators whose studies enable them shrewdly to judge and even anticipate values. Here again dealers are useful in discovering objects and calling them to the attention of museums or museum patrons. Occasionally, museums make dramatic news at auctions, as when the Metropolitan Museum of Art in 1961 acquired Rembrandt's *Aristotle Contemplating the Bust of Homer* with a then record bid of $2.3 million.

Museums also obtain collections by field work and expeditions. Natural history museums often send curators to gather scientific specimens in many parts of the world. Some anthropological museums obtain the bulk of their collections by means of archaeological expeditions, and art museums also collect archaeological and ethnographic materials in this manner. Historic preservation projects depend on archaeological digs to help provide historical authenticity for their architecture, furnishings, gardens, and interpretive activities; this historical archaeology results in collections of materials to be used for research and interpretation.

Still another way that museums acquire collections is by exchange or loan. Enlightened museum professionals like to see objects used well and fittingly. Sometimes, exchanges will mutually benefit and improve several collections. Formal exchange is difficult, however, because materials to be traded are usually uneven in value; often outright sale or extended loan is more feasible.[7]

The Need For a Plan

"The decision establishing the scope of the museum's collections is probably the most important one that the governing board can make," wrote Carl E. Guthe, in discussing small history museums, but the statement applies equally well to all types and sizes of institutions.[8] The relevance of a museum's holdings distinguishes it from a household attic filled with obsolete and often broken and useless discards. In making a plan, the museum should first of all consider its purposes and define them succinctly but clearly. What is it to collect? How preserve, authenticate, and research its collections? How exhibit and interpret them? How does the present collection fit into this plan? Wise answers to these basic questions can provide the framework that results in a first-class, high-quality museum.

Art museums must decide what period to cover, what geographic area to encompass, and what kinds of materials to gather. A small American regional museum may confine its collections to paintings and sculpture produced in its area during the era since European settlement. Yet at once pressures will arise to enlarge the chronological period so as to cover prehistory, to expand the geographic area to include the art of the countries from which the first settlers and their successors came, and to widen the art forms to embrace architecture, furnishings, folk art, photographs, and perhaps motion pictures. Local collectors will probably urge the museum to accept and enlarge their collections, no matter how inappropriate for the museum's field. Large comprehensive art museums have similar problems, aggravated by deciding what to do about prehistoric and classical archaeology, arms and armor, musical instruments, folk art, and contemporary art. The smaller art museum can sometimes solve its collection problem by keeping to a strictly prescribed scope for its own holdings but covering much wider periods and areas by means of temporary exhibits obtained on loan from private collectors, other museums, or traveling exhibition services. Museums may also decide to devote themselves to a special field such as modern art, American art, decorative art, furniture, textiles, glass, or ceramics or to a single artist, for example, Rodin, Saint-Gaudens, or Remington. A museum also should consider co-operative collecting by the museums of a region, with each responsible for certain fields so as to eliminate waste of money and resources in competition.

The history museum can define its field of collection rather readily; its period will extend from prehistory to the present or will cover some portion of that era, and its area will be determined chiefly by its location and geographic field—municipality, region, or nation. Then difficulties begin, however, for the inhabitants of the area have belonged to various jurisdictions from locality to nation and have had connections with, and imported materials from, other areas. The best plan will be to outline in considerable detail the history of the chosen period and area and then subject materials sought by the museum and offered to it to careful and rigorous analysis. A midwestern state history museum, for example, will confine its collection of American Indian materials to cultures that once inhabited the area, except for a few objects from outside cultures to be used for comparison. It will accept a few decorative art objects brought back by a state resident who once served as Minister to Spain but will not take an extensive collection of Spanish barber bowls amassed by the same diplomat. History museums may also be specialized—devoted to whaling or the sea, the military services, railroads or canals, and, of course, historic houses and sites.

Certain guidelines will help determine whether objects have historical value. In general, relics ("something left behind after decay, disintegration, or disappearance") are not suitable; a piece of the Charter Oak, a lock of Washington's hair, or a shell fragment picked up at Gettysburg tells us almost nothing of historical significance. On the other hand, objects with complete documentary records frequently have great value; a labeled piece of colonial furniture can transmit much social history, and even one with a well-defined family tradition can be helpful. Association pieces also have worthwhile emotional overtones; the portable writing desk on which Jefferson composed the Declaration of Independence or the "star-spangled banner" that Francis Scott Key saw flying at Fort McHenry are precious treasures of the National Museum of History and Technology. Equally important are everyday objects used by ordinary men and women, such as authentic log cabins or sod huts with their crude and meager furnishings.[9]

Art and history museums share an especially acute collection problem in deciding what to gather from the contemporary scene. Living artists and their work continue a major concern of the art museum. History is interested in the typical objects of everyday life, and they are exceedingly difficult to find for past ages; beautiful and unusual artifacts tend to survive, but not the commonplace ones. Thus century-old wedding dresses, ball gowns, and officer's uniforms are comparatively plentiful, but not everyday house-dresses or men's work clothes. The passage of time assigns values to material culture that do not always satisfy the needs of the social historian. Gaps in the future museum collections can be avoided if museums will adopt an outline of the history they wish to follow and a rational system of collecting designated contemporary objects. Some of these materials can be reviewed and weeded out every five or ten years. Also, in many instances, photographs of objects may be retained rather than the objects themselves.[10]

Science museums must also define their scope. The small natural history museum may limit itself to telling a broad scientific story with the flora and fauna of its locality or region; sometimes it can take advantage of the living specimens of the botanical gardens and zoos of the area. The technical museum or science center must decide how many historical objects to gather or whether to devote itself solely to explaining natural and physical phenomena and technological equipment and processes.[11]

These decisions by a museum governing board will apply to all future collection policies. The question will then remain of what a museum should do with materials acquired in the past that do not conform to the new policy. The best advice here is that the board proceed cautiously and adhere scrupulously to the conditions under which such objects were acquired until legal remedies can be found.

Obviously, whatever plan a museum adopts should ideally be written down as completely and clearly as possible. It should be understood by both governing board and staff and be revised periodically to incorporate decisions made in day-to-day policy determination and implementation. In developing such a program, the experience of the National Park Service may prove helpful, especially for history and natural science museums. The Park Service has worked out definite procedures to provide each of its properties with a master plan. This guide may include a topographic contour map of present conditions, a general physical development plan, an environmental or historical base map (with interpretive statement and plan), measured drawings and floor plans, and a furnishing plan. The extensive area of the typical park property has made these detailed guides desirable. Most museums (except for larger outdoor ones) require a much simpler plan, but they can better understand the planning process and elucidate their own objectives by examining Park Service procedures.[12]

The Ideal of Unrestricted Ownership

Negotiations between a prospective donor and a museum that wishes to acquire his collection may often result in complex and delicate bargaining. Should the collection be kept intact, not intermixed with objects from other collections? Should the collection remain always on exhibition? Should it have its own wing or gallery with the name of the donor prominently displayed? Should the collection be accepted as an extended or long-term loan in the hope that it may eventually ripen into a gift or bequest? The museum may be tempted to agree to such conditions in order to obtain possession of important articles or collections.

Any of these restrictions, however, offers possible future trouble for the museum. Whether the collection be old master paintings, the uniform and equipment of a prominent Revolutionary general, or South American butterflies, what happens if the museum in a generation or so obtains a larger and better collection in the same field? From a logical and psychological viewpoint, it would be far better to combine the old and new materials (and place some items in storage) in order to obtain a more effective exhibit. Also intensive study of museum objects frequently results in new attributions of artists or makers, and even exposes out-and-out fakes. Is the dead hand of the donor to prevent needed revisions and adjustments?

From the museum's point of view, it is usually best not to accept gifts with conditions attached. Museums, of course, should have proof of ownership of each article in their holdings, and they are well advised to have a standard gift-agreement form with a paragraph that makes clear that articles are given outright and unconditionally, the form to be signed in duplicate by the donor with one copy for him and the other for the museum. Occasionally, a governing board may decide that a collection (or a single object) is so important that it will be accepted with conditions. In such instances, a formal agreement should make clear the terms, again to be signed in duplicate, this time by both donor and museum representative.

Extended loans from individuals are even more likely to give a museum difficulties. Sometimes lenders use the loan device as a means of receiving free and safe storage for their possessions and have even been known to leave them in their wills to other museums than the one storing them. Loans may be terminated at inconvenient times, and disputes may develop over the treatment the museum gives the objects. In general, a museum is wise to avoid taking extended loans from individuals, but if it decides to do so, it should devise a legal agreement signed in duplicate by lender and museum that clearly makes provision for security, insurance, inspection, exhibition, and termination of the loan.

Two kinds of loans, however, are most useful and should be encouraged. The first is the loan for temporary exhibits that are so common today and desirable when they add to knowledge by showing objects in new and significant relationships. Here again, the museum must cover the whole loan process carefully with mutually agreed-upon provisions for packing, transportation, care, and insurance. Extended loans from one museum to another are also entirely legitimate. Sometimes a museum lends articles outside its field of collection to a museum that will exhibit and use them appropriately; the conditions under which the lending museum originally received the objects may make it difficult to relinquish ownership, but an extended or permanent loan allows the materials to be put to desirable use. Sometimes, too, a large museum will lend materials from storage to a smaller museum that will exhibit them well; in this situation, the lending museum may check on the loan and renew it periodically. Again, in both instances, careful records agreed to by both parties should be kept.[13]

The Place of the Dealer

In Roman days, there were dealers in art objects, good ones and untrustworthy ones. During the Middle Ages, second-hand dealers and jewelers bought and sold art. Until the seventeenth century, the dealer was usually an agent, often a courtier, rather than a shopkeeper. Some of the great artists also served as dealers; the most successful of all, perhaps, was Rubens. Art objects have been auctioned from early times, and there is the story of the Roman collector who fell asleep during a sale and whose nodding head was taken to mean that he was approving bids. He awoke to find he had bought unwanted items worth 1,800,000 sesterces. Paintings and art objects were sold at trade fairs in the Middle Ages and even later; but by the sixteenth century, artists had organized exhibitions of art for sale, and cities began to regulate auctions. For a time, Amsterdam was the chief art sales center, to be followed by Paris, which, after the French Revolution, was joined by London. Two great auction houses had been founded there—Sotheby's, by Samual Baker, in 1744; and Christie's by James Christie, in 1766.[14]

During the nineteenth century, many changes took place in the developing profession of the art dealer. He found, authenticated, promoted, and sold art, often becoming a connoisseur and critical authority in the process. Some dealers, such as Paul Duran-Ruel in Paris, the friend of the Impressionists, began to manage a group of artists, discovering new talents, buying paintings on speculation, exhibiting and promoting, and serving as bankers and confidants.

Dealers, both European and American, became important in the United States after the Civil War in persuading wealthy collectors to acquire old master paintings and other art objects. They sought outstanding works of art, enlisted art history experts such as Bernard Berenson, Wilhelm von Bode, and W. R. Valentiner to validate them, and took advantage of rivalries among the collectors to demand high prices from which they reaped great profits. Sir Joseph (later Lord) Duveen of London was one of the most enterprising, enthusiastic, and entertaining of all the dealers; his adventures in uncovering masterpieces and playing upon the sensitivities of his wealthy clients make dramatic and diverting reading. Robert C. Vose, Michel Knoedler, Jacques Seligman and his son Germain are other examples of those who helped make New York City a great international art mart, while William MacBeth and Robert Macintyre served collectors of American art well. Parke Bernet, established in 1937, became the leading American auction firm and in 1964 was purchased by Sotheby's of London. Today Sotheby's-Parke Bernet has branches also in Melbourne, Buenos Aires, Toronto, Paris, Florence, Beirut, Edinburgh, Johannesburg, Houston, and Los Angeles.[15]

Dealers proved invaluable to art museums, though less frequently to history or science ones. They played upon their clientele's desire to preserve and use their collections to the greatest advantage. Duveen knew that if his wealthy customers generously gave their holdings to museums, he would not be called upon to repurchase them in case of faulty attributions or worse calamities. Knowledgeable dealers working with experts sometimes made important research discoveries; like collectors and museum curators, they were in a strategic position to study the numerous paintings and art objects they handled.[16]

Determining Authenticity

In deciding to add items to their collections, museums must be on guard against forgeries and fakes. Forgeries are copies of paintings or objects made for fraudulent, usually profitable purposes. Fakes are genuine art works of little worth that are altered, or added to, so as to enhance their value. Forgers are occasionally driven by psychological obsession—a desire to commit a perfect fraud that will fool the greatest authorities. Han van Meegeren, for example, thought that the world failed to recognize his great talent and vowed to take in the experts by creating paintings in Vermeer's exact style. D. G. van Beuningen, the great Dutch collector whose motto was "Rely on your own taste and never ask advice," paid 1,600,000 florins for van Meegeren's spurious *Last Supper*, and the prestigious Boymans Museum of Rotterdam bought his *Christ and the Disciples at Emmaus* for 520,000 florins.[17]

There are three chief ways of authenticating objects—by scientific, historical, or stylistic analysis—and a museum should use all three of them in considering accessions. The first method is the newest and has obtained some spectacular results. It analyzes the physical nature, composition, and structure of an object. The laboratory examination may begin by using physical or optical methods, nondestructive because they do not require that a minute sample be taken. Visual examination with raking light and by using a binocular microscope of low magnification will explore the field of visible radiation. Then X-rays or gamma rays will reveal an object's condition throughout its depth, including repairs or restorations. Ultraviolet and infrared rays are used to determine many invisible characteristics of objects, for example, the age of varnish, presence of restoration, nature of patina, or repairs. X-ray fluorescence spectroscopy is a recently developed technique that shows the chemical composition of an inorganic object and is entirely nondestructive. Other methods require a tiny sample, often obtained with the prick of a hypodermic needle. These include ultraviolet and infrared spectrography that show the composition of inorganic substances and some organic compounds, microchemistry, microscopy or examination under powerful magnification combined with microphotography, and carbon 14 or thermoluminescence examination to estimate the age of ancient materials.

Such scientific processes are helpful in detecting fraud. For example, many forgers have been tripped up by using inauthentic paint colors. The dates of introduction of several of the pigments used by artists are well known: Prussian blue, 1704; zinc white, 1781; cobalt blue, 1802; cadmium yellow, 1817; artificial ultramarine, 1824; and titanium oxide, 1920. Spectroscopy or chemical analysis can identify the makeup of colors.[18]

Historical analysis tries to establish the provenance of an object by tracing its history through surviving records or oral testimony. Many times this may be difficult because of missing records, but a museum should always try to gather as much of the object's history as possible. Historical analysis also examines the authenticity of the details shown in the painting or object; the forger or faker may make mistakes about costumes, decorative arts, or inscriptions for the period he is trying to represent. Stylistic analysis compares the object with known productions of the same maker or in the same cultural era; a knowing connoisseur or art historian may be able to see differences in style that reveal an object's fraudulent nature.

Maurice Rheims gives an example of the way different types of analysis can interact. A French picture dealer some years ago acquired a panel of the Italian school said to be of the fifteenth century that might justify an attribution to Uccello. Scientific examination determined that the wood, preparation, surface, and even the cracks seemed of the right date. A great expert on the period hung the painting on the wall where he saw it over a period of time, but he remained uneasy about its style, which seemed somehow out of fashion for the period it represented. Finally he showed it to another dealer who, it turned out, knew the painting well and knew that it had been done by one of the best modern forgers. The forger had worked on an old panel, leaving the background intact and using only materials authentic for its day. Thus modern science failed to detect the fraud, but stylistic analysis was suspicious and historical knowledge of the actual facts proved what connoisseurship suspected.[19]

Importance of Records

Museum collections lose much of their value if they are not properly recorded. As soon as a work of art, scientific specimen, or historical object enters a museum, it should be identified immediately and recorded accurately and permanently. As Carl Guthe says, "The primary purpose of collection documentation is to insure the permanent and individual absolute identification of each item in the collections."[20] The important thing is that every object have its own individual number painted on or attached to it and that this number be entered in the museum register.

Most museums keep at least three important records. The permanent accession record (possibly with a two-unit number, as for example, *75.38*—the thirty-eighth object or lot received in the year 1975) shows source, date of receipt, brief description, origin, and remarks. When the accession consists of more than one object, the record also assigns a number to each individual object (a three-unit number, say *75.38.15*—the fifteenth item in the accession just described). This individual number may be assigned at once or added later, perhaps at the time the catalogue cards are made. The accession records as bound or filed together constitute the museum register. The second important record is the catalogue card for each object, which contains the object's number, artist or maker, provenance, period, description, source, date received, value, location of photograph, exact measurements, marks, condition, publications, and history. The catalogue may be in numerical order according to object numbers with duplicate files arranged by donor, location, subject, or special research topics. The third record will be a folder containing all correspondence, legal documents, newspaper clippings, and other miscellaneous records concerning the object.

This simple system may need to be expanded in the case of larger museums, but the minimum records described should be maintained by all museums. There also should be similar records covering loans for special exhibits or for longer terms. A museum will do well to keep duplicate records of its register and its main catalogue in a separate location safe from fire, theft, or other hazard; in some instances, such records may be microfilmed and kept in a bank vault, being brought up to date periodically.[21]

Museums are beginning to experiment with placing their catalogue records on computers. The Museum of Modern Art, for example, has its entire art catalogue computerized. The advantages are the ease of maintaining records, the improved access to data, the speed of retrieval of information, and the removal of the need for duplicate files. While using a computer is expensive at present, the Museum of Modern Art estimates that its system has cost about the same as having the catalogue prepared and maintained by hand. The National Museum of Natural History at the Smithsonian Institution has also computerized its crustacean collection, which contains 500,000 specimens occupying ten and one-half miles of shelves and with registration and cataloguing years behind. As the computerization process becomes cheaper, many more museums will use it, and computers will become more and more valuable, especially for research purposes. The Museum Computer Network, Inc., begun in 1967 and reorganized in 1972 at the State University of New York College in Stony Brook, Long Island, is dedicated to creating a National Data Bank for museums and has twenty-one institutional members, including the Metropolitan Museum of Art, the Museum of Modern Art, the American Museum of Natural History, and the Smithsonian museums. The museums of Great Britain are planning to develop a nationwide catalogue system by using computers.[22]

Dual Arrangement

Most museums arrange their collections in two ways—for display or public exhibition and as study or reserve collections. In general, about the same amount of space will be given to the two functions; some museums now are alloting approximately 30 percent of their buildings to each and using the remaining 40 percent for office space and educational and visitor services. The science museums were the first to use dual arrangement; their emphasis on systematics and taxonomy caused their numerous specimens to be arranged in series for study that usually occupied much greater space than the popular exhibits.

The Bavarian National Museum in Munich, about the turn of the century, arranged its period rooms in historical sequence for the ordinary visitor and its reserve collections separately according to technical classification as furniture, ceramics, metals, textiles, and the like. The National Museum of History and Technology of the Smithsonian has treated cultural history somewhat similarly. Its galleries on "Everyday Life in the American Past" tell the story of American decorative arts with big dramatic themes that are backed up by large study collections of the different classes of objects in storage not seen by the public but open to scholars. Art museums have experimented with dual arrangement, especially in Boston and Philadelphia. Better storage methods employing sliding picture storage frames have greatly improved reserve collections in the art field.

In general, the principle of dual arrangement is accepted today, with the popular exhibit open freely to the general public and the study collection well arranged in storage and readily available to the scholar, but art museums are still slow to adopt the ideal except in the case of prints, drawings, textiles, or other easily handled materials. Clearing inaccessible attics of objects and placing them either on exhibition or open study-storage would improve their protection and preservation, cause the staff to know and utilize them better, and increase the research done on them by either staff or visiting scholars.[23]

Ethics of Acquisition

American museums are becoming more and more concerned about illicit trade in foreign art and archaeological objects. Mexican and other pre-Columbian Middle American sites have been pillaged by poverty-stricken peasants who have sold objects to unscrupulous "pickers" for a mere pittance. Similar looting has taken place in Peru, the Middle East, Southeast Asia, and elsewhere. Paintings and art objects have also been stolen from Indian temples, Italian churches, and African royal sanctuaries, as well as from many foreign museums.[24]

Objects from these lootings and thefts have been smuggled into the United States, have turned up in the art market, and have found their way into museums by purchase or through gifts and bequests by private collectors. Some of the more notable cases have caused foreign governments to retaliate by closing down archaeological projects conducted by American institutions. In the past, the attitudes of American museums toward the situation have differed. Museums with anthropological collections urged all museums to take great care in investigating the provenance of objects so as to guarantee that none acquired had broken laws protecting the national patrimony of the country of origin. Art museums, however, pointed out that the United States is composed of people of many ethnic origins who should have their cultural heritages represented in American museums. While they were willing to take reasonable precautions against acquiring objects illicitly exported from foreign lands, they argued that the primary responsibility for enforcing these laws rested with the countries of origin and that the situation could be improved if those nations would agree to release, for acquisition, long-term loan, or exchange, materials of high artistic quality for display in this country. They pointed out that a museum acquiring objects by field collection or excavation could be much surer of their provenance than a museum purchasing objects in the art market or receiving them by gift or bequest.[25]

Three recent sensational cases have shown the difficulties that may accompany the acquisition of objects of doubtful provenance. In December 1969, on the eve of its celebration of the centennial of its founding, the Museum of Fine Arts in Boston announced that it had acquired an apparently unknown small portrait by Raphael, probably of Eleonora Gonzaga and probably painted in 1505. Early in 1971 United States Customs officials came to the museum to seize the tiny painting as stolen property, eventually to be returned to Italy. A trustee, the director, and a curator of the museum had bought it in Genoa (reportedly for about $600,000). The dealer from whom they obtained the portrait turned out to have a police record, and they had not declared it at customs when it entered the United States in the curator's suitcase.[26]

In 1972 the Metropolitan Museum of Art announced that it had purchased a previously unknown Greek calyx krater of the sixth century B.C. made by the potter Euxitheos and the painter Euphronios. The price paid was about $1 million. The Italian police soon made the accusation that the krater had been looted from an Etruscan tomb there in 1971. The museum had inquired about its origin from the dealer who sold it. He said he had secured it from an Armenian dealer, whose father (also a dealer) had acquired the vase in fragments in London in 1920. The Armenian dealer furnished a letter and sworn affidavit to these facts; the Swiss (the vase had been reassembled in Zurich) and United States customs laws were observed in importing the krater; and the Italian police have not proved their accusation.[27]

Another dispute surfaced in 1973 involving the Afo-A-Kom, a sixty-four-inch-tall carved male wooden figure sheathed in reddish-brown and blue beads that had belonged for more than a century to the Kom nation in the United Republic of Cameroon. This most sacred object was stolen from the royal sanctuary by tribal thieves and smuggled out, apparently to Paris. It was then acquired by a New York dealer, who advertised it for sale for $60,000. After the *New York Times* revealed the story, no museum or collection would buy the object. In fact, the Museum of African Art at Washington took the lead in returning the sacred statue to the Kom, and another museum helped raise funds to pay the dealer his actual expenses in securing the carving.[28]

The United Nations Educational, Scientific and Cultural Organization in 1970 adopted a Convention on the Means of Prohibiting and Preventing the Illicit Export, Import and Transfer of Ownership of Cultural Property. Under it, each ratifying state would establish an export certificate for important cultural property and no state would import such property without a certificate. Provision is also made for the return of stolen property to the state of origin. The United States ratified the convention with certain reservations in 1972 but has not yet passed implementing legislation; it it does so, many of its provisions would apply only to federally controlled museums. The United States entered into a unilateral treaty with Mexico in 1971 to protect both countries' pre-Columbian and colonial art and artifacts as well as documents from official archives up to 1920 and to provide joint archaeological work and exchanges of antiquities. The two countries will return property illegally imported into either one.[29]

The leading United States cultural organizations concerned have adopted a joint Professional Policy on Museum Acquisitions, recommending that American museums refuse "to acquire through purchase, gift, or bequest cultural property imported in violation of the laws obtaining in the countries of origin," and that they support and be guided by the principles of the UNESCO Convention. The policy also urges that the governing board of each individual museum adopt an appropriate acquisition policy. The organizations joining in the policy statement were the American Association of Museums; United States Committee, International Council of Museums; College Art Association of America; Association of Art Museum Directors; Archaeological Institute of America; American Anthropological Association; and Society for American Archaeology.

Despite these actions, the whole question of acquisitions involving the patrimony of other nations remains a thorny one. As long as the countries of origin are too weak and too poor to enforce protective laws, smuggling and illicit sales are sure to take place. The decision of museums not to acquire objects of doubtful provenance will not cause the market for such materials to dry up, and in some cases may result in collections of value being kept from public knowledge and even destroyed. Still, responsible museum professionals and governing boards certainly cannot condone the acquisition of stolen and looted objects, and individual museums are adopting statements of policy in which they pledge to acquire only materials the provenance of which can be established. Leaders in this movement include the University Museum of the University of Pennsylvania, Harvard University, the Field Museum of Natural History, American Museum of Natural History, Brooklyn Museum, Smithsonian Institution, and University of California, Berkeley.[30]

Ethics of Dispersal

Just as a museum has a right (and indeed a duty) to define its field of acquisition and adopt clear policies relating to accessions, so also it ought to establish principles of disposing of materials that are outside its scope or that it cannot use for exhibition, study, or loan. Collection management certainly includes out-go, as well as in-flow. The difficulty here, however, is that a museum is a kind of public trust and that deaccession and disposal of objects can lead to public criticism. Even the boards of museums that accept no public funds occupy a trusteeship relationship that is subject to some state supervision.

Many museum objects offer little difficulty if they are deaccessioned. Some museums (especially those dealing with history and science) may even accept objects with the understanding that they may not be accessioned but will be sold or otherwise disposed of for the benefit of the museum. Other objects may have been received years earlier and lie outside a museum's agreed-upon field (for example, stuffed birds or seashells in a small art museum); if such objects cannot be returned to the donors, no one can reasonably oppose their disposal. Items damaged beyond reasonable repair or actual duplicates also arouse little controversy. Similarly, objects more useful in other collections (for example, Egyptian scarabs in a local history museum) can be placed on long-term loan, given, or even sold to another, more appropriate, museum.[31]

Major problems are encountered, however, when items are sold for financial reasons or traded or sold to upgrade the quality of a collection. Art museums often experience special difficulties because of varying opinions of the importance and monetary value of art objects. Museums follow three general practices in this area. Some, for example, the Louvre and London's National Gallery, sell or exchange nothing. A second policy permits sales or exchanges only with other museums or similar nonprofit institutions. The third practice is for the museum freely to sell or exchange works of art to which the museum has unrestricted title in order to refine and enhance its collections.

The Metropolitan Museum of Art has recently stirred considerable controversy in deaccessioning some of its holdings. In 1970 the city of New York reluctantly approved plans for a major expansion of the museum's physical plant into Central Park, with the understanding that it would not continue to increase the over-all size of its collections but would concentrate on improving their excellence and representative quality. In the fall of the same year, the museum bought at auction in London the superb portrait by Velásquez of *Juan de Pareja* for $5,592,000. Though part of the purchase price was contributed by the trustees, some of it was raised by deaccessioning and selling other art. Many of the paintings sold were from the Adelaide Milton de Groot Collection. Miss de Groot, in her will, "without limiting in any way the absolute nature of this bequest," requested the museum not to sell any of the works of art but to keep what it wished and give the remainder to one or more important museums that it should select. In interpreting the will, outside legal counsel confirmed the opinion of the Metropolitan trustees that the De Groot bequest was absolute and her precatory request not legally binding.

When the De Groot sales were discovered, acrimonious arguments filled the newspapers and art journals about whether certain paintings should have been deaccessioned and if so, whether the Metropolitan, which sold them to a private dealer, had received enough money. The attorney general of New York state made an intensive investigation into the matter. The Metropolitan issued a White Paper that gave a detailed history of all disposals, 1971 to 1973, and adopted, with the participation of the attorney general's office, new procedures for deaccessioning and disposal of works of art.

The process included (1) promptly informing the attorney general whenever the museum deaccessioned any work of art worth more than $5,000; (2) requiring that any sale, except to another museum, of a deaccessioned work of art worth more than $5,000 be at public auction; (3) giving adequate public notice prior to sale of a deaccessioned work of art worth $25,000 on exhibition within the past ten years; (4) stipulation that the museum would deviate from a nonbinding restriction of a donor only with the consent of the donor or his heirs and on notice to the attorney general; and (5) binding restrictions could be removed only with court authority and appropriate notice to the attorney general. Thus, the Metropolitan's deaccessioning process underwent considerable change as a result of the New York attorney general's intervention. Not all museums agreed with the revision. The Museum of Modern Art, which had forty years of experience with frequent disposal of paintings and sculpture, argued that professionals and specialists in the field of modern art—its own staff, outside art historians, and professionals on its board—were better qualified to make judgments about dispositions than the attorney general's office. Also, the museum had used public auction, private auction by sealed bids, direct sales, and consignment for disposal; of these, public auction had proved least advantageous for both prices and flexibility.[32]

All legal considerations aside, the museum profession would do well to ponder certain guidelines on disposal as suggested by Sherman E. Lee, director of the Cleveland Museum of Art. They include the following points:

1. If there is a reasonable doubt about the propriety or necessity for such a removal, don't do it.
2. Never remove excellent works on the basis of changes in taste.
3. Always remember that a "series" may well be a positive good and that a "series" consists of a number of duplicates or near-duplicates.
4. Deletions from a collection should be replaced by much more desirable works of the same category.
5. A careful check on values in any sale or trade is mandatory, and outside expert consultation is insurance against error or criticism.
6. The process of deaccessioning should be more rigorous than that for acquisition. If the latter requires only accession committee approval, then the former should require full board action, preferably by a two-thirds vote.
7. If the work to be removed would be a desirable and hard-to-obtain acquisition for another public institution, full consideration should

be given to making the work available to such an institution at a price commensurate with the object's value.

8. Removals should only be permitted where no legal obligations imposed by the giver are in force. Where moral obligations are involved, they must be evaluated within a moral content. Consultation with near relations is always a generous and wise procedure.
9. The principle of deaccessioning is not in question. The practice of deaccessioning should be the object of careful and wise study and regulation.[33]

Ideally, museums should design their own disposal procedures based on the highest professional ethics, both in deciding upon the deaccessioning and carrying out the sales or exchanges. If museums do not handle these procedures well, government is likely to step in. The attorney general of New York state in the case of the Metropolitan Museum asserted that if the voluntary and co-operative understanding arrived at there did not fully serve the public purposes, he would consider suggesting corrective legislative action.

The Museum as Conservation

An art conservation student rebacks a painting, University of Delaware/Winterthur Museum Program

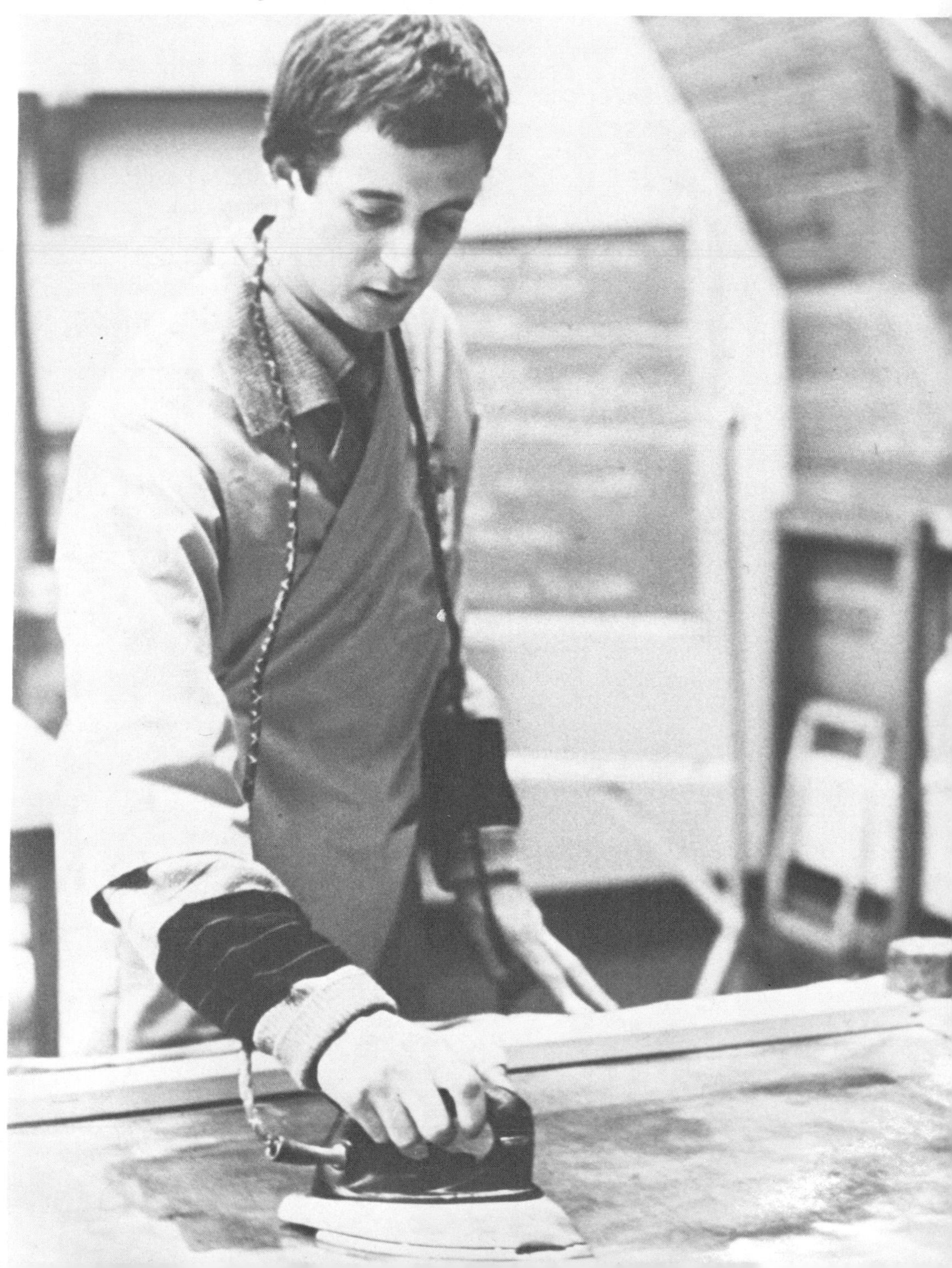

Not until the twentieth century did museums clearly realize that one of their chief functions as well as an all-important duty was to pass on their collections in pristine condition to succeeding generations. By that time science was far enough advanced to point out that, just as all human beings must die, so all objects must deteriorate. At the same time, scientists learned to slow the degradation of museum materials, and a new profession of scientifically knowledgeable "conservators" began to replace the artists and craftsmen commonly known as "restorers." Conservators knew how to preserve materials, that is, to prevent, stop, or retard deterioration, and also how to restore objects that had undergone decay or alteration. Unfortunately, conserving museum objects is an expensive business, and the American Institute of Conservation maintains that a museum needs to set aside at least 10 percent of its annual budget for this function. Only the wealthiest museums have been able to establish their own conservation laboratories, while others have been forced to send their ailing objects to private conservators. Experiments have been made with regional conservation laboratories, and they may offer a feasible solution to the problem.[1]

The Physical Nature of Museum Objects

The conservator is interested in the materials of which museum objects are made—not primarily their aesthetic form, but their molecular/atomic composition and structure. He wants to know about their condition—how much they have deteriorated and how they can be stabilized for a long future. In doing his work, he is dealing with four chief classes of substances: organic materials, metals and their alloys, siliceous and equivalent materials, and easel and mural paintings. The classic treatment of scientific museum conservation was written by Harold J. Plenderleith, former keeper of the British Museum research laboratory. In the revised second edition, A. E. A. Werner, then the keeper of the laboratory, collaborated with Mr. Plenderleith. The volume remains the basic reference tool in this field.

Organic materials include hides, leather, parchment, paper, bone, ivory, textiles, and wood. They are of animal or vegetable origin, carbon-based, and with cellular structure. They are susceptible to deterioration by light, variations in humidity and temperature, dryness or brittleness, and excessive humidity (damp) that produces molds, mildew, and other biological reactions.

Gold, silver, lead, tin, copper and its alloys, iron, and steel are the chief metals. They are inorganic, much more stable than organic materials, and little affected by light, temperature variations, and biological reaction. They differ in their resistance to deterioration from variations in humidity and from impurities in the air or the ground. Gold is the only metal that remains virtually intact under all conditions. The others suffer from corrosion that may produce a pleasing patina or heavy incrustation that ultimately transforms the metal into the mineral ore from which it was extracted. Silver exposed to air tarnishes and if underground for a long period may take on a patina. Copper and iron are easily oxidized in air or especially in the ground. Copper and bronze show brown, blue, or green patinas, and iron can be completely transformed into rust.

Siliceous and equivalent materials consist of natural stone, bricks, pottery and other ceramics, and glass. Natural stone varies in its resistance to deterioration. Granite and basalt are relatively impervious, but limestone and sandstone are vulnerable to industrial sulfur fumes, automobile emissions, temperature and humidity variations, saline efflorescences, and cryptomatic vegetation (molds and mosses). Bricks and pottery, both of clay, are similar to natural stone in their resistance. If baked at higher temperatures, they are equivalent to stone of average resistance; if baked at low heat or air dried, they correspond to soft natural stone. Ceramics fired at high temperatures have great resistance to deterioration, but water with salt in solution can produce efflorescences in them. High humidity can dull the transparency of normally stable glass and lead to crizzling with a multitude of small cracks.

Easel and mural paintings are complex chemical compounds that contain in their various layers both organic and inorganic materials. The outer layer of varnish is completely organic; the paint layers and ground or coating are usually a combination of organic and inorganic; the support, if wood or canvas, is organic, or if metal or a wall substance, inorganic. Adhesives used between the layers are organic. Varnish, which normally lasts only twenty to fifty years before losing its elasticity, also turns yellow. Mediums or vehicles of oil or distemper in the paint layers become brittle and subject to damp, while the ground or foundation is susceptible to high humidity. Soft wood and canvas supports of easel paintings attract insects and are distorted by damp, and saline efflorescences and mold attack murals. Decay also weakens the adhesives between layers and results in unsticking and blisters.[2]

Proper Museum Environment

Environment has a powerful influence on objects, which tend to establish an equilibrium with their surroundings. Whenever the environment is changed, the objects are likely to suffer. Thus when archaeologists open a tomb, objects apparently in perfect condition may shrink or warp and sometimes even turn to dust. The changes in the relative humidity and temperature of the atmosphere cause such deterioration.

Museums therefore need to provide a stable environment with constant relative humidity and temperature for the varied objects in their collections. The two qualities are closely related; in fact, relative humidity is defined as the ratio of the amount of water vapor present in the air to the greatest amount possible at the same temperature. As those familiar with central heating so well know, increasing the temperature of a building in winter reduces the humidity markedly and may result in too dry an atmosphere, while lowering the temperature may raise the humidity so much that it reaches the dew point and water condenses on walls and objects.

A temperature of sixty to seventy-five degrees Fahrenheit or about twenty degrees centigrade is comfortable for museum visitors year round. At that temperature the relative humidity should not fall below 50 percent, or organic materials such as paper, parchment, and leather will become brittle; canvas will go slack; and textiles and the adhesives used in making furniture will dry out and deteriorate. Similarly, if the relative humidity exceeds 65 percent, mold and mildew will grow on glue, leather, and paper; wood will swell and canvas tighten; and oxidation of metals will increase. The ideal relative humidity for most museum objects at temperatures of about seventy degrees Fahrenheit is 50 to 65 percent.

Atmospheric pollution also causes museum objects to decay. Museums near the sea must cope with minute salt crystals blown inland that promote the growth of micro-organisms. Museums in industrial districts suffer greatly from sulfur fumes produced by burning coal, coke, or oil; these gases attack all metals save gold, as well as paint films that include white lead, building stones, paper, textiles, and leather. Exhaust emissions from automobiles add greatly to pollution problems.

Modern filtered air-conditioning systems will provide the constant relative humidity and temperature desirable for the museum environment and will avoid atmospheric pollution. Obviously, every museum should strive to obtain such climate control for its entire buildings, but especially for its exhibition and storage spaces. Though it may be difficult to raise money for such a purpose (the saying goes that nobody ever gave a museum a ton of coal in memory of his mother), air conditioning in the long run is more important for the museum than the acquisition of million-dollar objects. The smaller museum that cannot afford this protection can go part way by securing a hygrometer to measure relative humidity and by using humidifiers, dehumidifiers, silica gel, tightly closed museum cases, and other devices.

Another important part of the museum environment is lighting. Strong light or ultraviolet rays damage watercolors, paintings, paper, textiles, and other materials, usually by fading or embrittlement. Sunlight is especially destructive because of ultraviolet radiation and should be controlled by blinds, curtains, or special glass. Incandescent bulbs give off heat, which must be lessened in museum cases. The ultraviolet emissions of fluorescent tubes can be reduced to safe levels by plastic sleeves. Too much light intensity from spotlights or too high a general illumination should also be avoided.[3]

Preventive Conservation

The curator is the first line of defense in conserving museum materials. The very word *curator* means someone who has the care of something; British museums use *keeper* as an equivalent word. Thus, the museum curator, no matter what his scholarly research, exhibition, and educational functions may be, is responsible for the safety and good condition of the museum objects entrusted to him. He will, of course, be sure that the museum administration provides fire protection and security precautions. After he has seen that proper control has been obtained of humidity, temperature, atmospheric pollution, and lighting, he will institute regular procedures that will insure that the controlled environment is maintained to protect the objects no matter where they may be found in the museum.[4]

When the materials first come to the museum, they should receive careful inspection, routine cleaning, and fumigation. Close visual examination will determine their general condition and whether they need to undergo scientific scrutiny by experts. Removal of dirt and dust, perhaps by careful use of a vacuum cleaner or, in some instances, by gentle washing, will follow and a decision can be made as to whether more complex cleaning is required under expert supervision. Fumigation can probably be done on the museum premises in a tank or vault; ethylene oxide may be used against insects, and thymol crystals heated by a forty-watt electric bulb will destroy mold and fungus. More powerful toxic gases can be used by experts for more complex and stubborn infestations. The museum should also employ an exterminating service to make regular inspections and take protective action against insects and vermin.[5]

After the museum objects have been examined, cleaned, and fumigated (and, of course, properly recorded), they are ready for display or storage. In either instance, the curator will devise good housekeeping methods for regular cleaning and inspection; everyday care is exceedingly important. If placed on exhibition, safe and protective methods of framing, matting, case design, and pedestal mounting are required.[6]

If in storage, the objects should be properly placed so that they are safe, stable, and accessible. The physical nature of the material will determine how it is stored; a few examples will show the varied conditions required. Textiles should be placed in darkness, never folded, and systematically inspected to avoid damage from insects; they can be rolled, hung from retractable frames, or, in the case of costumes, mounted on manikins or special padded hangers in transparent plastic bags. Metal objects must be kept dry (silica gel is often useful here), on shelves not touching each other, in padded areas to avoid scratches, and the silver must not be polished too often. Paintings can be hung on both sides of heavy-gauge wire screens that travel on overhead tracks and in floor channels. If it is necessary to stack paintings against walls, they should rest on padded blocks with face outwards and corrugated boards separating the paintings. Watercolors, engravings, or other art works on paper must use acid-free paper for backing and matting.[7]

Any museum employee who handles or moves objects for exhibition, storage, study, or shipping should be carefully trained to observe certain fundamental rules. These differ for the many materials involved and are best studied in detail in the American Association of Museums' publication on *Museum Registration Methods*. A few examples will show the general tenor of these procedures. Hands should be washed, gloves kept clean, no smoking allowed, and work areas neatly arranged and clean. Haste is to be avoided, especially when using hand trucks or dollies; they should not be overloaded, nor should objects protrude beyond the edges of trucks. Only one object is to be carried at a time, and that with both hands. Resilient padding should line carrying boxes, packing materials be searched before being discarded, and all fragments saved. In every instance a careful plan must be worked out for each object to be moved.[8]

The curator, then, is in charge of preventive conservation for the objects in his care. His general understanding of their physical nature and the optimum conditions of environment they need will lead to largely common-sense procedures of inspection, recording, cleaning, storage, and handling.

Packing and Shipping

Special exhibitions are increasingly used by museums to promote scholarly research, increase public enlightenment, and attract popular attention. They usually involve borrowing materials from several museums, and a curator ought to have a leading role in deciding when objects in his care should be lent. He may approve highly of the purposes of a temporary or traveling exhibit and also know that his own museum may wish to borrow materials from other museums from time to time. Sometimes the pressure on him to approve a loan may be great, and the ultimate decision may rest upon the director and board of trustees. The curator, however, should carefully consider the dangers to which such exhibits expose objects. Can they stand the jolting and jarring of travel and the changes in humidity and temperature they are sure to encounter? Can they be properly packed for both going and coming? Will the borrower provide careful handling, dependable environmental control, and protection against fire, vandalism, and theft? These practical questions will help the curator decide whether the proposed exhibit is important enough to justify the risks to the objects in his care.[9]

In order to respond rationally to requests for loans, the wise curator may well decide, with advice from conservators, to classify the objects he cares for as to their ability to travel safely. Some objects will be too delicate and fragile to stand any shipping. Others may be allowed to travel only occasionally to exhibits of exceptional importance with strictly specified conditions of packing, handling, and protection during transit and on exhibition. In another category will be placed objects sound, stable, and structurally strong enough to be included in traveling exhibitions.[10]

Once the decision has been made to lend objects, arrangements must be made for their packing, transport, exhibition, repacking, and return travel. The whole transaction must be covered by written agreements and by insurance.

The packing can be as elaborate as the situation requires. If the distances involved are short, the objects may be taken by car, station wagon, or van with abundant padding and careful separation but without special cases. Caroline Keck's *Safeguarding Your Collection in*

Travel will show the small museum how to instruct a carpenter to build a solid, water-tight, shock-absorbing case in which objects can be "floated" with inner cushioning provided by some of the new plastic foam materials. A reliable commercial packing firm may be used, though its work should be carefully supervised. A larger museum will have its own trained packing staff. In instances of important international exhibitions of extremely rare objects, as Nathan Stolow points out, conservators know how to build ideal containers with preconditioned packing materials or silica gel panels that will maintain about the same humidity and temperature that the objects enjoy in the best air-conditioned museum.

Transport should be as carefully planned. The small museum may use the director's automobile, if the distance is not too great, and larger museums may send their own vans. If a carefully checked and reliable household-moving company is used, the lending and receiving museum staffs should supervise the loading and unloading. If railroad, water, or air transport is involved, the sending museum should deliver the boxes to the station, ship, or aircraft, and the receiving museum should pick them up. In any instance—truck, railway, ship, or air—the transportation should be direct, without layovers or transshipments. For extremely rare objects, a museum staff member should accompany the shipment, going and coming.

Unpacking and re-packing of loans should be done by trained packers because, at these points, the most damage to objects is likely. Instructions will be attached to the inside of shipping cases. Packing material should be stored in the same kind of space in which the loan is installed, preferably air conditioned. The repacking should be done by those who did the unpacking, and the same materials should be used.

The installation of borrowed materials is the responsibility of the curator of the borrowing museum; he should see that they have the same protection as those of his own museum. All of the arrangements should be clearly written down and agreed to by both parties. The lending museum will photograph the objects before they leave and describe any weaknesses or defects, and the borrowing museum will do likewise before returning them. The insurance must be carefully arranged from wall to wall of the lending museum—at the lender's valuation and with the lender's policy to be paid for by the borrower or with the borrower's policy agreed to by the lender.

Thus the curator is responsible for deciding which of his objects ought to travel and seeing that they are properly packed, safely transported, treated carefully in the places they are exhibited, are repacked correctly, and returned in good condition.[11] These curatorial responsibilities are combined with the ones described under preventive conservation above. Beyond this, the curator without training as a conservator should not venture. Sheldon Keck, in an article properly entitled, "A Little Training Can be a Dangerous Thing," tells of a curator who, in cleaning a Corot painting, inadvertently removed a tree from the landscape.[12] Cleaning and relining paintings, removing stains from paper or textiles, consolidating wood sculptures, treating corroded metals, or repairing broken ceramic or glass objects requires special skills based on understanding of chemistry and physics, as well as a high degree of manual dexterity. Most manipulative techniques take at least three years to learn. For such specialized tasks, the curator should call upon well-trained and experienced conservators.

The Conservator

The conservator as we know him today has developed during the last thirty or forty years. His predecessor, the restorer, took an empirical approach to conservation. He knew certain practical treatments to use on deteriorating art and historical objects and with skilled hands applied them. The conservator was a new breed, in that he used knowledge of science (especially chemistry and physics) to institute preventive treatment, diagnose factors responsible for deterioration, conduct scientific examination, and devise improved methods of repair. With the shift from the restorer's studio to the conservator's laboratory came the ideal of establishing central laboratories conducting advanced scientific research and regional treatment centers manned by conservators trained in science, knowledgeable of history and art history, and with manual dexterity.[13]

The conservator has two classes of museum duties. As adviser on preventive conservation, he helps the curator work out operating procedures, and as skillful scientist and craftsman he diagnoses and treats deteriorated or altered objects. This second role begins with inspection of a museum's holdings in co-operation with the curator and assignment of priorities for objects that need treatment; it often becomes a continuing responsibility with periodic inspections of which written records are kept.

In his treatment work, the conservator observes several guiding principles. One of these is that he will examine with the latest scientific methods objects to be worked upon in order to understand as thoroughly as possible the nature and prognosis of the deterioration and alteration. The methods of scientific examination discussed for the detection of frauds in the preceding chapter will be applied to the objects to be restored.

A second major principle requires the conservator to make as few changes as possible and to keep anything he does reversible in the future. For example, fifty years ago a rash restorer might have decided that a polychrome wood sculpture was so worm-eaten that he would replace a considerable portion with new wood shaped and painted as nearly like the original as he could make it. Such overdrastic action would be much regretted today, when the use of a beeswax or synthetic resin impregnation would make it possible to save the original form. A more conservative kind of restoration—say, fumigation of the statue to stop worm damage and minimum repainting with soluble paint—would have preserved it for the better treatment that could be given now. Conservators, of course, need to make judgments in such areas. Some modern synthetics used to impregnate and consolidate objects made of porous material are almost impossible to remove, but as Elizabeth C. G. Packard puts it, "When there is a choice between losing the work of art completely or treating it with a non-reversible product, it may be necessary to take a chance on the latter course."

Another of the conservator's rules is that he not use conjecture in restoration or reconstruction of objects. If he cannot find out by research what their actual appearance was, he should not proceed with restoration. This area is a very dangerous one, for conservators sometimes know so much about objects and their normal appearance in a historical period that they are tempted to go ahead intuitively, even when they lack authentic evidence. In general, the conservator should not aim to make the object appear as it did when new (its original state) but rather as if it had been well cared for (its actual state). Another pitfall here is to use today's taste in restoring an object. For example, the H. F. du Pont Winterthur Museum acquired an early-nineteenth-century wood-sculptured man's bust with several bad cracks; it had been cleaned down to the wood. In restoring it, the question arose whether to paint it a stone color or to use a natural finish that would show off the wood grain. Modern taste would have dictated the latter course, but research into the early nineteenth-century practice and faint traces of paint led to painting it stone color.

Conservators should write a detailed account of everything they have found out about the object, good or bad, and every step they have taken in repairing or restoring it, and a copy of this account should become part of the museum record of the object. If further work is needed in the future, sounder judgments can be made, based on the record.

A good conservator sometimes discovers new properties of objects and develops improved methods of treating them. In such instances, should he pass on his research by publication in a professional journal or book, even though he realizes that a forger may use the new knowledge for dishonest purposes? In general, such publication would seem to be in order if it advances the science of conservation, even though some misuse may result. In some instances, withholding exact details or formulas may be justified.[14]

The Care of Paintings

Conservators probably have given more attention to easel paintings than to any other art form and for a longer time. They have learned to examine the paint surface in the laboratory—in normal or raking light, through the canvas with transmitted light, under the microscope, and with ultraviolet and infrared rays. They have used X-rays to penetrate into the paint layers and have taken tiny samples of the cross-section of the painting, sometimes under the microscope showing some five layers from auxiliary support to surface varnish. All these examinations can be photographed and thus made available for future study.[15]

The conservator can learn the physical composition of the painting, the state and extent of deterioration, and whether it has been altered by human hands. Raking light may show a painting in fragile condition with tiny bits of lifted paint. Ultraviolet, infrared, and X-rays may establish how much of the original remains and how much has been lost or changed in previous repairs. Sometimes the rays reveal other painting below the surface—preliminary sketches by the artist or much more surprising images. Sheldon and Caroline Keck, in examining a nineteenth-century American portrait of an older woman, found beneath it a likeness of the subject at a younger age; only the eyes were the same. When the black dress and prim bonnet of the upper painting were removed, an appealing and glamorous young woman was revealed with auburn hair and golden satin gown. Apparently she had had the portrait redone much later when she became a widow.[16]

Once the painting is fully understood, the conservator can determine what needs to be done to preserve it. If the paint layers are in good condition, careful cleaning may be enough—removal of the varnish with solvents, filling in paint losses, inpainting, and revarnishing. If the adhesives holding the layers together or the canvas itself has weakened, the painting may require relining or rebacking by adding a strong new canvas behind the original one. This complex process will probably use a heated wax-resin (or older glue-paste) that is flowed through the paint layers with lining irons or with an electric hot table and a vacuum pump. Methods of relining are changing today as new synthetics undergo experimentation and testing; for example, fiberglass is being substituted for canvas and new heat sealers such as Beva 371 are being employed instead of the customary wax-resins. After relining, the cleaning process can follow safely. Finally, the frame will be added with the picture properly placed in the rabbet molding and a protective backing board attached to the stretcher with screws.[17]

Caroline Keck gives an exciting example of the way the process works in describing the treatment of an oil painting that belonged to the Newark Museum. The painting on canvas was attached by thick glue to a wooden panel. The fabric had pulled away from the panel, to produce multiple blisters on the surface, which also contained layers of grime and discolored varnish. The blisters were so high that a plaster cast had to be made before the painting could be placed face down and the panel chiseled away. The conservators then decided to remove the badly distorted canvas and effect a complete transfer of the painting layers to a new fabric. The face of the painting was covered with paper and attached with wax to a rigid white process board that could later be removed. The old canvas at the back was gently peeled away, the paint layers carefully flattened and a new fabric attached by heated wax-resin. All the paint layers were firmly bonded now, and the facing materials could be removed. When cleaning took place, much to everyone's surprise and joy, the painting was found to be signed and dated, "William Williams, 1772."[18]

These methods, especially when accompanied by a favorable museum environment and periodic inspection, may preserve a painting indefinitely, though it may require cleaning every half century or so, and perhaps relining every century or two.

Art works on paper often are exceedingly fragile. Paper made without neutralization of acid-forming materials is highly impermanent, no matter how carefully handled and stored. Excessive humidity will bring mold, sometimes in rusty spots called "foxing" that discolor the sheet. Too much light, especially the ultraviolet rays contained in sunlight or fluorescent tubes, causes fading and embrittlement; five to fifteen footcandles is considered the highest light level to which works on paper should be exposed. High temperature accelerates deterioration and embrittlement, while pollution creates sulfur dioxide that discolors and disintegrates the paper. Insects—silverfish, termites, woodworms, and cockroaches—eat paper, as do rats and mice.

Preventive conservation will do much to preserve paper, and curators can take positive steps to be sure that watercolors, pastels, and drawings (as well as prints) are matted and framed correctly. Acid-free museum board should constitute the backing and picture-window front of the mat, and they should be hinged together. The picture should hang free from the backing by two hinges attached to the upper edge of the picture's reverse side. Unmatted pictures should be stored in acid-free folders and matted ones in solander boxes or insect-proof drawers. They should be fumigated occasionally, possibly with thymol crystals. Such pictures should be framed with glass at the front, then the matted picture, and one or more layers of acid-free backboard.

Other treatment of art works on paper should be left to the conservator. Cleaning by dry or wet methods, bleaching and removing stains, treating pastels for mildew, flattening creases, repairing tears, and sizing and retouching are delicate operations not to be attempted by the untrained and inexperienced. An example of an unusually complex restoration was the successful transfer of a fifteenth-century Flemish print from a badly deteriorated wood panel to a specially made paper backing by Francis W. Doloff at the Museum of Fine Arts, Boston.[19]

Organic Materials

Textiles, until recently, were of animal (wool, silk) or vegetable (cotton, linen, hemp) origin. The conservator must wash and dry-clean them, bleach and remove stains, fumigate and fight mold and moths, and protect them from light and air pollution. Repairing and mounting them is easier today because of the development of synthetic fibers such as nylon and teryline; the synthetics are stronger and more permanent than natural fibers and impervious to mold or insects. Dramatic repairs sometimes take place because of them; Plenderleith and Werner describe a frail fifteenth- or sixteenth-century pyx cloth of drawn-thread work reinforced successfully by a teryline net, and a crumpled thirteenth-century woven fragment from an archbishop's tomb consolidated with soluble nylon until it could be relaxed and become flexible, revealing a striking pattern of threads covered with silver gilt.[20]

Wood, often an important art material, must be protected from warping and cracking, as well as from fungus and insect attack. Fumigation will get rid of insects for the moment, and impregnation with liquid insecticides can make wood proof against further attack. Impregnated wax or synthetic resins will consolidate and strengthen deteriorated wooden objects. Waterlogged wood is a special problem; the water must be removed slowly over a period of time to prevent shrinkage and distortion, while synthetic materials are absorbed to give mechanical strength. An unusual example in this field is the Swedish frigate *Vasa*, which sank in Stockholm harbor on its maiden voyage in 1628. Brought to the surface in 1961, with most of its equipment intact, it has had a museum barge built around it so that visitors may observe the restoration work being done. A high humidity is maintained while the oaken timbers slowly absorb the polyethylene glycol that will eventually permit the ship to be visited in a normal air-conditioned atmosphere.[21]

Bone and ivory objects are less common in museums but require special care. They are easily warped and stained and, when buried in the ground, become fossilized and difficult to restore. Washing will get rid of surplus dirt and soluble salts, while insoluble salts can sometimes be removed by extremely rapid cleaning successively by distilled water, alcohol, and ether. Synthetic resins can then be used for consolidation. An outstanding restoration took place at the Museum of Fine Arts, Boston, when William J. Young patiently put together about fifty fragments (originally kept by the owner in a cigar box) of an exquisite ivory-and-gold figurine from Crete of the sixteenth century B.C. This Minoan snake goddess, only 6½ inches high, was housed in a special case, its humidity kept low by silica gel. Plenderleith was able to preserve and restore a beautiful Phoenician ivory carving of the ninth century B.C. from Nimrud. It was found at the bottom of a well and thought to be part of a throne. The carving, with a floral background embellished with gold, lapis lazuli, and carnelian, depicted a lioness killing a Nubian clad in a gleaming gold loincloth, his curly hair tipped with gold.[22]

Metals

Metals (except for gold) are vulnerable to corrosion produced by chemical or electrical reactions and enhanced by high humidity, air pollution, or burial underground. Corrosion often results in heavy or total incrustation, the metal seeking to return to a mineral form similar to that from which it was refined. The three chief treatments for corrosion (often used in combination) employ chemical reagents, electrochemical or electrolytic reduction, and mechanical washing, brushing, picking, and the like.

Preliminary examination with a needle under a lens, a magnet for ferrous metal, or X-rays enables the conservator to determine the thickness of the incrustation, strength of the remaining metal, and presence of ornament. One form of electrochemical reduction uses granulated zinc and caustic soda to soften the incrustation. In electrolytic reduction, an electric current may employ the corroded object as the cathode, a sodium carbonate solution as the electrolyte, and two stainless steel anodes. Both processes will be accompanied by brushing and scraping under running water.[23]

The electrolytic process sometimes provides almost magical results. A large silver lyre of about 2500 B.C. excavated in the Great Death Pit of the Royal Graves at Ur in 1927 was put on display at the British Museum largely as found. The original silver had almost disappeared, having been converted to silver chloride of a dark brown hue. By using a consolidative electrolytic reduction, R. M. Organ succeeded in converting the silver chloride back to metallic silver and restored the bending strength to the brittle metal so that it could be properly shaped.[24]

The so-called "bronze disease," characterized by green powdery spots, occurs upon copper and any of its alloys. When conservators realized that the condition was caused by the formation of cuprous chloride while the objects were underground and that it was activated in the new museum environment by high humidity, its treatment, though difficult, could be accomplished. Electrochemical or electrolytic reduction could be employed but would remove the patina. The spots could be dug out, dry silver oxide used to form a chemical seal, and then the object exposed to 78 percent relative humidity for not more than twenty-four hours to see whether the reaction had stopped; if so, the object, the patina largely intact, was then placed in a case under low relative humidity. Plenderleith and Werner cite the case of a Greek bronze head of a barbarian dated about 400 B.C. and with a fine patina that had remained stable in the British Museum for a long period but was suddenly attacked by the disease. A leaky roof had resulted in damp in the wall against which the head was placed. The spots of cuprous chloride were excavated individually with dental tools, the indentations treated with lacquer, and the head placed in its own case, kept dry by silica gel.[25]

Iron gives much trouble because it rusts easily in the air as well as underground. It can be treated by some of the methods outlined above, then impregnated with oils and greases, microcrystalline wax or beeswax, or lacquers. A shield boss found in the seventh-century Sutton Hoo ship burial now in the British Museum was badly encrusted and rusted but was discovered to conceal ornaments of gold, bronze, and garnets. Treated locally with dilute nitric acid, it was then washed, dried in alcohol and ether baths, and lacquered. An axe in the same find suffered from massive rust with no metal left. Its original shape was studied microscopically and recovered enough by picking and grinding so that an accurate reconstruction could be made.[26]

Stone, Ceramics, and Glass

Granite and basalt, though hard and nonporous, cannot stand the sulfur fumes and automobile emissions of modern civilization. Granite monuments such as the Egyptian obelisks known as Cleopatra's Needles in London and New York can be cleaned and then waterproofed with paraffin wax but it is almost impossible to keep them clean. Monuments from Honduras shown in the portico of the British Museum had to be moved indoors because of frost damage. Sandstone and limestone are relatively porous and absorb soluble salts when buried in the ground; in the museum, fluctuations of relative humidity cause these stones to crystallize, that is, the soluble salts make their way to the surface and can deface ornamental detail and inscriptions. Immersion in water, extraction with moist paper pulp, and vacuum transpiration of distilled water through stone are some of the treatments used to clean the stone, which is then impregnated with wax, resins, or silicon ester. Marble is difficult to clean and to consolidate, but various chemical and mechanical methods can accomplish it. Some large stone objects may be reassembled by using stainless steel or metal dowels.[27]

Ceramics, whether glazed or unglazed, frequently suffer through soluble salts working to the surface and causing efflorescence and flaking. The salts may be removed by soaking with water and the surface can be consolidated by impregnation with synthetics, sometimes liquid nylon. Repairs to broken pottery can be made by strengthening the pieces by impregnation and then putting them together with doweling, a bandage along the back, or an epoxy resin adhesive. If pieces are missing, they can be filled in with colored plaster or a synthetic preparation.[28]

Glass, though usually stable, sometimes suffers from the "weeping" or "sweating" that accompanies the "glass disease." The sodium and potassium in the glass become mobile and susceptible to attack by moisture. If nothing is done to stop the process, the glass becomes cloudy or crizzled. Washing in tap water, distilled water, and alcohol helps, and in some cases organic lacquers will resist the damp. The only sure protection, however, is to place the glass in a relative humidity of under about 40 percent, obtained by using silica gel, sometimes with a small electric fan. Glass also suffers from devitrification, in which the surface becomes partially crystallized and flakes off; this condition can be treated with a surface consolidant such as polyvinyl acetate or polyvinyl alcohol. Broken glass is difficult to repair, but various synthetic adhesives can be used, though epoxy resin must be employed with great caution because it can be softened only by heat and in the process old glass may become crizzled.[29]

These brief descriptions of the way the conservator uses science to protect and restore art and historical objects make clear his importance to the museum. For too long, museums have not taken proper care of their holdings, but conservators are making hopeful changes. With their help, more museum objects can last indefinitely to inspire and instruct future generations.

9

The Museum as Research

Scientists examine embryo coelacanth, American Museum of Natural History

There are three distinct kinds of museum research, and they may be defined as programmatic or applied, general or basic, and audience research. The first has to do with authenticating every part of the museum's collection and program. The second consists of the scholarly contributions of the museum and its staff for the purpose of increasing knowledge in those fields in which the museum has collections or programs. This general, basic, or pure research seeks to serve broader scholarship. Research is essential, to adapt the words of the Smithsonian bequest, for "the increase" as well as the "diffusion of knowledge." The third kind of research is psychological or sociological; it examines the demographic and cultural composition of the museum audience, samples its behavioral response to exhibits and other activities, tests the effectiveness of various segments of the museum's educational program, and experiments with increasing the interaction of exhibits and viewers in teaching displays. It often closely resembles the marketing research done for industry.[1]

Programmatic Research

Programmatic or applied research begins with a thorough examination of the objects belonging to the museum—their physical nature, their history or provenance, and their use and significance. How have they been acquired? If natural specimens, where were they found? If man-made, who created them? Can their history or provenance be traced? What do documentary literary sources reveal about them? In what publications have they been described and pictured? Can living authorities comment on them, possibly through the oral history technique? If man-made, what does the examination of the conservator/scientist show their physical composition to be? (This kind of scientific investigation is sometimes called "technical research.") What are their stylistic characteristics according to the curator/scholar? These questions will take somewhat different forms for art, natural history, technical, or history museums, as well as for botanical or zoological gardens, but the big aim in every instance will be accurately to identify, authenticate, and describe the objects for the museum registration and cataloguing system. Scholars, whether on the museum staff or outside, can make use of this basic object-centered research.

For the museum itself, programmatic research may take a second form. Special reports will be written to support important museum programs and activities. If a natural history museum holds a seminar on some scientific subject based on its collections, a planning paper will outline the general scope of the event, and individual reports may be accumulated or published based upon both the museum collections and outside sources. Every special exhibition at an art museum will be built upon research notes that will result in proper labeling and often a printed catalogue. The history, anthropology, or technical museum will also use research to organize and interpret its exhibits and other activities. The outdoor museum, whether preservation project or assembled historical village, will use voluminous research reports of historian, archaeologist, architect, landscape designer, and decorative arts curator to establish the authenticity of each building, furnishing, and garden; research reports will also buttress this museum's activities—crafts, vehicles, livestock, period foods, music, military drills, sports days, and the like. In other words, research should undergird every part of the museum's interpretation program.[2]

The Research Team

Programmatic research in the museum is often a team effort. It is not confined to the customary examination of manuscripts, books, newspapers, and oral sources but uses a more intensive in-depth approach, with contributions made by experts familiar with specimens or objects. The art museum, for example, may call upon one or more curators, outside art historians, the registrar, and the conservator to secure factual information for its catalog. The history museum, in working out its themes, may enlist anthropologists, geographers, and numerous other specialists to co-operate with its historians and designers. The botanical garden may employ the different viewpoints of the botanist/taxonomist, the geneticist, and the plant breeder/gardener. The outdoor museum uses specialists in history, archaeology, architecture, landscape design, and decorative arts in preparing and interpreting its buildings, settings, and furnishings.

This broad-based, interdisciplinary kind of research is necessary for a museum, the stock in trade of which is objects. These objects are so believable, so convincing in their full-scale, three-dimensional reality that, if used irresponsibly or carelessly, they can easily mislead their viewers. Sophisticated members of the public are accustomed to exert a certain amount of skepticism toward words, whether spoken or written, but are not so prepared to argue with objects. Thus a museum has a special responsibility for the truthfulness of its exhibits and activities that can best be fulfilled by intensive team research. Sometimes, too, the team approach is used for general research.

Co-ordinating team research presents some problems because different components of the team usually have their individual points of view and may wish their way of looking at a situation to prevail. A feasible way of handling such arguments is through a central research committee with the different disciplines represented and appeal allowed to the museum director in case of stalemate.[3]

General Research

The natural history museum has employed a different definition of the museum from that followed by art, history, and science and technology museums. While it may recognize the primacy of a museum's archival function—its collection, conservation, and classification of objects—it has considered the museum a research center, rather than a place of exhibition. In fact, some university natural history museums have done almost no exhibition, and their entire collections have been used for research purposes rather than being separated into exhibition and reserve or storage collections. Even the large American natural history museums in New York, Washington, and Chicago, with their high-quality exhibits, have considered research superior to exhibition, and their most prestigious curators have been research scientists.[4]

Natural history museums, as Laurence V. Coleman has observed, have had a better record of doing general, basic, or pure research than art, history, or technical museums. The chief reason for this accomplishment has been that the natural history museum in collecting, identifying, and classifying botanical and zoological species from throughout the world was for a time the leading scientific institution in the biological field. Its extensive collections made systematics or taxonomy most important in the early development of scientific biology. Later, for a time, these specialties seemed less rewarding for research, and functional studies in embryology, physiology, animal behavior, ecology, and genetics were better done in the field or in universities or scientific institutes than in museums. More recently, however, scientists have realized the great amount of work still needed in systematics and the value of studying both dead and living specimens. Thus, natural history museum collections today offer great research opportunities in biology as well as in mineralogy, petrology, paleontology, physical anthropology, ethnology, and archaeology. Museums with skilled scientific staffs, well-arranged collections, and excellent laboratories and libraries constitute ideal research centers, from which well-planned field or study trips can be conducted to supplement the central resources.[5]

Basic research has occurred more infrequently in museums of art, history, and science and technology. Part of this neglect has been occasioned by the emphasis placed by these museums upon exhibition. Art galleries, since they opened to the public in the latter part of the eighteenth century, have displayed pictures, sculpture, and other art objects largely for aesthetic purposes and more recently as historical documentation. History museums have shown disparate objects with small reference to great historical movements and only recently, chiefly in their outdoor form, have emphasized social history and the everyday life of the common man. Only a few large technical museums are interested in historical objects connected with the physical sciences; most science centers devote themselves to participatory interpretation to show how atomic power, computers, submarines, coal mines, and other forms of modern technology work.

The development of the discipline of art history is resulting in more research activity in the art museum because art historians are always ultimately concerned with objects. The general historian, however, traditionally has depended upon written documentation and seldom understands or tries to use objects. G. Carroll Lindsay is right in thinking that research in history museums must start with the museum, but most history museums are small and poorly financed. The science centers also take little interest in research, and many of them do not even have scholarly curators on their staffs. Thus general research seems to face an uncertain future in many American museums.[6]

William N. Fenton, sometime director of the New York State Museum, believes that, in the natural history museum, research even tops collection as a function. He says:

> I am firmly convinced that the staff of a museum takes precedence over its collections. I believe that this relationship expresses essentially the character of the research museum where the collections accumulate as a by-product and directly reflect the research interests of the scientists. Then as the scientific collections grow and become a resource for research, the museum attracts scientists and it attains stature proportionate to its resources and its publications.[7]

This type of museum offers its curators a distinctive kind of general or basic research opportunity well described by Albert E. Parr, sometime director of the American Museum of Natural History. Parr argued that a curator resembles a university professor in that he devotes half his time to museum archival and exhibition matters and half to personal research, just as a university professor gives half his time to teaching and other university service and half to personal research. In either instance, research is to be regarded as a right left entirely to the individual, rather than a duty dictated by the institution. The museum or university should be content because the research results in better curatorship or better teaching. Because personal research is a right, it matters not that a New York curator investigates bats in New Guinea or a Boston curator, fleas on an elephant. Parr, perhaps somewhat unrealistically, justified the right of curators to do personal research because they work for a considerably smaller financial return than they could receive if employed in industry.[8]

This kind of research arrangement means that natural history curators and university professors have the same kind of scholarly training (usually demonstrated by their holding Ph.D. degrees) and move freely between museum and university or, in some university museums, hold joint appointments in both institutions. Not all natural history museums can afford to allow their curators to give half time to research, but it is a goal toward which they aspire. In some instances, curators, by taking the last six months of one year together with the first six months following, have spent an entire year on personal research, often working far from the museum. In these instances, the curators must arrange to have their regular museum duties covered, usually by other staff members or by visiting authorities paid by the museum.

Many museums, both inside and outside the natural history field, cannot afford to be so liberal and may allow curators only one day a week for personal research or direct all curatorial research to the needs of the museum. In the latter case, however, the curator usually is allowed to work in the field of his specialty, given his choice of several projects in which the museum is interested, and provided full travel, incidental, and publication expenses. Still, thus far, this system sometimes fails to produce high-quality general research.

A museum must realize that an effective research and publication program demands that curators be given time for defined research projects on prescribed schedules and with high priorities. Not much will be accomplished if a curator is expected to do research on his time off or during occasional moments taken from regular responsibilities; nor should other duties be permitted to interrupt his research schedule. In many instances, in order to conduct an excellent research program, a museum will need to hire special researchers and writers either as permanent or temporary staff members to devote full time to important projects.

Publication opportunities must always be considered in developing a research program. They stimulate staff research and writing, as well as adding to the scholarly reputation of the museum itself. If possible, the museum should maintain a quarterly magazine, year-book, or other periodical as an outlet for staff research, and the larger museum ought to issue not only catalogues and other programmatic publications but also varied pamphlets, picture texts, books, and monographs for both its popular and scholarly audiences.[9]

Organization of Research

The well-run museum not only encourages its staff to do general research in its fields of interest but also arranges its holdings in such a way as to attract responsible outside scholars. Objects or specimens in the collections should be available to them in comfortable studies, alcoves, or library space. They should be accorded use of the catalogue, other registration materials, and finding aids. The museum's library, large or small, should welcome them and give them access to special library collections of books, manuscripts, microfilms, and iconographic materials. If the museum has a publication program, it may include suitable articles by outside scholars in its periodical or publish their relevant books or monographs.

A museum will do well, also, to assist graduate or postgraduate students working on general research topics of interest to the museum. A small grant to the student (perhaps during the summer) will insure his understanding of the museum's particular interests and use of museum research resources. It will bring the museum a brief progress report and a copy of the final study—if printed, with an acknowledgment of the museum's grant in aid. Such a program can forward the general research the museum wishes to accomplish and at a reasonable cost.

The small museum can provide occasional research help to outside scholars with a minimum of staff organization, but the larger institution will work out more regular procedures, perhaps using its library with its staff as a research center. In any instance, the director of the museum's research program should co-ordinate staff and outside general research and, whenever the result appears promising, see that proper avenues of publication are explored.

The larger museum with extensive collections, considerable financing, and staff of specialists obviously has the best chance to develop a significant program of general or basic research.[10] Other museums necessarily must devote most of their time and resources to exhibition, interpretation, and other forms of public service and may need to concentrate on the programmatic research that only they can provide. Still, they may occasionally contribute to general research in their chosen field. Any museum with one well-trained professional on its staff or with one or more outside scholars using its resources should regard itself as part of a community of scholars—alert and creative, no matter how small.

Audience Research Beginnings

As educational institutions, museums face a difficult task. They deal with a heterogeneous audience that differs widely in age, education, and cultural background. They teach permissively, that is, their visitors come when they wish, stay as long as they like, move about freely with no ordered viewing, and look at only objects that interest them, on an average, for only a few seconds per exhibit. There are no instructional objectives, textbooks, grades, or examinations to outline or evaluate a learning experience. Still, museums often have great impact upon their visitors and stir interests that may lead to true self-education.

Working with such an open learning approach, museum curators, designers, and educational staff should know how to build exhibits that attract and instruct their audience and how to devise other programs that will help motivate lasting understanding. Thus the museum needs to consider the psychological, sociological, and motivational aspects of its permissive and informal educational efforts and to fashion research methods that will test and improve their effectiveness. Otherwise, as Stephan F. de Borhegyi observed, "museums will fail in their function to provide mass education and will become simply glorified warehouses, recreational facilities, or exclusive clubs for the learned."[11]

In 1924, at the urging of Clark Wissler, the American Association of Museums called in the psychologist Edward S. Robinson to do carefully controlled time-and-motion studies of museum visitors. With stopwatch and clipboard, Robinson, his associates, and their students scientifically and unobtrusively observed the reactions of visitors in museums at Chicago, Milwaukee, Philadelphia, New York, and Buffalo. They made some surprising discoveries. Robinson, for example, found that visitors spent an average of nine seconds looking at a single exhibit in large museums and twelve to fifteen seconds in small ones. Arthur W. Melton discovered that about 75 percent of visitors, on entering an exhibit hall, turned to the right, progressed counter-clockwise, and, if an exit was encountered by the time they reached the back of the hall, looked only at the right hand wall. Exhibits to the left, next to the entrance, were likely to be ignored entirely. He also observed the magnetic power of the exit; many visitors who saw one ahead made straight for it, not bothering to look at any exhibits in the hall.

Perhaps the most important concept established by these pioneer investigative psychologists of the 1920s and 30s was that every display in a museum competes with every other display. The placement of objects and the number of objects are important in determining how long each item will be examined. In science and industry museums, Melton found that adding motion to a display drew visitors immediately and that the attraction was even stronger when they activated the motion by pressing a button or turning a crank. Such scientific observation promised to enable museums better to understand the reaction of their audiences, give their exhibits maximum exposure, and experiment with mock-ups before making final installations.[12]

Museum Demographic Research

Another type of research examined the demography of the museum audience by means of sampling surveys conducted by interviews using questionnaires or by questionnaires alone. Some of the best-known of these projects were conducted at Milwaukee Public Museum (1952–1953), Royal Ontario Museum at Toronto (1959–1960), New York State Museum at Albany (1966), and the Smithsonian's National Museum of History and Technology and National Museum of Natural History (1968–1969). The British also began to use this kind of research at Ulster Museum in Belfast (1968–1970) and the Antiquities Gallery in Dundee (1970).

These surveys usually worked out percentages of the visitors by sex, race, age, educational background, occupation, income level, place of residence, how many times visited, length of stay, whether alone or accompanied, and reason for coming. In general, the museum audience was white, younger (though the Smithsonian visitors were middle-aged), upper middle class in income, above average in education, came to the museum with friends or family, and stayed about one-half hour to two hours. This visitor profile raised a basic question: Should the museum adapt its offerings to this somewhat elite audience, or should it take measures to attract older persons, minority groups, and less privileged classes? Obviously, a museum administration should determine its purposes and not adopt programs just because they are popular.

Sometimes the survey included questions that helped a museum solve practical problems. The Milwaukee study found that having to climb stairs interfered with the popularity of exhibits; those on the second floor lost about 25 percent of the total audience, and those on the third floor another 25 percent. Thus the new Milwaukee building included escalators to meet that problem. At Toronto, the survey studied the image that the museum staff had of the audience, which was considerably better educated and wealthier than the staff had thought. Only 1 percent of the New York State Museum's audience had heard of the museum by radio, television, or press (as compared with 66 percent by word of mouth), demonstrating a need for better publicity through mass media. Also a large percentage wished for a restaurant or coffee shop, important to know in planning the museum's new building. Of the Smithsonian visitors, 63 percent wanted more information on exhibits.

The Ulster Museum, engaged in a major expansion, not only surveyed its own audience, but went out on the streets to sample the community attitude. Some 87 percent of the nonvisitors had heard of the museum, but 63 percent did not know its location, 38 percent had no interest in the museum, and 40 percent could not find time to visit (perhaps Sunday or night openings should be experimented with). Also it was clear that the museum attracted chiefly students and not older persons. The Antiquities Gallery at Dundee, planning a renovation, was discouraged to find that 85 percent of its audience liked the existing jumble of archaeology, local history, and natural history; 43 percent of the adults had no recommendations for a new gallery.[13]

Some demographic research has examined problems outside the museum itself and of much broader significance. The Regional Planning Association for the New York Metropolitan Region in 1969 did an elaborate survey related to the cultural growth of the thirty-one-county area of New York, New Jersey, and Connecticut. The survey studied a carefully selected statistical sample of 2,500 visitors on a Thursday and a Sunday at the Metropolitan Museum, Museum of Modern Art, and Whitney Museum in Manhattan and the Brooklyn Museum, Newark (New Jersey) Museum, and Hudson River Museum at Yonkers. Many visitors were from professional and managerial families, the most affluent and best-educated of the community. Few blue-collar workers attended the Manhattan museums, but the other three attracted many. Clerical and sales persons visited the museums near their places of employment. A substantial majority of the attendance was from the area, but the Manhattan museums attracted more than 20 percent from outside. Annual visits totaled about 20 million.

The planners expected museum visits to reach 80 million in A.D. 2000. They recommended that the twenty-four metropolitan communities that would probably number more than one-half million then have at least one museum with works of the region, traveling exhibits (some of them containerized), and loans from the larger museums. Public financing would be needed so that central museums could reach lower-income groups with traveling exhibits to schools and neighborhoods.[14]

Another unusual survey with a demographic base was done in Toronto between 1965 and 1967 to determine attitudes toward modern art. It was planned by the Committee for Museums of Modern Art of the International Council of Museums and designed as a pilot study that could be extended to other countries. Participants were interviewed in their homes by a marketing research firm. After supplying demographic information, they examined four out of twenty-three packs of ten postcards each of paintings done between 1900 and 1960. They ranked one pack by preference from ten to one and answered several questions about it and then chose the painting they liked best and the one they disliked most in the other three packs.

The respondents chose the most conservative, least radical pictures as their favorites (Millet's *Angelus* ranked first with 51 percent of the vote). They resented paintings they thought unintelligible or meant to confuse them. A work by Dubuffet received 78 percent unfavorable votes, and forty-one of the most eminent painters of the twentieth century were in the two bottom ranks of preference. Familiarity with a painting or types of painting had some favorable effect on choices. The public was consistent in what it liked and (vehemently) disliked. It was unable to identify themes of the sets of cards as chosen by the art historians, for example, figures in silent communion, landscapes with mountains or clifflike forms, the tower form, or track forms (movement and recession). There was no relationship between the age, sex, occupation, or education of those interviewed and the general findings.[15]

Some European audience research has examined the attitude of the general public toward museums and tried to understand the social and cultural processes in which museums are involved. Manfred Eisenbeis in 1972 reported on a sample of 1,917 persons in West Germany. He found that 9 percent had never attended a museum, 23 percent had visited while in school, 18 percent had gone once or twice since, 30 percent went occasionally on a chance visit, 8 percent whenever they had an opportunity, and 2 percent regularly and as often as possible. Museums compared closely with the theater in popularity, did slightly better than concerts or art exhibitions, and ran far behind sight-seeing, fairs, zoos, or botanic gardens. Going to museums was considered as informing/improving by 57 percent, entertaining/relaxing by 6 percent, and partly one and the other by 34 percent. The cinema and the theater were judged far more entertaining. The image of the museum was identified with that of a palace (30 percent), monument (19 percent), library (16 percent), school (12 percent), church (9 percent), theater (9 percent), department store (2 percent), and bank (2 percent).

The survey found that the art museum attracted a special public, an educated and cultural elite. It was not a purely recreational institution with no pressure to learn. On the other hand, zoos, castles and country houses, large museums of technology or natural history, and open-air museums offered leisure opportunities and places for family excursions with children's playgrounds, cafes, and parks that had little to do with the museum collection itself. They also attracted tourist groups and trade union and society outings. Similarly, museums with amateur painting classes, libraries, courses and lectures, films, and cafeterias overcame the image of elitism and served as general leisure-time centers.[16]

Ross J. Loomis in his article, "Please! Not Another Visitor Survey," is right in stating that many demographic projects (not the ones cited above) have been amateurishly done. Often the descriptive data obtained was not followed up by periodic measurement of the audience. He also properly emphasized that professional help should be obtained in devising the questionnaire and the method of sampling.[17] In general, a large museum ought to keep careful attendance figures on a day-to-day basis so that it could answer practical questions of staffing needs or the best time to close exhibits for repairs, special events, television shows, and the like. It also should survey its audience regularly so as to be sensitive to changes that would affect its interpretation program.

Interactive Exhibits and Their Viewers

Modern communication-system theory begins with a source or *transmitter* that sends a *message* by means of a *medium*. It overcomes distracting *noise* and reaches a *receiver*, which through *feedback* allows the transmitter to determine whether the message has been understood. The museum constitutes such a communications system. Its curatorial and educational staff forms the transmitter, decides upon a message or script, and with the help of design specialists transmits the message through an exhibit. Imaginative and artistic use of objects, art work, labels and appeal to sensory perception will avoid or reduce distracting influences (noise) so as to make the message clear to the museum visitors, who constitute the receiver. Their reactions—or feedback—enable the originating staff to determine whether the message is getting across and how to reduce objectionable noise still further. The feedback loop, then, is the area of audience research. Exhibitions are not the only medium museums use to transmit messages; lectures, demonstrations, seminars, publications, and audiovisual productions are some of the others that deserve careful study.[18]

Much audience research continues to be devoted to display problems, some of it on governmental exhibits at world's fairs and similar exhibitions and much of it in the museums themselves. James B. Taylor and his associates did a thorough study of the United States Science Exhibit at the Seattle World's Fair in 1962. They found an exhibit to be a process in which a series of displays leads to an over-all impression; individual exhibits should be planned for their sequence in the process and not for static orientation. Crowd flow and pressure are most important; areas of constant crowd flow should have terse, quickly understood displays, areas of crowd stoppage more general and complex ones, and areas of variable crowd flow exhibits on at least two levels, either to be glimpsed on the run or perused at leisure. The exhibit planner should provide a general framework with a sequence of displays carefully programmed so that the general theme and messages are crystal clear. Display mood and rhythm should vary, and humor and textural effects be used. Some exhibits should be designed to arouse visitor curiosity and motivation rather than to communicate information. De Borhegyi at the Milwaukee Public Museum experimented in applying these principles and produced some ingenious floor plans for his new museum.[19]

Testing an exhibit's effectiveness ideally should be done before it is finally in place. Such tests can be made with mock-ups of inexpensive, temporary materials that can easily be changed in the permanent exhibition. Elizabeth H. Nicol's exciting study, published in 1969, concerned an exhibit on the teeth of mammals (especially shearing and grinding molars) viewed by nine-year-olds at the Children's Museum in Boston. Various displays were discarded or modified in the light of the reactions of the children in the sample until eventually a permanent installation was achieved. The validating technique saved time and money, while greatly increasing learning effectiveness.[20]

Psychologists are doing much experimental work on analyzing the interaction of viewers and exhibits. As Harris H. Shettel points out, not every display is a teaching exhibit. Some have primarily aesthetic appeal and speak directly to the beholder with little interpretation required. Other landmark objects are so intrinsically attractive that they secure the close attention of nearly all viewers; a huge locomotive, the Hope Diamond, or Lindberg's *Spirit of St. Louis* are a few examples. Instructional or teaching exhibits are different, however, because they are designed to convey understanding—to tell a story, show historical development, or explain a process or scientific principle. They attempt to increase the viewer's knowledge or change his attitude.[21]

Psychologists maintain that an instructional exhibit must have goals that can be tested; they need to go beyond generalizations such as enabling the viewer to *understand, discover,* or *grasp the meaning of*. Goals should lead to behavioral action, such as *name, arrange, compare, distinguish, identify,* and the like. Chandler C. Screven describes an objective for audience research on an exhibit of Greek and Roman pottery as follows:

> Given six pairs of color slides of pottery, presented one pair at a time in a test machine, each pair containing an example of one Greek and one Roman piece, the visitor will correctly identify the Greek (or Roman) example in five out of six pairs.[22]

When objectives have been determined and the exhibit installed, the experimental process, in its simplest form, involves selecting a scientifically correct sample of the intended audience, giving it a pretest, exposing it to the exhibit, and conducting a post-test. These tests can be written or they can be given on a testing machine, in some instances with projected slides; the viewer can choose answers by pressing buttons. During the visitor's exposure to the display, various devices can enable the exhibit to direct him to do something; he responds and is told whether he is right or wrong; and then the exhibit directs him to proceed to the next step. A simple device for such visitor guidance is a self-scoring card of printed questions that the viewer fills out at certain points. If he marks the right square, it turns pink, while the wrong one turns blue. Another device is a punchboard with choices to be punched with a stylus; it may be connected with a tape cassette. A right answer causes the tape to say something like: "Good! Go on to the next number," or to make no response to a wrong answer. The self-test machine at the end may be coin-activated and return the coin if a set percentage of correct answers is given.[23]

A word of caution should be added about such testing. Even though visitors do not need to participate unless they wish, these experiments should remain just that—experiments to improve the effectiveness of museum displays. All teaching exhibits in the museum should not be ordered in this way. One of the chief reasons for the attractiveness of the museum is its permissive character, the way it allows its viewers voluntary observation—the informal type of education it provides. Walter Dorwin Teague, the industrial designer, once remarked about exhibits at world's fairs that the designer did not regiment visitors or force them to do anything; he simply "made it easy for the marbles to roll downhill." Sometimes an interactive learning exhibit can be kept permanently as a kind of game for viewers, or a self-test can be built into an exhibit at the end to let one know how well he has understood. Usually, however, the experimentation with the learning process should be used for the purpose of designing or improving the exhibit.

A large museum will do well to assign some of its staff the duty of testing the various parts of its program—exhibits, guidebooks, guide presentations, audiovisual aids, and the like—on a regular continuing basis. The staff can do the testing itself, employing a psychologist consultant to advise on sampling, questionnaires, statistical treatment, and the like. Most visitors are delighted to participate in such testing and to know that their efforts may lead to improvement of the museum's programs. Testing done over a period of time allows fruitful comparisons with the first baseline studies. The museum should also be certain to publish significant contributions of its audience research program, because this rapidly growing field has important implications for the future of all museums.[24]

The Museum as Exhibition

Exhibit of adornment and jewelry throughout the world, Museum of Ethnography, Neuchâtel, Switzerland

Several forces have changed museum attitudes toward exhibition. Perhaps strongest has been the steady democratization of Western society, which transformed museums into cultural and educational institutions serving the general public. Also important was the influence of world's fairs that demanded less cluttered exhibits, often with large objects that could be easily seen and walked around, as well as dramatic displays to attract and hold popular attention. The rise of department stores with compelling, sales-producing arrangements influenced museum exhibit designers, as did the modern art and contemporary architecture movement that began to flourish in the 1920s.[1] The German Bauhaus School in the field of exhibition aimed to make objects on display all-important and play down exhibit techniques. Clean and simple shapes would lead to more powerful and direct visual communication. As Herbert Bayer explained, "The total application of all plastic and psychological means . . . makes exhibition design an intensified and new language. It becomes integrated use of graphics with architectural structure, of advertising psychology with space concepts, of light and color with motion and sound."[2]

Kinds of Exhibits

An exhibit may be defined as a showing or display of materials for the purpose of communication with an audience, often the general public. Yet exhibits have different aims. In museums, they employ original objects to inspire or inform, and incidentally to entertain; in world's fairs, they show objects or processes that illustrate the industrial, technological, and artistic attainments of the different nations; in trade fairs, commercial exhibits, or department stores, they frankly advertise and try to sell various products; and in amusement parks, they entertain and amaze.

These differing purposes affect the nature of the exhibits and the display techniques used. Museum exhibits usually are less dramatic and gaudy than those of world's fairs and commercial shows. The art museum tries to let the work of art communicate directly with the viewer and to use exhibition techniques unobtrusively and with taste. Other types of museums stress the authenticity of the object and its meaning; they strive for totally honest presentation of original specimens or artifacts and avoid the gimmicks and hoopla that may accompany commercial displays.

Museums have two chief classes of exhibits—permanent and temporary. Many of their collections, including their masterpieces and landmark objects, are on display at all times, unless being repaired or on loan to another museum. Temporary exhibits on special themes may feature objects from the museum's collection brought from storage or their usual display places, perhaps supplemented by loans from other museums and collectors. Other special exhibits may consist chiefly of loans or of prepackaged displays obtained from a traveling exhibition service. Permanent and temporary exhibits are often much the same in their theme-centered plan, circulation layout, and design techniques; sometimes, in fact, a new museum will create a series of temporary exhibits that are transferred to its permanent galleries with a minimum of revision. Yet temporary exhibits often justifiably use somewhat more theatrical display techniques because their points must be made more rapidly for viewers who will see the exhibit only once.[3]

The ordinary exhibition in an indoor museum can usually be classified as didactic or teaching. It is carefully organized to present a theme and subthemes through a series of objects arranged in ordered sequence and supported by interpretive aids such as labels, diagrams, art work, photographs, models, and perhaps multimedia devices. The chief components of such an exhibition are a concept or story line, objects to be displayed, and an area or setting using various exhibit methods.

Preparing the Exhibit Script

The exhibit starts with a concept, an idea, or a point of view that is developed in one of two ways. First, it may be stated as a theme and through careful study and research analyzed and divided into subthemes. Then objects can be sought and arranged in exhibit units to elucidate the story. A second approach begins with a collection of objects and from them develops a theme and subthemes. Often both approaches are used simultaneously, and a kind of storyboard arrangement results, with themes listed in one column and appropriate objects in another; exhibition devices may be added later in a third column.[4]

A good example of the theme-dominant approach took place when the Smithsonian Institution's National Museum of History and Technology installed a Hall of Civil Engineering in 1964. The planners first decided to limit the exhibit to bridges and tunnels. An extensive search found only a few original objects, such as fragments of the chain cables of Telford's

Menai Strait suspension bridge (1825) and cased models of ejector pumps used by Eads on his Saint Louis bridge over the Mississippi (1870). Thus models supplemented by diagrams, photographs, and other illustrations comprised the chief exhibit materials. They dealt with structures such as the famed Pont du Gard at Nîmes built by the Romans (A.D. 14), the steel tubular arch chord of the Saint Louis bridge, and the Kentucky River bridge (1876) when under construction on the cantilever principle. Models illustrating building techniques were especially effective. The result was an instructive exhibit but one almost barren of three-dimensional original objects.[5]

On the other hand, many American museums have used their extensive costume collections to show the historical development of dress. The Brooklyn Museum, for example, has arranged many costume exhibitions, even staging an occasional style show with carefully protected old dresses on living models and contrasted with the collections they inspired from contemporary couturiers. The problem in arranging costume exhibitions is not scarcity of original materials but avoidance of unhistorical and elitist emphasis because the more elaborate costumes have survived.

Art museums often use a curatorial order in organizing their shows. This arrangement may be chronological, historical, geographic, or based on some other principle, but it makes judgments of quality, value, and aesthetic compatability. In assembling such a display, a curator may lean art works against the walls of the exhibit area according to one of these general principles and then make changes because of aesthetic considerations, such as placing attractive works in vistas framed by doorways, adjusting the spacing between works, and giving special consideration to entrance and summary areas. He tries to exhibit the works so as to bring out their aesthetic quality and show respect for the artist.[6]

Developing a clear exhibition concept with subthemes and exhibit units obviously requires intensive research. The researcher must be able virtually to write an authoritative essay on the subject of the exhibition. To do this, the normal methods of historical and scientific research will be employed with careful examination of primary sources. Then exhibit units must be devised to make the story abundantly clear—preferably with actual objects enhanced by unobtrusive but effective exhibition techniques. In a small museum, the curator or even the director may do the whole job—research, exhibition design, and installation. In a larger institution, a research assistant may assemble the literary materials, a curator the objects, and a designer the presentation plan.

In preparing the exhibit script, the purposes of the exhibit should be written out as clearly and specifically as possible. The audience for the exhibit should be defined and preferably sampled; the exhibit planner should get out of his office and talk with members of his prospective audience to find what they want to know about the subject and how they respond to some of his tentative design ideas.[7]

An effective museum exhibition needs relevant objects, preferably original ones but at least three-dimensional reproductions or models. Objects constitute the essence of the museum; they may require enhancement, but they themselves tell much to their beholders. A display that consists only of art work, photographs, labels, and multimedia devices can be confusing and difficult to remember; the museum staff often would have done better to devote its energies to producing a book or film program that the audience could have absorbed while seated in comfortable chairs at home or in an auditorium. A recent example of such an exhibition was *The World of Franklin and Jefferson* (1975–1976), a bicentennial extravaganza designed by Charles and Ray Eames and shown at the Grand Palais in Paris, the National Museum in Warsaw, the British Museum in London, and the Metropolitan Museum in New York. It contained few objects but chiefly glossy color photographs with explanatory labels containing 40,000 words. Charles Eames was right to call it "the world's greatest walk-in tabloid."[8]

Creating the Layout

Once the exhibit script has been agreed upon, the designer is ready to consider space requirements. Often he will need to work with a less-than-ideal area prescribed by the rigid nature of a monumental building. Occasionally, he may have a special exhibits gallery with maximum flexibility of partitions, cases, panels, and lighting, perhaps even with a light-weight and flexible structural framing system with spring-loaded supports between ceiling and floor and easily accessible light tracks.

The first big decision is whether the viewers should take a prescribed path or wander at will. For many years world's fairs, commercial exhibits, and museums paid little attention to circulation. In the twentieth century, however, Bauhaus-trained designers, intent upon obtaining maximum communication, began to study circulation carefully and to organize the floor plan to obtain uninterrupted flow of traffic and to encourage the visitor to view all exhibits. In the *German Werkbund* show (1930) at Paris, Walter Gropius used a bridge to give visitors an overview of the exhibit and to draw them forward, and sometimes a ramp was employed to define a circulation pattern. Bayer painted decorative shapes and even footprints on the floor of the Museum of Modern Art in 1938 to direct visitors, and he argued that exhibits with labels required viewers to move from left to right since reading was from left to right.

Controlled circulation remains controversial. Designers like James Gardner, especially when working on commercial exhibitions, fear long waiting lines and crowds that obscure displays. They argue that controlled circulation should be used only when absolutely essential and should not extend for more than one hundred yards at a time. Paul Smith, director of the tiny but innovative Museum of Contemporary Crafts in New York, opposes a "one-way street" circulation, thinks viewers should be allowed to backtrack, and prefers "a free-form environment where people can move around at their own pace and not get tied up in visitor traffic."

On the other hand, teaching exhibitions break displays down into small units to be viewed in definite sequence. The designer then may try to organize the floor plan so as to induce the visitor to view all exhibits. They may be placed on only one side of a passage, and maze arrangements are even used occasionally, though they tend to give an oppressive feeling of constriction. Probably the wisest general plan is to vary the circulation pattern with controlled order for a few concepts that demand sequential viewing and free circulation elsewhere. Highly technical displays that appeal to specialists may be placed in separate rooms or alcoves where they can be skipped by less-interested viewers.[9]

René d'Harnoncourt, late director of the Museum of Modern Art, presented his famed exhibit of *Indian Arts in the United States* (1941) to the trustees two months in advance, with scale models of the museum's three floors and each of a thousand objects scaled in place, the lighting precisely conceived, and the backgrounds painted in their final colors. He believed in using both a two-dimensional floor plan and a three-dimensional scale model; the latter can be made of cardboard very economically. These devices allow the designer to see how his displays will work and to avoid costly mistakes.

The mention of Gropius, Bayer, and the Bauhaus, of d'Harnoncourt and the Museum of Modern Art should remind us how much contemporary museum exhibition design owes to the modern art movement. Alfred H. Barr, Jr., the first director of the Modern, and d'Harnoncourt made that institution an exciting and pioneering leader of the museum world that organized 820 exhibitions in its first twenty-five years, 567 shown in the museum and 252 traveling exhibits prepared by it. The modern designer always emphasized the desirability of keeping the techniques and paraphernalia of display simple, direct, and inconspicuous and using them only to enhance the materials displayed. Bayer was delighted with his propagandistic *Road to Victory* exhibit (1942) at MOMA because the giant blown-up photographs of the American war effort selected by Edward Steichen with captions by Carl Sandburg had almost no structural exhibition elements to interfere with the images themselves. The photographs, free-standing or suspended by wires from the ceiling, formed their own partitions and subject divisions. D'Harnoncourt thought that a museum designer "shouldn't *add* to a work of art; he must not prostitute the whole thing and finally make a peepshow of it." He decried an exhibit of primitive ivory figures played upon by shifting blue and green lights and recommended that museums doing "that sort of thing . . . use eggs, not works of art."[10]

Choosing the Design Techniques

For many years museums presented their exhibits in rectangular or square rooms, utilizing the four walls and floor for pictures and cases. This arrangement could become monotonous and dull and has sometimes been called "the tyranny of the rectangular room"; modern designers prefer curved, angled, or screen walls, movable panels, varied divisions, angles, and directions, and platforms "to reduce the sheer acreage of floors." Such devices add appeal and change of pace, thus diminishing museum fatigue and boredom. Varying the floorscape is important, also—using random-width boards, parquet, carpeted, brick, or stone surfaces, a step or two up or down, or an occasional ramp or bridge.

In placing exhibits on walls or in cases, the designer must remember that the average eye level for a man is about five feet, five inches; for a woman, near five feet; and for a six-year-old, about three feet, six inches. An elliptical cone of vision restricts comfortable head movements to about thirty degrees from the eye level up or down and about forty-five degrees from side to side. Large objects such as dinosaurs or heroic statues must be placed so as to allow the viewer space enough to back away. Bayer also pointed out that a greatly enlarged field of vision can be obtained by placing objects to be viewed at an angle in either the vertical or horizontal plane so as to fall comfortably within the cone of vision.[11]

For long, museums protected most exhibited objects in cases—wall or table types, usually rectangular or square and free-standing. New materials, better ways of mounting glass and plexiglas, and contained lighting have improved standardized cases and made them less bulky and more attractive, though they often pick up confusing reflections. It is better wherever possible to show objects without cases, protecting them by suspending them out of reach or by placing them so that a platform or pebbled surface keeps back the visitor. If a case must be used, its shape can be individually tailored—perhaps polyhedral, bubble, or pyramidal—so as to give an object the space most appropriate for its nature. Old-fashioned wall or table cases often acquired from stores can be remodeled with light boxes above and sloping front glass to reduce reflection, and they and modern standard cases can be placed in a continuous gallery wall that also contains panel displays.

When extremely valuable objects are exhibited on important occasions with no expense spared, elaborate cases can be devised that give the highest protection. Thus the Soviet loan of forty-one French impressionist and postimpressionist paintings toured the United States in 1973 mounted in shadow boxes behind one-half-inch-thick bulletproof plexiglas. The touring exhibition of archaeological finds of the People's Republic of China in 1974–1975 used cases, the relative humidity of which was adjusted to the nature of the objects shown and constantly monitored.[12]

Another display technique is the diorama. It began as a life-sized exhibit with three-dimensional specimens or objects in the foreground amid realistic surroundings and contained in a curved, painted background. The habitat groups of natural history museums—for example, one portraying an African watering hole—showed animals in a proper setting. In some instances man was portrayed in his physical and cultural milieu; thus the historic Iroquois Indian groups in the New York State Museum at Albany were modeled from tribal descendants with settings carefully reproduced from authentic historical sites. Full-scale groups are expensive, however, and take up much space, so that miniature dioramas—scale groups of sculptured figures and lifelike details blending almost indistinguishably with a curved, realistic painted background—have almost taken over the definition of the word.

The miniature diorama employs perspective and is intended to be viewed only from the front. It can well portray an important and dramatic historical or natural event; a detailed historical, ethnographic, or ecological setting; or an industrial plant or process with or without animation. The scale of one and a half inches equaling one foot has been used frequently, since it works well with a housing about six feet wide. The figures are usually modeled from hard wax on a wire framework, with clothing modeled from the wax. The diorama aperture is about forty-two inches wide, thirty-six inches high, and placed at an eye level of five feet;

the glass in front is slanted inward at the bottom to reduce reflection. Dioramas can be made to present an alternating scene through the same aperture by using two dioramas, mirrors, and alternating light sources. A series of dioramas has sometimes been installed side by side, for example, showing the career of Abraham Lincoln at the Chicago Historical Society, but such an arrangement tends to become monotonous, and today dioramas are usually employed more sparingly and intermixed with other kinds of displays.[13]

Lighting is one of the chief tools of the exhibit designer. For many years, art museums considered natural daylight, preferably from above, the ideal light for paintings, but today artificial light, either incandescent or fluorescent, is usually favored because it remains uniform and can be controlled. Lighting may give the object on display a proper setting, for example, the light under which it was created. D'Harnoncourt liked to approximate the original light and color backgrounds of primitive art works—"the green of the jungle, the white light of the full sun, the red of rocks and tan of desert." Lighting also makes museum audiences feel comfortable; in northern countries, they prefer the warm tungsten light; in the tropics, the cool fluorescent.

For the general exhibit designer, lighting is, as Gardner asserts, "the most flexible and forceful display technique available." No longer is viewing to be left to chance; lighting will emphasize roundness, solidity, or surface qualities. It can be directed to a painting or figure exactly, to light it and nothing more, as the *Winged Victory* at the head of the Louvre's grand staircase. Lighting also is all-important for the temporary exhibition; changes in intensity from dimness to sparkle and in color from subdued to bright (and back again) on the exhibition path lure the visitor on and persuade him to look more closely at the displays. An artful mixture of general and spotlighting adapted to individual objects brings out qualities that would be missed under bland, over-all illumination.

Lighting also need not embrittle or fade art works on paper or textiles, so long as the intensity is controlled. Protective sleeves on fluorescent tubes will filter out harmful irradiation, the heat of incandescent lighting can be dissipated, and special glass or curtains will diffuse natural light.[14]

Creative exhibit designers provide fresh ways of looking at objects that enhance their impact and meaning. D'Harnoncourt's American Indian exhibit brought out the sculptural magnificence of a tiny, eight-inch-high Adena smoking pipe by placing it beside a huge, enlarged photo-mural of itself. Bayer in the *German Werkbund* show suspended chairs from the wall at an angle, a device used again by Ivan Chermayeff and his team in *American Arts and the American Experience* (1973), a permanent installation at the Yale University Art Gallery. In *Airways for Peace* (1943) at the Museum of Modern Art, for a focal exhibit Bayer suspended an outside-in, walk-in globe from the ceiling with a map of the world on the inside surface so that the viewer could grasp the whole at a glance. Erberto Carboni, the brilliant Italian, did a Television Exhibit (1953–1954) at Milan that used the familiar curved television screen and sending and receiving towers as design motifs.[15]

Labels

Labels are a basic means by which a museum transforms a collection of objects into a storytelling exhibition that communicates effectively with its chosen audience. They must attract the viewer's attention, convey information about the objects on display in a concise, yet understandable way, and, by successfully provoking his curiosity, motivate the visitor to look at the whole exhibition. Actual objects have their own character; in a good exhibit, words are often redundant and should be kept incisive. The viewer who must stand while reading quickly experiences museum fatigue and will skip long labels entirely.

There are several classes of labels. The main label, sometimes called the room or gallery label, briefly and clearly states the theme of the exhibit. This label will be prominently placed and may consist of a symbol, art work, or headline of large three-dimensional letters with perhaps a subhead of smaller letters and somewhat greater length; it is similar to the title of a book. A secondary topic label (sometimes a case label) will be used for the exhibition's subthemes; though not so prominent as the main label, its headline will have large letters and its subhead, while brief, will be long enough to give the gist of the subtheme. The main and the secondary labels are essential to understanding the exhibition and will carry its over-all message to viewers who do no more than read them and look at the objects.

Other explanatory labels, longer and of smaller type size, give facts, figures, and explanations for interested viewers and specialists but can be ignored by less-interested visitors. Caption labels also are usually supplied for most individual objects; they briefly give the chief facts, such as name of the object, maker, date, and place of origin. If a donor's name must be included, it should come last and in smaller type.

George Brown Goode was right when he wrote in 1895 that "the preparation of labels is one of the most difficult tasks of the museum man." It involves two distinct processes—literary composition and visual appearance. On the literary side, the problem is to translate the detailed knowledge and often the jargon of the curator into a short explanation using language readily understood by the layman. This approach calls for straightforward literary style and clarity of content so as to obtain maximum readability. Often, a curator will be wise to consult a journalist, editor, or advertising copywriter accustomed to making every word count, for the greatest fault of most labels is verbosity. The Smithsonian museums have decided that no explanatory label is to exceed seventy-five words; this difficult standard is met by skillful use of charts, diagrams, or cutaway models and by dividing a necessarily long label into two or more shorter ones.

The second requirement of a label is typographic legibility. Lettering must be large enough to be readable at the distance from which it is observed (ordinary typewritten labels cannot be read from more than fifteen inches away). Easily recognized Roman serif or sans serif typefaces (no boldface) should be used consistently and with capitals and lower case letters, short paragraphs with proper indentation, no excessively long width of line, and the colors of letters contrasting with the background color (black letters against white are most legible). Labels can be produced by hand or with Leroy, Wrico, or other letter guides; with plaster, paste-on, other types of pre-formed letters, or photolettering; by label typewriter or regular printing; or, perhaps best of all, by silk-screening.

The exhibit designer also may play a part in producing high-grade labels. He wants them to fit into his general design tastefully, but he must respect their typographical legibility and place the labels close enough to the objects they describe that their relationship is readily apparent. The labels must be well lighted, the essential ones placed high enough not to be obscured by crowds, and the others kept at an easy-to-read height.

Goode considered "the art of label writing in its infancy," and one sometimes wonders how much museums have learned about it since that day. Still, labels remain the basic means of enabling viewers to understand exhibitions. Guidebooks and catalogues help, and oral labels (whether by radio or tape recording) are useful adjuncts, but thus far no one has found a satisfactory substitute for a well-written, visually attractive label.[16]

Functional Arrangement

During the last half of the nineteenth century, European museums began to experiment with a new kind of exhibition arrangement. In natural history museums, the habitat group developed—nesting birds mounted with parents, eggs, and young in a proper geographic and botanical setting, or a lion group shown devouring its prey in an authentic African environment. The period room, whether found in innovative museums using the culture history approach or in the popular new outdoor folk museums, was a humanistic version of the habitat group. Later, museums of science and industry tried a similar approach with exhibits such as a reproduced salt or coal mine or a full-scale submarine that one could walk through.

Combining dozens or even hundreds of individual objects into a meaningful whole understandable to the viewer at a glance produced a powerful exhibit, but one that did not emphasize its separate components. Benjamin Franklin's original printing press would not stand out so well if it were part of a three-press, fully equipped colonial printing shop, perhaps demonstrated by working craftsmen, as it would if shown in its own highlighted setting.

There were also different kinds of period rooms. The artistic period room contained original architectural elements, furniture, and furnishings of high excellence in design and workmanship, all of the same period and tastefully placed so as to please modern connoisseurs and observers. The historical period room, on the other hand, tried to show an actual or typical room as research found that it once had appeared. Furnishings of an earlier period might be included as they often are in any home today, and everything was arranged according to the taste of the day. Pictures were hung higher than eye level or in rows, if that was the way they were customarily placed then. Nor was the room necessarily beautiful. If it belonged to a colonial governor or prosperous merchant, it might have great aesthetic appeal, but almost certainly not if it was a simple room of a frontier cabin, a slave quarter, or a jail cell. Albert E. Parr, sometime director of the American Museum of Natural History, considers the less fashionable units sociological period rooms and observes that he has found them chiefly in European museums.

Other variations of the functional approach include the composite faunistic habitat group (again, Parr's term) and the period setting as defined by Mrs. Nina Fletcher Little. The faunistic habitat does not show any particular landscape, but rather a synthetic, continuous group of environments; thus at the Biologiska Museet in Stockholm, a visitor enters a two-level central observation tower, from which he may see preserved, as he walks around, all the most important animals of Sweden, each in its proper environment. The period setting recreates only the architectural features of a period room—ceilings, walls, floors, and fireplaces—as a background for furniture and furnishings of the same era but not arranged as the contents of a room.

Habitat groups and period rooms are expensive and use much space, and they do not let the observer inspect individual pieces closely. To overcome the first two handicaps, miniature dioramas are sometimes used, as, for example, Mrs. James Ward Thorne's famed miniature rooms at the Art Institute of Chicago. The National Museum of History and Technology in its "Hall of Everyday Life in the American Past" uses a chronological arrangement with labeled objects displayed on panels or in cases as well as occasional period rooms using some similar objects. This kind of display allows both close examination of individual pieces and the unity of vision provided by the period room. Still another approach is found at Plimoth Plantation. Here the buildings, furniture, and furnishings have all been reconstructed. Visitors are encouraged to touch anything that interests them, to sit on chairs, or to open chests. The interpretation also tries to reproduce Pilgrim life of about 1627; the interpreters tend animals, carry water in and out, keep up the fires, cook, spin, weave, sew, make soap and candles, practice crafts, and do the many homely tasks of a small rural village. Thus the period room at places like Plimoth takes on new, more realistic dimensions.[17]

Multimedia Exhibits

Another approach to exhibition employs modern electronic communication devices. In 1969 Marshall McLuhan and Harley Parker of Toronto, two leading students of these media, met with museum leaders at a seminar in New York to explore ways in which museums could improve communication with their visiting public. To supplement its spirited discussions, the seminar visited conventional exhibits at the American Museum of Natural History and a special light-and-sound orientation show designed by Parker for a Dutch gallery at the Museum of the City of New York, complete with mixed-media devices that included multiple slide and motion picture projectors and strobe lights.[18]

McLuhan and Parker made their educational philosophy abundantly clear. According to them, museums in the nineteenth century had adopted a story-line type of exhibition that was sequential, linear, logical, and pictorial, but also one-thing-at-a-time and detached. They had concentrated upon objects but paid little attention to their audience. As a result, according to McLuhan, most museum viewers "walk up to an object and look at it casually, read the label, give it [the object] a cursory glance, and walk on. They have not really looked at anything, because they are data oriented."[19] A remedy for this situation, the two men argued, would be electronic bombardment of the viewer's senses—certainly sight and hearing and possibly touch, smell, and taste. Such communication is random, shared, and instantaneous. The recipient who uses all his senses absorbs information more readily and retains it longer. The human mind can comprehend about 400 words per minute, while the human voice can utter only 150.[20]

Thus, Parker recommended that the carefully done exhibits of the American Museum of Natural History be phased out and replaced. He said:

> Take photographs of all this stuff, put them in printed form, and you have a book. . . .
>
> Museums are still feeding on the book. What I'm asking for is, please, let us recognize that this [the exhibition] is a unique medium. Explore it and begin to exploit it.[21]

Combining the objects-and-multimedia appeal to the senses, McLuhan and Parker argued, would give museums new impact and attract new audiences. Primitive man for thousands of years had acquired information chiefly by sensory, immediate stimuli; not until Gutenberg's printing press and the renaissance painters had literate and pictorial presentation become predominant. Thus humankind still instinctively understands the powerful sensory approach. Children raised with television readily comprehend sophisticated audiovisual devices, and so do beats, hippies, and teenagers, often in revolt against literate and linear life-styles. The multimedia could bring new audience participation and involvement to the exhibition.[22]

The basic building blocks of multimedia programs are numerous and readily available. First of all is the live performer who can narrate, sing, or act. Then come images of various kinds—color slides that are relatively inexpensive and can be made to dissolve smoothly from one to another; illuminated transparencies lighted or darkened according to a program; film loops that run for about two minutes, conveying a basic message or directing the viewers along a route; images projected not from film but from the objects themselves by means of opaque or overhead projectors; and story-line films or videotapes, often shown by rear projection. These images can appear on multiple screens or various surfaces. Lighting used with objects themselves or with the various images can produce varied effects—flashers, dimmers, strobes that freeze movement into fragmented parts, black or ultraviolet light that reacts only to fluorescent materials, and polarized lenses that produce intensely bright spectral colors. Sound comes in stereophonic effects with multiple tracks or can be distorted. Special effects can convey aroma, temperature, or a sensation of movement. A program using these varied devices can be synchronized and kept in sequence by optical or magnetic film, punched tape, or one with inaudible signals, or by other devices.[23]

Two rather recent exhibits have used mixed media effectively. In 1969 the American Museum of Natural History installed a special exhibit (open for two years) in honor of the centennial of its founding. Entitled *Can Man Survive?* it did much to bring the question of their deteriorating environment to the attention of Americans. At the beginning of the display, two four-minute color films, projected side by side, showed that all life on earth depends on food, water, and oxygen and that it exists in a complex and delicate balance. The remainder of the exhibit described the increasing overpopulation and pollution with which modern man is upsetting this balance. At the very end, the question "Can Man Survive?" was asked for a last time, as the viewer turned a corner to see, in a mirror, who it is that holds the answer.

The exhibition subtly worked upon the emotions of the viewer. He saw the two introductory films in spacious, air-conditioned comfort, but as he went along, the dim illumination, narrow and somewhat claustrophobic passages, and floors that tilted slightly so as to keep him off balance gave him a feeling of physical unrest that unconsciously aroused a sense of concern for what he saw happening to the environment in the displays. The exhibition depended mainly on mixed media—models, films, slides, and tape recorders, but as Joseph Wetzel, the chief designer, put it: "The gadgets are not what's important. The big point is that the American Museum had something really important to say, and chose to say it in an appropriate way. A way that could have some impact."[24]

The second exhibition, a permanent one of *The Story of the Earth* (1972), is the chief feature of the Geological Museum in London. One enters it through a towering rockface, reproduced in realistically painted plaster taken from castings of a highway cut in the northwest Scottish Highlands. Though the display contains some rocks that can be handled, its chief exhibits are spectacularly achieved by mixed media—a curved panorama of galaxies in space; a continuous filmstrip showing the semimolten surface of the earth as it appeared 4,500 million years ago; a push-button animated diorama of the Surtsey volcano that erupted off Iceland in 1964 with realistic-looking lava flowing from the crater; and a shaking platform accompanied by fearful rumblings that simulates the 1964 Alaskan earthquake, the greatest ever recorded. Gardner, the designer, combined models and dioramas with ingenious multimedia components such as back projection, film loops, slide sequences, polaroid animations, and sound effects. So complex was the electronic layout that a technician had to be employed to keep everything running.[25]

Obviously, multimedia exhibits can have tremendous impact and make a subject vivid and spectacular. They must be used, however, with caution. The story-line or message, despite the beliefs of McLuhan and Parker, must not be discarded but made crystal-clear and developed with infinite care. One should notice that the two exhibitions described contained few original objects and developed independent themes for interpretive purposes. The New York show had little connection with the collections of its museum, and the London one was only a general introduction to geology. Mixing traditional linear didactic displays with sometimes raucous multimedia is risky business. The museum must keep control, not the design firm; multimedia devices are tools and techniques for communicating clearly defined ideas and concepts, not gimmicks to be admired for their novelty and ingenuity. A designer can keep an exhibition from becoming mediocre and stodgy, but a curator must see that it retains its truthfulness and sincerity.

Mobile Museums

Since World War II, many museums have been trying to reach audiences that do not come to their doors. Sometimes a big-city museum has developed outreach programs to appeal to inner-city urban poor, ethnic, or minority groups. In other instances, a state-supported museum in a capital city has taken programs to small villages and remote rural areas. In developing countries with many illiterates, museum exhibits have proved invaluable in transmitting information on health, agriculture, modern science, ecology, and social welfare.

Part of this outreach program can be accomplished by traveling exhibits sent out by the central museum, but then provision must be made for exhibition space, installation and dismantlement, security, and community participation. Often, an easier way to accomplish the objectives of a museum extension program is to install an exhibit in a trailer or railroad train and circulate it with someone from the museum to see that it is properly protected and used.

The Illinois State Museum sent out its first museumobile in 1948; five years later, the Virginia Museum of Fine Arts put an art-mobile on the road, and in 1954 the history-mobile of the State Historical Society of

Wisconsin began its travels. Today there are more than forty such programs in the United States and Canada. Perhaps the Virginia version has been the most successful, with four art-mobiles in action—two devoted to thirty local art organizations affiliated with the central museum in Richmond, one serving the small communities of the state, and one earmarked for its fifteen colleges and universities. Michigan has an "artrain" of four railroad coaches that tours the state, and Manitoba a "Rolling Stock" that takes history and other displays to small towns and Indian reservations.

Most mobile museums emphasize an exhibit that is carefully installed with provision for protection against fire, theft, or other damage. A specially trained curator either accompanies the vehicle or drives to the site to work with community leaders, teachers, and students to secure its maximum utilization, together with orientation and curriculum guides, slide sets, and films. About one-fifth of the mobile programs operate in cities, using smaller vehicles outfitted with supplies for participatory activities in neighborhood centers, playgrounds, parks, and housing projects; the emphasis here is upon creative workshops in art, history, or science.[26]

A pioneer museobus was constructed in Poland in 1949 by the National Museum of Warsaw. In the Ukraine a similar vehicle takes information about natural phenomena, history, and archaeology to hamlets and even to farm workers resting during harvesting times. UNESCO built a museobus to reach rural workers in tropical Africa with displays on modern agricultural techniques, public health measures, and demonstrations of scientific principles. The Birla Industrial and Technological Museum of Calcutta has used a two-decker museobus, once for an exhibit on "Transformation of Energy."

European users of museum vehicles have been ingenious in enlarging their exhibit space. In 1954 an expandable trailer was designed for use in arid regions, and in 1972 the Linder museobus in France would triple the 8-foot-3-inch (2.50 meters) width prescribed by highway regulations and provide more than 600 square feet of interior space with room to hang thirty normal-size pictures. The steep increase in petroleum prices experienced since 1975 may make it more feasible to take mobile museums to the schools than to bring school buses to the museum.[27]

The Future of Exhibition

Museum exhibition has come a long way, particularly in the last fifty years. Exhibits must now meet exacting standards—authenticity as enforced by the curator; attractiveness as provided by the designer; and effectiveness of communication, the prime purpose of both.[28] The experimental work of the psychologist in the field of audience research is also of great importance; by using mock-ups and observing closely the reaction of a sample of the intended audience, museums can greatly improve exhibition impact. Multimedia devices, used with ingenuity and care, will heighten the visitors' sensory perception and produce a feeling of mood.

Most museums today conduct a changing special exhibition program that may offer a dozen or more shows each year. This activity is often the main function of small or medium-sized museums and constitutes the major commitment of the time of their entire staff. A changing exhibition program furnishes numerous opportunities for the museum to seek new acquisitions for its collection, do fresh research on the objects it shows, issue a catalogue or other publications, mount promotional and public relations campaigns, and conduct a host of educational activities—an opening ceremony, special tours for adult and school groups, lectures, panels, seminars, and the like. There is no better way to keep the museum fresh and attractive for both its regular patrons and new audiences.

Museum objects, however, can be greatly harmed when transported to new environments without proper attention to relative humidity, lighting, and security. Packing, unpacking, transportation, and installation also present hazards, and even though insurance will provide some protection against financial loss, the destruction or deterioration of valuable museum objects is a serious matter. Thus museums must exercise great care to insure that exhibitions do not damage the objects. In addition, too vigorously changing an exhibit program may also throw the purposes of the museum out of balance. If the entire staff devotes most of its time to frenetic installation and utilization of shows, less spectacular functions such as conservation and research get neglected. Despite these caveats, exhibition will remain the most basic activity for most museums, and creative museum personnel should devote major attention to devising ways in which objects may add to human understanding and enjoyment.

11

The Museum as Interpretation

Shingle-making in the eighteenth-century manner, Colonial Williamsburg

American museums have for long been known around the museum world for their educational programs. More conventional European institutions had regarded exhibition as their basic and in some instances their only educational activity. True, the Scandinavian open-air folk museums had made their displays lively with operating windmills and crafts, animals and crops in their fields, music and folk-dancing, and costumed guides performing household tasks, but were they real museums or only ethnographic parks, first cousins to Tivoli-like amusement centers? As American museum education programs blossomed and historic houses and villages spread over the countryside, some reaction set in against the very word *education*. Certain museum leaders feared that it connoted an authoritarian type of learning with classrooms, textbooks, assigned reading, examinations, and grades. They considered *interpretation* a better word to describe the learning process that went on in museums; it was informal and voluntary and contained a large measure of recreation.

What Is Interpretation?

Freeman Tilden, in his pioneering book *Interpreting Our Heritage*, written for the National Park Service in 1957, defined interpretation as "An educational activity which aims to reveal meanings and relationships through the use of original objects, by firsthand experience, and by illustrative media, rather than simply to communicate factual information."[1] Twenty years later, we can expand this definition somewhat and decide that good interpretation contains at least five basic elements:

1. It seeks to teach certain truths, to reveal meanings, to impart understanding. Thus, it has serious educational purpose.

2. It is based on original objects, whether animate or inanimate; natural or man-made; aesthetic, historical, or scientific. Objects have been around much longer than language and, when properly arranged, have innate powers to impart and inform.

3. It is supported by sound scientific or historical research that examines each museum object, undergirds every program, analyzes the museum's audience, and evaluates its methods of presentation so as to secure more effective communication.

4. It makes use, wherever possible, of sensory perception—sight,

hearing, smell, taste, touch, and the kinetic muscle sense. In the case of three-dimensional natural or historical environment, sensory perception can create a mood that allows the visitor to feel attuned with the natural scene or to glimpse what it was like to live in another age. The sensory approach, with its emotional overtones, should supplement but not replace the customary rational avenue to understanding provided by words and verbalization; together they constitute a powerful learning process.

5. It is informal education without the trappings of the classroom, is voluntary and dependent only on the interest of the viewer, and is often enjoyable and entertaining. It may furnish one with strong motivation to read further, to visit other places, and seek other ways of satisfying one's newly aroused curiosities.

Those who carry out the interpretation process in museums have at hand a whole panopoly of methods from which to choose—sensory experiences, multimedia and audiovisual productions, personable guides, demonstrations, self-guided tours, labels, lecturers, publications, and many others.[2]

Orientation

Large museums with varied exhibits and complex circulation patterns should provide museum-goers with an over-view before they start their tours. They should understand the chief collections and the ways in which they are arranged so that they may make choices of what they wish to see and know how to find their way. Orientation can be achieved in many ways. A lecture or some other kind of oral presentation, a selective exhibition arranged to illustrate general themes and building locations, a printed piece with key illustrations, a slide show or filmstrip—any of these approaches, when imaginatively and tastefully conceived, can provide a proper introduction to a museum.

Occasionally, orientation can be moving and even spectacular. The Museum of Anthropology in Mexico City has an automated show that begins with a darkened stage and the exotic pre-Columbian music of reed flutes and drums. The lights come on to reveal beautiful models of early Mexican pyramids and other landmarks, sometimes illustrated with interior scenes projected on screens behind the stage. The scene darkens again to allow the models to fold down into the floor and new ones to replace them. The strange music continues throughout the fifteen-minute performance. Thus the early history of the Toltecs,

Aztecs, and Mayas unfolds and provides a central theme that frequently recurs to the visitor as he goes about the exhibits in the museum galleries that tell the story in much greater detail with a wealth of subthemes.[3]

Other effective orientation programs use wide-screen motion pictures with a multiple-channel sound track. The National Air and Space Museum of the Smithsonian Institution, opened on July 4, 1976, has a spectacular thirty-minute film, *To Fly*, that makes the viewer feel he is aboard various aircraft, from an early hot-air balloon to the latest space rocket. The earth below, viewed from tree-top height or from outer space, is always thrilling, and the film in some instances produces realistic vertigo in the viewers. The program is an excellent introduction to the full-scale air and space craft and other striking exhibits of the museum.

At Colonial Williamsburg in Virginia, another wide-screen film in about thirty-five minutes tells *The Story of a Patriot*. John Fry, the fictitious hero, participates in the events leading to the Revolution in Virginia and gradually decides, after considerable emotional conflict, to give up his loyalty to the king and go along with his patriot friends—Washington, Jefferson, Patrick Henry, and George Wythe. The film also, as part of the story-line, shows the chief features of the historic area and exhibition buildings of Colonial Williamsburg; these details provide the visitor with many a pleasant shock of recognition as he later makes his tour.[4]

The chief components of really successful orientation programs are: (1) over-all themes that add meaning to the regular museum exhibits; (2) emotional impact that makes the orientation program itself a feature of the museum visit; and (3) details of exhibits that intrigue the visitor's interest, make him decide what he wishes to see, and serve as recognizable guideposts during his tour.

The Tour

Museum tours may be divided into two chief classes—self-guided and personally conducted. In the first, the visitor makes his way about the museum at his own pace, stopping as he likes to view exhibits and read labels. He may be assisted by some kind of printed piece—a guidebook that he reads at will as he goes about, or a printed sheet describing the artists, paintings, or objects in each gallery. He may press a button in order to hear a talking label, or he may rent a small radio receiver or tape recorder so as to carry his private interpretation with him. Various devices may provide background music appropriate for the period or place of the exhibits or may reproduce the music of rare instruments as he views them.

These self-guided tours can be enriched at various points by other automatic or visitor-activated audiovisual or multimedia devices. They include short films (often shown by rear projection); slide and sound sequences; multimedia combinations of images, lights, and sounds; and odors, such as the delicious aroma of chocolate in a period candy store.

Personally conducted tours, though more expensive to operate, are usually more effective than self-guided ones, provided the guides are good. Perceptive teacher-guides—well prepared, wise, flexible, friendly, and unrehearsed—can make museum tours a pleasant, even memorable, learning experience. The guides should have at their command human interest materials that emphasize colorful personalities, lively happenings, and underlying concepts. Excellent guides possess personal warmth of communication, like people, and consider their interpretation "an act of love toward humanity, not a specialized message to the initiated few." Both men and women can make excellent interpreters; sensitivity and friendliness are the needed qualities.

Training such a guide force is a continuing process. The curatorial or research staff needs to provide subject matter that possesses both accuracy and human interest, upon which the interpretation is based. A syllabus or manual of questions and reading material can be the start, followed by group discussions, observation of tours, and then trial tours by the beginner commented upon by more experienced guides. In a large museum, the curatorial, research, and educational staff may give more formal courses to the guides, or they may be encouraged to attend college or university classes in their subject-matter fields. Group visits to other museums to observe how they conduct their interpretation are of much value. The important thing is to develop an esprit de corps in the guide force that inspires its individual members to continue to learn and to take pride in their own distinctive presentations. They may joke about attending a college from which no one ever graduates, but their continuing search for knowledge makes them better interpreters.

This kind of interpretation is often best done by professionals, because guides paid for their preparation and tour leadership constitute a more reliable and more manageable group. The possibility of using volunteers, however, should not be disregarded; though they present more problems in maintaining uniform standards of preparation and presentation and in scheduling, proper professional supervision can frequently make excellent use of the pool of well-educated, talented, and enthusiastic men and women of a community. Such volunteers make many smaller museums economically possible, and they also help interpret a museum to its community.

The complex and difficult mechanics of administering a guide force are usually best handled by a professional. Scheduling can be a frustrating business and in larger museums demands records of daily past attendance in order to provide the right number of guides. The physical handling of groups requires much thought and care to see that they are gathered efficiently and that they move about the museum with dispatch and a minimum of disturbance to touring individuals or other groups. In many museums the guides also serve as guards and protect the objects from damage or theft. They must be trained to meet emergencies such as fire, illness of visitors, and rare confrontations with militants. Should guides wear uniforms? In larger museums, perhaps a distinctive blazer for both men and women may be desirable, so as to set them off from the ordinary public; and in history and outdoor museums, guides may wear reproduced period costumes to display them for the public.[5]

Bringing Exhibits to Life

Museum tours can be enhanced by demonstrations of processes. This maxim accounts for the increasing use of crafts and industrial operations by both indoor and outdoor museums. The manufacture of cloth with its carding, spinning, and weaving done by hand or by early machines can be far more enlightening and exciting than the best verbal presentation of these processes by talented guides. So can setting type by hand, inking with balls or rollers, positioning the hand-made paper, and pulling the "devil's tail" of the heavy press. In the botanical garden, cultivation, harvesting, potting, pruning, and plant-propagation techniques arouse great interest in the visitors. In a museum of science and industry, a visit to an enlarged human heart, a farm with live animals, or a demonstration of electricity that literally makesa volunteer's hair stand on end captures the rapt attention of nearly every visitor. Playing period music on authentic instruments in person or on well-made tapes is another mood-producing practice, for music calls forth rich emotional response in almost everyone.

The outdoor museum is especially fortunate in finding opportunities to provide demonstrations and activities. Visitors can ride in horse-drawn vehicles, oxcarts, canal boats, or early railroad trains. Horses, cattle, sheep, chickens, ducks, geese, and other animals can be observed and sometimes petted. Military drills, sports, games, period plays or dramatic skits, dancing, and even fireworks can enliven special occasions. The serving of food and meals reminiscent of a period or area is both evocative and popular.

All these activities involve a high degree of visitor participation, either psychological or actual. They better explain processes; they combine sensory perception with rational analysis; and they dramatize collections of objects. A basic underlying problem with them is that of authenticity. Even if the equipment, processes, and costumes are thoroughly researched, is the demonstrated craft over-romanticized? Are the frequent quarrels between master craftsmen and their apprentices understood? Are the long hours and grinding tedium of much of the work? Are the early industrial demonstrations too neat and clean? Is the tyranny of the machine understood and the social evils of the labor of women and children? There is also sometimes a problem of commercialism. The craft program can become so engrossed in selling the popular items it produces that it gives too little attention to interpretation.

Another process of interpretation becoming popular especially in outdoor history museums is that of role-playing by the guides. Here the interpreter tries to learn everything possible about the historical period involved and to conduct himself as if he were living then; the interpretation is normally given in the first person. Often the guide performs everyday tasks of the period; the housewife may kill a chicken, scald it and pluck the feathers, cut it up, and fry it. The farmer may fell a tree with an axe, cut it to size by chopping and wedging, and carry other seasoned wood to the fireplace. Meanwhile, each one talks about his or her daily life and chores. About noon, they may prepare their customary dinner and eat it, meanwhile discussing the weather, their newlyborn calf, a neighbor's approaching wedding, news of a historical event, or other period happenings. This interpretation sometimes involves the visitors and may extend to "live-in" situations where students don period costumes, occupy a historic house or shop, and participate in activities such as cooking or the crafts. Role-playing thus is included in the "living history" approach along with craft demonstrations, historical rides, and other period participatory activities.

This kind of interpretation has a novelty and immediacy that makes it appealing. On the other hand, it has certain defects. Role-playing, unless most artfully carried on, often seems overdramatic and unconvincing. It sometimes cannot stand the full light of day, but is better done at night, with flickering candles or other forms of dim illumination. The matters discussed by the interpreters may also not answer the questions of the visitors and may take much more time than a well-organized, didactic commentary. Practical personnel problems may arise with such a program. Should blacks, for example, be restricted to showing the often-times demeaning life of slaves, or should they be allowed to play white Anglo-Saxon roles? With a more conventional interpretation, the interpreter's job can be defined as dispensing information and explanation, and modern civil-rights problems can largely be avoided.

On balance, bringing exhibits to life is an effective, oftentimes powerful, teaching technique, and any museum is wise to consider its purposes and exhibits from this point of view. Demonstrations, rides, processes, music, role-playing, and other activities can be accurately presented and used to secure maximum visitor participation.[6]

Lectures, Forums, Seminars

A tested and reliable form of museum interpretation is the lecture or its variations, such as slide or film showings, field trips, or campfire talks. The storyteller has exercised a popular human role from the earliest times; a skilled, personable speaker can communicate effectively and distinctively with his audience. Thus a museum will do well to organize general or specialized lecture series to develop understandings of its fields of interest and of its collections. Such lectures may also be taken outside the museum walls; a museum speaker's bureau can furnish programs for universities and schools, women's and service clubs, and other organizations. In some instances, also, television or film may increase enormously the range of the lecturer.

Operating a lecture program demands careful planning and attention to details. The selection of pertinent subjects; the preparation of the talks with excellent slides, other visual materials, or actual objects; the arrangement for proper projection and sound-amplification equipment; and routine details such as comfortable seating, proper room temperature, and light for note-taking must all be considered. Some one person should be responsible for the program who combines efficiency, ability to work with people, and a regard for showmanship.

A museum will do well to develop a series of conferences, forums, workshops, and seminars that presents aspects of its program in considerable depth and appeals to specialized and sometimes scholarly audiences. Such activity can build a core of enthusiastic and loyal supporters of the museum, whether they be members, organized Friends of the Museum, or regular attendants of a special event. These supporters may make gifts to the museum and back its programs in other ways. The special event also has strong promotional overtones and gives much opportunity for publicity.

Such a program of specialized interpretation may take many forms. A smaller museum may organize only an occasional event of this kind, perhaps taking advantage of an anniversary or the fact that some current movement gives its collection or field of interest special relevance. Larger museums will do well to offer annual conferences that interpret their various fields of interest.

Planning such events should be done with great care. Sometimes the museum will do well to work with a college or university, a special society, a magazine, or other outside experts in order to obtain broadly based ideas and better promotion. An advisory committee composed of staff and outside members may be used; if so, the outsiders should be appointed for limited, overlapping terms, so that rotation is guaranteed. Each conference should be planned well in advance; a museum staff member should act as the responsible executive; and a planning paper, careful minutes of committee meetings, and a detailed daily schedule for the proposed event should be required.

The program itself must be developed in considerable detail. The speakers are the most important single ingredient. Before they are invited, they should be checked as to command of subject matter, speaking ability, and terminal facilities. In addition to their expenses, should they be paid an honorarium and should their spouses be included in the invitation? Change of pace in the conference schedule is also important, and the planners can skillfully combine the program components—talks, discussions, films, demonstrations, tours behind the scenes or in the region, musical events, banquets, and the like.

In carrying out the event, the registration of those who will attend; the development of the program; the hotel, restaurant, tour, and other logistical arrangements; and the publicity should be co-ordinated. When the conference opens, attention must be given to meeting and welcoming the speakers, providing for their entertainment, and letting them test the microphones and other equipment and run through their slides. The acoustics and projection facilities, as well as each feature on the program, need to be carefully checked. Publicity stories, pictures, and interviews must be provided. After the conference ends, speakers should be written thank-you notes and asked for suggestions for improving the event and for future speakers. Any publication resulting from the event must be edited and seen through the press.

To put it simply, the secrets of success of any conference, forum, workshop, or seminar are (1) imaginative and thorough planning;

(2) efficient execution, with great attention to detail; and (3) much emphasis upon friendly hospitality shown by all members of the museum staff. When these events succeed, the museum acquires a large group of backers who understand its objectives and program in considerable depth. They constitute the kind of preferred support that every museum seeks and needs.[7]

Publications

The interpretation described thus far has taken place in the museum, and there can be no real substitute for the museum visit to show objects in all their vivid three-dimensional reality. But there are ways to take the museum story beyond its walls and to reach even larger audiences than its visitors. The first useful medium here consists of publications.

Publications are a form of communication with the public. Books, periodicals, and pamphlets tell the museum story in a carefully considered, thoughtful manner. They often act as long-term ambassadors for the museum on the shelves of research, public, and private libraries. Even if an owner has read a publication from cover to cover, he may consult it from time to time and pass it along to new readers. Publications also are valuable for the internal organization of a museum in that they stimulate staff members to do research and writing.

The museum should control all printed pieces that it issues and should give careful attention to securing high quality in their design and production. These standards should extend to all job printing done for the museum, including labels, stationery, invitations, monthly calendars, programs, posters, and lists of materials sold at sales desks. All these ephemera should show good taste and uphold a typographic image of high quality for the museum.

The museum will also probably publish a newsletter for its members and, if it is large and affluent enough, an annual report, a quarterly magazine, or a yearbook. The newsletter, usually issued monthly or quarterly, can conceivably be produced by some near-print process, though it should have a well-designed, printed title heading. The annual report, magazine, or yearbook should meet all the design requirements of book printing and should carry as many excellent illustrations as the museum can afford, at least some of which are in color. These publications will offer a good outlet for staff-written articles.

For some museums with an active special-exhibition program, the exhibition catalogue may take the place of the magazine or yearbook. Catalogues, whether of special exhibitions or permanent collections, deserve well-designed printing and abundant illustration, and they, of course, are important avenues for staff research. Each museum should also have an excellent and attractive guidebook, perhaps, in the larger museum, with sections bound and sold separately, covering the different collections.

The larger museum may also have a regular book-publication program. Some books will have general interest and can be sold as souvenir items at the museum sales desk. Many of these can be of pamphlet format—paper-bound, abundantly illustrated, and reasonably priced. The museum should consider establishing other series of books in its general field—art, science, or history—and they may include scholarly studies, specialized popular treatments, and books for younger readers.

In building such a program, the museum will do well to use a planning outline for each publication. It should include details on the author, title, target date, and audience to be reached; a summary outline of the subject-matter content; the estimated number of pages, size, binding, and illustrations; the cost of authorship, illustration, composition, printing, paper, and binding; the retail price, actual cost, and wholesale and retail profit per volume, the size of edition, estimated sales for the first three years and life of the printing; and the distribution plan through museum alone or in co-operation with a national distributor. Such an outline gives top management an opportunity to understand and control a publications program.

In securing manuscripts, the museum can look to its own staff or to outside authors. In order for a staff member to write an article or book. it must be placed high among his job priorities and, often, made his sole assignment. Sometimes recognized outside writers can be put under contract to produce books for the museum. In other instances, an author may be added to the museum staff with the sole duty of writing one or more books. If a museum has a large enough program, it may have its own editorial and design staff, though these functions can usually be performed outside, under contract. In nearly any instance, it is not economical for the museum to do its own printing; it should, instead, hire a printer well qualified for the kind of publication to be produced.

The museum can well handle the local distribution of its publications through its sales desk and other local outlets, but national distribution is a specialized and demanding business. A large museum can possibly build up an effective mail-order business, but it is usually wiser to try to arrange with an established book publisher to distribute museum titles. A balanced distribution system may be feasible with the museum handling in-house and possibly local sales, as well as pamphlets and other low-priced items; a commercial publisher distributing general publications and books for younger readers that have a trade appeal for bookstores; and a university press carrying books of more scholarly interest.

A word may be added about books by outside publishers. In general, a museum can offer for sale at its own sales desk all worthy publications in its field of interest. A large art or science museum should carry good books covering the areas of its collections. An outdoor history museum should stock books on the architecture, gardens, furnishings, and history of its area. All these books help interpret the museum and its field, and this is the primary reason for carrying them. If, in the process, the museum makes a reasonable profit, so much the better.[8]

Film and Television

Another way to reach the public outside the museum walls is through the audiovisual medium. The motion picture or television is most effective in this area because of the manner in which the viewer concentrates his attention upon images so realistic and true to life that he identifies with the situations and feelings being portrayed there. Color slides, filmstrips with or without sound, sets of photographs, phonograph recordings, and soundtapes are other productions in this field—not so powerful in their effect, but less difficult and expensive to make.

Motion pictures and television videotapes have advantages other than their forceful impact. They produce largely uniform effects wherever shown, and they are comparatively easy to transport and to project. Though their production costs are high, individual prints can be shown many times and thus reach huge audiences. From the standpoint of cost per viewer, films may be comparatively economical; if properly distributed, they may cost less per viewer than publications or other audiovisual products.

Museums can produce motion pictures in several ways. If large and well endowed enough, they may set up their own program. In such instances, they should have a small production staff that can make their own documentary-type films over a period of time and with minimum disturbance of the normal museum activities. If museums embark upon more ambitious films employing acting talent and a complex story line, they should use their audiovisual staff as a production unit and import a writer, director, actors, and editor from the outside. Still other approaches to museum film-making involve commercial producers, university film units, and television stations, most frequently educational ones.

All film projects, whether museum or outside-controlled, should use a planning outline somewhat similar to the one described above for publications. It will cover title, outline of content, and audience; schedule for scripting, production, and completion; length, use of narration, and use of dialogue; script budget, production budget including crew, principals, extras, props, costumes, film stock, sound, and internal museum charges; completion cost of editing titles, music, and sound; and distribution plan with estimated sales and rentals.

With such a guide, a museum can decide whether it can afford to make a film with its own production unit, whether it can subsidize an outside producer, or whether it can pay the heavy indirect costs incurred in the disruption of its activities by an outside producer who pays his direct costs. The museum that produces or obtains such films also needs to decide whether to promote and distribute them itself to schools, clubs, and television stations, or to arrange for their sale and rental by a commercial distributor. In either instance, the museum should try to make the users pay for the distribution costs and to amortize at least a part of the production expense.

The rapid growth of television has given museums new opportunities to reach mammoth audiences. In some instances, the museum has worked with a local station to develop regular programs based upon the museum collection. Sometimes the television cameras have come to the museum, but more frequently paintings and objects have been transported to the television studio. At first, museum directors thought that such programs might reduce museum attendance, but they actually have had the opposite effect. Those who view the television program often come to the museum to see the original objects.

There can be no doubt that television gives the museum new opportunities to take its collections and expertise to an ever-widening audience, both adults and students. The museum must be careful to protect its collections from breakage or from deterioration caused by excessive heat or light, but television cameras and lighting improve continually. Museum television programs, whether produced regularly by a local station or occasionally by a network, require much staff time, but the rewards are great and can be worth the expenditure. And once a program is on film, just like the museum motion picture, it can be distributed widely to schools and clubs, as well as being used occasionally for other television broadcasts.

In making films or producing television programs, the museum must be sure to see that it retains control of the script to guarantee the subject-matter accuracy and the good taste of the result, whether it be in the field of art, science, or history. Keeping this control is not an easy matter, for working with film or television is a highly technical and expensive process, and the professional film writers, directors, and technicians are accustomed to making the key decisions, often on the basis of supposed popular appeal. This approach can result in simplistic and unpleasant gimmicks and a consequent loss of truthfulness and sincerity. Thus the museum must exert great caution in participating in this advanced audiovisual field, not only in productions of its own but also in those where out-of-pocket costs are paid by an outside film or television maker. Despite the need for great care, the creative museum that dares to work with film can develop its themes with vividness and reach an audience of millions.[9]

Publicity and Merchandising

Telling the museum story to the mass audience has obvious promotional overtones. The museum public relations department turns out, or persuades outside journalists to turn out, newspaper and magazine articles dealing with the never-ending stream of changing exhibits and special programs. Acting as a speaker's bureau, it sends museum curators, educators, and administrators to women's or service clubs or to appear on radio or television programs. News film clips, videotapes, or a museum film appear on television to take the museum program to the general public.

Then there is the matter of merchandising. The museum may possess beautiful and charming paintings, prints, or objects that appeal to visitors who are looking for souvenirs. Thus postcards, slides, notepaper, Christmas cards, and the like are developed and then attractively framed reproduction prints and authentically reproduced objects and jewelry. Some museums with collections of furnishings even start reproduction programs and license manfacturers to produce authentic copies of furniture, ceramics, silver, pewter, glass, fabrics, wallpaper, and other materials.

The museum sales desk and merchandising program is more than a source of revenue. It is an extension of the museum collection outside its walls, a form of interpretation. And it is a kind of taste-making, with strict canons of authenticity and appropriateness. No miniature Indian canoes with the name of the town on the side, but tasteful objects treasured in the museum and suitable for modern living.[10]

Youth Activities

Young people, remarked a European museum director, "lack the background knowledge possessed by adults but nevertheless prove such excellent spontaneous observers that nine-to-twelve-year-old children may be considered the brightest and most inspiring of all museum guests."[11] And Freeman Tilden has this admonition: "Interpretation addressed to children (say up to the age of twelve) should not be a dilution of the presentation to adults, but should follow a fundamentally different approach. To be at its best will require a separate program."[12] Thus, museums can offer great discovery experiences to young people when their programs are carefully tailored to the interests and attention span of this specialized audience.

A museum should provide special tours for individual youthful visitors of different ages. These tours should put a premium on activity and audience participation and be conducted by guides who understand and appeal to the youthful audience. At Colonial Williamsburg, for example, young people (age seven to twelve) on the Tricorn Hat Tour bowl on the green, try on wigs at the peruke-maker's, get lost in the holly maze, put themselves in the pillory and stocks at the gaol, drink lemonade in a tavern, and eat gingerbread at the bakery.

Usually, however, the best way to reach the young audience is through the schools. The traditional method is the school journey, but advance planning and close co-operation between museum and school are required if this approach is to be effective. School group visits that are warmed-over or diluted versions of the regular adult tour can deteriorate into boredom or become a meaningless lark. Yet the combining of words and objects, of classroom and museum resources, offers opportunities for real learning.

The first thing to do is to adapt museum interpretation to the school curriculum. This means working out different story-lines for different school subjects and for different grade levels. The museum educational staff should take the lead and invite innovative teachers and curriculum advisers to participate in planning workshops. When themes and programs are agreed upon, the museum should send traveling exhibits, classroom kits, publications, and audiovisual materials to the school, and staff members, too, in the case of projects involving several or lengthy museum visits. The museum also should build a guide force with the flexibility and skill to deal with young people.

The classroom teacher should co-operate in developing the museum project so that it enables the students to obtain new insights into the subject (whether art, science, or history) through their experiences with objects. Another product of student learning can be obtained by having the group work on committees to make all the practical arrangements for the journey—finance, transportation, meals, overnight stay (if any), code of conduct, and the like. Post-tour activities are also most important. The class will prepare thank-you letters; summaries that include diaries, photographs, drawings, slides, and soundtapes; and a public presentation to parents and friends. The teachers and museum staff will evaluate the project and make suggestions for its improvement.

School visits to museums can be improved greatly by employing nonverbal methods of communication. Art museums are using improvised dance, movement, music, and sketching to further student understanding of art, as well as less didactic verbal approaches of creative writing and storytelling. Role-playing, as described above, is also of great value for students.

Especially effective with history museums is the inquiry or discovery approach. Here the emphasis is placed on providing the students in their classroom with a wealth of historical primary source materials—duplicated inventories, wills, letters, travel accounts, drawings and other graphic materials, and three-dimensional objects. Experts from the museum or outside are brought into the classroom to contribute detailed information and lore and to demonstrate processes. When the class has studied and absorbed this information, it then visits the museum, where interpreters skillfully elicit information from the students by well-conceived questions.

Always the burden is placed on the students. They are asked to "read" period rooms—to decide, for example, how large a family used them, what its economic status was, what life for young people was like. Or walking down the street of an outdoor museum, the students are asked to comment upon food, shelter, clothing, transportation, education, religion, crafts, and other aspects of life of that time from the hints they find in the historical environment. Thus the primary sources studied in advance are combined with the actual museum visit to stir the students' imagination. Especially valuable will be opportunities to sample farming chores or handicrafts, to play games of the period, to ride in authentic conveyances, and to eat food prepared after old recipes. Combining primary sources—written or graphic documents, objects, and processes—can result in poignant learning experiences that will be long remembered.[13]

Another way in which museums and schools can work together is through the museum club, a voluntary activity that takes place after school, on weekends, or during holidays. A science club may prepare individual projects in the museum for a science fair, and the hard core of interested youngsters may serve as junior curators of the museum. At the school, a history club may do research and writing on local history, collect library and museum materials, take field trips, mark sites, or make a motion picture. Many state historical societies sponsor statewide organizations of such clubs—called, for example, Yorkers, Tar Heels, Badgers, or Gophers—with their own magazine, tours, fairs, yearly convention, and awards. In some instances, the state historical societies have gone on to work with state education departments to devise curriculums and materials for required courses in state history for elementary and secondary schools.[14]

Then, there are the children's museums, a distinctive American contribution. The Brooklyn Children's Museum (1899) was the first one in the world, and there are about five hundred in the United States today. A dispute has raged about what to call them—children's, junior, youth, or family museums. Fort Worth has dropped "Children's" from its name and is now the Fort Worth Museum of Science and History, with 100,000 square feet of exhibits and a planetarium on a 10-acre site with another 400-acre nature center. The neighborhood museum in the inner city is, in a sense, an extension of the children's-museum concept.

The collections of these museums put emphasis upon usable, rather than rare, objects. The permanent collection is often not of great monetary value and changes rapidly. It usually contains small live animals that the children may handle. Programs may include a planetarium, science demonstrations, puppets, see-and-touch shows, music, dance, theater, painting and drawing, and crafts demonstrations. Workshops may be held on anthropology, astronomy, anatomy, dance, music, photography, art, poetry, creative writing, theater, and public speaking. The children's museum is relatively unstructured. While there are occasional lectures and workshops, the main approach is individual; a student sees something that interests him, and the museum instructor responds informally to help the young person develop a project on his own.[15]

Interpretation Problems

In this age of rapid change, marked by revolt against established institutions and by violent clashes of opinion, a museum's interpretation program must seek to be relevant and to appeal not only to the affluent and the elite, but also to the underprivileged and the discontented.

Experimentation with improvisation of performing arts activities, role-playing, and the inquiry method of discovering the past—all these developments offer fresh opportunities for good interpretation. The sensitivity and social commitment of the younger generation also can help the museum in these exciting experimental fields.

A set of serious problems affecting future interpretation programs develops as a museum's attendance curve goes up. Obviously, the warm, personal, somewhat leisurely interpretation that works well for a few hundred persons per day will need to be changed to be effective for ten times that number. Long waiting lines and crowded conditions in galleries that make viewing objects difficult are serious handicaps. Perhaps the museum can remain open longer hours. Perhaps it can open regional centers. Perhaps it can use effective multimedia methods. Crowded conditions inevitably demand a different kind of interpretation, though not necessarily a poorer interpretation.

12

The Museum as Cultural Center and Social Instrument

The Rat: Man's Invited Affliction, exhibit at Anacostia Neighborhood Museum, Washington, D.C.

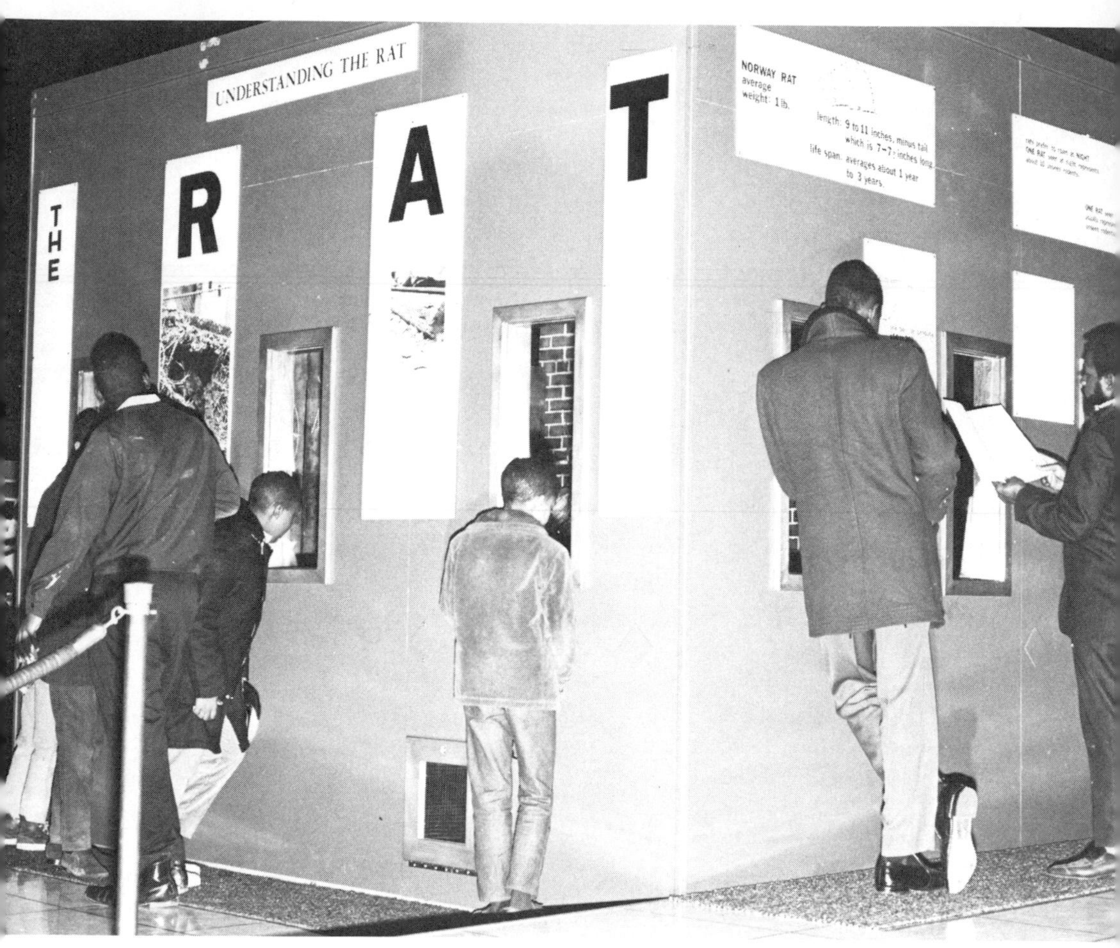

The typical nineteenth-century museum with its emphasis on objects and specimens was sometimes a static and even forbidding place for the general public. It was dead quiet and could be musty; visitors felt constrained to talk in hushed tones there. The rise of varied education and interpretation programs began to change all that. They brought in hordes of visitors, many of them young and lively. A large portion of the museum staff had to give attention to people as well as objects. During the last half of the twentieth century, many museums began to become community cultural centers; in fact, numerous art institutions even dropped the word *museum* and adopted the term *art center.* Some of this emphasis was found in other kinds of museums; children's museums stressed activities instead of rare objects, most technical museums became science centers, and many general museums offered various combinations of visual and performing arts, history, and science. Considerable ferment arose to take museum outreach programs into the slum-ridden inner cities or to form neighborhood museums there for the social betterment of new audiences—the poor, the disadvantaged, and ethnic or minority groups.

Performing Arts

An editorial in the American Association of Museum's *Museum Work* in 1920 looked back over the previous quarter-century and thought that museums in this country had adopted, in order, the following practices: exhibition of objects and specimens, publication of popular bulletins, loans of duplicate materials, docent service, storytelling, music, and loans of rare objects.[1] If the writer could have looked ahead, he would doubtless have been astonished to see museums conducting theater programs; showings of documentary, classic, and avant-garde motion pictures; dance recitals; costume balls and galas; and festivals, fairs, and assorted happenings.

With their spacious galleries and entrance halls, it was natural for museums to offer musical concerts from time to time. By 1919, the Pennsylvania Academy for the Fine Arts was staging such events at the head of its main staircase, and the Metropolitan Museum was attracting to its free Saturday evening concerts as many as 8,000 listeners who sat on the stairs or upon straw mats on the floor and overflowed into the galleries. Toledo, Minneapolis, Cleveland, and Providence had similar programs. Some conservatives grumbled about using "circus or Salvation Army techniques" and asked, "Why not employ properly or improperly clad classic dancers or a trained seal or two?" Still, the American Association of Museums at its annual convention in 1919 endorsed including music among the activities of art and other museums as an appropriate addition to their educational programs.[2]

During the next half-century, many museums acquired their own auditoriums to present music, drama, film, and the dance. At the Toledo Museum of Art, 117,350 children and adults attended such performances in 1965. The Cleveland Museum of Art's endowed music program added a May Festival of Contemporary Music to its May Show for area artists. The Los Angeles County Museum of Art dedicated its new building in 1965 with Handel's *Music for the Royal Fireworks* accompanying actual fireworks and had appropriate Japanese music and American jazz performed for openings of special exhibitions. The Walker Art Center in Minneapolis co-operated with the adjoining Tyrone Guthrie Theatre to reinforce the exhibition of contemporary visual art with children's programs of performing and plastic arts, lecture demonstrations of modern dance, panels on contemporary dramatic art, and concerts of ethnic, jazz, baroque, and contemporary music.[3]

Many smaller art centers sprang up throughout the country, more recently stimulated by state art councils and the National Endowment for the Arts. A few are endowed, for example, the Paine Art Center and Arboretum (1947) in Oshkosh, Wisconsin, with ten shows a year, lectures, films, and concerts. The Kingsport (Tennessee) Fine Arts Center (1968) is situated in a former church; serves an art guild, theater guild, and symphony orchestra; offers classes in arts and crafts; and conducts public jam sessions. The Appalachia (Virginia) Community Art Center (1973) occupies a one-room storefront in a town of about 2,000 and instructs in basketweaving, apple-butter-making, and sand-casting. A far-out project that says it is not a museum is Artpark, which opened in 1974 on a 172-acre site in Lewiston, New York, near Niagara Falls. Summer visitors there can picnic, fish, hike, or work with artists and craftspeople. Performing art programs include theater, ballet, opera, and a film series.[4]

The Harris survey of the National Endowment for the Arts examined the educational and cultural activities of museums for 1971–1972 in some detail. Performing arts presentations prepared by the museum were offered regularly by 6 percent of all museums, occasionally by 12 percent, and not at all by 82 percent. For art museums, however, comparable figures were 16 percent, 25 percent, and 59 percent. These percentages refer to programs prepared by museums and need to be interpreted in the light of a Toledo Museum of Art survey of 1966 that, upon examining 160 art museums, found only 23 percent had their own performing arts programs, though 69 percent cosponsored such activities and 8 percent used outside sponsors.[5]

A 1974 study backed by the University of Wisconsin Center for Arts Administration discovered that 124 museums offered the following types of activities—chamber music (53 museums), film (47), instrumental recital (42), drama (41), vocal recital (34), folk music (29), poetry (26), guest artist series (21), ethnic dance (20), and fewer for jazz, modern dance, orchestra, ballet, opera, rock music, municipal band, electronic music, blues, mime, and puppet shows. One-third of the programs were sponsored by museums founded since 1960. The chief reasons for initiating these activities, according to the museums, were to demonstrate the interrelationship of the arts and to complement exhibit programs, to attract visitors and develop a new and more diversified audience, and to respond to a community need.[6]

Often these activities were more or less independent of the museum collections, exhibits, and programs, but sometimes they were employed as interpretive devices. Thus the National Museum of History and Technology believed that its musical instruments should be heard as well as seen and gave frequent programs and demonstrations. The Metropolitan went even further by renting electronic receivers to visitors so that they could stand in front of a rare harpsichord, one-keyed flute, or other exotic instrument and listen to a recording that had been made on that very device. The Cloisters branch of the Metropolitan helped interpret medieval times by offering appropriate concerts and an occasional drama. Colonial Williamsburg used music to bring the eighteenth century alive with tavern songs, candle-lit concerts, and militia musters and staged authentic plays and occasional short operas.[7]

Similarly, performing arts are more widely used as part of museum tours, especially with school groups. At the National Collection of Fine Arts, students made improvisation tours and workshops, dramatizing situations and ideas. At the neighboring National Portrait Gallery, after studying portraits and paintings, they took roles in the trial of John Brown with partly scripted, partly improvised parts. The Metropolitan has had an arts awareness program for black and Puerto Rican high school students involving nonverbal reaction to paintings as well as taking photographs, playing simple musical instruments, painting, and dancing. At the High Museum of Art in Atlanta, fourth-graders participated in a discovery program in eight visits that involved responding to art works with body movement and dancing; it used music—chamber, country, western, and jazz. These activities did not lose contact with art objects or historical ideas, but added light-hearted movement workshops and improvisational role-playing to the customary lectures and discussions.[8]

The museum also is a natural center for social events. Openings of special exhibits furnish occasions for cocktail parties, lectures, and performances. A museum restaurant can serve the staff, visitors, and indeed the whole community at lunchtime and be open for special members' dinners before openings, plays, or other performances. Historical museums can add to their interpretation by serving food typical of their region and period. Balls or galas may be put on to raise money for museum projects as well as house tours or visits to museums in the region. More ambitious travel in this country or abroad may be organized with the museum furnishing expert guidance and receiving a tax-exempt contribution from each tour member.[9]

Obviously, the performing arts offered the museum an opportunity to enhance its influence as a community cultural center. Otto Wittman, sometime director of the Toledo Museum of Art, summed it up this way:

> In our largest metropolitan centers, there are theaters, concert halls, specialized art and music schools, as well as museums. However, along the Main Streets of most American cities . . . the museum is often the community's only cultural center. They give added dimension and meaning to the lives of many of us. They enrich and broaden our children's education. They are on the front lines of America's cultural growth.[10]

A visiting Polish museum director found it "amazing and fascinating to observe the varied educational programs of American museums, which make them real social and cultural centers in their communities," and another director from the Netherlands remarked upon the rich fare of lecture, concert, ballet, and film the American museum offered its visitors and thought that it reached the whole population of a city, starting with the youngsters.[11]

Broader Cultural Centers

Museums that serve as cultural centers frequently not only put visual and performing arts together but also combine art, history, and science subject matter and sometimes reach a regional audience. Perhaps the best way to make this kind of broadened function clear is to examine some actual cases.

The Munson-Williams-Proctor Institute (1919) in Utica, New York, occupies a complex of buildings that includes a Museum of Art (1960) designed by Philip Johnson, with sculpture court, galleries, and auditorium seating 271; "Fountain Elms" (1850), a Tuscan villa-style house with four Victorian period rooms and the institute's growing collection of American decorative art as well as the exhibition area and offices of the Oneida Historical Society; two carriage houses containing a School of Art with studio classrooms, display space, and offices; another building used for ballet and modern dance classes; and a Meetinghouse with small meeting rooms and kitchen used by community cultural, charitable, and educational groups.

The institute's program includes a dozen or more special art exhibitions per year, art lectures, film series, extensive music program with lecture/recitals provided by a resident musician and great-artist music and dance series, and excursions to other American cultural centers. A ten-day summer Utica Arts Festival offers sidewalk art exhibits by area artists and performances including band, chamber music, symphony, voice, opera, jazz, dance, theater, and circus. This active program is backed by some 6,000 members and attracts a yearly attendance of about 200,000.[12]

The Roberson Center for the Arts and Sciences (1954) at Binghamton, New York, presents an even more varied cultural mix of visual and performing arts, natural sciences and astronomy, history and humanities. This combination of museums, arts council, and education center serves eleven counties in south-central New York and upper Pennsylvania. The building, Richard J. Neutra, architect, joins the Victorian Roberson Mansion as hall of history to a contemporary-style museum and service center with auditorium or theater seating 310 and with a small planetarium. The center also operates the Two Rivers Gallery nearby, where exhibited artwork may be purchased or rented, and the Kopernik Observatory several miles away in Vestal Center. The Roberson constituent organizations include an astronomical society, civic theater, fine arts society, folk dancers, garden center, historical society, performing arts society, photographic center, and world affairs council.

The Roberson Center has had an artist in residence, has conducted workshops and seminars for teachers, dispensed vocational information to students and parents, originated television and radio programs, circulated package exhibits designed for classroom use, and taken live performances to the schools of the region. Neutra said that in all his wide experience around the world he had seen nothing like the center, that it was "simply a unique educational experiment" which showed "that all human concerns are capable of fascinating integration."[13]

An even more ambitious cultural center is the Virginia Museum of Fine Arts (1934) in Richmond. Generously supported by the commonwealth that has paid for its building and numerous expansions and contributes the operating expenses, this museum serves the entire state with a staff of more than a hundred and a budget that exceeds $2 million. Its handsome galleries with useful orientation theaters exhibit a comprehensive collection of art works, and it has good studio space for classes in arts and crafts for both adults and children. A well-equipped modern theater seats five hundred, is served by a fully accredited professional company, and presents both traditional and modern plays. Other performances include lectures, concerts, film, and dance. Fine restaurant facilities are available for members, staff, and the general public.

The Virginia Museum has thirty affiliate and chapter organizations situated throughout the state and more than 12,000 members, about one-half with joint membership in the local affiliate or chapter. A corporate patrons program includes about a hundred industries and businesses that pay dues of at least $500 per year. Active interplay takes place between central museum and affiliates and chapters. Richmond circulates more than a hundred traveling exhibits of art objects, photographs, slide sets, television cassettes, and films, and sends to the localities artists to conduct workshops, lectures, and some performances. Affiliates and chapters organize safaris to attend openings, plays, and other special events in Richmond, often dining in the pleasant members' suite. The museum's four art-mobiles carry high-grade exhibits throughout the state; two are reserved for affiliates and chapters, one for localities organized by the Virginia Federation of Women's Clubs, and one for the colleges and universities of the state.[14]

Other statewide programs have been pioneered by historical agencies that frequently operate a central museum along with regional historic houses, outdoor museums, and historical parks. These state historical agencies often stimulate and assist local historical societies that may become their virtual branches, and they also may encourage the formation of history clubs, usually by secondary school students. They may combine the visual and performing arts in demonstrations, special events, and re-enactments. Some leading historical agencies of this type are the Minnesota Historical Society, with some twenty branch museums; the North Carolina Division of Archives and History, with thirteen; the Ohio Historical Society, with twenty-nine; the Pennsylvania Historical and Museum Commission, with fifty-two; and the State Historical Society of Wisconsin, with seven.[15]

Museums in other parts of the world are joining this movement. The outdoor museums of Scandinavia and elsewhere have always used music, drama, and dance to enliven their collections of folk materials. Louisiana (1958), the modern art museum north of Copenhagen near the Sound separating Denmark from Sweden, is an outstanding cultural center. The architects began there with a century-old mansion set in a park with many rare trees and used a glass corridor to join it to three interconnected buildings of contemporary architecture. The natural beauty of the site, which could be glimpsed from the galleries, formed an excellent background for the art. Louisiana strives to fuse architecture, landscape gardening, painting, sculpture, graphic art, and handicrafts to create what Knud W. Jensen, its founder, calls "the meeting place for the arts." Concerts, recitals, lectures, dramatic performances, and films are part of the program. There is a studio for children and a tasteful cafeteria. Jensen argues that Louisiana should act as a "mother-museum" for its region, "sort of a cultural chain-store with branches in the suburbs, the dormitory towns, or out in the county." The Louisiana Club has 5,000 members, and the museum's yearly attendance exceeds 200,000.[16]

A Social Instrument

When Theodore L. Low wrote his *The Museum as a Social Instrument* in 1942, he advocated that museums make popular education their predominant goal, superior to, but including, acquisitions, preservation, and scholarly study. He opposed having museums confine their attention to the upper strata of society and urged that they vigorously seek to serve "an intellectual middle class."[17] Low, of course, had no way of looking ahead to see how events of the 1960s would change the meaning of "social instrument." He had been thinking in the same general terms that John Cotton Dana had used in conceiving the Newark (New Jersey) Museum as a vehicle for community pride and betterment. But the civil-rights movement, the immigration of dispossessed agricultural workers, chiefly blacks and Latin Americans, to the inner cities, the mushrooming of white suburbs, and the rise of radical student and counterculture movements against the Vietnam War and the establishment had marked effects upon all cultural institutions, including museums.

The transformation of many museums into cultural centers was not designed usually to include the poorer and underprivileged classes. A 1974 survey of twenty-six affiliates and chapters of the Virginia Museum of Fine Arts, for example, found that not a single organization saw a part of its goals to include securing social change. The Harris survey discovered that museum directors shared this viewpoint. They were asked to evaluate the two museum purposes most important to themselves, the public, and trustees, and most successfully carried out by their museums. The encouraging of positive social change ranked at the bottom of six suggested purposes, in the directors' opinions of most importance to only 6 percent of the directors, 2 percent of the public, and 3 percent of the trustees, and successfully accomplished by 3 percent of the museums.[18]

The fight to make museums institutions of popular education, as Low conceived them, has been largely won. The movement toward museum outreach and neighborhood museums among the disadvantaged and alienated of the inner city is less accepted, though it receives support from federal programs dealing with urban problems and from private foundations. Perhaps as museums take on an ever-stronger public character and receive more public funds, they are more likely to become social instruments in today's meaning of the term.

Museum Outreach

Some museums can secure new audiences with programs that attract ethnic or minority groups to the museum. The Grand Rapids (Michigan) Public Museum organized community festivals and an annual Christmas observance beginning in 1967 that involved Polish, Mexican, Dutch, Afro-American, French, British, German, Latvian, and other groups. The Mexican festival, for example, began with a temporary exhibit of Mexican history, arts, and crafts that resulted in a smaller permanent installation. The exhibit opened with a parade from St. Andrew's Cathedral to the museum followed by guitar music, dancing, singing, and traditional refreshments. Enthusiasm ran so high that the Mexican community organized a committee to stage an annual fiesta that attracts Latin Americans from throughout western Michigan. The different ethnic groups not only took fresh pride in their distinctive cultural history, customs, and creativity but displayed a co-operative spirit toward the whole community and continued to participate in the museum's programs.[19]

The Oakland (California) Museum has presented an Asian Festival featuring Chinese, Japanese, and Philippine visual and performing arts, crafts, and foods, a Mexican Independence Fiesta, Soul Vibrations for Afro-American culture, and Pow-Wow Weekend for the American Indian. The museum leaves the planning of these educational ethnic happenings to the communities involved but furnishes staging, equipment, and support staff when requested. An African festival organized by the Newark Museum included "Art in Africa," 112 items chiefly from the museum's collection; photographs of the people, terrain, and animals of Africa; and prints, paintings, and collages of local artists who called themselves "Black Motion." Then there were African films; costumes for men, women, and children designed by Black Motion after African dress and textiles; an African drummer and his dance company; and a lecture demonstration of African music. The black community responded enthusiastically; museum attendance that had dropped following 1967 riots in Newark went up again.[20]

New York City museums had somewhat spotty success in wooing the new audience. The Museum of the City of New York, once a traditional historical museum, began in 1971 to stage community-oriented programs that attacked social problems with a special exhibit, *Drug Scene in New York*. The facts of drug addiction were presented clearly, and former addicts warned viewers of its perils; the show created a sensation. Three years later came an exhibit on venereal disease. A seventy-second clock rang loudly to remind visitors that someone contracts syphillis or gonorrhea that frequently, and free blood tests were offered. A third special show dealt with alcoholism. Labels in the exhibits were in Spanish as well as English. The American Museum of Natural History added staff members to develop programs appealing to blacks, Puerto Ricans, and American Indians with exhibits, lectures, dance recitals, and music festivals at the museum. The program also co-operated with the city schools and sent instructors with demonstration materials to community centers, block events, drug rehabilitation units, and prisons. Art museums joined the movement, but the Metropolitan exhibit, *Harlem on My Mind*, met strong resistance because blacks were not consulted in assembling it, and its catalogue had to be withdrawn on account of an antisemitic remark. The museum sent out a mobile unit, *Eye Opener*, and provided modular exhibits to community centers. It lent art objects, staff know-how, and cases and equipment to several community museums including El Museo del Barrio (on Puerto Rican history and culture), the

Bronx Museum of the Arts in Bronx County Courthouse, and Tom Lloyd's Storefront Museum in South Jamaica.[21]

The Philadelphia Museum of Art has had unusually successful outreach experience that began in 1970. It has observed well the basic principles of community-oriented programs: to respect the wishes and ideas of the groups, to help them whenever feasible, provided assistance is asked, and to keep the museum in the background. Working with black, Puerto Rican, Italian, Chinese, Jewish, and other ethnic groups in the inner city, the museum's department of urban outreach furnished the neighborhoods with videotape equipment and staff so that they could produce news-style documentary films examining the quality of life and environmental problems of their communities. Chalk-ins were held for children at playgrounds, and murals were painted on prominent neighborhood walls. The museum worked through cultural centers in the inner city and with community groups such as the teenage Potentials and the Young Great Society.[22]

Neighborhood Museums

Another approach to the inner-city audience was for museums to establish branches. One of the earliest and most successful of these was the Anacostia Neighborhood Museum created as a bureau of the Smithsonian Institution in 1967 to serve a predominantly black slum area of Washington, D.C. The Smithsonian with great wisdom provided financing (supplemented by federal and foundation funds) and expert consultation (when asked) for the new institution situated in an old movie theater. The planning and administration were left to the community, which operated through an advisory committee of forty-six local residents but with its meetings open to everyone. It also used a youth-advisory committee of about twenty high school students. John R. Kinard, social worker and resident of the inner city, became director of the museum and furnished inspiring leadership.

The museum assembled exhibits dealing with the African heritage of the blacks, the local history of Anacostia, and current urban and black problems. Perhaps its most spectacular exhibit that traveled to other cities and was the subject of a network television show treated *The Rat: Man's Invited Affliction.* Centerpiece of the display were rats, acclimatized so as to be awake during daytime hours, prowling about a large case strewn with discarded junk and garbage, and coming up to portholes where they could be viewed eye to eye. The exhibit made clear the life cycle of the rat; its evil role as destroyer of food, disease carrier, and attacker of small children; and how it could be controlled by community action for cleanliness, proper food storage, and building construction.

Anacostia is, however, much more than exhibits. It is a cultural arts center with workshops in arts and crafts, a useful small library, its own bus that transports children and exhibits, and much music, dance, drama, and films. It also provides a meeting place for community groups, an urban planning center that distributes educational materials throughout the community, and a skill-training facility that teaches the design and fabrication of museum exhibits. In short, "the museum's role is to enliven the community and enlighten the people it serves."[23]

When the Brooklyn Children's Museum's two Victorian mansions were condemned in 1967, it decided, while awaiting construction of its new building, to open a neighborhood museum in a two-story converted automobile warehouse in the Stuyvesant-Crown Heights section of Brooklyn. Appealingly named MUSE, the project was to test the feasibility of setting up small neighborhood museums in the metropolitan area. Lloyd Hezekiah, director, considers a museum a theater, rather than a cathedral or temple, and thus MUSE offered a rich variety of programs—planetarium shows, live animals, see-and-touch exhibits, science and craft demonstrations, puppet shows, music, dance, theater presentations, and take-home collections. Workshops for children and adults treated anthropology, astronomy, anatomy, dance, photography, art, poetry, consumer education, sex education, drug abuse, aviation, creative writing, theater, public speaking, music, and other subjects. In addition there were school group visits, traveling cases for classroom use, innovative exhibits including space science and liquid-light mixing, and street festivals. The museum stationed its staff members near all this activity so as to help children and adults make the most of it.

Though MUSE was an obvious success, its audience came from all parts of the metropolitan area, and the Children's Museum decided to go ahead with its plans for a strikingly original building, which opened in 1977 at its former location. MUSE was left to the community to develop as it saw best, beginning with the community leadership, planning boards, and advisory council that had co-operated with the Children's Museum.[24]

There are probably at least one hundred ethnic minority neighborhood museums or art centers in existence throughout the country, serving blacks, Puerto Ricans, Chicanos, Orientals, American Indians, and others. Many of them are in the inner cities and have converted a brownstone house, movie theater, garage, warehouse, or store-front to their uses. Some of them collect objects and install exhibits, for example, El Museo del Barrio in New York or the International Afro-American Museum in Detroit. Some of them are mainly workshops that give inner-city residents access to art, such as the Selma Burke Art Center of Pittsburgh or Neighborhood Arts in Akron. Still others offer free-form art activity; Studio Watts in Los Angeles or the Adept New American Folk Gallery in Houston are examples here, or City Arts of New York or the Chicago Mural Group that specialize in mural paintings for inner-city buildings.

All these organizations are fiercely independent; they will accept financing, materials, and technical help from large, well-established museums, but they insist on developing their own programs and doing their own thing. They often are headed by charismatic leaders; Kinard and Hezekiah have been mentioned, and others include Topper Carew of the New Thing Art and Architecture Center in Washington, the Reverend John Farmer of the Afro-American Development Center in Jacksonville, and James M. Woods of Studio Watts. The neighborhood centers are financed chiefly by grants from urban-improvement programs, the National Endowments, and private foundations; in times when federal and state support is being reduced, they are sometimes in peril of closing down.

The movement recently has become especially active among Native Americans, both on and off the reservation. No one knows how many Indian-run museums and centers exist, and they vary from small family operations to huge, multimillion-dollar complexes. The Pueblo Cultural Center in Albuquerque (1976), for example, occupies an 11.6-acre downtown site and received an Economic Development Administration grant of $1.6 million; it includes a museum, an educational program, a theater, a shop selling work of individual artists, a restaurant, and office space for lease. From these activities it hopes to generate income for operating expenses. In Seattle the Indians of the Tribes Foundation obtained a 99-year lease on 17 acres at nearby Fort Lawton to develop an educational and cultural Discovery Park with an art center called Daybreak Star (1976). It is to include a theater, restaurant, library, museum, a Long House for community dinners and ceremonial events, and a Large Circle outdoors for traditional athletic contests, craft demonstrations, and tepee encampments. These museums and centers deal with a basic problem—to try to help Native Americans retain their cultural identity and religious beliefs in the midst of an incompatible industrial civilization. The American Indian Movement (AIM) is as militant a defendant of

Native American rights as other organizations for blacks, Puerto Ricans, or Chicanos.[25]

Conflict and Problems

The rise of militant minorities sometimes brought turbulence to museums, especially those devoted to art and situated in a metropolis. A Seminar for Neighborhood Museums held at MUSE in Brooklyn in 1969 was virtually taken over by blacks and Puerto Ricans who "presented to a sympathetic but startled audience a strong case for their anger and frustration and a challenge to the white museum establishment." Topper Carew insisted that black people knew how to live, how to improve the quality of life, and were nonmaterialistic. "Community museums," he said, "have always existed in the black community, on street corners, in backyards, on stoops. It's just that it's a living museum." John Hendricks of the Guerilla Art Action Group thought "The problem is not to impose the white cultures on the poor but rather to find a way to allow these cultures of the poor to flourish to their direct benefit without the interference of an uptight white elite." The seminar voiced a favorite minority demand that museums decentralize their holdings and distribute them among the inner cities with artists and the people of the community controlling the decentralized collections.[26]

The revolutionary Art Workers' Coalition made up of dissident artists and art theorists in 1969 demanded that the Museum of Modern Art sell art from its collection worth $1 million and give the proceeds to the poor of "all races in this country." The museum was to close its doors until the Vietnam War was over. The coalition issued manifestoes, picketed the museum, and spilled cans of blood in its galleries. Black groups also picketed the Metropolitan's *Harlem on My Mind* show, and someone damaged ten paintings in the permanent galleries by scratching "H" (for Hoving, the director) on them; another extremist group tossed cockroaches on the buffet table at a Metropolitan party.[27]

A somewhat amusing incident in these confrontations occurred in 1970 when members of the Coalition and Art Strike Against War, Racism, Sexism and Repression grabbed the microphone at the annual convention of the American Association of Museums in New York and disrupted the meeting. They announced that war, racism, sexism and repression was to be the theme of the convention. Their chief speaker, Ralph Ortiz, director of El Museo del Barrio, accused museums of complicity in the atrocities of our day and failure to take a stand on the vital issues of our times. The Art Strike demanded that all urban museums earmark 15 percent of their funds the first year, 20 percent the second, and 40 percent ultimately for decentralizing their facilities and services for the benefit of inner-city museums, community art programs, and training internships for blacks, Mexicans, American Indians, Puerto Ricans, and other oppressed people. The AAM was called upon to demand the immediate release of Black Panthers and all political prisoners in this country. Some of the startled museum professionals entered into informal dialogue with the dissidents, but many thought they were addressing only the New York City art museums, and the AAM later cancelled a conference to be held at the Metropolitan to discuss how museums should deal with current social issues.[28]

The radical extremists made conservative art museum directors even more apprehensive about making museums into cultural centers or engaging in outreach social programs. The directors insisted that a museum's first duty was to preserve its collections and hand them down to posterity. Research and exhibition/interpretation were important also, but ought not to imperil the basic preservation functions. Daniel Catton Rich, former director of the Art Institute of Chicago and of the Worcester Art Museum, thought that ever larger buildings and many new services including outreach and socially oriented programs would eventually lead a museum to bankruptcy or government take-over with bureaucratic waste and lack of imagination and energy. The remedy would be for the art museum to drop many such programs and, instead of splitting up collections and scattering them around the city, to shed some of its expanded holdings. Primitive art, for example, could go to museums of natural history; decorative art could be cut back, with Americana released to historical museums; and art schools and theaters were better attached to a university. These transfers would make the museums more manageable and more enjoyable for the public. Rich concluded that the art museum

> should return to first principles . . . which remain collecting, preserving, exhibiting, and above-all educating. Collecting in the future is bound to slow down, preservation with modern methods to increase, exhibiting to become more selective, and education, the last of these to be taken seriously, greatly to expand. Its emphasis will be less on audiovisual apparatus than fresh and innovative thinking on how the art experience can become aesthetically and psychologically satisfying. To adapt a McLuhanism, "the museum *is* the message."[29]

Wise museums should steer a course somewhere between these extremes. The lively cultural center has many advantages, especially for the smaller city, and museum attempts to reach new audiences among underprivileged and ethnic minorities are praiseworthy. Still, there are limits to what collections of objects and museum techniques can accomplish for social uplift, and museums must be sure to preserve their precious holdings for future as well as contemporary use.

13

The Museum Profession

Paul J. Sachs and his Museum Studies students, Harvard University, 1943–1944

A museum employee in the United States who applies for a passport to travel abroad is in a quandary when filling out the blank on "Occupation." To list *Director, Curator, Registrar,* or *Business Manager* obviously is not specific enough. To choose *Art Historian, Historian,* or *Scientist* may be a bit pretentious. So one falls back on *Museum Director, Museum Scientist,* or *Museum Editor,* and all appears fitting and well. Perhaps this very process suggests that a museum profession exists. Of course, Albert E. Parr is right when he argues that museums encompass "A Plurality of Professions."[1] They hire administrators, art historians, historians, scientists, educators, exhibit designers, editors, registrars, librarians, public relations directors, and many other specialists. But so do universities, industries, and businesses. In our complex culture, numerous workers follow two (or even more) callings; thus a person trained in history may be at once a member of the historical, museum, university teaching, and historic preservation professions and an archivist, librarian, or other related specialist. Museum professionals do not keep their roles as separate as did Chekhov when he wrote: "Medicine is my lawful wife, literature my mistress. When I am tired of the one, I spend a night with the other."

What Is a Profession?

The fact that museum studies courses are springing up in great numbers and that frequent references are made to "the museum profession" does not mean, as Dr. Parr seems to think, that someone is "attempting to homogenize our careers and force us all into the mold of a single profession."[2] Directors, curators, educators, designers, and other museum professionals will always have varied specialities, just as do doctors or lawyers. The paramount essence of the museum profession is a common cause and goals. Objects are still important, whether artistic, historical, or scientific, and well-tested standards have been developed for their collection, conservation, and interpretation.

A professional must, of course, possess specialized knowledge usually acquired after intensive academic or equivalent training. He should receive financial remuneration, and fortunately most museum professionals now do so. The day is about over when a wealthy amateur might serve without pay as curator of an important museum department. Not that museums do not welcome volunteers and encourage them to take a professional attitude toward their work; however, they usually are part-time and under professional supervision.

American museums have greatly increased their professionalism in the last half-century by improving their published literature, adopting an accreditation program, laying down guidelines for museum studies courses, and agreeing upon an internal code of ethics. In all these and many other endeavors they have acted chiefly through their leading professional organization, the American Association of Museums (AAM), also assisted at times by the International Council of Museums (Icom) with headquarters in Paris.[3]

Museums USA

In order to understand the museum profession in this country, one should take an over-all look at the museums themselves. Fortunately, the National Endowment for the Arts hired an affiliate of the Louis Harris Poll organization to make the most thorough survey of these museums yet attempted, using 1971–1972 fiscal year figures. Six criteria were employed in selecting museums for the survey. They had to have permanent facilities available to the public on a regular schedule, be open for three months or more for at least twenty-five hours per week, have an operating budget of $1,000 or more for each month open, own a part of the collection they exhibited, have at least one paid employee with academic training or special knowledge relating to the major subjects represented in the collection, and be nonprofit and tax exempt. Only 1,821 museums met these rather modest requirements, even though the *Official Museum Directory, 1977*, sponsored by the AAM, listed about 5,000 institutions in the United States. The difference in totals meant that more than 3,000 museums could not attain the criteria of the survey; most of them stayed open only a few days a week with volunteer help.[4]

Of the 1,821 museums, more than one-third (37 percent) were exclusively or predominantly devoted to history, 19 percent to art, 16 percent to science, and the remainder to combinations of the three disciplines. Laurence Vail Coleman, in a similar survey in 1938, listed 2,489 museums, of which about half were for history, 30 percent for science, 16 percent for art, and the rest general. Thus, in the last forty years, art museums have overtaken those dedicated to science.[5] The total museum work force in 1971–1972 was about 113,300. Of this number, 30,400 were full-time paid personnel with 11,000 professionals and 19,400 nonprofessionals. Part-time paid personnel numbered 18,700. Volunteers totaled 64,200, that is, more than full- and part-time paid staffs combined.[6]

These figures are enough to establish the general nature of the American museum profession. It is a small calling only emerging as a profession, though it is unlikely that the part-time and volunteer segments of its work force will ever disappear. Volunteerism is a strongly established American institution, and the creative, self-fulfilling nature of museum work will continue to attract volunteer men and women with strong cultural and community interests. Indeed, many museums could not exist without their talented and devoted volunteers.

Museum Publications

One test of a profession, according to Wilbur H. Glover, is that it possess a learned literature, and he asserts that the museum profession meets this standard.[7] It is true, however, that most museum publication is done in periodicals, though recently more books are appearing.

The AAM has been an important source of publication. From 1918 to 1926, it issued the bimonthly *Museum Work,* with articles and the proceedings of its annual meetings. In 1923 it started *Museum News,* a semimonthly bulletin of four to twelve pages that included short articles, sometimes papers read at the annual meeting. In 1959 *Museum News* became a much larger, well-illustrated magazine (monthly, September to June) of longer articles and special departments. A monthly *Bulletin* with "Washington Report," placement listings, and classified ads began in 1968, greatly enlarged and renamed *Aviso* in 1975, when *Museum News* began to appear only six times yearly.

Reading *Museum News* and *Aviso* regularly will keep museum professionals au courant with their field, but there are other useful periodicals. *Curator,* the quarterly published by the American Museum of Natural History since 1958, covers the whole museum field in considerable depth and prides itself on using plentiful and excellent illustrations. *History News,* the monthly of the American Association for State and Local History since 1940, is especially valuable for its eight-to-twelve-page practical *Technical Leaflets,* often dealing with museum practices and problems and bound separately into the magazine. *Historic Preservation,* the quarterly established in 1949 by the National Trust for Historic Preservation, has frequent articles on museums. Specialized but important is the *Journal* (begun in 1960 as the *Bulletin*) of the American Institute of Conservation. Several of the six regional conferences of the AAM have publications, including the *Museologist* (1935) of the Northeast Conference, *Midwest Museums Quarterly* (1940), and *Western Museum Quarterly* (1962).

An international quarterly of great importance is *Museum* (1948), published by UNESCO in Paris with the assistance of Icom. This well-edited and beautifully illustrated magazine covers the activities of the museum movement throughout the world. *ICOM News* (1948), a quarterly bulletin, contains shorter articles. The International Council of Monuments and Sites (Icomos) issues annually *Monumentum* (1967), devoted to historic preservation, while the International Institute for Conservation of Historic and Artistic Works (IIC) publishes *Studies in Conservation* (1954) quarterly and *Art and Archaeology Technical Abstracts* (1967) twice yearly. The Museums Association of Great Britain has a quarterly (formerly monthly), *Museums Journal* (1901), of exceptional value, with stimulating articles and discerning reviews of exhibitions and books. The Canadian Museums Association's *C.M.A. Gazette* (1966) appears quarterly and reflects the renaissance in museum construction and operation that has taken place in Canada since its 1967 centennial.

Most of the publishers of museum periodicals also issue books. Coleman, as director of the AAM, wrote a series of museum manuals between 1927 and 1950 on small museums, museums and outdoor recreation, historic houses, the museum in America, college and university museums, company museums, and museum buildings.[8] Since his day, the association has published the standard book on museum registration methods and established an official museums directory now issued every two years. It examined museums and the environment and the new inner city minority audiences of museums, prepared the Belmont Report for President Johnson on museum needs, and issued studies on museum accreditation, salaries, training courses, museum studies curriculums, and an accounting handbook.[9]

The American Association for State and Local History during the past few years has instituted a promising museum publication program. To sound practical books on the management of small museums, safeguarding collections in travel, the care of paintings, and the administration of manuscripts, the association has added a multivolume bibliography on historical organization practices; manuals on the care of manuscripts, historical photographs, and historical collections; and titles on introduction to museum work, interpretation of historic sites, cataloguing in the computer age, and exhibits for the small museum. Its *Technical Leaflets* now number more than one hundred, and it offers twenty-two tape cassettes of authoritative talks on museum problems and twenty-five slide/tape training kits on various museum techniques.[10]

Important in the international museum field are the UNESCO publications. One of these is virtually a textbook on the organization of museums. Others deal with the conservation and restoration of archival materials; conservation of cultural property with special reference to tropical conditions; a field manual for museum expeditions for archaeology, ethnology, botany, geology, and zoology; museum techniques in fundamental education; museums, imagination, and education; preserving and restoring monuments and historic buildings; and temporary and traveling exhibits.[11] Icom has published a book on museum security and papers presented at its triennial conferences, recent ones dealing with the training of museum personnel, research, and education.[12]

Bibliographies of museum literature include the pioneering Milwaukee Public Museum's *A Bibliography of Museums and Museum Work, 1900–1961* and the New York State Historical Association's *Guide to Historic Preservation, Historical Agencies, and Museum Practices* (1970), in process of being brought up to date in the bibliographical series of the American Association for State and Local History. Icom since 1967 is issuing an *International Museological Bibliography* as a supplement of *ICOM News*.[13]

Accreditation

A most important step in strengthening the museum profession was the decision of the American Association of Museums to accredit museums that met accepted standards. A panel of leading museum officials worked with the Federal Council on the Arts and Humanities to produce *America's Museums: The Belmont Report* in 1968 for President Lyndon Johnson. It called for limited federal support for museums and urged "that the American Association of Museums and its member institutions develop and agree upon acceptable criteria and methods of accrediting museums."[14] Representative John Brademas of Indiana, in an address to the association's annual meeting in 1969, said: "The museum community should develop standards of accreditation against which the excellence of individual museums can be measured. Federal support should not be provided to museums which do not reach a level of quality accepted in the museum field."[15]

Meanwhile, the AAM in 1968 appointed a committee to study accreditation, and its plan was adopted in 1970. Under it an individual museum undertook a rigorous self-examination of its administration, curatorship, exhibitions, interpretive program, and future plans. It answered a long and searching questionnaire devised by an accreditation commission composed of seven experienced museum leaders appointed by the association. If the answers to the questionnaire were satisfactory, the commission would send an on-site evaluation committee of two or more museum professionals to verify the facts by talking with museum board and staff members and examining plant and procedures. After reviewing the questionnaire and visiting committee report, the commission would then grant accreditation, table it for a maximum of one year, while specific weaknesses were corrected, or refuse it entirely.

For the purposes of accreditation, a museum was defined as "an organized and permanent non-profit institution, essentially educational or aesthetic in purpose, with professional staff, which owns and utilizes tangible objects, cares for them, and exhibits them to the public on some regular schedule."[16] Accreditation meant that a museum met this definition and the accepted standards of the profession, without presuming to distinguish among various grades of achievement or excellence beyond the established minimums.

Some 400 museums have been accredited in the six years beginning in 1971, while 33 have been rejected, 29 tabled or awaiting action, and 77 in process.[17] When these figures are compared with the total of 1,821 museums listed by the National Endowment for the Arts survey or the 1,192 institution members of the American Association of Museums in 1977, it is clear that while considerable progress is being made, some well-established instititions have not deigned to apply for accreditation or have withdrawn their applications. The restrictive definition of a museum as one "which owns and utilizes tangible objects" until recently excluded and angered planetariums, science and technology centers, and art centers. Since 1975 they have begun to be accredited, however, so long as they meet the other parts of the definition and attain "acceptable standards both in the utilization of material and resources and for the care of objects borrowed for exhibition and interpretation."[18]

The accreditation commission steadily has refined and improved its materials and procedures, giving special attention to training visiting committee members so as to secure more uniform results. It is about to begin reaccrediting every five years with a simpler process than that used in the original accreditation. The greatest problem facing the program remains the participation of the museums themselves. If a much larger number are accredited, the foundation and governmental funding agencies may come to require that only accredited or accreditable museums may receive grants. In any event, the accreditation process has done much to establish generally accepted standards for museums, to increase public respect for them, and to create a sense of pride in the museum profession.[19]

Museum Studies

Previous generations of American museum workers received their training in traditional academic subjects, usually at the graduate level, in art or art history for art museums, history for history museums, and science for science museums. The nuts-and-bolts side of museum operation they learned on their first job. Since American museums were numerous and intensely individualistic, with the majority privately controlled, many staff members had unorthodox backgrounds, sometimes with no degrees at all. An agreeable pastime at meetings of museum professional organizations was discussing how those present had entered the profession.

This system was uncertain, haphazard, and wasteful for both individuals and institutions. Yet American museums were not willing to devise in-service training courses similar to those inaugurated in Great Britain in 1932 by the Museums Association. A museum worker there, after employment for at least six months, could attend short courses for two or three years, receive guidance from a senior museum staff member, write a thesis, and pass a rigorous written examination. He would then receive a diploma from the Museums Association.[20]

An exception to the loosely organized American system was the graduate course in museum work and problems taught for a quarter-century beginning in 1923 at Harvard and the Fogg Art Museum by Paul J. Sachs. A collector and connoisseur himself, Sachs insisted that his students be solidly grounded in art history and thoroughly familiar with art objects. He brought in museum directors and curators to speak to his classes; took them to visit museums, private galleries, and auction halls; and introduced them to leading collectors and dealers. Students participated in organizing exhibits at the Fogg and served as interns there and elsewhere under close professional supervision. Little wonder that they came to hold high positions as directors and curators at the National Gallery of Art, Metropolitan Museum of Art, Museum of Modern Art, Boston's Museum of Fine Arts, and many other prestigious places.[21]

Since that day, about two dozen graduate museum studies programs have been organized, still following many principles established by Professor Sachs, but preparing students for careers in all kinds of museums. In addition, undergraduate courses, internships conducted by museums themselves, and in-service training seminars—some of the best organized by the American Association for State and Local History, American Association of Museums, National Trust for Historic Preservation, and Smithsonian Institution—have proliferated. Grants from the National Endowments for the Arts and Humanities and the National Museum Act have supported internships at the museums as well as fellowships for joint university-museum training programs.[22]

Some college and university courses have been hastily conceived to seek alternate careers for students having difficulty finding work as professors or secondary school teachers. The AAM appointed a committee to study the situation and devise suggested guidelines. It reported in 1973 and recommended that good graduate programs should

1. be taught in concert by an accredited college or university and one or more accredited museums;
2. include subject-matter courses in relevant academic disciplines (to be waived if the student already had an advanced degree in the subject);
3. use museum objects to impart understanding of the subject-matter fields;
4. touch all aspects of theoretical museum work—history, purposes, management, collection, conservation, research, exhibition, interpretation, and professional ethics; and
5. provide internship experience in one or more accredited museums under professional supervision for a period of at least two months and up to one year.[23]

In 1977 another AAM committee on museum studies was formed to review the situation, since about three hundred courses of some kind were being offered at graduate, undergraduate, internship, and in-service levels. The AAM seems wisely to have recognized the importance of frequent review of such courses and periodic reports by competent committees.

How long graduate museum studies programs should last is still debatable. Those that include subject-matter courses should run at least one full year, or, better, two, before the master's degree. Those training specialists may require longer; for example, conservators need two years in residence and then one year of actual work with an experienced conservator. Curators planning to enter a special department in a large museum should complete a Ph.D. or its equivalent for the sake of their full scholarly development, even though a master's degree may enable them to secure a museum position. Well-conceived undergraduate courses also have their place, usually for exploration of the field and preparation for graduate work but occasionally, where strong museum support is available, fitting students for general work in small museums or for technical positions requiring craft skills such as those used in exhibition or by preparators.

What should one say about the value of museum studies and their future? There can be little doubt of their usefulness for students who wish museum careers. Quality courses combine essential subject-matter knowledge, museum theory and bibliography, and actual practice of accepted techniques. Graduates understand the common history, philosophy, and purposes of museums, what their chosen personal role involves, and how specialists with varied interests constitute a team that can produce an excellent, effective organization. This strong sense of common purpose and staff interdependence may be the most valuable contribution of a sound program in developing a true profession.

Museums themselves gain much from the programs because their young staff members come to them with an understanding of both the ideal and the real museum worlds, ready to devote themselves to the opportunities of their positions without taking time and energy to find out what museums are all about.

Code of Ethics

Most professions pride themselves on possessing a system of principles and rules, self-enforced and peculiar to their calling. What is usually referred to as a code of ethics takes its place somewhere between the dictates of ordinary morality and the actual laws of the land. One can also argue that a great portion of an ethical code is unwritten in that it must be applied to situations that arise spontaneously and are not covered clearly by statements previously set down.

The AAM adopted a Code of Ethics unanimously at its twentieth annual meeting in 1925, but for many years it was largely forgotten. It set forth principles to be followed in relations of museums to the public, between museums, of the director to the trustees, of the director to the staff and vice versa, and between members of the staff. Some of its injunctions—for example, that museum workers not accept commissions or gifts from businesses, that museums refuse to acquire objects obtained through vandalism, and that trustees be discreet in discussing administrative and executive matters with staff members—are still relevant today.[24]

About fifty years later, the association again appointed a committee to examine ethical questions relating to museums and museum personnel. The committee report was adopted, again unanimously, at the 1978 annual meeting of the association. The present Code of Ethics first considered the collection—the need for its physical care and conservation, the avoidance of acquiring objects illegally excavated or stolen and smuggled from their country of origin, and the proper disposal of objects in museum collections. Appraisals, commercial use, availability of collections, truth in presentation, and the use of human remains and sacred objects were also examined. Each museum was urged to develop and make public a statement of policy in these fields.[25]

Conflicts of interest have been lately much in the public consciousness in many fields, and the museum code needed to consider them. Trustees must not be financially negligent, of course, and they ought not to indulge in self-dealing, take insider advantage, or collect in such a way as to compete unfairly with their museum. Curators may be allowed to collect personally because this practice sharpens their professional judgment and thus their worth to the museum, but all dealing is out, the museum should be given the option to purchase objects they collect at the price paid, and full disclosure should be made of all transactions. Similar rules apply to directors, other professional staff, and volunteers; matters such as outside employment, consulting activities, teaching, lecturing, and writing should be subject to disclosure and prior approval from a supervisor.[26]

These are only a few examples of the principles the new code of ethics examines. There are also sections of great importance on museum management and governance. Such a code is highly desirable, both for its educational effect on trustees, director, and staff and for its reassurance to the public. It is far better for the profession to consider, agree upon, and enforce ethical principles and rules rather than letting a state attorney general, acting in his capacity as supervisor of charitable trusts, seek legislative regulation. The increasingly public nature and accountability of museums have made the code both desirable and necessary.

American Association of Museums

The emerging museum profession has two main objectives—internally to build a sense of unity in the institutions and individuals that comprise it, and externally to secure recognition and aid from the general public, philanthropic foundations, businesses, and federal, state, and municipal governments. The AAM, organized with both institutional and individual members, has problems in attaining professionalism. Museums are highly independent and individualistic, with diverse subject-matter fields and of varied size and financial strength. Museum workers of differing backgrounds are generalists in small museums but highly specialized experts in the larger ones—curators, educators, designers, administrators, and many others. To weld these divergent, sometimes clashing, institutions and their creative, often opinionated, individuals into a profession is not easy.

Other professional organizations touch upon the museum field and sometimes enlist loyal followers who find them more helpful than the AAM. The American Association for State and Local History has been soundly financed and skillfully administered, and its activities such as annual meetings, publications, seminars, and panels of consultants have served history museums, especially the small ones, exceedingly well. Then there are the College Art Association, the National Trust for Historic Preservation, the Association of Art Museum Directors, the Directors of Systematic Collections, the Association of Science Museum Directors, and the Association of Science-Technology Centers. The six regional conferences of the AAM—New England (1919), Midwest (1928), Western (1942), Northeast (1947), Southeast (1951), and Mountain Plains (1954)—draw more attendance from the small museums than the association's annual meeting.

From the first, the AAM held an annual meeting, established working committees, and issued publications. In 1923 it received a three-year challenge grant from the Laura Spellman Rockefeller Memorial of $10,000 annually and established a paid staff at rent-free headquarters at the Smithsonian Institution. For the next thirty-five years, the association, with the scholarly Laurence Vail Coleman as executive secretary and then director, gathered data on American museums by correspondence and interview and initiated programs such as those that established so-called trailside museums in national and state parks or did research on audience response to exhibits. The program, however, failed to attract strong financial support. Until 1951, foundations (chiefly the Laura Spellman Rockefeller Memorial and Carnegie Corporation of New York) paid about one-half the operating budget, with annual supporting grants of $10,000 to $15,000; they also took care of the research and publishing costs of its books. The $250,000 to $500,000 endowment that Coleman pleaded for did not materialize. In 1958 there were 620 institutional and 1,625 individual members paying only $27,000 in dues.[27]

Joseph Allen Patterson was the next director, from 1958 to 1967. He had

had promotional experience with the Museum of Modern Art and, according to the association's president, Charles Parkhurst, made the organization "far more vigorous than one would have dreamed from its relatively quiet existence . . . for many, many years."[28] Patterson transformed the *Museum News* from a small news-sheet into a first-rate magazine that attracted stimulating articles by leaders throughout the profession. He established a useful *Museums Directory* that listed institutions in the United States and Canada. He revitalized the regional conferences, visiting their sessions regularly. He set up museum training seminars, brought foreign museum professionals to the annual meeting, arranged strong annual sessions of museum trustees, sponsored annual group flights to Europe, and began consideration of an accreditation program. Most promising of all, he appeared before congressional committees that secured the National Museum Act and included museums in the legislation leading to the establishment of the National Endowments for the Arts and Humanities. Patterson worked closely with the Smithsonian Institution, Office of Education, and National Science Foundation in forwarding museum goals.[29]

Patterson's successor was a young lawyer skilled in government advocacy, Kyran M. McGrath. McGrath energetically continued the varied program of the AAM with ever more stress on influencing legislation and the administrative agencies of the federal government. His seven years as director, 1968 to 1975, were extremely busy. On the internal side, McGrath's major accomplishment was the beginning of accreditation and externally, the strengthening of federal support. Not only did the National Science Foundation, National Museum Act, National Endowments for the Arts and Humanities, and other federal agencies provide funds for approved projects, but McGrath fought to obtain a National Museum Services Act that would furnish money for operating expenses.[30] In 1975 Joseph Veach Noble became president of the association, with Richard McLanathan as director. With strong trustee support, they secured in 1977 the authorization of an Institute of Museum Services in the Department of Health, Education and Welfare and began to try to obtain an annual appropriation for it of at least $25 million. Lee Kimche became director of the Institute of Museum Services in December, and Lawrence L. Reger succeeded McLanathan as director of the AAM in May 1978.[31]

The association had held two planning conferences on its future organization—at Aspen, Colorado, in 1973 and at Woodstock, Illinois, in 1974—and they resulted in a new constitution unanimously adopted at the annual meeting in 1976. The chief effect of this document is to decentralize and democratize the governance of the association. Each of the six regional conferences elects three members of the council (a total of eighteen), while only fifteen councillors are chosen at large. The hope is that giving the conferences and discipline groups, such as curators, educators, small museums, and security officers, more responsibility will increase the involvement of both conferences and individual members. The AAM also has found, through experience, that the conferences (and their appointed state representatives) are important in backing favorable legislation for museums. On April 30, 1977, association membership was 5,583 with 1,194 institutions, 3,512 individuals, 315 libraries, 422 trustees, and 140 foreign members, and total dues collected for the previous year exceeded $352,000. The number of institution members constituted a much larger proportion of the 1,821 museums listed by the National Endowment for the Arts survey than did the individuals when compared with the 11,000 full-time professionals found by the same survey.[32]

All things considered, the AAM seems to have made considerable progress, especially in the last twenty years. If its new constitution succeeds in increasing grass-roots participation and support and in providing wise and skilled councillors and officers, the association should be able to cope with its organizational, financial, and legislative problems so as to strengthen museums and achieve a true museum profession.

International Council of Museums (Icom)

The movement of American museum workers toward professionalism has been assisted by international developments. In 1946 UNESCO was constituted, promptly set up a Museums Division, and partially subsidized the nongovernmental Icom, also organized in 1946. Icom established National Committees in seventy-six countries around the world, and a score of International Committees devoted to subjects such as archaeology and history, modern art, costume, regional museums, and security.[33]

Museums were an especially valuable avenue for international communication in a world of hundreds of languages and dialects, as well as widespread illiteracy. Georges Salles of France, president of Icom, put it well in 1956:

> Unesco's aim is to bring people together through cultures and the exchange of their spiritual heritage. And museums are most advantageously placed to help in

the good work. They are the only place in the world where, with the object as interpreter, a language is spoken that everyone can understand.[34]

Dr. Grace L. McCann Morley, on leave as director of the San Francisco Museum of Art, in 1946 was counsellor for the UNESCO Preparatory Commission and then for two years was in charge of the Museums Division. Chauncey L. Hamlin, president of the Buffalo Museum of Science and a past president of the American Association of Museums, was Icom's first president. Georges-Henri Rivière of France headed the secretariat as director, from 1947 to 1965, and then became its permanent adviser.

UNESCO in 1948 began to publish *Museum* in French and English (with résumés in Spanish and Russian). Icom was determined to see that museums improved their exhibition and educational programs. To mark its first ten years, it launched an International Campaign for Museums in 1956 and reviewed the progress made in the decade thus:

> Some institutions tried to transform themselves, others to modernize their appearance completely. . . . Some museums met with brilliant success. The public, roused from indifference, began to visit them. The word "museum" recovered its full meaning. . . . Museums of art or of science . . . should become more active and be so arranged as to bring the public into real contact with exhibits and documents, experiments and history.[35]

UNESCO and Icom early created a documentation center in Paris that attempted to gather all important museum publications. The triennial conferences begun in 1948 enabled museum leaders from around the world to know each other and to inspect first-hand the museums of the regions where the meetings were held. Special museum education seminars have been organized since 1952 at Brooklyn, Athens, Rio de Janiero, Tokyo, and New Delhi. Exchanges have been arranged of exhibits, museum personnel, and technical missions. An Icom Regional Agency for Southeast Asia was set up in 1967, and similar organizations are in formation for Africa and Latin America. A Training Centre for Museum Technicians opened at Jos, Nigeria, in 1963 to teach museum practices such as exhibition, photography, sound recording, conservation, and registration.[36]

UNESCO was also interested in historic preservation and in 1949 enlarged its Museums Division into the Division of Museums and Monuments. The International Centre for the Study of Preservation and Restoration of Cultural Property (known as the Rome Centre) was established in 1959. The International Council of Monuments and Sites (Icomos) appeared in 1965 as a kind of sister organization to Icom but with its own headquarters in Paris. UNESCO (always with the help of Icom) formulated and sought world adoption of international agreements such as the Hague Convention for the Protection of Cultural Property in the Event of Armed Conflict (1954) and the Convention on the Means of Protecting and Preventing the Illicit Export, Import and Transfer of Ownership of Cultural Property (1970).[37]

The Future

The relationship of a museum's board of trustees, director, and staff is critical for the professionalization of museum workers, as the sociologist, Dorothy A. Mariner, has pointed out.[38] It is unrealistic, however, to think that the board can be replaced; lay boards are a fact of life for most hospitals, universities, libraries, and other nonprofit organizations. The trick is to define properly the duties of each segment of the museum governance system and to obtain acceptance by those involved.

The board is legally responsible for the very survival of the museum and should see that financial support is provided, set down broad policies and programs, and choose a director to implement them. Trustees should be especially sensitive about their individual relationships with director and staff. In dealing with the former, they must remember that they are acting as a full board, not upon individual responsibility. They may possess special information and skills of value to staff members but in any contact with staff should work through the director or with his knowledge and consent.

The director is the museum's administrator or executive who carries out the policies of the board. He hires the staff and is responsible for seeing that its expertise is transmitted to the board and that it understands the board's policy decisions. The director, of course, calls upon trustees for advice, but they are not to meddle in administrative matters or interfere with the director and staff in carrying out their regular duties according to high professional standards. The skilled director understands the varied capabilities of his staff members and tries to provide a working environment in which they can function effectively. He must always remember the necessity for continuous communication—to make clear the objectives of the various programs along with individual staff responsibilities. The director is in a sense Janus-headed—responsible for the smooth interchange between trustees and staff, between policy and fulfillment. The Association of Art Museum Directors has devised a valuable statement of professional practices for art museums, much of which can be followed by other institutions. The AAM's professional practices committee considers disputes between trustees and directors or directors and staffs that concern its membership.[39]

A new aspect of museum governance arises when professional workers become unionized. Nonprofessional museum staff members responsible for maintenance, housekeeping, or security, especially when government employees, have belonged to unions for many years, but not curators, educators, and other professionals. In May 1971, however, the Professional and Administrative Staff Association of the Museum of Modern Art in New York received a charter from the Distributive Workers of America and staged a strike in order to obtain what it considered a fair contract. That December, employees at the Minneapolis Institute of Arts formed a second professional museum union. At the Metropolitan Museum of Art in New York, instead of unions, innovations of governance have included a Curatorial Forum of curators, conservators, and cataloguers; an Educational Assembly of educators, librarians, lecturers, and technical staff; and a third group from the administrative and service areas. Each of these organizations elects a representative to attend meetings of the board of trustees. If the rapid unionization of college and university faculties furnishes any guidance, however, more museum unions seem likely.[40]

Less than twenty years ago, Maurice Rheims could write that "Museums are the churches of collectors. Speaking in whispers, groups of visitors wander as an act of faith from one gallery to another."[41] Under that concept, museums were reserved for the happy few—chiefly the wealthy, the cultured, the elite. With the great growth of museums and their ever-increasing educational appeal to the general public, all that is changing. More and more, it is agreed that museums must be operated for all the public. Of course, objects valuable to humanity must be collected and conserved, but also studied, exhibited, interpreted, and used as part of a holistic cultural environment and sometimes for the general social welfare.

Museums devoted to the public interest require ingenious and inspired governance in order to obtain the intellectual and financial support they need. Talented lay persons from different walks of life should constitute their boards and help steer them for the public benefit. But most important of all, if museums are to survive, are well-trained, dedicated, and thoroughly professional museum men and women. They alone can keep museums moving in right directions and achieving higher standards of proven excellence.

Notes
Bibliography
Index

Notes

Notes, Chapter 1

1. American Association of Museums, *America's Museums: The Belmont Report* (Washington, 1969), pp. 3, 17–20.
2. Douglas A. Allan, "The Museum and Its Functions," in United Nations Educational, Scientific and Cultural Organization [UNESCO], *The Organization of Museums: Practical Advice* (Paris, 1967), p. 13.
3. American Association of Museums, *Museum Accreditation: Professional Standards* (Washington, 1973), pp. 8–9. For a European definition of museum, see Kenneth Hudson, *A Social History of Museums: What the Visitors Thought* (London, 1975), pp. 1–3.
4. Thomas P. F. Hoving, "Branch Out!" *Museum News* 47 (September 1968):16.
5. Daniel S. Greenberg, "There's a Windmill in the Attic: S. Dillon Ripley Is Blowing Dust off the Smithsonian," *Saturday Review* 48 (June 5, 1965):48.
6. Benjamin Ives Gilman, *Museum Ideals of Purpose and Method,* 2nd ed. (Cambridge, Mass., 1923), p. xvii; F. T. Marinetti, "The Foundation and Manifesto of Futurism, 1908" in Herschel B. Chipp, *Theories of Modern Art: A Source Book of Artistic Concepts by Artists and Critics* (Berkeley and Los Angeles, 1968), pp. 286–288.
7. Barry Schwartz, "Museums: Art for Who's Sake?" *Ramparts* 9 (June 1971):44.
8. George Sarton, *A History of Science: Hellenistic Science and Culture in the Last Three Centuries B.C.* (Cambridge, Mass., 1959), pp. 29–34; Germain Bazin, *The Museum Age* (New York, 1967), p. 16; Alma S. Wittlin, *Museums: In Search of a Usable Future* (Cambridge, Mass., 1970), p. 221; David E. H. Jones, "The Great Museum at Alexandria . . . ," *Smithsonian* 2 (December 1971):53–60, (January 1972):59–63.
9. Bazin, *Museum Age,* pp. 12–14, 18–23; Wittlin, *Museums: In Search,* pp. 4–7, 12–13; Niels von Holst, *Creators, Collectors and Connoisseurs: The Anatomy of Artistic Taste from Antiquity to the Present Day* (New York, 1967), pp. 21–40.
10. Bazin, *Museum Age,* pp. 29–39; Wittlin, *Museums: In Search,* pp. 7–8; Francis Henry Taylor, *Babel's Tower: The Dilemma of the Modern Museum* (New York, 1945), p. 11.
11. Bazin, *Museum Age,* pp. 28, 34–35.
12. J. Mordaunt Crook, *The British Museum* (London, 1972), p. 32; Hudson, *Social History of Museums,* p. 6; Bazin, *Museum Age,* pp. 129–130; Holst, *Creators,* pp. 92, 94–96, 103–105; Taylor, *Babel's Tower,* pp. 12–17; Silvio A. Bedini, "The Evolution of Science Museums," *Technology and Culture* 5 (1965):1–29; Helmut Seling, "The Genesis of the Museum," *Architectural Review* 141 (1967):103–114.
13. Edward S. Hyams and William MacQuitty, *Great Botanical Gardens of the World* (New York, 1969), pp. 16–23, 34–43, 87, 102–103, 107; A. W. Hill, "The History and Functions of Botanic Gardens," *Annals Missouri Botanical Garden* 2 (1915):185–240.
14. Bazin, *Museum Age,* pp. 141–191; Hudson, *Social History of Museums,* pp. 3–6.
15. Douglas and Elizabeth Rigby, *Lock, Stock and Barrel . . .* (Philadelphia, 1944); Maurice

Rheims, *The Strange Life of Objects: 35 Centuries of Art Collecting and Collectors* (New York, 1961); Sherman E. Lee, "The Idea of an Art Museum," *Harper's Magazine* 237 (September 1968):76–79; Hudson, *Social History of Museums*, pp. 2–6. The museum authority mentioned, Frank O. Spinney, taught in the Cooperstown (N.Y.) Graduate Programs.

16. Bazin, *Museum Age*, pp. 12–14, 89, 116–118, 176.
17. Paul Coremans, "The Museum Laboratory" in UNESCO, *The Organization of Museums: Practical Advice* (Paris, 1967), pp. 83–118, plates 3–33; H. J. Plenderleith and A. E. A. Werner, *The Conservation of Antiquities and Works of Art*, 2nd ed. (New York, 1972).
18. Hiroshi Daifuku, "Museums and Research" in UNESCO, *Organization of Museums*, pp. 68–72; American Association of Museums, *Belmont Report*, pp. 6–8.
19. Bazin, *Museum Age*, pp. 177–180, 230–234; Charles R. Richards, *Industrial Art and the Museum* (New York, 1927), pp. 10–12.
20. Richards, *Industrial Art and the Museum*, pp. 12–19.
21. Mats Rehnberg, *The Nordiska Museet and Skansen: An Introduction to the History and Activities of a Famous Swedish Museum* (Stockholm, 1957), pp. 9–14.
22. Kenneth W. Luckhurst, *The Story of Exhibitions* (London and New York, 1951).
23. Laura M. Bragg, "The Birth of the Museum Idea in America," *Charleston Museum Quarterly* 1 (1923):3–13.
24. Charles Coleman Sellers, *Charles Willson Peale* (New York, 1969).
25. Paul H. Oehser, *The Smithsonian Institution* (New York, 1970).
26. Geoffrey T. Hellman, *Bankers, Bones & Beetles: The First Century of the American Museum of Natural History* (Garden City, N.Y., 1969); Calvin Tomkins, *Merchants and Masterpieces: The Story of the Metropolitan Museum of Art* (New York, 1970); Walter Muir Whitehill, *Museum of Fine Arts, Boston: A Centennial History*, 2 vols. (Cambridge, Mass., 1970).
27. Laurence Vail Coleman, *Historic House Museums: With a Directory* (Washington, 1933).
28. Reprinted, with permission of the author, from *And What's More*, by David McCord. Copyright 1941 by Coward, McCann; copyright 1973 by David McCord.
29. George Brown Goode, "A Memorial of . . . ," in Smithsonian Institution, *Annual Report for 1897*, Part II (Washington, 1901), pp. 72–73; Gilman, *Museum Ideals*, pp. 80–81, 88–102, 279–316; Whitehill, *Museum of Fine Arts*, 1:293–294.
30. Freeman Tilden, *Interpreting Our Heritage*, rev. ed. (Chapel Hill, N.C., 1967); American Association of Museums, *Belmont Report, pp. 8*–23; E. P. Alexander, "The Regional Museum as a Cultural Centre," *Museum* 23 (1970–71):274–284; Hudson, *Social History of Museums*, pp. 48–73.
31. Newark Museum, *A Survey: 50 Years* (Newark, N.J., 1959), p. 9. See also Richard Grove, "Pioneers in American Museums: John Cotton Dana," *Museum News* 56 (May–June 1978):32–39.
32. American Association of Museums, *Museums: Their New Audience: A Report to the Department of Housing and Urban Development . . .* (Washington, D.C., 1972).
33. Albert Ten Eyck Gardner, "Museum in Motion," Metropolitan Museum of Art *Bulletin*, 24 (Summer 1965):21.
34. Bazin, *Museum Age*, pp. 260–261.

Notes, Chapter 2

1. Francis Henry Taylor, *The Taste of Angels: A History of Art Collecting from Rameses to Napoleon* (Boston, 1948), pp. 50–51; Germain Bazin, *The Museum Age*, pp. 37–39;

Germain Bazin, *The Louvre* (New York, 1958), p. 12; Alma S. Wittlin, *Museums: In Search of a Usable Future*, pp. 8, 18.

2. Niels von Holst, *Creators, Collectors and Connoisseurs*, pp, 58–66; Taylor, *Taste of Angels*, pp. 55–72: Bazin, *Museum Age*, pp. 44–46, 58–62; Wittlin, *Museums: In Search*, p. 75; Helmut Seling, "The Genesis of the Museum," p. 103.
3. Holst, *Creators*, pp. 69–74; Taylor, *Taste of Angels*, pp. 85–109; Bazin, *Museum Age*, pp. 46–52; Wittlin, *Museums: In Search*, p. 101; Seling, "Genesis of the Museum," p. 103.

Frank Herrmann, *The English as Collectors: A Documentary Chrestomathy* . . . (London, 1972), pp. 57–68; Holst, *Creators*, pp. 116–129, 168; Taylor, *Taste of Angels*, pp. 208–241; Bazin, *Museum Age*, pp. 83–84, 90–91; Bazin, *Louvre*, pp. 25–26; Wittlin, *Museums: In Search*, p. 101; Kenneth Hudson, *A Social History of Museums*, pp. 11–12.

5. Taylor, *Taste of Angels*, pp. 277–278, 324–337; Bazin, *Museum Age*, pp. 92–95; Bazin, *Louvre*, pp. 21–28; Holst, *Creators*, pp. 157–160; Wittlin, *Museums: In Search*, pp. 57–59.
6. Holst, *Creators*, pp. 86–90, 107–116, 128–139, 157, 161–163, 169–177, 179, 187–189, 190–198, 202–203; Taylor, *Taste of Angels*, pp. 140–182, 279–290; Bazin, *Museum Age*, pp. 75–80, 101; Wittlin, *Museums: In Search*, pp. 10–11, 92–93.
7. Holst, *Creators*, pp. 144–146; Taylor, *Taste of Angels*, pp. 403–409, 420–464, 511–531; Bazin, *Museum Age*, pp. 118–126.
8. Wittlin, *Museums: In Search*, pp. 92–93; Taylor, *Taste of Angels*, p. 469; Bazin, *Museum Age*, p. 89; Holst, *Creators*, pp. 153–154.
9. Bazin, *Museum Age*, pp. 166–167; Taylor, *Taste of Angels*, pp. 382–383; Seling, "Genesis of the Museum," p. 105; Holst, *Creators*, pp. 209–214.
10. Bazin, *Museum Age*, pp. 163–166.
11. Bazin, *Museum Age*, pp. 162–163.
12. Bazin, *Museum Age*, pp. 158–159; Seling, "Genesis of the Museum," p. 109; Holst, *Creators*, pp. 161–163, 206–209; Hudson, *Social History of Museums*, pp. 28–29.
13. Bazin, *Museum Age*, pp. 150–156; Bazin, *Louvre*, pp. 39–45; Taylor, *Taste of Angels*, p. 371; Christiane Aulanier, *Histoire de Palais et du Musée du Louvre*, 9 vols. (Paris, 1947–64).
14. Bazin, *Museum Age*, p. 144.
15. Bazin, *Museum Age*, pp. 159–160; Taylor, *Taste of Angels*, pp. 511–525; Holst, *Creators*, pp. 166–167, 169–178, 184–185.
16. Bazin, *Museum Age*, pp. 144–145; Taylor, *Taste of Angels*, pp. 414–416; Wittlin, *Museums: In Search*, p. 46.
17. Bazin, *Museum Age*, pp. 145–150; Taylor, *Taste of Angels*, pp. 417–420, 475–476; Holst, *Creators*, pp. 194, 205–206.
18. Bazin, *Museum Age*, pp. 171–172; Bazin, *Louvre*, pp. 46–48; Holst, *Creators*, pp. 215–217; Taylor, *Taste of Angels*, p. 539; Seling, "Genesis of the Museum," p. 109; Linda Nochlin, "Museums and Radicals: A History of Emergencies," in Brian O'Doherty, editor, *Museums in Crisis* (New York, 1972), pp. 7–41; Cecil Gould, *Trophy of Conquest: The Musée Napoléon and the Creation of the Louvre* (London, 1965), pp. 13–29, 70–71; Wilhelm Treve, *Art Plunder: The Fate of Works of Art in War and Unrest* (New York, 1961), 139–199.
19. Bazin, *Museum Age*, p. 174; Bazin, *Louvre*, p. 48; Taylor, *Taste of Angels*, pp. 540–541; Nochlin, "Museums and Radicals," p. 11; Gould, *Trophy of Conquest*, pp. 30–40.
20. Bazin, *Museum Age*, p. 174; Bazin, *Louvre*, pp. 48–49; Holst, *Creators*, pp. 217–218; Taylor, *Taste of Angels*, pp. 544–547; Nochlin, "Museums and Radicals," p. 13; Gould, *Trophy of Conquest*, pp. 41–66.
21. Bazin, *Museum Age*, p. 176; Gould, *Trophy of Conquest*, pp. 67–69.

22. Bazin, *Museum Age*, pp. 176–180; Bazin, *Louvre*, pp. 50–51; Taylor, *Taste of Angels*, pp. 548–560; Holst, *Creators*, pp. 218–220; Gould, *Trophy of Conquest*, pp. 86–115.
23. Bazin, *Museum Age*, pp. 180–185, 190; Bazin, *Louvre*, pp. 52–56; Taylor, *Taste of Angels*, pp. 561–562, 572–573; Holst, *Creators*, pp. 220–224; Gould, *Trophy of Conquest*, pp. 75–80.
24. Bazin, *Museum Age*, pp. 185–191; Bazin, *Louvre*, pp. 57–60; Taylor, *Taste of Angels*, pp. 571–589; Gould, *Trophy of Conquest*, pp. 80–85, 116–135. For the activities of Hitler and Goering, see David Roxan and Ken Wanstall, *The Rape of Art: The Story of Hitler's Plunder of the Great Masterpieces of Europe* (New York, 1965).
25. Bazin, *Museum Age*, pp. 201, 204, 207, 209; Bazin, *Louvre*, pp. 61–85; Holst, *Creators*, pp. 260–261.
26. Herrmann, *English as Collectors*, pp. 263-273; Philip Hendy, "The National Gallery," in *Art Treasures of the National Gallery, London* (London, 1959), pp. 9–25; Holst, *Creators*, pp. 224–225.
27. Bazin, *Museum Age*, pp. 195–197, 270; Herrman, *English as Collectors*, 202–209, plate 61; Seling, "Genesis of the Museum," pp. 112–114; Holst, *Creators*, pp. 231–232, 257, 279; A. Mahr, "The Centenary Celebrations of the Prussian State Museums," *Museums Journal* 30 (March 1931):253–260; Berlin State Museums Curatorial Staff, *Art Treasures of the Berlin State Museums* (New York, 1964), pp. 7–22, 91, 99–104, 122–126, 130–131, 133.
28. Bazin, *Museum Age*, pp. 198–199, 270; Seling, "Genesis of the Museum," pp. 111–112, 114; Holst, *Creators*, pp. 227–230; Munich Art Galleries Staff and University of Munich Art Historians, *Munich* (South Brunswick, N.J., 1969), pp. 1–60.
29. Bazin, *Museum Age*, pp. 214–215, 269; B. B. Piotrovsky, editor, *Art Treasures of the Hermitage* (Leningrad, 1969), pp. 15–16; Mikhail Artamonov, "The State Hermitage Museum, Leningrad," *Museum* 10 (1957):97–113.
30. Bazin, *Museum Age*, 217–218; Raymond Charmet, *The Museums of Paris* (New York, 1967), pp. 5–6; National Gallery, Millbank [Tate Gallery], *Illustrated Guide: British School* (London, 1928), pp. viii–ix; Hendy, "National Gallery," pp. 24–25.
31. Bazin, *Museum Age*, 230–234; Kenneth W. Luckhurst, *The Story of Exhibitions*, pp. 83–116; Eugene S. Ferguson, "Technical Museums and International Exhibitions," *Technology and Culture* 6 (1965):30–46; Winslow Ames, "London or Liegnitz?" *Museum News* 43 (October 1964):27–35; Charmet, *Museums of Paris*, p. 11; Victoria and Albert Museum, *Masterpieces in the Victoria & Albert Museum* (London, 1952), pp. iii–iv; Sir Leigh Ashton, "100 Years of the Victoria & Albert Museum," *Museums Journal* 53 (May 1953):43–47.
32. Laurence Vail Coleman, *The Museum in America: A Critical Study*, 3 vols. (Washington, 1939), 1:10, 11, 14–15, 112; 2:230; 3:429–432; Walter Pach, *The Art Museum in America* (New York, 1948), pp. 32, 33, 38, 40, 42; Calvin Tomkins, *Merchants and Masterpieces*, p. 38.
33. Pach, *Art Museum*, pp. 40–41; Eloise Spaeth, *American Art Museums and Galleries: An Introduction to Looking* (New York, 1960), pp. 217–229; Holst, *Creators*, pp. 257–259, 271–272.
34. Tomkins, *Merchants and Masterpieces*, p. 21.
35. Walter Muir Whitehill, *Museum of Fine Arts, Boston: A Centennial History*, 2 vols., 1:9–13; Tomkins, *Merchants and Masterpieces*, p. 23.
36. Whitehill, *Museum of Fine Arts*, 1:31; Tomkins, *Merchants and Masterpieces*, p. 70.
37. Winifred E. Howe, *A History of the Metropolitan Museum of Art . . .* , 2 vols. (New York, 1913, 1946), 1:138–139; Coleman, *Museum in America*, 1:106–111; Tomkins, *Merchants and Masterpieces*, pp. 39–41.

38. Whitehill, *Museum of Fine Arts,* 1:19–20; Howe, *Metropolitan History,* 1:153–156, 180–181, 281–283; 2:8–14; Tomkins, *Merchants and Masterpieces,* pp. 44, 47, 49–59, 95–182.
39. Howe, *Metropolitan Museum* 2:14–17, 210–223; Tomkins, *Merchants and Masterpieces,* pp. 285–289, 292, 355–358; Leo Lerman, *The Museum: One Hundred Years of the Metropolitan Museum of Art* (New York, 1969), p. 276.
40. Whitehill, *Museum of Fine Arts,* 1:chaps. 4, 5, 8; 2: chaps. 14, 19, 21; Pach, *Art Museum,* pp. 65–68; Newsweek, *Museum of Fine Arts, Boston* (New York, 1969), pp. 9–15, 162–165.
41. National Endowment for the Arts, *Museums USA: Art, History, Science, and Other Museums* (Washington, D.C., 1974), p. 5; Nathaniel Burt, *Palaces for the People: A Social History of the American Art Museum* (Boston, 1977); Russell Lynes, *Good Old Modern: An Intimate Portrait of the Museum of Modern Art* (New York, 1975); Avis Berman, "Pioneers in American Museums: Juliana Force," *Museum News* 55 (November/December 1976):45–49, 59–62.
42. Lerman, *Museum,* p. 14; Tomkins, *Merchants and Masterpieces,* pp. 115–120; Stephen Mark Dobbs, "Dana and Kent and Early Museum Education," *Museum News* 50 (October 1971):38–41; Barbara Y. Newsom, *The Metropolitan Museum as an Educational Institution* (New York, 1970).
43. Whitehill, *Museum of Fine Arts,* 1:10, 41, 288–301.
44. National Endowment for the Arts, *Museums USA,* p. 25.
45. Nochlin, "Museums and Radicals," pp. 7–41. See also Ernest van den Haag, "Art and the Mass Audience," in Brian O'Doherty, editor, *Museums in Crisis,* pp. 65–74; American Assembly, *On Understanding Art Museums* (Englewood Cliffs, N.J., 1975), pp. 131–140; George Nash, "Art Museums as Perceived by the Public," *Curator* 18 (1975):55–67.
46. Lynes, *Good Old Modern,* pp. 288–291; Tomkins, *Merchants and Masterpieces,* pp. 297–310; Berman, "Juliana Force," pp. 45–49, 59–62; Carl Wittke, *The First Fifty Years: The Cleveland Museum of Art, 1916–1966* (Cleveland, 1966), pp. 121–124; American Assembly, *Art Museums,* pp. 163–184. For the political ramifications of modern art, see Jane de Hart Mathews, "Art and Politics in Cold War America," *American Historical Review* 81 (October 1976):762–787.
47. Gilman, *Museum Ideals,* pp. 86–87, 92; John Cotton Dana, *The New Museum* (Woodstock, Vt., 1917); Francis Henry Taylor, *Babel's Tower,* pp. 23, 25–27; Sherman E. Lee, "The Idea of an Art Museum," pp. 76–79; W. G. Constable, "Museums in a Changing World," *Museums Journal* 55 (January 1956):259–262.
48. Brian O'Doherty, "Introduction," in O'Doherty, editor, *Museums in Crisis,* pp. 2–5; John Canaday, *Culture-Gulch: Notes on Art and Its Public in the 1960's* (New York: 1969), pp. 163–181.

Notes, Chapter 3

1. David Murray, *Museums: Their History and Their Use, with a Bibliography and List of Museums in the United Kingdom,* 3 vols. (Glasgow, 1904), 1:45–73; Alma S. Wittlin, *Museums: In Search of a Usable Future,* pp. 17–22; P. J. P. Whitehead, "Museums in the History of Zoology," *Museums Journal* 70 (1970–1971):51.
2. Murray, *Museums,* 1:25, 27, 78–80; Wittlin, *Museums: In Search,* pp. 39–53; Whitehead, "Museums in Zoology," pp. 51–52; Silvio A. Bedini, "The Evolution of Science Museums," pp. 2–6, 11–12; Germain Bazin, *The Museum Age,* pp. 62, 144; Willy Ley, *Dawn of Zoology* (Englewood Cliffs, N.J., 1968), pp. 121–161, 268–273.

3. Murray, *Museums*, 1:95–96, 103–104, 115–117; Whitehead, "Museums in Zoology," p. 52; Bedini, "Science Museums," pp. 2–6; Holger Jacobaeus, *Muséum Regium, seu Catalogus rerum . . .* (Hafniae, 1696).
4. Bedini, "Science Museums," pp. 4–6, 11–17; Murray, *Museums*, 1:2, 106–107.
5. Bazin, *Museum Age*, p. 115; Wittlin, *Museums: In Search*, pp. 64–65; Bedini, "Science Museums," pp. 25–26; Murray, *Museums*, 1:205–230.
6. Robert William Theodore Gunther, *Early Science in Oxford*, 15 vols. (Oxford, 1923–1967), 1:43–47; 3:280–333, 346–366; 391–447; Mea Allan, *The Tradescants: Their Plants, Gardens and Museum, 1570–1662* (London, 1964); Bazin, *Museum Age*, pp. 141, 144–145; Whitehead, "Museums in Zoology," pp. 54–55; Murray, *Museums*, 1:107–111; Ley, *Dawn of Zoology*, pp. 202–203; Ashmolean Museum, University of Oxford, *Treasures of the Ashmolean Museum: An Illustrated Souvenir of Art, Archaeology and Numismatics . . .* (Oxford, 1970), pp. ii–iii, no. 24; F. J. North, "On Learning How to Run a Museum," *Museums Journal* 51 (April 1951):4–5; (June 1951):63–66; D. B. Harden, "The Ashmolean Museum—Beaumont Street," *Museums Journal* 52 (February 1952):265–270.
7. G. R. de Beer, *Sir Hans Sloane and the British Museum* (London, 1953), pp. 13–49; E. St. John Brooks, *Sir Hans Sloane: The Great Collector and His Circle* (London, 1954), pp. 13–77; Edward Miller, *That Noble Cabinet: A History of the British Museum* (Athens, Ohio, 1974), pp. 36–37.
8. De Beer, *Sloane*, pp. 50–95, 123–124; Brooks, *Sloane*, pp. 78–118, 192; Miller, *That Noble Cabinet*, pp. 37–39; James Mordaunt Crook, *The British Museum*, pp. 42–49.
9. De Beer, *Sloane*, pp. 125–128; Brooks, *Sloane*, pp. 209–210; Murray, *Museums*, 1:171–172; Miller, *That Noble Cabinet*, pp. 26, 39; Kenneth Hudson, *A Social History of Museums*, p. 18.
10. De Beer, *Sloane*, pp. 108–134, 148, 160–161; Brooks, *Sloane*, pp. 176–201; Miller, *That Noble Cabinet*, pp. 38, 40; Crook, *British Museum*, pp. 42–43; Hudson, *Social History of Museums*, pp. 18–21; Murray, *Museums*, 1:127–144; Frank Charlton Francis, *Treasures of the British Museum* (London, 1967), p. 10; James Britten, *The Sloane Herbarium . . .* rev. ed. by J. E. Dandy (London, 1958).
11. De Beer, *Sloane*, pp. 138–139; Brooks, *Sloane*, pp. 218–221; Miller, *That Noble Cabinet*, p. 41.
12. De Beer, *Sloane*, pp. 143–153; Brooks, *Sloane*, pp. 221–223; Miller, *That Noble Cabinet*, pp. 42–46, 70–71, 74, 77–79, 86–87, 92; Crook, *British Museum*, pp. 48–49, 52–54, 65–66; Hudson, *Social History of Museums*, pp. 8–10; Henry C. Shelley, *The British Museum: Its History and Treasures* (Boston, 1911), pp. 59–62; Wittlin, *Museums: In Search*, pp. 102–105.
13. Miller, *That Noble Cabinet*, pp. 74–76, 85–86, 96–108, 111–115, 191–223, 299–320, 327, 336–339, 355–356; Crook, *British Museum*, pp. 62, 66–71, 118, 128, 216, 226–229; Francis, *Treasures of the British Museum*, pp. 22, 25; Hermann Justus Braunholtz, *Sir Hans Sloane and Ethnography* (London, 1970), pp. 19–20, 37–45; Hudson, *Social History of Museums*, pp. 39–40.
14. Miller, *That Noble Cabinet*, pp. 224–244; Crook, *British Museum*, pp. 199–200; Edward Edwards, *Lives of the Founders of the British Museum: With Notices of Its Chief Augmentors and Other Benefactors, 1570–1878* (1870; reprint ed., New York, 1969), pp. 333–336, 487–510, 601–607; Francis, *Treasures of the British Museum*, pp. 14–15, 20–21; Karl P. Schmidt, "The Nature of the Natural History Museum," *Curator* 1 (January 1958):23; Sir William Henry Flower, *Essays on Museums and Other Subjects Connected with Natural History* (New York, 1898), pp. 15–22, 37–41; James A. Bateman, "The Functions of Museums in Biology," *Museums Journal* 74 (March 1975):159–164, esp. p. 161.

15. W. H. Mullens, "Some Museums of Old London: I. The Leverian Museum; II. William Bullock's London Museum," *Museums Journal* 15 (1915–1916):120–129, 162–172; 17 (1917–1918):51–56, 132–137, 180–187; Hugh Honour, "Curiosities of the Egyptian Hall," *Country Life* 115 (1954):38–39; Whitehead, "Museums in Zoology," pp. 156–159; Murray, *Museums*, 1:175–179; Hudson, *Social History of Museums*, pp. 17–18, 24–26.
16. Whitehead, "Museums in Zoology," p. 156; Flower, *Essays on Museums*, pp. 41–47; René Taton, editor, *History of Science*, 3 vols. (New York, 1963–1965), 3:325–326; *Museums of the World: A Directory of 17,000 Museums in 48 Countries . . .* Comp. by Eleanor Braun (New York, 1973), pp. 78–79; *Guide des Musées de France* (Fribourg, 1970), pp. 136–137; *Blue Guide: Paris* (London, 1968), pp. 108–110; Libraire Larousse, *Dictionnaire de Paris* (Paris, 1964), pp. 285–286, 358; Murray, *Museums*, 2:93; Hermann Heinrich Frese, *Anthropology and the Public: The Role of Museums* (Leiden, 1969), pp. 20, 26–29; Paul Lemoine, "National Museum of Natural History . . . Paris," *Natural History Magazine* (London) 5 (January 1935):4–19; Bateman, "Museums in Biology," p. 161.
17. Flower, *Essays on Museums*, pp. 41–47; *Museums of the World*, p. 21; Murray, *Museums*, 2:245–246; Karl Baedeker, *Austria . . . Handbook for Travellers*, 12th ed. (Leipsig, 1929), pp. 103–108.
18. Maria Luisa Azzarol Puccetti, "La Spècola, the Zoological Museum of the University of Florence," *Curator* 15 (1972):93–112; Bazin, *Museum Age*, p. 163.
19. Laura M. Bragg, "The Birth of the Museum Idea in America," *Charleston Museum Quarterly* 1 (First Quarter, 1923):3–13; Paul M. Rea, "A Contribution to Early Museum History in America," American Association of Museums *Proceedings* 9 (1915):53–65; William G. Mazyck, *The Charleston Museum: Its Genesis and Development* (Charleston, 1908), pp. 5–28; Hudson, *Social History of Museums*, pp. 31–33.
20. William E. Lingelbach, "An Early American Historian [Pierre Eugène du Simitière]," in New York Public Library, *Bookmen's Holiday: Notes and Studies Written and Gathered in Tribute to Harry Miller Lydenberg* (New York, 1943), pp. 355–361; Hans Huth, "Pierre Eugène du Simitière and the Beginnings of the American Historical Museum," *Pennsylvania Magazine of History and Biography* 69 (October 1945):315–325.
21. Charles Coleman Sellers, *Charles Willson Peale*, pp. 203–211. See also E. P. Alexander, "Bringing History to Life: Philadelphia and Williamsburg," *Curator* 4 (1961):61.
22. Sellers, *Peale*, pp. 212–217, 219, 221–222, 264–265, 303, 335; Hudson, *Social History of Museums*, pp. 33–36.
23. Sellers, *Peale*, pp. 216, 230, 241, 263, 281, 293–301, 333, 340–341.
24. Sellers, *Peale*, pp. 282–283, 289–291, 305, 335, 337–338, 341, 342, 350–351, 361–362, 377–380, 406–407.
25. Sellers, *Peale*, pp. 245, 256, 331, 337, 350–351, 380, 386, 394, 401, 408.
26. Sellers, *Peale*, pp. 257–258, 330, 347–348.
27. P. T. Barnum, *Struggles and Triumphs: or, Forty Years' Recollections of P. T. Barnum Written by Himself* [1869] (New York, 1930), pp. 66–73, 102–103, 180–181; John Rickards Betts, "P. T. Barnum and the Popularization of Natural History," *Journal of the History of Ideas* 20 (1959):353–368; Morris Robert Werner, *Barnum* (New York, 1923), pp. 43–50.
28. Barnum, *Struggles and Triumphs*, pp. 74, 84, 105–106, 251–252, 392, 406–409; Werner, *Barnum*, 235–252; Neil Harris, *Humbug: The Art of P. T. Barnum* (Boston, 1973), pp. 33–57.
29. Barnum, *Struggles and Triumphs*, pp. 465–475, 514–517; Werner, *Barnum*, pp. 302–303; Betts, "Barnum and Popularization," pp. 357–368.
30. Paul H. Oehser, *The Smithsonian Institution*, pp. 3–25; Walter Karp, *The Smithsonian:*

An Establishment for the Increase and Diffusion of Knowledge Among Men (Washington, D.C., 1965), pp. 7–19; Geoffrey T. Hellman, *The Smithsonian: Octopus on the Mall* (Philadelphia, 1967), pp. 26–55; Wilcomb E. Washburn, "Joseph Henry's Conception of the Purpose of the Smithsonian Institution," in Whitfield J. Bell, Jr., and others, *A Cabinet of Curiosities: Five Episodes in the Evolution of American Museums* (Charlottesville, Va., 1967), pp. 106–166, esp. pp. 106–108.

31. Washburn, "Purpose of the Smithsonian," pp. 106–108.
32. Oehser, *Smithsonian*, pp. 26–40; Karp, *Smithsonian*, pp. 19–27; Hellman, *Octopus*, pp. 56–58; Washburn, "Purpose of the Smithsonian," pp. 108–166.
33. Oehser, *Smithsonian*, pp. 40–44; Karp, *Smithsonian*, pp. 29–43; Hellman, *Octopus*, pp. 89–116; Washburn, "Purpose of the Smithsonian," pp. 129–152; James M. Goode, "A View from the Castle," *Museum News* 54 (July/August 1976):38–45.
34. Oehser, *Smithsonian*, pp. 44–47 (the quotation is on p. 45); Karp, *Smithsonian*, pp. 76–80; Hellman, *Octopus*, pp. 94–95, 97, 198; G. Carroll Lindsay, "George Brown Goode," in Clifford L. Lord, editor, *Keepers of the Past* (Chapel Hill, N.C., 1965), pp. 127–140. See also "A Memorial of George Brown Goode . . . ," in Smithsonian Institution, *Annual Report for 1897*, Part II (Washington, D.C., 1901); National Museum of History and Technology, *1876: A Centennial Exhibition*, Robert C. Post, editor (Washington, D.C., 1976), esp. pp. 11–23.
35. Oehser, *Smithsonian*, pp. 87–95; Karp, *Smithsonian*, pp. 44–49; Hellman, *Octopus*, pp. 198–201, 207–208, 215–216.
36. Oehser, *Smithsonian*, pp. 96–111, 134–155; Karp, *Smithsonian*, pp. 75–117; Hellman, *Octopus*, pp. 159–192, 207–216.
37. Oehser, *Smithsonian*, pp. 72–86, 203–217, 225–232; Karp, *Smithsonian*, pp. 119–125.
38. Geoffrey T. Hellman, *Bankers, Bones and Beetles*, pp. 9–28; *Natural History: The Journal of the American Museum* 30 (September/October 1930):452.
39. Hellman, *Bankers, Bones, and Beetles*, p. 28.
40. Hellman, *Bankers, Bones, and Beetles*, pp. 35–36; *Natural History*, 27 (July/August 1927):309–391.
41. Hellman, *Bankers, Bones and Beetles*, pp. 57–115; quotation on page 63.
42. Hellman, *Bankers, Bones, and Beetles*, pp. 117–206; *Natural History*, 30 (September/October 1930):451–525.
43. Hellman, *Bankers, Bones, and Beetles*, pp. 207–244; Geoffrey T. Hellman, "The Hidden Museum [American Museum of Natural History]," *New Yorker*, May 19, 1975, pp. 42–74.
44. Hellman, *Bankers, Bones, and Beetles*, p. 256.
45. Ralph W. Dexter, "The Role of F. W. Putnam in Founding the Field Museum," *Curator* 13 (1970):21–26; George A. Dorsey, "The Department of Anthropology of the Field Columbian Museum—A Review of Six Years," *American Anthropologist* (n.s.), 2 (1900):247–265; Field Museum of Natural History, *Annual Report of the Director to the Board of Trustees, 1960* (Chicago, 1961); Donald Collier, "Chicago Comes of Age: The World's Columbian Exposition and the Birth of the Field Museum," Field Museum *Bulletin* (May 1969):2–7; "The Museum's First Million," Field Museum *Bulletin* (August 1970):13–15.
46. Chesly Manly, *One Billion Years on Our Doorstep: . . . Six Articles on the Chicago Natural History Museum Reprinted from the Chicago Tribune* (Chicago, 1959), pp. 17–22; Field Museum, *Annual Report of Director, 1911, 1926, 1929, 1940* (Chicago, 1912, 1927, 1930, 1941); John R. Millar, "1921–1961: 40 Years Recalled," Field Museum *Bulletin* (May 1961):6–7; "Stanley Field, 1875–1964," Field Museum *Bulletin* (December

1964):2–3, 8; E. Leland Webber, "Field Museum Again: Name Change Honors Field Family," Field Museum *Bulletin* (March 1966):203; Joyce Zibro, "About Field Museum," Field Museum *Bulletin* (October 1971):2–8.

47. A. E. Parr, *Mostly About Museums . . .* (New York, 1959), pp. 45–73; Parr, "The Functions of Museums: Research Centers or Show Places," *Curator* 6 (1963):20–31; Parr, "Museums in Megalopolis," Canadian Museums Association *Gazette* 4 (August/November 1970):19–25; Parr, "On Museums and Directors," *Curator* 16 (1973):281–285; Dean Amadon, "Natural History Museums—Some Trends," *Curator* 14 (1971): 42–49; Bateman, "Museums in Biology," pp. 159–164.
48. Frese, *Anthropology and the Public,* pp. 15–35.
49. Frese, *Anthropology and the Public,* pp. 7, 12, 24, 28, 134–136, 163, 183–186; P. H. Pott, *National Museum of Ethnology, Leiden, 1837–1962* (The Hague, 1962), pp. 1–15; Hudson, *Social History of Museums,* pp. 52–53, 74–75.
50. Paul Rivet, "Organization of an Ethnological Museum," *Museum* 1 (1948):113.
51. Frese, *Anthropology and the Public,* pp. 7, 20, 26–29, 64, 66, 68, 154; Rivet, "Organization of Ethnological Museum," pp. 68–70, 112–113; Roger Falck, "Methods of Case Display at the *Musée de l'Homme," Museum* 1 (1948):70–75, 114–115.
52. Frese, *Anthropology and the Public,* pp. 23, 140, 203; Froelich Rainey, "The Archaeology Explosion," *Expedition* 9 (Spring 1967):2–7 and "Editorial," 11 (Fall 1968):2–3.
53. Ignacio Bernal and others, *The Mexican National Museum of Anthropology* (London, 1968); Pedro Ramirez Vasquez and others, *The National Museum of Anthropology, Mexico: Art, Architecture, Anthropology* (New York, 1968).

Notes, Chapter 4

1. Silvio A. Bedini, "The Evolution of Science Museums," pp. 1–29, esp. the table on pp. 2–6; Germain Bazin, *The Museum Age,* pp. 37–39, 75–76.
2. Bedini, "Science Museums," pp. 11–18; Bazin, *Museum Age,* pp. 86–87, 144; Martha Ornstein, *The Role of Scientific Societies in the Seventeenth Century,* 3rd ed. (Chicago, 1938), pp. 77–90, 219.
3. Bedini, "Science Museums," pp. 18–20; Ornstein, *Scientific Societies,* pp. 112–115; Eugene S. Ferguson, "Technical Museums and International Exhibitions," pp. 30–46, esp. pp. 32, 45; Bazin, *Museum Age,* 144–145.
4. Charles R. Richards, *The Industrial Museum* (New York, 1925), pp. 7–11; "Imperial Conservatory of Arts and Trades at Paris," *American Journal of Education* 21 (1870):439–449; H. W. Dickinson, "Museums and Their Relation to the History of Engineering," Newcomen Society for the History of Engineering and Technology, *Transactions* 16 (1933–1934):4–6; Bedini, "Science Museums," pp. 20–21; Ferguson, "Technical Museums," p. 31; Ornstein, *Scientific Societies,* p. 155; *Museums of the World: A Directory,* compiled by Eleanor Braun, pp. 78–79; *Guide des Musées de Paris . . .* (Fribourg, Switzerland, 1970), p. 135; Alexis Blanc, "The Technological Museum of the Conservatoire des Arts et Métiers, Paris," *Museum* 20 (1967):208–213. Concise but up to date and perceptive is Victor J. Danilov, "European Science and Technology Museums," *Museum News* 54 (July/August 1976):34–37, 71–72
5. *Musées de Paris,* p. 135; Archie F. Key, *Beyond Four Walls: The Origins and Development of Canadian Museums* (Toronto, 1974), pp. 46–47; Louis de Broglie, "Scientific Museology and the Palais de la Découverte," *Museum* 2 (1949):141–149; André Léveillé, "The History of Sciences in the Palais de la Découverte," *Museum* 7 (1954): 195–201; A. J. Rose, "The Palais de la Découverte, Paris," *Museum* 20 (1967):204–207; Danilov,

"European Science and Technology Museums," p. 37; International Committee, Museums of Science and Technology, *Guide-Book of Museums of Science and Technology* (Prague, 1974), pp. 201–208.

6. Kenneth W. Luckhurst, *The Story of Exhibitions*, pp. 83–116; Christopher Hobhouse, *1851 and the Crystal Palace* (New York, 1937), 1–9, 24–40, 43–61, 150–165; Hector Bolitho, *Albert, Prince Consort* (Indianapolis, 1964), 117, 119–120, 125–128; Ferguson, "Technical Museums," pp. 30, 32–33, 35–39; Lord Amulree, "The Museum as an Aid to the Encouragement of Arts, Manufactures, and Commerce," *Museums Journal* 39 (November 1939):350–356; Kenneth Hudson, *A Social History of Museums*, pp. 41–47.
7. Dickinson, "Museums and Engineering," pp. 1–12; Ferguson, "Technical Museums," pp. 38–39; Richards, *Industrial Museum*, pp. 12–19; W. T. O'Dea, "The Science Museum, London," *Museum* 7 (1954):154–160 and "New Galleries at the Science Museum, London," *Museum* 16 (1963):198–204; W. T. O'Dea and L. A. West, "Editorial: Museums of Science and Industry," *Museum* 20 (1967):150–157, 190–193; H. W. Dickinson, "The New Buildings of the Science Museum," *Museums Journal* 27 (May 1928):336–341; "The Children's Gallery at the Science Museum," *Museums Journal* 31 (January 1932):442–444; E. E. B. Mackintosh, "Special Exhibitions at the Science Museum," *Museums Journal* 37 (October 1937):317–327; Herman Shaw, "Science Museums," *Museums Journal* 46 (December 1946):169–173 and "The Science Museum and Its Public," *Museums Journal* 49 (August 1949):105–113; F. Sherwood Taylor, "The Physical Sciences and the Museum," *Museums Journal* 51 (October 1951):169–176 and "Children and Science in the Museum," *Museums Journal* 55 (November 1955):202–207; Frank Greenaway, "A New Chemistry Gallery at the Science Museum . . . ," *Museums Journal* 64 (June 1964):59–67; International Committee, Museums of Science and Technology, *Guidebook, 1974*, pp. 373–381.
8. Richards, *Industrial Museum*, pp. 20–32, 70–110; Ferguson, "Technical Museums," pp. 30, 41–42; Karl Bassler, "Deutsches Museum: Museum of Science and Technology," *Museum* 2 (1949):171–179 and "Heavy Current Electrotechnology: A New Department of the Deutsches Museum," *Museum* 7 (1954):161–166; three articles by Hermann Auer: "The Deutsches Museum, Munich," *Museum* 20 (1967):199–201; "Problems of Science and Technology Museums: The Experience of the Deutsches Museum, Munich," *Museum* 21 (1968):128–139; "Museums of the Natural and Exact Sciences," *Museum* 26 (1974):68–75. See also "Oskar von Miller," *Museums Journal* 34 (June 1934):76–79.

Richards, *Industrial Museum*, pp. 33-45, 111-117; "Technisches Museum fur Industrie und Gwerbe, Wien," *Museum* 5 (1952):198; H. Philip Spratt, "Tekniska Museet; A New Science Museum Opened in Stockholm," *Museums Journal* 36 (September 1936):243–245; "The Technical Museum, Stockholm," *Museums Journal* 45 (April 1945):4–6; Thorsten Althin, "The Automarium of the Tekniska Museum, Stockholm," *Museum* 7 (1954):167–173; S. Strandh, "The Museum of Science and Technology, Stockholm," *Museum* 20 (1967):188–190; International Committee, Museums of Science and Technology, *Guidebook, 1974*, pp. 81–104, 253–276.

10. Charles S. Keyser, *Fairmount Park and the International Exhibition at Philadelphia* (Philadelphia, 1876), pp. 1–82; Lynne Vincent Cheney, "1876: The Eagle Screams," *American Heritage* 25 (April 1974):15–35, 98–99; Luckhurst, *Story of Exhibitions*, pp. 52, 124–125, 136–137, 175, 190, 202, 206.
11. Paul H. Oehser, *The Smithsonian Institution*, pp. 49–57, 189–190, 193–194, 196–197; Geoffrey T. Hellman, *The Smithsonian Institution, pp. 97–98*; Walter Karp, *The Smithsonian Institution*, pp. 55–69, 75–93; Gene Gurney, *The Smithsonian Institution: A Picture*

Story of Its Buildings, Exhibits and Activities (New York, 1964), pp. 7–22, 62–97, 99–102; National Museum of History and Technology, *Exhibits in the Museum of History and Technology: An Illustrated Tour* (Washington, 1968), pp. 40–41, 45–51, 60–63, 74–127; O'Dea and West, "Museums of Science and Technology," pp. 150–157; Frank A. Taylor, "The Museums of Science and Technology in the United States," *Museum* 20 (1967):158–163; *Museums Journal* 27 (April 1927):327; *Museums Journal* 28 (December 1928):204; *Museums Journal 48* (November 1948):174; Robert P. Multhauf, "A Museum Case History: The Department of Science and Technology of the United States Museum of History and Technology," *Technology and Culture* 6 (Winter 1965):47–58; Finn, "Science Museum Today," pp. 74–82.

12. Herman Kogan, *A Continuing Marvel: The Story of the Museum of Science and Industry* (Garden City, N.Y., 1973), p. 10.
13. Kogan, *Continuing Marvel*, p. 95.
14. Kogan, *Continuing Marvel*, esp. pp. 9–11, 18–19, 30, 43, 45–55, 71, 87, 89, 95, 98–101, 111–113, 115, 117–120, 124–129, 131–133, 134, 138–143, 145–157, 162–163, 174, 185, 194–195, 197–199, 205; Lenox Riley Lohr, "Publicity and Public Relations," *Museum* 4 (1951):229–233; Daniel M. MacMaster, "The Museum of Science and Industry, Chicago," *Museum* 20 (1967): 167–168; Brooke Hindle, "Museum Treatment of Industrialization: History, Problems, Opportunities," *Curator* 15 (1972):206–219, esp. 216; Ferguson, "Technical Museums," pp. 42–46; Victor J. Danilov, "Under the Microscope," *Museum News* 52 (March 1974):37–44, esp. p. 37; International Committee, Museums of Science and Technology, *Guidebook, 1974*, pp. 169–176.
15. Henry Ford Museum Staff, *Greenfield Village and Henry Ford Museum* (New York, 1972), p. 6; Greenfield Village and Henry Ford Museum, *Selected Treasures* (Dearborn, Mich., 1969), pp. 4, 6.
16. Henry Ford Museum Staff, *Greenfield Village and Henry Ford Museum*, pp. 6–25, 46, 50–53, 70–91, 98–103, 142–217; Greenfield Village and Henry Ford Museum, *Selected Treasures*, pp. 1–79; William Greenleaf, *From These Beginnings: The Early Philanthropies of Henry and Edsel Ford, 1911–1936* (Detroit, 1964), pp. 71–112; Allan Nevins and Frank Ernest Hill, *Ford: Expansion and Challenge, 1915–1933* (New York, 1957), pp. 497, 500–506; Ferguson, "Technical Museums," p. 42; Hindle, "Museum Treatment of Industrialization," pp. 210–211.
17. Bruce Sinclair, *Philadelphia's Philosopher Mechanics: A History of the Franklin Institute, 1824–1865* (Baltimore, 1974), pp. 39–41, 93–96, 100–103, 259–261; I. M. Levitt, "The Science Teaching Museum of the Franklin Institute, Philadelphia," *Museum* 20 (1967): 169–171; Robert W. Neatherby, "Education and the Franklin Institute Science Museum," *Museums Journal* 64 (June 1964):50–58; Ferguson, "Technical Museums," pp. 34–35; Hindle, "Museum Treatment of Industrialization," p. 216; Danilov, "Under the Microscope," pp. 37–38; International Committee, Museums of Science and Technology, *Guidebook, 1974*, pp. 145–154.
18. Key, *Beyond Four Walls*, p. 264.
19. Key, *Beyond Four Walls*, pp. 263–265; Archie F. Key, "Canada's Museum Explosion," *Museums Journal* 67 (June 1967):26–27; O'Dea and West, "Museums of Science and Technology," pp. 150–157; International Committee, Museums of Science and Technology, *Guidebook, 1974*, pp. 121–128; Douglas N. Ormand, "The Ontario Science Centre, Toronto," *Museum* 26 (1974):76–85.
20. Ainar Stenklo, "The Stora Kopparbergwerks Museum, Falun (Sweden)," *Museum* 20 (1967):218–219; D. E. Hogan, "The Pilkington Glass Museum, St. Helens (United Kingdom)," *Museum* 20 (1967):220–221; J. F. Schouten, "The Philips Evoluon, Eindho-

ven (Netherlands)," *Museum* 20 (1967):222–225; International Committee, Museums of Science and Technology, *Guidebook, 1974*, pp. 285–292.

21. Hindle, "Museum Treatment of Industrialization," pp. 206–219; George Basalla, "Museums and Technological Utopianism," *Curator* 17 (1974):105–118; N. W. Bertenshaw, "Museums of Science and Industry—Whither?" *Museums Journal* 64 (June 1964):68–78; Finn, "Science Museum Today," pp. 74–82; Victor J. Danilov, "Science/Technology Museums Come of Age," *Curator* 16 (1973):183–219 and his "Under the Microscope," pp. 37–44 and "European Science and Technology Museums," pp. 34–37, 71–72.

Notes, Chapter 5

1. Niels von Holst, *Creators, Collectors and Connoisseurs*, pp. 92, 106; Francis Henry Taylor, *The Taste of Angels*, pp. 77–78; Germain Bazin, *The Museum Age*, pp. 56–58; Alma S. Wittlin, *Museums: In Search of a Usable Future*, p. 37.
2. Taylor, *Taste of Angels*, p. 193; Bazin, *Museum Age*, pp. 65–67.
3. Bazin, *Museum Age*, pp. 102–104; Holst, *Creators*, p. 92.
4. Bazin, *Museum Age*, p. 230; Hans Huth, "Pierre Eugène du Simitière and the Beginnings of the American Historical Museum," pp. 315–325; Charles Coleman Sellers, *Charles Willson Peale*, pp. 213, 264–265, 303, 334–344; John H. Demer, "The Portrait Busts of John H. I. Browere," *Antiques* 110 (July 1976):111–117; E. P. Alexander, *The Museum: A Living Book of History* (Detroit, 1959), pp. 4–5, 7–8; E. P. Alexander, "An Art Gallery in Frontier Wisconsin," *Wisconsin Magazine of History* 29 (March 1946):281–300.
5. Wittlin, *Museums: In Search*, p. 15.
6. Bazin, *Museum Age*, pp. 225–227; Germain Bazin, *The Louvre*, pp. 61–66; Gerald Van der Kemp, "The National Museum of Versailles," *Museum* 12 (1959):159–164.
7. Robert L. Scribner, "Born to Battle," *American Heritage* 5 (Spring 1954):32–40.
8. Bazin, *Museum Age*, p. 225; Ned J. Burns, "The History of Dioramas," *Museum News* 17 (February 15, 1940):8–12; E. V. Gatacre, "The Limits of Professional Design," *Museums Journal* 76 (December 1976):95; Sellers, *Peale*, pp. 205–211; Oliver W. Larkin, *Art and Life in America* (New York, 1949), pp. 112–113.
9. Larkin, *Art and Life*, p. 13; Sellers, *Peale*, pp. 204–211; Porter Butts, *Art in Wisconsin . . .* (Madison, Wisc., 1936), pp. 53–63, 178–181.
10. Bazin, *Museum Age*, pp. 173–174; Holst, *Creators*, pp. 234–241.
11. John Summerson, *Heavenly Mansions; and Other Essays on Architecture* (London, 1949), pp. 135–158; H. F. Chettle, "Ancient Monuments," *Quarterly Review* 269 (October 1937):228–245; Paul Leon, *La vie des monuments français: destruction, restoration* (Paris, 1951), pp. 63–117, 188–211; Henry James, *A Little Tour of France* (Boston, 1900), pp. 191–207.
12. Hermann Heinrich Frese, *Anthropology and the Public*, pp. 11, 12; P. H. Pott, *National Museum of Ethnology, Leiden, 1837–1962*, pp. 4–5; Mats Rehnberg, *The Nordiska Museet and Skansen;* Bo Lagercrantz, "A Great Museum Pioneer of the Nineteenth Century," *Curator* 7 (1964):179–184; Iorwerth C. Peate, *Folk Museums* (Cardiff, 1948), pp. 15–21; Peter Michelson, "The Outdoor Museum and Its Educational Program," in Seminar on Preservation and Restoration, Williamsburg, Va., 1963, *Historic Preservation Today* (Charlottesville, Va., 1966), pp. 201–217 and also comment by E. P. Alexander, pp. 218–224; F. A. Bather, "The Triumph of Hazelius," *Museums Journal* 16 (December 1916):136; Holger Rasmussen, editor, *Dansk Folkemuseum und Frilandsmuseet . . .*

(Copenhagen, 1966), pp. 7–10; *The Sandvig Collections: Guide to the Open Air Museum* (Lillehammer, 1963); Reidar Kjellberg, "Scandinavian Open Air Museums," *Museum News* 39 (December 1960/January 1961):18–22; Peter Holm, "The Old Town: A Folk Museum in Denmark," *Museums Journal* 37 (April 1937):1–9. The growth of the outdoor museum in Europe is well shown in Adelhart Zippelius, *Handbuch der europaischen Freilichtmuseen* (Köln, 1975).

13. Kenneth W. Luckhurst, *The Story of Exhibitions*, pp. 83–116; Charles R. Richards, *Industrial Art and the Museum*, pp. 5–8, 10–20; *Das Schweizerische Landesmuseum, 1898–1948 . . .* (Zurich, 1948).
14. Alexander, *The Museum*, pp. 1–9; Julian P. Boyd, "State and Local Historical Societies in the United States," *American Historical Review* 40 (October, 1934):10–37; Leslie W. Dunlap, *American Historical Societies, 1790–1860* (Madison, Wis., 1944); R. W. G. Vail, *Knickerbocker Birthday: A Sesquicentennial History of the New-York Historical Society, 1804–1954* (New York, 1954), pp. 33, 52–53, 93, 108–111, 126–128; Walter Muir Whitehill, *Independent Historical Societies: An Enquiry into Their Research and Publication Functions and Their Financial Future* (Boston, 1962).
15. New York (State) Legislature, Assembly, *Select Committee on the Petition of Washington Irving and Others to Preserve Washington's Headquarters in Newburgh*, No. 356, March 27, 1839, pp. 1–5; Richard Caldwell, *A True History of the Acquisition of Washington's Headquarters at Newburgh, by the State of New York* (Salisbury Mills, N.Y., 1887), pp. 7–41; Charles B. Hosmer, Jr., *Presence of the Past: A History of the Preservation Movement in the United States Before Williamsburg* (New York, 1965), pp. 35–37.
16. Gerald W. Johnson, *Mount Vernon: The Story of a Shrine . . .* (New York, 1953), pp. 8–11; Hosmer, *Presence of the Past*, pp. 44–62.
17. Hosmer, *Presence of the Past*, pp. 255–257; E. P. Alexander, "Sixty Years of Historic Preservation: The Society for the Preservation of New England Antiquities," *Old-Time New England* 61 (1970–71):14–19.
18. William C. Everhart, *The National Park Service* (New York, 1972), pp. 33, 74–79, 249–260; U.S. Council of Mayors, *With Heritage So Rich: A Report . . . on Historic Preservation . . .* (New York, 1966), pp. 204–208; American Association of Museums, *The Official Museum Directory, 1977: United States and Canada* (Washington, 1976), pp. 819–871.
19. Raymond B. Fosdick, *John D. Rockefeller, Jr.: A Portrait* (New York, 1956), pp. 272–301; E. P. Alexander, *The Interpretation Program of Colonial Williamsburg* (Williamsburg, 1971), pp. 1–46; E. P. Alexander, "Restorations," in William B. Hesseltine and Donald R. McNeil, editors, *In Support of Clio: Essays in Memory of Herbert A. Kellar* (Madison, Wis., 1958), pp. 195–214.
20. William Greenleaf, *From These Beginnings*, pp. 71–112; Allan Nevins and Frank Ernest Hill, *Ford: Expansion and Challenge, 1915–1933*, pp. 497–506, 614; *Guidebook of Greenfield Village* (Dearborn, Mich., 1957), p. 1; *Greenfield Village and the Henry Ford Museum;* Alexander, "Restorations," pp. 201–204.
21. George Brown Goode, "Museum History and Museums of History," in Smithsonian Institution, *Annual Report for 1897*, Part II (Washington, D.C., 1901), pp. 63–82; Lelja Dobronić, "In Search of a New Type of Historical Museum," *Museum* 7 (1954):235–242; G. R. Lowther, "Perspective and Historical Museums," *Museums Journal* 59 (January 1959):224–228; Loris S. Russell, "Problems and Potentialities of the History Museum," *Curator* 6 (1963):341–349; John Hale, "Museums and the Teaching of History," *Museum* 21 (1968):67–68; Jean-Yves Veillard, "The Problem of the History Museum from an Experiment in the Musée de Bretagne, Rennes," *Museum* 24 (1972):193–203;

George-Henri Rivière, "Role of Museums of Art and Human and Social Sciences," *Museum* 25 (1973):26–44.

Notes, Chapter 6

1. American Association of Museums, *Museum Accreditation: Professional Standards*. By Marilyn Hicks Fitzgerald (Washington, 1973), p. 8; A. W. Hill, "The History and Functions of Botanic Gardens," pp. 185–240; Edward S. Hyams and William MacQuitty, *Great Botanical Gardens of the World*, pp. 12–13; Edward S. Hyams, *A History of Gardens and Gardening* (New York, 1971), pp. 9–125; George H. M. Lawrence, "The Historical Role of the Botanic Garden," *Longwood Program Seminars* 1 (1968–69):43–44; Howard S. Irwin, "Botanical Gardens in the Decades Ahead," *Curator* 16 (1973):45–55; Ulysses Prentice Hedrick, *A History of Horticulture in America to 1860* (New York, 1950), pp. 3–4; Donald Wyman, "The Arboretums and Botanical Gardens of North America," *Chronica Botanica* 10 (Summer 1947):405–408.
2. Hyams and MacQuitty, *Great Gardens*, pp. 18–22; Hill, "History and Functions," pp. 191–192, 194, 225; Lawrence, "Historical Role," pp. 34–35.
3. Hyams and MacQuitty, *Great Gardens*, p. 23; Hyams, *Gardens and Gardening*, pp. 126–128; Hill, "History and Functions," pp. 192–195, 226; Lawrence, "Historical Role," p. 34.
4. Hyams and MacQuitty, *Great Gardens*, pp. 34–43; Hyams, *Gardens and Gardening*, pp. 128–130; Lawrence, "Historical Role," pp. 34–35.
5. Hyams and MacQuitty, *Great Gardens*, pp. 23, 82–85, 102–103; Hill, "History and Functions," pp. 192, 194, 197–201, 233; Lawrence, "Historical Role," p. 34; William C. Steere, "Research as a Function of a Botanical Garden," *Longwood Program Seminars* 1 (1968–69):43–47.
6. Hyams and MacQuitty, *Great Gardens*, pp. 107–108; Hill, "History and Functions," pp. 197, 203–206; Lawrence, "Historical Role," p. 35; Steere, "Research as a Function," p. 44. On the Wardian case, see Kenneth Lemmoy, *The Golden Age of Plant Explorers* (London, 1968), pp. 54, 183–184, 217.
7. W. B. Turrill, *The Royal Botanic Gardens, Kew: Past and Present* (London, 1959), pp. 18–21; Mea Allan, *The Hookers of Kew, 1785–1911* (London, 1967), pp. 36, 151; Hyams and MacQuitty, *Great Gardens*, pp. 104–105; Hyams, *Gardens and Gardening*, pp. 250–251; Hill, "History and Functions," pp. 206–207, 235.
8. Turrill, *Kew*, pp. 21–34; Mea Allan, *Hookers*, p. 36; Hyams and MacQuitty, *Great Gardens*, pp. 108–109; Hill, "History and Functions," p. 207.
9. Turrill, *Kew*, pp. 23–24; Mea Allan, *Hookers*, p. 36; Hyams and MacQuitty, *Great Gardens*, pp. 108–109; Lawrence, "Historical Role," pp. 35–36; Hill, "History and Functions," pp. 207–208.
10. Turrill, *Kew*, pp. 20–21, 24–32, 86–89; Mea Allan, *Hookers*, pp. 77–79, 88–89, 105–106, 109–110, 138–141, 146–152, 178–179, 200–201, 205–206; Hyams and MacQuitty, *Great Gardens*, pp. 109–110; Hill, "History and Functions," pp. 208–209.
11. Turrill, *Kew*, pp. 30–35, 47–55, 59–61, 65–66; Mea Allan, *Hookers*, pp. 211–236; Hyams and MacQuitty, *Great Gardens*, pp. 110–115.
12. Turrill, *Kew*, pp. 237–239.
13. Turrill, *Kew*, pp. 35–37; Mea Allan, *Hookers*, pp. 224, 228, 230–231, 237; Hyams and MacQuitty, *Great Gardens*, pp. 115–121; Steere, "Research as a Function," pp. 44–45; Lanning Roper on Wakehurst, *London Times*, July 27, 1975.
14. Harold Roy Fletcher and William H. Brown, *The Royal Botanic Garden, Edinburgh,*

1670–1970 (Edinburgh, 1970); Hyams and MacQuitty, *Great Gardens*, pp. 44–53; Hyams, *Gardens and Gardening*, p. 287; Hill, "History and Functions," pp. 201–203.

15. Hyams and MacQuitty, *Great Gardens*, pp. 82–85.
16. Hyams and MacQuitty, *Great Gardens*, pp. 92–101.
17. Hyams and MacQuitty, *Great Gardens*, pp. 76–81; Hill, "History and Functions," p. 209.
18. Hyams and MacQuitty, *Great Gardens*, pp. 122–125.
19. Hyams and MacQuitty, *Great Gardens*, pp. 174–177; Hyams, *Gardens and Gardening*, p. 281; Stanwin G. Shetler, *The Komarov Botanical Institute: 250 Years of Russian Research* (Washington, D.C., 1967), pp. 127–128, 180–183.
20. Hyams and MacQuitty, *Great Gardens*, p. 211; Hill, "History and Functions," pp. 210–212.
21. Hyams and MacQuitty, *Great Gardens*, pp. 220–227; Hill, "History and Functions," pp. 212–213.
22. Hyams and MacQuitty, *Great Gardens*, pp. 200–210; Hyams, *Gardens and Gardening*, p. 258; Hill, "History and Functions," p. 214.
23. Hyams and MacQuitty, *Great Gardens*, pp. 194–199, 211–219, 244–253; Hill, "History and Functions," pp. 210–211, 213–215.
24. Hyams and MacQuitty, *Great Gardens*, pp. 254–265; Hill, "History and Functions," p. 215.
25. Hyams and MacQuitty, *Great Gardens*, pp. 232–238.
26. Hedrick, *History of Horticulture*, pp. 71–72, 85–92, 207–209, 423–424; Joseph Ewan, editor, *A Short History of Botany in the United States* (New York and London, 1969), pp. 2–5, 33–34, 38–39, 132–133; Christine Chapman Robbins, *David Hosack, Citizen of New York* (Philadelphia, 1964), pp. 26, 44–99, 195–197; Hyams, *Gardens and Gardening*, p. 209.
27. Hyams and MacQuitty, *Great Gardens*, pp. 148–152; Carroll C. Calkins, editor, *Great Gardens in America* (New York and Waukesha, Wis., 1969), pp. 242–251; Ewan, *Short History*, pp. 43–44; Wyman, "American Arboretums and Botanical Gardens," pp. 437–438.
28. Hyams and MacQuitty, *Great Gardens*, pp. 132–136; Stephane Barry Sutton, *Charles Sprague Sargent and the Arnold Arboretum* (Cambridge, Mass., 1970); Wyman, "American Arboretums and Botanical Gardens," pp. 430–433.
29. Hyams and MacQuitty, *Great Gardens*, p. 137; Irwin, "Botanical Gardens in the Decades Ahead," pp. 45–55; Wyman, "American Arboretums and Botanical Gardens," pp. 442–444.
30. Hyams and MacQuitty, *Great Gardens*, pp. 156–163; Calkins, *Great American Gardens*, pp. 272–281; Wyman, "American Arboretums and Botanical Gardens," pp. 422–423; William Hertrich, *The Huntington Botanical Gardens, 1905–1949* (San Marino, Calif., 1949).
31. Hyams and MacQuitty, *Great Gardens*, pp. 137–141; Charles Stuart Gager, "The Educational Work of Botanic Gardens," Brooklyn Botanic Garden, *Contributions* 1 (1911):73–85; Frances M. Miner, "The Botanic Garden—from the Educator's Viewpoint", *Longwood Program Seminars* 4 (1972):14–19; Wyman, "American Arboretums and Botanical Gardens," pp. 429–431.
32. Hyams and MacQuitty, *Great Gardens*, pp. 142–147; Hyams, *Gardens and Gardening*, p. 312; Calkins, *Great American Gardens*, pp. 168–175; Wyman, "American Arboretums and Botanical Gardens," pp. 447–448; Longwood Gardens, *A Visit to Longwood Gardens*, 8th ed. (Kennett Square, Pa., 1970); Longwood Gardens, *Fountains*

of Longwood Gardens (Kennett Square, Pa., 1960); Lanning Roper, "Longwood Gardens: A Twentieth-Century American Pleasure Ground," Royal Horticultural Society, *Journal* 82 (May 1957):1–9.

33. Hyams and MacQuitty, *Great Gardens*, pp. 164–169; Wyman, "American Arboretums and Botanical Gardens," pp. 425–426.
34. Irwin, "Botanical Gardens in the Decades Ahead," pp. 45–55; George S. Avery, Jr., "Botanic Gardens—What Role Today?: An 'Operation Bootstraps' Opportunity for Botanists," in William Campbell Steere, editor, *Fifty Years of Botany: Golden Jubilee Volume of the Botanical Society of America* (New York, 1958), pp. 536–544; Russell J. Seibert, "Arboreta and Botanical Gardens in the Field of Plant Sciences and Human Welfare," in Steere, editor, *Fifty Years of Botany*, pp. 545–549.
35. James Fisher, *Zoos of the World: The Story of Animals in Captivity* (Garden City, N.Y., 1967), pp. 21–57; Bernard Livingston, *Zoo: Animals, People, Places* (New York, 1974), pp. 15–35, 71, 233; Harry Gersh, *The Animals Next Door: A Guide to Zoos and Aquariums of the Americas* (New York, 1971), pp. 1–14; *International Zoo Yearbook* 14 (1974):257–327; Wilfrid Blunt, *The Ark in the Park: The Zoo in the Nineteenth Century* (London, 1976), pp. 10, 16–31.
36. Fisher, *Zoos of the World*, pp. 138, 164–169; Livingston, *Zoo*, pp. 137–152; Gersch, *Animals Next Door*, pp. 14–15.
37. William Bridges, *Gathering of the Animals: An Unconventional History of the New York Zoological Society* (New York, 1974), pp. 382–383.
38. *International Zoo Yearbook* 14 (1974):257–327; Livingston, *Zoo*, pp. 236, 239–240, 280–282; Gersch, *Animals Next Door*, pp. 15–16, 70, 78, 85, 95–96, 111, 115, 120–121, 135, 141, 148–149.
39. Bridges, *Gathering of of the Animals*, esp. pp. 16–17, 20–38, 57–60, 99–122, 223–230, 387–388, 412, 414, 440–486, 505; Livingston, *Zoo*, pp. 263–279; American Association of Zoological Parks and Aquariums, *Zoos and Aquariums in the Americas* (Wheeling, W. Va., 1974), p. 97; "Elephant and Tiger and Rhinoceros Roaming the Bronx? Preposterous!" *New York Times*, August 17, 1977.
40. *International Zoo Yearbook* 14 (1974):273, 308; Livingston, *Zoo*, pp. 93–120; *Zoos and Aquariums in the Americas*, p. 23; William Mortison, "Afroamericanus: A New Species of Zoo," *Museum News* 51 (November 1972):28–33.
41. Randall L. Eaton, William York, and William Dredge, "The Lion Country Safari and Its Role in Conservation, Education and Research," *International Zoo Yearbook* 10 (1970):171–172; Livingston, *Zoo*, pp. 121–136.
42. The best publication to show the changing purposes of zoos and their detailed problems is *International Zoo Yearbook*, published by the Zoological Society of London, 1 (1961)—. Also helpful for the research side of the zoo is Heini Hediger, *Man and Animal in the Zoo: Zoo Biology* (New York, 1969). A concise discussion of the purposes and problems of zoos is Gersch, *Animals Next Door*, pp. 17–67. Extremely negative in its approach but a realistic listing of zoo deficiencies and problems that everyone should read is Peter Batten and Deborah Stanel, *Living Trophies* (New York, 1976).

Notes, Chapter 7

1. Quoted in Douglas and Elizabeth Rigby, *Lock, Stock and Barrel*, p. 6.
2. Maurice Rheims, *The Strange Life of Objects*, p. 43.
3. On the collector's drives, see Rigby and Rigby, *Lock, Stock and Barrel*, pp. 3–82; Rheims, *Strange Life of Objects*, pp. 17–49; Pierre Cabane, *The Great Collectors* (New York, 1963), pp. xii–xviii; Alma S. Wittlin, *Museums: In Search of a Usable Future*,

pp. 3–60; W. G. Constable, *Art Collecting in the United States of America: An Outline and History* (London, 1964), pp. 97–99. Two fascinating accounts of American collecting are Aline B. Saarinen, *The Proud Possessors: The Lives, Times and Tastes of Some Adventurous American Art Collectors* (New York, 1958) and Russell Lynes, *The Taste-Makers* (New York, 1954).

4. For contrasting points of view toward the place of the art museum, see Thomas P. F. Hoving, "Branch Out!" pp. 15–20, and Sherman E. Lee, "The Idea of an Art Museum," pp. 75–79. A good comprehensive summary is Joshua C. Taylor, "The Art Museum in the United States," in American Assembly, *On Understanding Art Museums*, edited by Sherman E. Lee (Englewood Cliffs, N.J., 1975), pp. 34–67.
5. E. McClung Fleming, "Early American Decorative Arts as Social Documents," *Mississippi Valley Historical Review* 45 (1958):276–284; John Chavis, "The Artifact and the Study of History," *Curator* 7 (1964):156–162. Thomas J. Schlereth, "Historical Houses as Learning Laboratories . . . ," *History News* 33 (April 1978): Technical Leaflet no. 104.
6. G. Ellis Burcaw, *Introduction to Museum Work* (Nashville, Tenn., 1975), pp. 47–83.
7. An exceptionally useful treatment of field collecting is United Nations Educational, Scientific and Cultural Organization, *Field Manual for Museums* (Paris, 1970).
8. Carl E. Guthe, *The Management of Small History Museums* (Nashville, Tenn., 1959), p. 16.
9. Guthe, *Small History Museums*, pp. 13–23; Eugene F. Kramer, "Collecting Historical Artifacts: An Aid for Small Museums," *History News* 25 (August 1970): Technical Leaflet no. 6; Arthur C. Parker, *A Manual for History Museums* (New York, 1935), pp. 9–29; Laurence Vail Coleman, *The Museum in America*, 1:118–121.
10. G. Ellis Burcaw, "Active Collecting in History Museums," *Museum News* 45 (March 1967):21–22 and his *Museum Work*, pp. 61–62; Coleman, *Museum in America*, 2:244–245.
11. Coleman, *Museum in America*, 1:120–121.
12. Ned J. Burns, *National Park Service Field Manual for Museums* (Washington, D.C., 1941), pp. 26–40, 343–408; Ralph H. Lewis, *Manual for Museums* (Washington, D.C., 1976), pp. 182–203; National Park Service, *Independence National Historic Park Interpretive Prospectus* (Philadelphia, 1970) and *Master Plan* (Philadelphia, 1971).
13. Coleman, *Museum in America*, 2:236–241; Burns, *Field Manual*, pp. 107–108; Guthe, *Small History Museums*, pp. 25, 27; Burcaw, *Museum Work*, pp. 50–51.
14. Germain Bazin, *The Museum Age*, pp. 16–17, 84–86, 107–114.
15. Rheims, *Strange Life of Objects*, pp. 98–101, 105–110, 173–202; Constable, *Art Collecting*, pp. 5–6, 42–43, 99–104, 145. A brilliant and entertaining biography is Samuel N. Behrman, *Duveen* (New York, 1952), and other excellent accounts by dealers themselves are René Gimpel, *Diary of an Art Dealer* (New York, 1966) and Germain Seligman, *Merchants of Art: 1880–1960: Eighty Years of Professional Collecting* (New York, 1961). For conditions today among dealers and auction houses, see Robert S. Warshaw, "Law in the Marketplace," *Museum News* 53 (May 1975):18–23, 50–51; Bonnie Burnham, *Art In Crisis* (New York, 1975), pp. 191–214.
16. Rheims, *Strange Life of Objects*, p. 152; Burnham, *Art in Crisis*, p. 204.
17. Otto Kurz, *Fakes: A Handbook for Collectors and Students*, 2nd ed., rev. and enl. (New York, 1967), pp. 329–334; George Savage, *Forgeries, Fakes, and Reproductions: A Handbook for the Art Dealer and Collector* (New York, 1963), pp. 206–209, 221–222, 227, 231–232; Cabane, *Great Collectors*, pp. 153–157; Lawrence Jeppson, *The Fabulous Frauds: Fascinating Tales of Great Art Forgeries* (New York, 1970), pp. 149–195.
18. Paul Coremans, "The Museum Laboratory," pp. 94–96; Richard Buck, "On Conserva-

tion," *Museum News* 52 (March 1974):16–19; Savage, *Forgeries, Fakes, and Reproductions*, pp. 34, 227, 231; Kurz, *Fakes*, pp. 22–31; Thomas B. Brill and George J. Reilly, "Chemistry in the Museum," *Chemistry* 45 (May 1972):6–9; Clements L. Robertson, "The Visual and Optical Examination of Works of Art," *Museum News* 46 (December 1967):47–52: Technical Supplement no. 20.

19. Rheims, *Strange Life of Objects*, pp. 161–162.
20. Guthe, *Small History Museums*, p. 35.
21. The definitive book in this field is American Association of Museums, *Museum Registration Methods*, by Dorothy H. Dudley, Irma B. Wilkinson, and others, 3rd ed. (Washington, D.C., 1978). Of value for its clarity is Guthe, *Small History Museums*, pp. 28–37. Other sources worth examination are Burns, *Field Manual*, pp. 110–117; Laurence Vail Coleman, *Manual for Small Museums* (New York, 1927), pp. 173–186; John M. Graham II, "A Method of Museum Registration," *Museum News* 42 (April 1964):Technical Supplement no. 2; Robert R. Macdonald, "Toward a More Accessible Collection: Cataloguing at the Mercer Museum," *Museum News* 48 (February 1969):23–26; Marilyn Pink, *How to Catalogue Works of Art: A Guide for Private Collectors* (Los Angeles, 1972).
22. Robert G. Chenall, *Museum Cataloguing in the Computer Age* (Nashville, Tenn., 1975); Metropolitan Museum of Art Conference, *Computers and Their Potential Applications in Museums* (New York, 1968); "Museums and Computers: Strange Bedfellows," Special Issue, *Museum News* 51 (April 1973):13–36; David Vance, "Computers and Registration" in *Museum Registration Methods*, pp. 283–290 and "Museum Computer Network: The Second Phase," *Museum News* 48 (May 1970): 15–20; Geoffrey Romney, "IRGMA [Information Retrieval Group of the Museums Association]," *Museums Journal* 75 (December 1975):124–125. The State University of New York College at Stony Brook has a bimonthly newsletter *Spectra* (November 1974—) that contains current news on computer use in museums.
23. Coleman, *Museum in America*, 2:249–256; William Henry Flower, *Essays on Museums and Other Subjects Connected with Natural History*, pp. 30–53; *Exhibits in the Museum of History and Technology: An Illustrated Tour* (Washington, D.C., 1968), pp. 12–18; Thomas S. Buechner, "The Open Study-Storage Gallery," *Museum News* 40 (May 1962):34–37.
24. The most recent and excellent treatments of the subject are Karl E. Meyer, *The Plundered Past* (New York, 1973) and Burnham, *Art Crisis*.
25. Ann Zelle, "Acquisitions: Saving Whose Heritage?" *Museum News* 49 (April 1971):19–26.
26. Meyer, *Plundered Past*, pp. 102–106; Burnham, *Art Crisis*, pp. 146–147; John L. Hess, *The Grand Acquisitors* (Boston, 1974), pp. 137–138.
27. Metropolitan Museum of Art, *Report on Art Transactions, June 20, 1973* (New York, 1973), pp. 23–24; Meyer, *Plundered Past*, pp. 86–100; Burnham, *Art Crisis*, p. 137; Hess, *Grand Acquisitors*, pp. 141–151; Metropolitan Museum of Art, *The Euphronios Krater: A Report to the Members of the Corporation, March 7, 1974;* Thomas Hoving, *The Chase, the Capture: Collecting at the Metropolitan* (New York, 1975), pp. 40–56.
28. *New York Times*, October 26, 31, 1973. A good discussion of the effect of western civilization on African art is Burnham, *Art Crisis*, pp. 132–134.
29. Franklin Feldman and Stephen Weil, editors, *Art Works: Law, Policy, Practice* (New York, 1974), pp. 525–572; Meyer, *Plundered Past*, pp. 42, 271–273, 281–301; Burnham, *Art Crisis*, pp. 166–167, 182, 185–186.
30. Feldman and Weil, *Art Works*, pp. 627–661; "More on Acquisitions," *Museum News* 52

(September 1973):46–48; Meyer, *Plundered Past*, pp. 74–75, 254–262; Hoving, *The Chase, the Capture*, pp. 2–6. Perhaps the best discussion of both sides of the problem is Burnham, *Art Crisis*, pp. 135–152. Other disputes have arisen about museum display of American Indian materials including religious objects and skeletons. Nancy Oestreich Lurie, "American Indians and Museums: A Love-Hate Relationship," *The Old Northwest: A Journal of Regional Life and Letters* 2 (September 1976):235–251.

31. Kramer, "Collecting Historical Artifacts"; Helmuth J. Naumer and Aubyn Kendall, "Acquisitions and Old Lace," *Museum News* 51 (May 1973):40–42.
32. Feldman and Weil, *Art Works*, pp. 1115–1134; John Jacob, "The Sale or Disposal or Museum Objects," *Museums Journal* 71 (December 1971):112–116; Metropolitan Museum, *Report on Art Transactions;* Metropolitan Museum of Art, *Procedures for Deaccessioning and Disposal of Works of Art, June 20, 1973* (New York, 1973); "White Paper Published—Guidelines Emerge," *Museum News* 52 (September 1973):6. For the Museum of Modern Art and deaccessioning, see Feldman and Weil, *Art Works*, pp. 1119–1122; Russell Lynes, *Good Old Modern*, pp. 295–297.
33. "Forum on Acquisitions and Deaccessioning," *Museum News* 52 (September 1973):23.

Notes, Chapter 8

1. Germain Bazin, *The Museum Age*, p. 176; Joshua C. Taylor, "The Art Museum in America," pp. 54–55; Sheldon Keck, "Training for Engineers in Conservation," in International Institute for Conservation . . . , *Recent Advances in Conservation: Contributions to the IIC Rome Conference, 1961* (London, 1964), pp. 199–201; Richard D. Buck, "An Experiment in Cooperative Conservation," *Studies in Conservation* 2 (1955–56):101–109, and "Conservation Co-op," *Museum News* 51 (December 1972):26–29.
2. Harold J. Plenderleith and A. E. A. Werner, *The Conservation of Antiquities and Works of Art*. Shorter summaries of value are Paul Coremans, "The Museum Laboratory," and Hiroshi Daifuku, "Collections: Their Care and Storage," both in UNESCO, *The Organization of Museums*, pp. 93–118, 119–125.
3. Plenderleith and Werner, *Conservation*, pp. 1–18; Per E. Guldbeck, *The Care of Historical Collections: A Conservation Handbook for the Nonspecialist* (Nashville, Tenn., 1972), pp. 16–25; Nathan Stolow, "Environmental Security" and "Light and Its Effect on Museum Security," in Caroline K. Keck and others, *A Primer on Museum Security* (Cooperstown, N.Y., 1966), pp. 39–51, and "The Action of Environment on Museum Objects—Part I: Humidity, Temperature, Atmospheric Pollution; Part II: Light," *Curator* 9 (1966):175–185, 298–306; Robert L. Feller, "Control of Deteriorating Effects of Light upon Museum Objects," *Museum* 17 (1964):57–98.
4. W. G. Constable, "Curators and Conservation," *Studies in Conservation* 1 (April 1954):97–102, esp. p. 98.
5. Plenderleith and Werner, *Conservation*, pp. 60–63, 129–134; Richard D. Buck, "The Inspection of Art Objects and Trial Glossary for Describing Condition," in American Association of Museums, *Museum Registration Methods*, edited by Dorothy H. Dudley and Irma B. Wilkinson, rev. ed. (Washington, D.C., 1968), pp. 164–170.
6. Sheldon Keck, "A Little Training Can Be a Dangerous Thing," *Museum News* 52 (December 1973):40–42; Constable, "Curators and Conservation," pp. 98–99.
7. Frieda Kay Fall, *Art Objects: Their Care and Preservation—A Handbook for Museums and Collectors* (LaJolla, Cal., 1973), pp. 17–35, 146–148, 214–219; Daifuku, "Collections," pp. 122–124; Guldbeck, *Conservation for the Nonspecialist*, pp. 3–6; Robert P. Sugden,

Safeguarding Works of Art: Storage, Packing, Transportation and Insurance (New York, 1948), pp. 11–33. Two American museums provide model storage facilities—the Henry Francis du Pont Winterthur Museum, Winterthur, Del., and the Colonial Williamsburg Foundation, Williamsburg, Va. Jentina E. Leene, editor, *Textile Conservation* (London, 1972), pp. 122–126; Margaret A. Fikioris, "A Model for Textile Storage," *Museum News* 52 (November 1973):34–41; John M. Graham II, "Solving Storage Problems," *Museum News* 41 (December 1962):24–29; Mildred B. Lanier, "Storage Facilities at Colonial Williamsburg," *Museum News* 45 (February 1967):31–33.

8. The whole of Caroline Keck and others, *Primer in Museum Security*, should be read, as well as American Association of Museums, *Museum Registration Methods*, pp. 63–82; Fall, *Art Objects*, pp. 9–11; Eric B. Rowlison, "Rules for Handling Works of Art," *Museum News* 53 (April 1975):10–13; Constable, "Curators and Conservation," pp. 97–102; Sheldon Keck, "A Little Training," pp. 40–42; Walter S. Dunn, "Storing Your Collections: Problems and Solutions," *History News* 25 (June 1970):Technical Leaflet no. 5.
9. Constable, "Curators and Conservation," p. 102; Peter Michaels, "Lender Beware!" *Museum News* 43 (September 1964):11–12.
10. Caroline K. Keck, *Safeguarding Your Collection in Travel* (Nashville, Tenn., 1970), pp. 10–17; Sheldon Keck, "A Little Training," pp. 41–42; Louis Pomerantz, "Art Consumption," *Museum News* 49 (November 1970):10–11.
11. American Association of Museums, *Museum Registration Methods*, pp. 83–109, 240–253; Caroline Keck, *Safeguarding in Travel*, pp. 17–42; Guldbeck, *Conservation for the Nonspecialist*, pp. 26–30; Nathan Stolow, *Controlled Environment for Works of Art in Transit* (London, 1966), and "Some Studies on the Protection of Works of Art During Travel," in IIC *Rome Conference, 1961*, pp. 9–12; United Nations Educational, Scientific and Cultural Organization, *Temporary and Travelling Exhibitions* (Paris, 1963), pp. 80–109; W. A. Baunhoft, "The Package Engineer in the Museum," *Museum News* 44 (December 1965): 27–28; Frieda K. Fall, "New Industrial Packing Materials: Their Possible Uses for Museums," *Museum News* 44 (December 1965):47–52: Technical Supplement no. 10; Huntington T. Block and John B. Lawton, "Insurance," in Caroline Keck and others, *Primer on Museum Security*, pp. 15–38.
12. Page 41.
13. Good summaries of today's attitude toward conservation are A. E. A. Werner, "Perspectives in Conservation," *Museums Journal* 61 (December 1961):201–203; George L. Stout, "Thirty Years of Conservation: A Summary of Remarks to the I.I.C. American Group in New York, June 1963," *Studies in Conservation* 9 (1964):126–129.
14. International Institute for Conservation of Historic and Artistic Works—American Group, *The Murray Pease Report/Code of Ethics for Art Conservators* (New York, 1968), pp. 53–68; United Nations Educational, Scientific and Cultural Organization, *The Conservation of Cultural Property with Special Reference to Tropical Conditions* (Paris, 1968), pp. 24–25, 113, 130–131, 206, 307; Paul Coremans, "The Conservation of Paintings," *Museums Journal* 61 (September 1961):105–109; Elizabeth C. G. Packard, "The Preservation of Polychromed Wood Sculpture by the Wax Immersion and Other Methods," *Museum News* 46 (October 1967):47–52: Technical Supplement no. 19.
15. An extremely sane and lucid treatment of painting conservation is Caroline K. Keck, *A Handbook on the Care of Paintings* (Nashville, Tenn., 1965). It is a model popular presentation of a complex technical subject. Also of value are Plenderleith and Werner, *Conservation*, pp. 162–186; William Bornstead, "The Conservation and Restoration of Easel Paintings," in *Conservation and Tropical Conditions*, pp. 191–208;

Coremans, "Conservation of Paintings," pp. 105–109; Clements L. Robertson, "The Visual and Optical Examination of Works of Art," pp. 47–52.

16. Caroline Keck, *Care of Paintings*, pp. 65–68.
17. Caroline Keck, *Care of Paintings*, pp. 70–85; Gustav A. Berger, "Heat-Seal Lining of a Torn Painting with Beva 371," *Studies in Conservation* 20 (August 1975):126–151. An excellent film showing how paintings are restored is Colonial Williamsburg Foundation, *The Art of the Conservator*, 16 mm. sound, color, 57 minutes.
18. Caroline Keck, *Care of Paintings*, pp. 98–102.
19. Plenderleith and Werner, *Conservation*, pp. 53–64, 76–99; Caroline Keck, *Care of Paintings*, pp. 23–25, 30–35; Guldbeck, *Conservation for the Nonspecialist*, pp. 63–72; Anne E. Clapp, *Curatorial Care of Works of Art on Paper*, rev. ed. (Oberlin, Ohio, 1973); Francis W. Doloff and Roy L. Perkinson, *How to Care for Works of Art on Paper* (Boston, 1971). The transfer of the Flemish print is described in the last reference, pp. 35–40.
20. Plenderleith and Werner, *Conservation*, pp. 100–123; E. R. Beecher, "The Conservation of Textiles," in UNESCO, *Conservation and Tropical Conditions*, pp. 251–264; Leene, editor, *Textile Conservation*; Guldbeck, *Conservation for the Nonspecialist*, pp. 117–125; Jane C. Giffin, "Care of Textiles and Costumes: Cleaning and Storage Techniques," *History News* 25 (December 1970):Technical Leaflet no. 2; Caroline K. Keck, "Care of Textiles and Costumes: Adaptive Techniques for Basic Maintenance," *History News* 29 (February 1974): Technical Leaflet no. 71.
21. Plenderleith and Werner, *Conservation*, pp. 124–147; International Institute for Conservation of Historic and Artistic Works, New York Conference, 1970, vol. 2: *Conservation of Wooden Objects*, 2nd ed. (London, 1971); Guldbeck, *Conservation for the Nonspecialist*, pp. 73–86; William Merrill, "Wood Deterioration: Causes, Detection, and Prevention," *History News* 29 (August 1974): Technical Leaflet no. 77; Anders Franzen, "The Warship 'Vasa'," *American Scandinavian Review* 51 (March 1963):12–26; "The Warship *Vasa* Rises Again," *Archaeology* 14 (September 1961):217–218. See also Sven Bergstrom, "Preservation of the 'Wasa' Sails," in IIC, *Conservation in Archaeology and the Applied Arts . . . Stockholm Congress, 1975* (London, 1975), pp. 33–35; Ray M. Seborg and Robert B. Inverarity, "Conservation of 200-Year-Old Water-Logged Boats with Polyethylene Glycol," *Studies in Conservation* 7 (1962):111–119.
22. Plenderleith and Werner, *Conservation*, pp. 148–161; A. E. A. Werner, "The Care of Leather, Wood, Bone and Ivory, and Archival Material," in UNESCO, *Conservation and Tropical Conditions*, pp. 265–290; Guldbeck, *Conservation for the Nonspecialist*, pp. 134–137; Fall, *Art Objects*, pp. 165, 169; Walter Muir Whitehill, *Museum of Fine Arts*, 1:376, 2:487–488.
23. Plenderleith and Werner, *Conservation*, pp. 189–296; H. J. Plenderleith and G. Toracca, "The Conservation of Metals in the Tropics," in UNESCO, *Conservation and Tropical Conditions*, pp. 237–250; Guldbeck, *Conservation for the Nonspecialist*, pp. 98–116; Harold L. Peterson, "Conservation of Metals," *History News* 23 (February 1968): Technical Leaflet no. 10; Mrs. Dean A. Fales, Jr., "The Care of Antique Silver," *History News* 22 (February 1967): Technical Leaflet no. 40.
24. Plenderleith and Werner, *Conservation*, pp. 224–227; R. M. Organ, "The Reclamation of the Wholly-Mineralized Silver in the Ur Lyre," in Research Laboratory, Museum of Fine Arts, Boston, *Application of Science in Examination of Works of Art* (Boston, 1965), pp. 126–144.
25. Plenderleith and Werner, *Conservation*, pp. 249–250; R. M. Organ, "Aspects of Bronze Patina and Its Treatment," *Studies in Conservation* 8 (1963):1–9.
26. Plenderleith and Werner, *Conservation*, pp. 292–293.

27. Plenderleith and Werner, *Conservation*, pp. 299–333; R. V. Sneyers and P. J. de Henau, "The Conservation of Stone," in UNESCO, *Conservation and Tropical Conditions*, pp. 209–236; International Institute for Conservation of Historic and Artistic Works, New York Conference, 1970, vol. 1: *Conservation of Stone*, 2nd ed. (London, 1971); Guldbeck, *Conservation for the Nonspecialist*, pp. 138–140.
28. Plenderleith and Werner, *Conservation*, pp. 334–342; Ione Gedye, "Pottery and Glass," in UNESCO, *Conservation and Tropical Conditions*, pp. 109–114; Guldbeck, *Conservation for the Nonspecialist*, pp. 126–130.
29. Plenderleith and Werner, *Conservation*, pp. 343–351; Gedye, "Pottery and Glass," p. 113; Guldbeck, *Conservation for the Nonspecialist*, pp. 131–133; Robert H. Brill, "Crizzling—A Problem in Glass Conservation," in IIC, *Stockholm Congress, 1975*, pp. 122–134.

Notes, Chapter 9

1. A thorough study of museum research that considers practices in the United States, western Europe, and eastern Europe, including the Soviet Union, is Jiri Neustupny, *Museum and Research* (Prague, 1968). For his discussion of basic and applied research, see pp. 13, 21–26, 38–63. A good short treatment is Hiroshi Daifuku, "Museums and Research," pp. 68–72. Somewhat outdated but still valuable is Laurence Vail Coleman, *The Museum in America*, 2:369–386.
2. Edward M. Riley, "Local History Contributions and Techniques in the Study of . . . Williamsburg," American Association for State and Local History, *Bulletin* 2 (February 1959):235–244; Daifuku, "Museums and Research," pp. 70–71; Charles F. Montgomery, "The Role of the Museum in Research," *Historic Preservation* 14 (1962):100–103.
3. Neustupny, *Museum Research*, pp. 13, 22, 102–106.
4. Two excellent discussions are "The Role of the Research Museum in Science," *Curator* 3 (1960):310–360; 4 (1961):184–189; and "Research Museums in Natural History," *Museum News* 41 (November 1962):29–37; (December 1962):30–37. Subsequent citations to these sources will be by separate authors and titles. See also Edwin H. Colbert, "What Is a Museum?" *Curator* 4 (1961):138–146, esp. pp. 141–142; James A. Bateman, "The Functions of Museums of Biology," pp. 159–164; Neustupny, *Museum Research*, pp. 52, 61, 90–101; Daifuku, "Museums and Research," pp. 69–70.
5. Coleman, *Museum in America*, 2:369, 375, 377–379; American Museum of Natural History, "Science Policy Reports," *Curator* 14 (1971):235–240; Hugo G. Rodeck, "The University Museum and Biological Research," *Curator* 3 (1960):311–312; Edwin H. Colbert, "The Museum and Geological Research," *Curator* 3 (1960):317–326; William N. Fenton, "The Museum and Anthropological Research," *Curator* 3 (1960):327–354; Theodore H. Hubbell, "Research Functions of Natural History Museums," *Museum News* 41 (November 1962):29, M. Graham Netting, "Objectives of Museum Research in Natural History," *Museum News* 41 (November 1962): pp. 30–34; A. E. Parr, *Mostly About Museums*, pp. 9–12, 20–21, 45–58; Daifuku, "Museums and Research," pp. 71–72.
6. G. Carroll Lindsay, "Museums and Research in History and Technology," *Curator* 5 (1962):236–244; Montgomery, "Role of Museum in Research," pp. 100–103; A. E. Parr, "The Functions of Museums: Research Centers or Show Places," pp. 26–31; John Chavis, "The Artifact and the Study of History," pp. 156–162; Victor J. Danilov, "America's Contemporary Science Museums," *Museums Journal* 75 (March 1976):145–148; Coleman, *Museum in America*, 2:375–376, 379–382; Daifuku, "Museums and Research," pp. 68–69.

7. Fenton, "Museum Anthropological Research," p. 328.
8. A. E. Parr, "The Right to Do Research," *Curator* 1 (Summer 1958):70–73; Parr, "Museums: Research Centers or Show Places," pp. 20–31; Parr, *Mostly About Museums*, pp. 45–73.
9. Neustupny, *Museum Research*, pp. 33–36; Colbert, "What Is a Museum?" p. 141; Daifuku, "Museums and Research," p. 70.
10. Neustupny, *Museum Research*, pp. 11, 104; Daifuku, "Museums and Research," pp. 68, 71–72; Coleman, *Museum in America*, 2:373–374, 383–384.
11. Stephan F. de Borhegyi, "Testing of Audience Reaction to Museum Exhibits," *Curator* 8 (1965):86–93 and in de Borhegyi and Irene A. Hanson, *The Museum Visitor: Selected Essays and Surveys of Visitor Reaction to Exhibits in the Milwaukee Public Museum* (Milwaukee, 1968), pp. 76–80, esp. p. 79. The latter is a key volume for the study of audience research and contains a good bibliography, pp. 175–187. More comprehensive and up to date is Pamala Elliot-Van Erp and Ross J. Loomis, *Annotated Bibliography of Museum Behavior Papers* (Washington, D.C., 1973). A good over-view of the subject is Kenneth Hudson, *A Social History of Museums*, esp. pp. 100–121. See also Hiroshi Daifuku, "The Museum and the Visitor," in UNESCO *The Organization of Museums: Practical Advice* (Paris, 1967), pp. 73–80.
12. Coleman, *Museum in America*, 2:384–386; Clark Wissler, "The Museum Exhibition Problem," *Museum Work* 7 (March/April 1925):173–180; Arthur W. Melton, *Problems of Installation in Museums of Art* (Washington, D.C., 1935); Melton, "Visitor Behavior in Museums: Some Early Research in Environmental Design," *Human Factors* 14 (October 1972):393–403.
13. Arthur Niehoff, "Characteristics of the Audience Reaction in the Milwaukee Public Museum" and "Audience Reaction in the Milwaukee Public Museum: The Winter Visitors" in de Borhegyi and Hanson, *Museum Visitor*, pp. 9–16, 21–31; D. S. Abbey and Duncan F. Cameron, *The Museum Visitor: I. Survey Design; II. Survey Results; III. Supplementary Studies*, 3 vols. (Toronto, 1959–61); New York State Education Department and Janus Museums Consultants, Toronto, *The 1966 Audience of the New York State Museum* (Albany, 1968); Carolyn H. Wells, *Smithsonian Visitor* (Washington, D.C., 1970), Philip S. Doughty, "The Public of the Ulster Museum: A Statistical Survey," *Museums Journal* 68 (1968):19–25, 47–53; David G. Erwin, "The Belfast Public and the Ulster Museum," *Museums Journal* 70 (March 1971):175–179; Herbert Coutts, "The Antiquities Gallery of Dundee Museum: A Visitor Survey," *Museums Journal* 70 (March 1971):173–174.
14. David A. Johnson, "Museum Attendance in the New York Metropolitan Region," *Curator* 12 (1969):201–230.
15. Duncan F. Cameron, David S. Abbey, Theodore Allen Heinrich, and William J. Withrow, "Public Attitudes Toward Modern Art," *Museum* 22 (1969):125–152. For a more subjective examination of the problem by directors of museums of modern art, see "Problems of the Museum of Contemporary Art in the West," *Museum* 24 (1972):2–59.
16. Manfred Eisenbeis, "Elements for a Sociology of Museums," *Museum* 24 (1972):110–119.
17. Ross J. Loomis, "Please! Not Another Visitor Survey," *Museum News* 52 (October 1973):20–26.
18. Duncan F. Cameron, "How Do We Know What Our Visitors Think?" *Museum News* 45 (March 1967):31–33; Cameron, "The Evaluator's Viewpoint," *Museum News* 46 (January 1968):43–45; Cameron, "A Viewpoint: The Museum as a Communications System and Implications for Museum Education," *Curator* 11 (1968):33–40; Eugene I.

Knez and A. Gilbert Wright, "The Museum as a Communications System: An Assessment of Cameron's Viewpoint," *Curator* 13 (1970):204–212; Elizabeth H. Nicol, *The Development of Validated Museum Exhibits* (Washington, D.C., 1969), pp. 6–13.

19. James B. Taylor, *Science on Display: A Study of the United States Science Exhibit, Seattle World's Fair, 1962* (Seattle, 1963), pp. 162–184; de Borhegyi, "Testing of Audience Reaction," pp. 76–80.
20. Nicol, *Validated Museum Exhibits*, esp. pp. 27–33, 99–101.
21. Harris H. Shettel, "Exhibits: Art Form or Educational Medium," *Museum News* 52 (September 1973):32–41, esp. p. 33.
22. Chandler G. Screven, "Learning and Exhibits: Instructional Design," *Museum News* 52 (January/February 1974):67–75, esp. p. 68; Screven, *The Measurement and Facilitation of Learning in the Museum Environment: An Experimental Analysis* (Washington, D.C., 1974), pp. 13–15; Shettel, "Art Form or Educational Medium?" pp. 68–69.
23. Screven, "Learning and Exhibits," pp. 69–75; Screven, *Measurement and Facilitation*, pp. 15–69; Shettel, "Art Form or Educational Medium?" pp. 39–41.
24. Cameron, "How Do We Know?" pp. 31–33.

Notes, Chapter 10

1. Neil Harris, "Museums, Merchandising, and Popular Taste: The Struggle for Influence," in *Material Cultural and the Study of American Life* [Winterthur Conference Report, 1975] (Charlottesville, Va., 1977).
2. Herbert Bayer, "Aspects of Design of Exhibitions and Museums," *Curator* 4 (1961):257–287 (quotations on pp. 258, 266); Lothar P. Witteborg, "Design Standards in Museum Exhibits," *Curator* 1 (January 1958):29–41. For more on Bayer's work, see his autobiographical *Herbert Bayer: Painter, Designer, Architect* (New York, 1967); Alexander Dorner, *The Way Beyond "Art"; The Work of Herbert Bayer* (New York, 1947), pp. 197–206; George Nelson, *Display* (New York, 1953), pp. 108–119. On the attitude of museums toward their visitors through the years, see Kenneth Hudson, *A Social History of Museums*.
3. United Nations Educational, Scientific and Cultural Organization, *Temporary and Travelling Exhibits;* James H. Carmel, *Exhibition Techniques, Traveling and Temporary* (New York, 1962); Margaret W. M. Schaeffer, "The Display Function of the Small Museum," *Curator* 8 (1965):103–118.
4. Arminta Neal, *Help! for the Small Museum: A Handbook of Exhibit Ideas and Methods* (Boulder, Colo., 1969), pp. 21–27, and *Exhibits for the Small Museum: A Handbook* (Nashville, Tenn., 1976), pp. 11–27; Jean-Yves Veillard, "The Problem of the History Museum from an Experiment in the Musée de Bretagne," pp. 193–203; Peter C. Welsh, "Exhibit Planning: Ordering Your Artifacts Interpretively," *History News* 29 (April 1974): Technical Leaflet no. 73.
5. Robert M. Vogel, "Assembling a New Hall of Civil Engineering," *Technology and Culture* 6 (Winter 1965):59–73.
6. Hal Glicksman, "A Guide to Art Installations," *Museum News* 50 (February 1972): 22–27; P. R. Adams, "The Exhibition," in UNESCO, *The Organization of Museums*, pp. 126–145, plates 41–77; Lothar P. Witteborg, "The Temporary Exhibit in Science Museums," in UNESCO, *Temporary and Travelling Exhibits* pp. 15–29; H. L. C. Jaffé, "Temporary Exhibitions in Art Museums," *Temporary and Travelling Exhibits*, pp. 30–43; Jean Gabus, "Aesthetic Principles and General Planning of Educational Exhibitions," *Museum* 18 (1965):2–97.

7. Joseph Wetzel, "Three Steps to Exhibit Success," *Museum News* 50 (February 1972):20; Witteborg, "Temporary Exhibits, Science Museums," pp. 15–17; Jaffé, "Temporary Exhibits, Art Museums," pp. 30–36.
8. E. V. Gatacre, "The Limits of Professional Design," pp. 93–99; Hilton Kramer, "What Is This Stuff Doing at the Met?" *New York Times*, March 14, 1976.
9. Bayer, "Aspects of Design," pp. 257–287; Nelson, *Display;* Carmel, *Exhibition Techniques*, pp. 75–76; Witteborg, "Temporary Exhibits, Science Museums," pp. 16–17; Jaffé, "Temporary Exhibits, Art Museums," pp. 37–40; James Gardner and Caroline Heller, *Exhibition and Display* (London, 1960), pp. 40–45; "An Interview with Paul J. Smith," *Museum News* 50 (February 1972):15–19.
10. Russell Lynes, *Good Old Modern*, pp. 267–269, 354–355, 412, 450–453; Adams, "The Exhibition," p. 151, plate 42; Bayer, *Autobiography*, pp. 30, 32, 35–37, 50–51, 64–65; Richard P. Lohse, *New Design in Exhibitions: 75 Examples of the New Form . . .* (Zurich, 1953), pp. 20–27, 142–143, 166–167, 230–233; Witteborg, "Temporary Exhibits, Science Museums," p. 17. Neal, *Exhibits for the Small Museum*, pp. 28–37, tells how to make scale models.
11. Adams, "The Exhibition," pp. 131, 134; Bayer, *Autobiography*, p. 30, 32, 35–37; Neal, *Help!*, pp. 33–36 and *Exhibits for the Small Museum*, pp. 137–146; Sir Hugh Casson, "The Future of the Past," *Museums Journal* 61 (September 1961):99–105; Gabus, "Aesthetic Principles and Educational Exhibitions," pp. 2–13.
12. Adams, "The Exhibition," p. 132; Lynes, *Good Old Modern*, p. 355; Carmel, *Exhibition Techniques*, pp. 56–57; Neal, *Help!*, pp. 52–79 and *Exhibits for the Small Museum*, pp. 37–102; Boston *Christian Science Monitor*, March 31, 1973; *The Exhibition of the Archaeological Finds of the Peoples Republic of China*, National Gallery of Art, Washington, D.C., December 13, 1974—March 30, 1975; George H. Rivière and Herman F. E. Visser, "Museum Showcases," *Museum* 13 (1960):1–23.
13. Ned J. Burns, *National Park Service Field Manual for Museums*, pp. 72–78, 85–86; and "The History of Dioramas," *Museum News* 17 (February 15, 1940):8–12.
14. Lynes, *Good Old Modern*, pp. 268–269; Bayer, "Aspects of Design," pp. 257–258; Gardner and Heller, *Exhibition and Display*, pp. 59–103, 112–123; Carmel, *Exhibition Techniques*, pp. 115–116; Adams, "The Exhibition," pp. 41–77; Misha Black, editor, *Exhibition Design*, rev. ed. (London, 1951), pp. 129–132, 147–153; Gabus, "Aesthetic Principles of Educational Exhibitions," pp. 3–7.
15. Adams, "The Exhibition," p. 131; Bayer, *Autobiography*, pp. 30, 56–59; Dorner, *Work of Bayer*, pp. 201–205; Lohse, *New Design*, pp. 26–30, 76–77; "American Arts and the American Experience," *Museum News* 53 (November 1974):36–41; Erberto Carboni, *Exhibitions and Displays* (Milan, 1957), pp. 196–201; Neal, *Exhibits for the Small Museum*, pp. 103–115.
16. George Weiner, "Why Johnny Can't Read Labels," *Curator* 6 (1963):143–156; Don W. Wilson and Dennis Medina, "Exhibit Labels: A Consideration of Content," *History News* 27 (April 1942): Technical Leaflet no. 60; Ralph H. Lewis, *Manual for Museums*, pp. 26–27, 121–123, 312–314; William Hayett, *Display and Exhibit Handbook* (New York, 1967), pp. 45–58; Adams, "The Exhibition," pp. 129–130; Carmel, *Exhibition Techniques*, pp. 101–109; Gabus, "Aesthetic Principles of Educational Exhibitions," pp. 16–23; Gardner and Heller, *Exhibition and Display*, pp. 104–111; Neal, *Help!*, pp. 95–99, 153–171 and *Exhibits for the Small Museum*, pp. 122–138; UNESCO, *Temporary and Travelling Exhibits*, pp. 23–25, 41–42, 64; Gatacre, "Limits of Design," p. 98.
17. Albert E. Parr, "The Habitat Group," *Curator* 2 (1959):107–128 and "Mood and Message," *Curator* 6 (1963):325–336; Nina Fletcher Little, "An Expanding Concept of

the Period Room," *Winterthur Seminar on Museum Operation and Connoisseurship* (Winterthur, Del., 1957), pp. 42–44; Gatacre, "Limits of Design," p. 96; E. P. Alexander, "Artistic and Historical Period Rooms," *Curator* 7 (1964):263–281; Museum of History and Technology, *Exhibits* (Washington, D.C., 1968), pp. 12–18; James Deetz, "The Reality of the Pilgrim Fathers," *Natural History* 78 (November 1969):32–45; James Deetz, George L. Wrenn III, and Mrs. Margaret B. Klapthor, "The Changing Historic House Museum," *Historic Preservation* 23 (January/March 1971):51–60.

18. Marshall McLuhan, Harley Parker, and Jacques Barzun, *Exploration of the Ways, Means and Values of Museum Communication with the Visiting Public: A Seminar . . .* (New York, 1969).
19. McLuhan and others, *Museum Communication*, p. 4.
20. McLuhan and others, *Museum Communication*, pp. 3, 14, 36–37, 51; William Kissiloff, "How to Use Mixed Media in Exhibits," *Curator* 12 (1969):83–95.
21. McLuhan and others, *Museum Communication*, pp. 29, 32.
22. McLuhan and others, *Museum Communication*, pp. 4–5, 10.
23. Kissiloff, "Mixed Media," pp. 86–92. For an unfavorable view of mixed media, see Gatacre, "Limits of Design," p. 98.
24. Michael Robbins, "Can Man Survive?: An Exhibit Asks the Question of the Century," *Museum News* 48 (September 1969):10–13 (direct quotation on p. 13); Wilfrid Sheed, "Evolution on a Bad Trip: 'Can Man Survive?' at the American," *Life* 67 (July 11, 1969):7; Wetzel, "Three Steps," p. 20.
25. Frederick W. Dunning, "The Story of the Earth: Exhibition at the Geological Museum, London," *Museum* 26 (1974):99–109; Geoffrey Tresise, " 'The Story of the Earth' at the Geological Museum," *Museums Journal* 73 (September 1973):71–72.
26. The most recent general treatment is Carol Supplee, "Museums on Wheels," *Museum News* 53 (October 1974):26–35, based on her essay written for the master of arts degree: Carol Supplee Butler, *The Mobile Museum: Its Role in the Museum Process* (Washington, D.C., 1973). Articles on individual projects include "Artrain," *Industrial Design* 19 (January 1972):48–49; Muriel B. Christison, "The Virginia Museum of Fine Arts' Artmobile, Richmond, Virginia," *Museum* 8 (1955):128–131; William Gaines, "Virginia Museum: Two Pioneer Programs," *Museum News* 50 (October 1971):22–25; "Rolling Museum Takes Education to Isolated Northern Canadians," *History News* 29 (January 1974):6–7.
27. For overseas experiments with mobile museums, see Abraham Beer, "Recent Developments in Mobile Units," *Museum* 5 (1952):186–195 and "Expandable Mobile for Arid Zones," *Museum* 7 (1954):127–140; Hiroshi Daifuku, "An Experimental Museum for Tropical Africa," *Museum* 18 (1965):126–129; S. K. Ghose, "Mobile Science Exhibitions of the Birla Industrial and Technological Museum, Calcutta," *Museum* 21 (1968):294–300; Maud Linder, "The Linder Museobus," *Museum* 24 (1972):232–235; Stanislaw Lorentz, "Mobile Museums in Poland," *Museum* 3 (1950):283–285; V. A. Sevcuk, "Traveling Exhibitions and Mobile Museums [in the Ukraine]," *Museum* 19 (1966): 156–159.
28. Vincent Ciulla and Charles F. Montgomery, "Creative Compromise: The Curator and the Designer," *Museum News* 55 (March/April 1977):31–37.

Notes, Chapter 11

1. Freeman Tilden, *Interpreting Our Heritage*, p. 8. See also William T. Alderson and Shirley Payne Low, *Interpretation of Historic Sites* (Nashville, Tenn., 1976), pp. 3–6.

2. E. P. Alexander, "What Is Interpretation?" *Longwood Program Seminars* 9 (1977):2–7, and *The Interpretation Program of Colonial Williamsburg*, pp. 11–12.
3. Pedro Ramirez Vasquez and others, *The National Museum of Anthropology, Mexico* . . . p. 38; Ignacio Bernal and others, *The Mexican National Museum of Anthropology*, p. 11.
4. Alexander, *Interpretation Program*, p. 23; Colonial Williamsburg, *Colonial Williamsburg Welcomes You to Its New Visitor Facilities* (Williamsburg, Va., 1957), 8 pp.
5. Ralph H. Lewis, *Manual for Museums*, pp. 311–318; Ned J. Burns, *Field Manual for Museums*, pp. 270–275, 300–302; Molly Harrison, "Education in Museums," in UNESCO, *The Organization of Museums*, pp. 81–92; Mrs. Shirley P. Low, "Historic Site Interpretation: The Human Approach," *History News* 20 (November 1965): Technical Leaflet no. 32, and "Training Interpreters," National Park Service, *Park Practice Guidelines* 30 (April 1969):1–14; Laurence Vail Coleman, *Historic House Museums*, pp. 261–286; Florence Montgomery, "The Training of Guides," *History News* 19 (March 1964): Technical Leaflet no. 18; Alderson and Low, *Interpretation*, pp. 40–62, 105–145; Tilden, *Interpreting Our Heritage*, pp. 3–10, 26–39, 68–77, 89–94; Huldah Smith Payson, "Volunteers: Priceless Personnel for the Small Museum," *Museum News* 45 (February 1967):18–21; "The Training and Utilization of Volunteers: A Symposium," *Curator* 8 (1965):287–301.
6. E. P. Alexander, "Bringing History to Life: Philadelphia and Williamsburg," pp. 58–68, and "A Fourth Dimension for History Museums," *Curator* 11 (1968):263–289; Burns, *Field Manual for Museums*, pp. 270–275; Alderson and Low, *Interpretation*, pp. 36–39, 42, 100–102; George R. Clay, "The Lightbulb Angel: Towards a Definition of the Folk Museums in Cooperstown," *Curator* 3 (1960):43–65; James Deetz, "The Reality of the Pilgrim Fathers," pp. 32–45; James Deetz and others, "The Changing Historic House Museum," pp. 51–60; Peter W. Cook, "The Craft of Demonstrations," *Museum News* 53 (November 1974):10–15, 63; Robert D. Ronsheim, "Is the Past Dead?" *Museum News* 53 (November 1974): pp. 16–18, 62–63; Holly Sidford, "Stepping into History," *Museum News* 53 (November 1974): 28–34; Thomas J. Schlereth, "It Wasn't That Simple," *Museum News* 56 (January/February 1978):36–44; Catherine Fennelly, *Life in an Old New England Village: An Old Sturbridge Village Book* (New York, 1969), pp. 129–148, 191–203; Louis B. Martin, editor, "Educational Programmes," *Arboretum and Botanical Garden Bulletin* 1 (July 1967):2–27; Brooke Hindle, *Technology in Early America: Needs and Opportunities for Study*. With a Directory of Artifact Collections by Lucius F. Ellsworth (Chapel Hill, N.C., 1966).
7. Alexander, *Interpretation Program*, pp. 30–33; Burns, *Field Manual for Museums*, pp. 275–279, 297–302; Hal Golden and Kitty Hanson, *How to Plan, Produce and Publicize Special Events* (Dobbs Ferry, N.Y., 1966), esp. chaps. 1, 7–8, 10, 16–17, 19; Tilden, *Interpreting Our Heritage*, pp. 3–10, 26–31.
8. Alderson and Low, *Interpretation*, pp. 63–69; Alexander, *Interpretation Program*, pp. 36–37, 40–43; William A. Bostick, "Solving the Problem of the Paper Explosion," *Museum News* 44 (May 1966):18–23; Charlotte S. Derby, "Reaching Your Public: The Historical Society Newsletter," *History News* 22 (January 1967): Technical Leaflet no. 39; Richard N. Gregg, "Art Museum Publications: Their Nature and Their Design," *Curator* 2 (1959):49–67; Allan Kullen, "The Printer and You," *Museum News* 44 (October 1965):24–30; Memory F. Mitchell, "Publishing in State Historical Journals," *Wisconsin Magazine of History* 59 (Winter 1975/76):135–142; John J. Walklet, Jr., "Publishing in the Historical Society," *History News* 21 (April 1966): Technical Leaflet no. 34.
9. Alderson and Low, *Interpretation*, pp. 79–84; Alexander, *Interpretation Program*,

pp. 37, 44–46; Jacques Durand, "The Use of Cultural and Scientific Films in the Museums of the World," *Museum* 16 (1963):82–114; Craig A. Gilborn, "Filmstrips and Slides," *Museum News* 36 (October 1967):24–27; Jerrold E. Kemp, *Planning and Producing Audiovisual Materials* (San Francisco, 1963); William Lillys, "Museum TV: Its Genesis," *Museum News* 51 (January 1973):15–19; Brian N. Rushton, "Producing and Selling a Quality Service to Education: Slides," *Museum News* 46 (January 1968):27–32; Arthur L. Smith, "Producing the Slide Show for Your Historical Society," *History News* 22 (June 1969): Technical Leaflet no. 42; Roy A. Smith, "Reaching Your Public Through Television," *History News* 20 (March 1965): Technical Leaflet no. 26.

10. Edward L. Bernays, editor *The Engineering of Consent* (Norman, Okla., 1955); Duncan F. Cameron, "Putting Public Relations in Its Place," *Curator* 4 (1963):103–107; Marguerite Gignilliat, "Reaching Your Public Through the Newspapers," *History News* 23 (April 1968): Technical Leaflet no. 45; Thomas G. McCaskey, "Reaching Your Public: Turning Travelers into Visitors," *History News* 20 (June 1965): Technical Leaflet no. 29; Somerset R. Water, "Museums and Tourism," *Museum News* 44 (January 1966):32–37; William G. Dooley, "A Modern Sales Desk in an Old Museum," *Curator* 2 (1959):348–355; David Henry Krahel, "Why a Museum Store?" *Curator* 14 (1971):200–204; Kathleen K. Newcomb, "The Museum Store: Organization and Sales Techniques," *History News* 23 (June 1968): Technical Leaflet no. 46; "Shops and Sales Desks: The Museum Shop as an Educational Service," *Museum News* 46 (December 1967):32–39; Roberta Faul, "Licensing Programs—A Second Life for Museum Collections," *Museum News* 54 (November/December 1975):20–25.
11. Peter Michelsen, "The Outdoor Museum and Its Educational Program," pp. 201–217.
12. Tilden, *Interpreting Our Heritage*, p. 47.
13. Paul L. Benedict, "Historic Site Interpretation: The Student Field Trip," *History News* 26 (March 1971): Technical Leaflet no. 19; Ellen Endter, "Museums, Learning and the Performing Arts," *Museum News* 53 (June 1975):34–37, 72; Barbara Newsom, *The Metropolitan Museum as an Educational Institution*, pp. 6–58, 79–85; Charles Russell, *Museums and Our Children: A Handbook and Guide for Teachers in Museums and Schools* (New York, 1956); Adele Z. Silver, "Education in a Museum: A Conservative Adventure," *Curator* 15 (1972):72–85; Sidford, "Stepping into History," pp. 28–34; Mary Sam Ward, "Henry Clay Day: The Ultimate Field Trip," *Museum News* 50 (October 1971):34–37; Barbara R. Winstanley, *Children and Museums* (Oxford, Eng., 1967).
14. Robert W. Montgomery, "History for Young People: Organizing a Junior Society," *History News* 22 (September 1967): Technical Leaflet no. 44; Doris Platt, "History for Young People: Projects and Activities," *History News* 21 (September 1966): Technical Leaflet no. 38.
15. American Association of Museums, *Museums: Their New Audience*, pp. 36, 73–76; Laurence Vail Coleman, *The Museum in America*, 2:341–354; Louise Condit, "A New Junior Museum," *Curator* 2 (1959):11–20; Molly Harrison, *Learning Out of School: A Teacher's Guide to the Educational Use of Museums* (London, 1970), and *Museum Adventure: The Story of Geffrye Museum* (London, 1950); Newsom, *Metropolitan as an Educational Institution*, pp. 6–24; Helmuth J. Naumer, "The Great Incorporation: The Youth Museum and Education," in Eric Larrabee, editor, *Museums and Education* (Washington, 1968), pp. 129–138; Alma S. Wittlin, "Junior Museums at the Crossroads: Forward to a New Era of Creativity or Backward to Obsoleteness?" *Curator* 6 (1963):58–63.

Notes, Chapter 12

1. *Museum Work* 2 (February 1920):130.
2. *Museum Work* 2 (February 1920):29–30, 145–160; 7 (March/April 1925):163–172; Winifred E. Howe, *A History of the Metropolitan Museum of Art,* 2:144–149.
3. Otto Wittmann, "Art Education at the Toledo Museum," *Museum News* 38 (February 1960):22–23; William J. Gravesmill, "Museums and the Performing Arts," *Museum News* 45 (January 1967):29–32; Walter Blodgett, "Music in Museums: The Why and How," *Museum News* 45 (January 1967):32–34; Lawrence Morton, "A Helping Hand to Art in Its Aspiration Toward the Condition of Music," *Museum News* 45 (January 1967): 37–39; John Ludwig, "The Role of the Performing Arts, *Museum News* 45 (January 1967):40–41.
4. Anthony V. Garton, "Art Centers Are Alive and Well," *Museum News* 53 (September 1974):20–23; "Artpark: The Non-Museum," *Museum News* 53 (June 1975):14–15.
5. National Endowment for the Arts,*Museums USA,* pp. 38–41; Gravesmill, "Museums and the Performing Arts," pp. 29–32.
6. "Museum Sponsorship of the Performing Arts," *Museum News* 53 (June 1975):24–29.
7. National Museum of History and Technology, *Exhibits,* pp. 60–63; Metropolitan Museum of Art, *Bulletin,* 29 (October 1970):89; 30 (October/November 1971):49; E. P. Alexander, *The Interpretation Program of Colonial Williamsburg,* pp. 25–26.
8. Ellen Endter, "Museums, Learning and the Performing Arts," pp. 34–37.
9. Carol A. King, "Let's Eat," *Museum News* 53 (June 1975):44–49.
10. "Museums at the Crossroads," *Museum News* 44 (September 1965):19.
11. Andrew Ciechanowiecki, "Visitor's View of American Museums," *Museum News* 37 (June 1959):20–21; Simon Levie, "As They See Us," *Museum News* 44 (October 1965):34–35.
12. Munson-Williams-Proctor Institute, *Year Book, 1975–76* (Utica, N.Y., 1976); Keith Martin, "Arts Council and Cultural Growth," *Museum News* 39 (December 1960):28–31.
13. Keith Martin, "A New Museum Concept, *Museum News* 45 (January 1967):23–28; Martin, "Arts Council," pp. 28–31; Roberson Center for the Arts and Sciences, *The Many Faces of Roberson* (Binghamton, 1978).
14. Muriel B. Christison, "25th Anniversary in Virginia," *Museum News* 39 (November 1960):36–39; William Gaines, "Virginia Museum: Two Pioneer Programs," pp. 22–25; Virginia Museum of Fine Arts, *The Mark Report: A Survey and Evaluation of the Virginia Museum's Statewide Programs.* By Charles C. Mark (Richmond, 1974).
15. American Association of Museums, *The Official Museum Directory, 1977: United States and Canada* (Washington, D.C./Skokie, Ill., 1976).
16. E. P. Alexander, "The Regional Museum as a Cultural Centre," pp. 274–284; *Louisiana: A Pictorial Reportage* (Humlebaek, Denmark, c. 1965); Knud W. Jensen, "Danish Museum by the Sea," *Museum News* 38 (June 1960):14–19.
17. Theodore L. Low, *The Museum as a Social Instrument* (New York, 1942), pp. 20, 29–36. See also his important *The Educational Philosophy and Practice of Art Museums in the United States* (New York, 1946). For criticism of Low's thesis and his rebuttal, see Wilcomb E. Washburn, "The Museum's Responsibility in Adult Education," *Curator* 7 (1964):33–38 and "Scholarship and the Museum," *Museum News* 40 (October 1961):16–19; Low, "The Museum as a Social Instrument: 20 Years Later," *Museum News* 40 (January 1962):28–30.

18. Virginia Museum of Fine Arts, *Mark Report*, p. 53; National Endowment for the Arts, *Museums USA*, pp. 25–35.
19. American Association of Museums, *Museums: Their New Audience*, pp. 35, 58–69; Weldon D. Frankforter, "The Community Festival as Practiced in Grand Rapids," *Museum News* 48 (January 1970):20–23.
20. AAM, *New Audience*, pp. 39, 83–89; Barry Schwartz, "Art for Who's Sake?," pp. 40–42; Samuel C. Miller, "An African Festival at the Newark Museum," *Museum News* 47 (May 1969):25–27.
21. Joseph Veach Noble, "Drug Scene in New York," *Museum News* 50 (November 1971):10–15; "The City Museum in a New Role Offers Multimedia V. D. Exhibit," *New York Times*, March 25, 1974; AAM, *New Audience*, pp. 31, 36–37, 50–51, 70–72; Sophy Burnham, *The Art Crowd* (New York, 1973), pp. 167–195; Susan Badder, "Three Fledgling Museums," Metropolitan Museum of Art, *Bulletin* 30 (February/March 1972):162–169; Schwartz, "Art for Who's Sake?," pp. 42–45.
22. AAM, *New Audience*, pp. 40, 90–95; David Katzive, "Museums Enter the Video Generation," *Museum News* 51 (January 1973):20–24; Penny Bach, "Rites of Passage," *Museum News* 55 (September/October 1976):36–42.
23. AAM, *New Audience*, pp. 32, 52–53; Caryl Marsh, "A Neighborhood Museum That Works," *Museum News* 47 (October 1968):11–16; Anacostia Neighborhood Museum, *Fifth Anniversary, September 15, 1972* (Washington, D.C., 1972); John R. Kinard and Esther Nighard, "The Anacostia Neighborhood Museum . . . ," *Museum* 24 (1972):102–109; John Kinard, "To Meet the Needs of Today's Audience," *Museum News* 50 (May 1972): 15-16; Schwartz, "Art for Who's Sake?,"pp. 47-49; Dillion Ripley, *The Sacred Grove* . . . (New York, 1969), pp. 104-111.
24. AAM, *New Audience*, pp. 36, 73–76; Lloyd Hezekiah, "Reflections on MUSE," *Museum News* 50 (May 1972):12–14.
25. AAM, *New Audience*, pp. 31, 38, 39, 46, 48–49, 77–82, 96–99; Elisabeth Stevens, "Black Arts Centers," *Museum News* 54 (March 1975):19–24; Ludy Biddle, "Keeping Tradition Alive," *Museum News* 55 (May/June 1977):35–42.
26. Emily Dennis Harvey and Bernard Freidberg, editors, *A Museum for the People: Neighborhood Museums—A Report from the Brooklyn MUSE Seminar* (New York, 1972), pp. ix, 35, 53.
27. Daniel Catton Rich, "Management, Power, and Integrity," in American Assembly, *On Understanding Art Museums* (Englewood Cliffs, N.J., 1975), pp. 140–144; John L. Hess, *The Grand Acquisitors*, p. 173; Burnham, *Art Crowd*, pp. 13–22, 192–193.
28. David Katzive, "Up Against the Waldorf-Astoria," *Museum News* 49 (September 1970):12–17.
29. Rich, "Management, Power, and Integrity," pp. 154–161.

Notes, Chapter 13

1. Albert E. Parr, "A Plurality of Professions," *Curator* 7 (1964):287–295. See also his "Policies and Salaries for Museum Faculties," *Curator* 1 (1958):13–17, and "Is There a Museum Profession?" *Curator* 3 (1960):101–106.
2. Parr, "Plurality," p. 294.
3. Wilbur H. Glover, "Toward a Profession," *Museum News* 42 (January 1964):11–14.
4. National Endowment for the Arts, *Museums USA*, p. 4; American Association of Museums, *The Official Museum Directory, 1977: United States and Canada*.
5. *Museums USA*, p. 7; Laurence Vail Coleman, *The Museum in America*, 3:661.
6. *Museums USA*, p. 83.

7. Glover, "Toward a Profession," pp. 11–14.
8. Mr. Coleman's books, unless otherwise indicated published at Washington by the American Association of Museums, include *Manual for Small Museums* (New York: G. P. Putnam's Sons, 1927); *Contributions of Museums to Outdoor Recreation* (Washington, D.C.: National Conference on Outdoor Recreation, 1929); *Historic House Museums; with a Directory* (1933); *Museum in America* (1939); *College and University Museums: A Message for College and University Presidents* (1942); *Company Museums* (1943); *Museum Buildings: A Planning Study* (1950).
9. Issued by American Association of Museums at Washington, D.C., unless otherwise indicated, are *Museum Registration Methods*, 3rd ed. edited by Dorothy H. Dudley and Irma B. Wilkinson (1978); *Official Museum Directory, 1977; Museums and the Environment: A Handbook for Education*, edited by Ruth N. Oliver (New York: Arkville Press, 1971); *Museums: Their New Audience* (1972); *America's Museums: The Belmont Report* (1969); *Museum Accreditation: Professional Standards*, by Marilyn Hicks Fitzgerald (1973); *Financial and Salary Review*, by Kyran McGrath (1971); *Museum Salary and Financial Review*, by Kyran McGrath (1973); *Museum Training Courses in the United States and Canada*, rev. ed., compiled by G. Ellis Burcaw (1971); *Museum Studies: A Curriculum Guide for Universities and Museums* (1973); *Museum Accounting Handbook*, by Malvern J. Gross, Jr., and William H. Daughtrey, Jr. (1977).
10. Published by the American Association for State and Local History at Nashville, Tenn.: *The Management of Small History Museums*, 2nd ed., by Carl E. Guthe (1964); *Safeguarding Your Collection in Travel*, by Caroline K. Keck (1970); *A Handbook on the Care of Paintings*, by Caroline K. Keck (1967); *The Care and Administration of Manuscripts*, 2nd ed., by Lucille M. Kane (1966); *Historic Preservation*, edited by Frederick L. Rath, Jr., and Merrilyn Rogers O'Connell (1975), vol. 1 of *A Bibliography on Historical Organization Practices; Modern Manuscripts: A Practical Manual for Their Management, Care, and Use*, by Kenneth W. Duckett (1975); *Collection, Use, and Care of Historical Photographs*, by Robert A. Weinstein and Larry Booth (1977); *The Care of Historical Collections: A Conservation Handbook for the Nonspecialist*, by Per E. Guldbeck (1972); *Introduction to Museum Work*, by G. Ellis Burcaw (1975); *Interpretation of Historic Sites*, by William T. Alderson and Shirley Payne Low (1976); *Museum Cataloging in the Computer Age*, by Robert G. Chenall (1975); *Exhibits for the Small Museum: A Handbook*, by Arminta Neal (1976). The association has a leaflet describing its Slide/Tape Training Kits and Tape Cassetts.
11. Published by UNESCO at Paris: *The Organization of Museums: Practical Advice*, 2nd ed. (1967); *Conservation and Restoration of Archive Materials*, by Yash Pal Kathpalia (1973); *The Conservation of Cultural Property with Special Reference to Tropical Conditions* (1968); *Field Manual for Museums* (1970); *Museum Techniques in Fundamental Education* (1956); *Museums, Imagination and Education* (1973); *Preserving and Restoring Monuments and Historic Buildings* (1972); *Temporary and Travelling Exhibits* (1963).
12. Icom publications (Paris, unless otherwise noted): *Museum Security*, edited by Robert G. Tillotson (1977); *Training of Museum Personnel* (London: Hugh Evelyn, 1970); *Museums and Research* (Munich: Deutsches Museum, 1970); *The Museum in the Service of Man . . . Museum Education and the Cultural Role* (1972).
13. Milwaukee bibliography by Stephan F. de Borhegyi, Elba A. Dodson, and Irene A. Hanson, 2 vols. (Milwaukee, 1960–61). New York State Historical Association bibliography by Frederick L. Rath, Jr., and Merrilyn Rogers O'Connell (Cooperstown, 1970); for its continuation, see note 10 above. The Icom bibliographies begin with the year 1967 and are issued in Prague and Paris.

14. AAM, *Belmont Report,* p. 62.
15. AAM, *Museum Accreditation,* p. 3.
16. AAM, *Museum Accreditation, pp. 7–9.*
17. "Looking at Accreditation," *Museum News* 55 (November/December 1976):15–41, esp. p. 16.
18. *Museum News* 55 (November/December 1976): 30–31.
19. *Museum News* 55 (November/December 1976): 32–37.
20. Brenda Capstick, "The Museum Profession in the United Kingdom," *Museum* 23 (1970–71):154–162.
21. E. P. Alexander, "A Handhold on the Curatorial Ladder," *Museum News* 52 (May 1974):23–25.
22. Office of Museum Programs, Smithsonian Institution, *Museum Studies Programs in the United States and Abroad* (Washington, D.C., 1976); Bret Waller, "Museum Training: Who Needs It?" *Museum News* 52 (May 1974):26–28.
23. AAM, *Museum Studies.*
24. AAM, *Code of Ethics for Museum Workers* (New York, 1925); reprinted in *Museum News* 52 (June 1974):26–29.
25. "Museum Ethics: A Report . . . ," *Museum News* 56 (March/April 1978):21–30. For a fuller treatment of questionable acquisitions and disposal of objects in museum collections, see chap. 7 above.
26. Key discussions of codes of ethics include W. G. Constable, "Museum Ethics," *Museums Journal* 41 (October 1941):145–151; R. Alan Douglas, "Museum Ethics: Practice and Policy," *Museum News* 45 (January 1967):18–21; Alan D. Ullberg and Patricia Ullberg, "A Proposed Curatorial Code of Ethics," *Museum News* 52 (May 1974):18–22; John Henry Merryman, "Are Museum Trustees and the Law Out of Step?" *Art News* 74 (November 1975):24–27; Thomas Vaughan, "A Simple Matter of Standards," *Museum News* 55 (January/February 1977):32–34.
27. American Association of Museums, *Museum Work: Including The Proceedings . . . ,* 8 vols. (Providence, R.I. and elsewhere, 1918–26); American Association of Museums, *Annual Reports* [with slightly varying titles], 34 vols. (New York City, Washington, D.C., 1924–58); Ellen C. Hicks, "The AAM after 72 Years," *Museum News* 56 (May/June 1978):44–48.
28. Charles Parkhurst in *Museum News* 45 (April 1967):4.
29. Patterson's career is best traced through *Museum News* 38 (March 1959) to 45 (April 1967), especially his column, "Points of View."
30. McGrath's administration can likewise be followed in *Museum News* 46 (1968) to 53 (May 75), mainly in his column "From the Director." He also started a monthly *Bulletin* in 1968 that contained Washington report, placement listings, and classified ads; it was superseded in September 1976 by the enlarged and renamed *Aviso.*
31. Richard McLanathan, "From the Director," *Museum News* 55 (January/February 1977):3; *Aviso* (November 1976):3; (December 1976):4; (June 1977):3; (April 1978):1; (June 1978):1–2.
32. Joseph Veach Noble, "The Future of the AAM," *Museum News* 55 (September/October 1975):34–36; Richard McLanathan, "Report on Membership," AAM Council Meeting, May 29, 1977; Ernst and Ernst, *AAM Audited Financial Statement,* April 30, 1977.
33. These developments are best followed through *Museum* and *Icom News.* See Grace Morley, "Museums and Unesco," *Museum* 2 (1949):11–12; Stephen Thomas, "Icom and AAM," *Museum News* 48 (October 1969):27–29; *Icom News* 29 (no. 3/1976):67–68.
34. "Unesco's Tenth Anniversary," *Museum* 9 (1956):133–134.

35. *Museum* 11 (1958):1.
36. "Unesco's Tenth Anniversary," pp. 133–143. On education seminars, see *Museum* 6 (1953):213–281; 8 (1955):201–238; 12 (1959):197–283; 16 (1963):206–260; 19 (1966):210–284; on Training Centre, 18 (1965):121–125; on Regional Agency, *Icom News* 26 (Spring 1973):28–33; 29 (nos. 1–2/1976):29.
37. Robert R. Garvey, "International Council of Monuments and Ṣites—Icomos," *Icom: Newsletter of U.S. National Committee* (Autumn 1972):5; "Unesco's Tenth Anniversary," pp. 133–143; *Museum* 12 (1959):64; *Icom News* 25 (December 1972):223–226; 26 (Spring 1973): special insert.
38. Dorothy A. Mariner, "Professionalizing the Museum Worker," *Museum News* 50 (June 1972):14–20.
39. Association of Art Museum Directors, *Professional Practices in Art Museums* (New York, 1971), 28 pp., reprinted in *Museum News* 51 (October 1972):15–20; Paul N. Perrot, "The Professional Relations Committee—Goals," *Museum News* 50 (December 1971):51–52.
40. Eileen Dribbin, "Museums Get a Taste of PASTA," *Museum News* 50 (June 1972):21–26; Ashton Hawkins, "Improving Governance at the Metropolitan Museum," *Museum News* 50 (June 1972):35; Ronald L. Miller, "Collective Bargaining in Museums," *Museum News* 54 (September/October 1975):26–29.
41. Maurice Rheims, *The Strange Life of Objects*, p. 29.

Some Basic Museum Books

General

Altick, Richard D. *The Shows of London.* Cambridge, Mass., and London: Harvard University Press, 1978. 553 pp.

American Association of Museums. *The Official Museum Directory 1977: United States, Canada.* Skokie, Ill.: National Register Publishing Co., 1976. 891 pp.

Bazin, Germain. *The Museum Age.* New York: Universe Books, 1967. 302 pp.

Bell, Whitfield, Jr., and others. *A Cabinet of Curiosities: Five Episodes in the Evolution of American Museums.* Charlottesville: University Press of Virginia, 1967. 166 pp.

Burcaw, G. Ellis. *Introduction to Museum Work.* Nashville, Tenn.: American Association for State and Local History, 1975. 202 pp.

Coleman, Laurence Vail. *The Museum in America: A Critical Study.* 3 vols. Washington, D.C.: American Association of Museums, 1939. 730 pp.

Everhart, William C. *The National Park Service.* New York: Praeger, 1972. 275 pp.

Hellman, Geoffrey T. *The Smithsonian Institution: Octopus on the Mall.* Philadelphia: Lippincott, 1967. 224 pp.

Key, Archie F. *Beyond Four Walls: The Origins and Development of Canadian Museums.* Toronto: McClelland and Stewart, 1973. 384 pp.

Lewis, Ralph H. *Manual for Museums.* Washington, D.C.: National Park Service, 1976. 412 pp.

National Endowment for the Arts. *Museums USA: Art, History, Science, and Other Museums.* Washington, D.C.: NEA, 1974. 203 pp.

Oehser, Paul H. *The Smithsonian Institution.* New York: Praeger, 1970. 275 pp.

Rogers, Lola Eriksen. *Museums and Related Institutions: A Basic Program Survey.* Washington, D.C.: Office of Education, 1969. 120 pp.

United Nations Educational, Scientific and Cultural Organization (UNESCO). *Field Manual for Museums.* Paris: UNESCO, 1970. 171 pp.

———. *The Organization of Museums: Practical Advice.* Paris: UNESCO, 1967. 188 pp.

Wittlin, Alma S. *Museums: In Search of a Usable Future.* Cambridge, Mass.: MIT Press, 1970. 295 pp.

Field Manual for Museums. Paris: UNESCO, 1970. 171 pp.
_____. *The Organization of Museums: Practical Advice*. Paris: UNESCO, 1967. 188 pp.
Wittlin, Alma S. *Museums: In Search of a Usable Future*. Cambridge, Mass.: MIT Press, 1970. 295 pp.

What is a Museum?

Dana, John Cotton. *The New Museum*. Woodstock, Vt.: Elm Tree Press, 1917. 52 pp.
Finlay, Ian. *Priceless Heritage: The Future of Museums*. London: Faber and Faber, 1977. 183 pp.
Gilman, Benjamin Ives. *Museum Ideals of Purpose and Method*. 2d ed. Cambridge: Harvard University Press, 1923. 462 pp.
Goode, George Brown. *A Memorial of . . . with a Selection of His Papers . . .* In Smithsonian Institution, *Annual Report for 1897*, part II. Washington, D. C.: 1901. 515 pp.
Hudson, Kenneth. *A Social History of Museums: What the Visitors Thought*. Atlantic Highlands, N.J.: Humanities Press, 1975. 210 pp.
O'Doherty, Brian, editor. *Museums in Crisis*. New York: Braziller, 1972. 178 pp.
Ripley, Sidney Dillon. *The Sacred Grove: Essays on Museums*. New York: Simon and Schuster, 1969. 150 pp.
Taylor, Francis Henry. *Babel's Tower: The Dilemma of the Modern Museum*. New York: Columbia University Press, 1945. 52 pp.
Weil, Stephen E. *Beauty and the Beasts: On Museums, Art, the Law and the Market*. Washington, D. C.: Smithsonian Institution Press, 1983. 272 pp.

The Art Museum

American Assembly, Columbia University. *On Understanding Art Museums*. Edited by Sherman E. Lee. Englewood Cliffs, N.J.: Prentice-Hall, 1975. 216 pp.
Burt, Nathaniel. *Palaces for the People: A Social History of the American Art Museum*. New York: Little, Brown, 1977. 446 pp.
Gould, Cecil. *Trophy of Conquest: The Musée Napoleon and the Creation of the Louvre*. London: Faber and Faber, 1965. 151 pp.
Hermann, Frank. *The English as Collectors: A Documentary Chrestomathy*. London: Chatto and Windus, 1972. 461 pp.
Holst, Neils von. *Creators, Collectors and Connoisseurs: The Anatomy of Taste from Antiquity to the Present Day*. New York: G. P. Putnam's Sons, 1967. 400 pp.
Howe, Winifred E. *A History of the Metropolitan Museum of Art . . .* 2 vols. New York: MMA, 1913, 1946.
Jackson, Virginia et. al. *Art Museums of the World*. Westport, Conn.: Greenwood Press, 1987. 1,696 pp.
Lerman, Leo. *The Museum: One Hundred Years of the Metropolitan Museum of Art*. New York: Viking, 1969. 400 pp.
Lynes, Russell. *Good Old Modern: An Intimate Portrait of the Museum of Modern Art*. New York: Atheneum, 1973. 490 pp.
Roberts, George, and Mary Roberts. *Triumph on Fairmount: Fiske Kimball and the Philadelphia Art Museum*. Philadelphia: Lippincott, 1959. 321 pp.
Taylor, Francis Henry. *The Taste of Angels: A History of Art Collecting from*

Rameses to Napoleon. Boston: Little, Brown, 1948. 661 pp.
Tomkins, Calvin. *Merchants and Masterpieces: The Story of the Metropolitan Museum of Art*. New York: E. P. Dutton, 1970. 383 pp.
Whitehill, Walter Muir. *Museum of Fine Arts, Boston: A Centennial History*. 2 vols. Cambridge, Mass.: Belknap Press, 1970. 888 pp.
Wittke, Carl. *The First Fifty Years: The Cleveland Museum of Art, 1916–1966*. Cleveland: Cleveland Museum of Art, 1966. 161 pp.

The Natural History Museum

Bernal, Ignacio, and others. *The Mexican National Museum of Anthropology*. London: Thames and Hudson, 1968. 216 pp.
Crook, James Mordaunt. *The British Museum*. London: Penguin Press, 1972. 251 pp.
De Beer, Gavin Rylands. *Sir Hans Sloane and the British Museum*. London, New York: Oxford University Press, 1953. 192 pp.
Frese, Hermann Heinrich. *Anthropology and the Public: The Role of Museums*. Leiden: E. J. Brill, 1969. 276 pp.
Harris, Neil. Humbug: *The Art of P. T. Barnum*. Boston: Little, Brown, 1973. 337 pp.
Hellman, Geoffrey T. *Bankers, Bones and Beetles: The First Century of the American Museum of Natural History*. Garden City, N. Y.: Natural History Press, 1969. 275 pp.
Miller, Edward. *That Noble Cabinet: A History of the British Museum*. Athens, Ohio: Ohio University Press, 1975. 400 pp.
Sellers, Charles Coleman. *Charles Willson Peale*. New York: Charles Scribner's Sons, 1969. 510 pp.

The Museum of Science and Technology

Danilov, Victor J. *America's Science Museums*. Westport, Conn.: Greenwood Press, 1990. 496 pp.
Greenleaf, William. *From These Beginnings: The Early Philanthropies of Henry and Edsel Ford, 1911–1936*. Detroit: Wayne State University Press, 1964. 235 pp.
Hindle, Brooke. *Technology in Early America: Needs and Opportunities. With a Directory of Artifact Collections by Lucius F. Ellsworth*. Chapel Hill: University of North Carolina Press, 1966. 145 pp.
Kogan, Herman. *A Continuing Marvel: The Story of the [Chicago] Museum of Science and Industry*. Garden City, N.Y.: Doubleday, 1973. 234 pp.
Luckhurst, Kenneth W. *The Story of Exhibitions*. London, New York: Studio Publications, 1951. 221 pp.
Orosz, Joel J. *Curators and Culture: The Museum Movement in America, 1740–1870*. Tuscaloosa and London: University of Alabama Press, 1990. 304 pp.
Richards, Charles R. *The Industrial Museum*. New York: Macmillan, 1925. 117 pp.

The History Museum

Angle, Paul M. *The Chicago Historical Society, 1856–1956: An Unconventional Chronicle*. New York, Chicago: Rand, McNally, 1956. 256 pp.
Coleman, Laurence Vail. *Historic House Museums; with a Directory*. Washington,

D. C.: American Association of Museums, 1933. 187 pp.

Fennelly, Catherine. *Life in an Old New England Country Village: An Old Sturbridge Village Book*. New York, 1969. 211 pp.

George, Gerald. *Visiting History: Arguments over Museums and Historic Sites*. Washington, D. C.: American Association of Museums, 1990. 118 pp.

Guthe, Carl E. *The Management of Small History Museums*. Nashville, Tenn.: American Association for State and Local History, 1964. 78 pp.

Henry Ford Museum Staff. *Greenfield Village and the Henry Ford Museum*. New York: Crown Publishers, 1972. 235 pp.

Hosmer, Charles B., Jr. *Presence of the Past: A History of the Preservation Movement in the United States Before Williamsburg*. New York: G. P. Putnam's Sons, 1965. 386 pp.

_____. *Preservation Comes of Age, From Williamsburg to the National Trust, 1926–1949*. Charlottesville: University Press of Virginia, 1981.

Johnson, Gerald W., and Charles Cecil Wall. *Mount Vernon: The Story of a Shrine*. New York: Random House, 1953. 122 pp.

Leon, Warren, and Roy Rosenzweig. ed. *History Museums in the United States: A Critical Assessment*. Urbana: University of Illinois Press, 1989. 344 pp.

Lord, Clifford L., editor. *Keepers of the Past*. Chapel Hill: University of North Carolina Press, 1965. 241 pp.

Lord, Clifford L., and Carl Ubbelohde. *Clio's Servant: A History of the State Historical Society of Wisconsin*. Madison: State Historical Society, 1967. 598 pp.

Rath, Frederick L., Jr. et. al. *Local History, National Heritage: Reflections on the History of AASLH*. Nashville, Tenn.: American Association for State and Local History, 1991. 128 pp.

Seminar on Preservation and Restoration, Williamsburg, Va., 1963. *Historic Preservation Today*. Charlottesville: University Press of Virginia, 1966. 265 pp.

U. S. Conference of Mayors. *With Heritage So Rich: A Report . . . on Historic Preservation . . .* Edited by Albert Rains and Lawrence G. Henderson. New York: Random House, 1966. 230 pp.

Vail, R. W. G. *Knickerbocker Birthday: A Sesquicentennial History of the New York Historical Society, 1804–1954*. New York: NYHS, 1954. 547 pp.

Whitehill, Walter Muir. *Independent Historical Societies: An Inquiry into Their Research and Publication Functions and Their Financial Future*. Boston: Boston Anthenaeum, 1962. 593 pp.

Yetter, George Humphrey. *Williamsburg Before and After: The Rebirth of Virginia's Colonial Capital*. Williamsburg: Colonial Williamsburg Foundation, 1988. 208 pp.

Botanical Gardens and Zoos

Allan, Mea. *The Hookers of Kew, 1785–1911*. London: Michael Joseph, 1967. 273 pp.

_____. *The Tradescants: Their Plants, Gardens and Museum, 1570–1662*. London: M. Joseph, 1964. 345 pp.

Blunt, Wilfrid. *The Ark in the Park: The [London] Zoo in the Nineteenth Century*. London: Hamish Hamilton, 1976. 276 pp.

Bridges, William. *Gathering of the Animals: An Unconventional History of the New*

York Zoological Society. New York: Harper and Row, 1974. 518 pp.
Fisher, James. *Zoos of the World: The Story of Animals in Captivity*. Garden City, N.Y.: Natural History Press, 1967. 245 pp.
Gersh, Harry. *The Animals Next Door: A Guide to Zoos and Aquariums of the Americas*. New York: Fleet Academic Editions, 1971. 170 pp.
Hediger, Heini. *Man and Animal in the Zoo: Zoo Biology*. New York: Seymour Lawrence/Delacorte Press, 1969. 303 pp.
Hyams, Edward S. *A History of Gardens and Gardening*. New York: Praeger, 1971. 345 pp.
Hyams, Edward S., and William MacQuitty. *Great Botanical Gardens of the World*. New York: Macmillan, 1969. 288 pp.
Livingston, Bernard. *Zoo: Animals, People, Places*. New York: Arbor House, 1974. 290 pp.
Sutton, Stephane Barry. *Charles Sprague Sargent and the Arnold Arboretum*. Cambridge: Harvard University Press, 1970. 382 pp.
Turrill, William Bartram. *The Royal Botanic Gardens: Kew, Past and Present*. London: Herbert Jenkins, 1959. 256 pp.

The Museum as Collection

American Association of Museums. *Museum Registration Methods*. By Dorothy H. Dudley, Irma B. Wilkinson, and others. 3rd ed., 3rd printing. Washington, D. C.: AAM, 1989.
Blackaby, James R., Patricia Greeno, and the Nomenclature Committee. *The Revised and Expanded Edition of Robert G. Chenhall's System for Classifying Man-made Objects*. Nashville, Tenn.: American Association for State and Local History, 1988. 253 pp.
Burnham, Bonnie. *The Art Crisis*. New York: St. Martins, 1975. 256 pp.
Chenhall, Robert G. and David Vance. *Museum Collections and Today's Computers*. Westport, Conn.: Greenwood Press, 1988. 177 pp.
Constable, William George. *Art Collecting in the United States . . . : An Outline of History*. London: T. Nelson and Sons, 1964. 210 pp.
Feldman, Franklin, and Stephen E. Weil, editors. *Art Works: Law, Policy, Practices*. New York: Practising Law Institute, 1974. 1,241 pp.
Kurz, Otto. *Fakes: A Handbook for Collectors and Students*. 2d rev. and enl. ed. New York: Dover, 1967. 348 pp.
Malaro, Marie C. *A Legal Primer on Managing Museum Collections*. Washington, D. C.: Smithsonian Institution Press, 1985. 352 pp.
Meyer, Karl Ernst. *The Plundered Past*. New York: Atheneum, 1973. 353 pp.
Metropolitan Museum of Art, New York City. *The Chase, The Capture: Collecting at the Metropolitan*. New York: MMA, 1975. 234 pp.
_____. *Computers and Their Potential Applications in Museums*. New York: Arno Press, 1968. 402 pp.
Reibel, Daniel B. *Registration Methods for Small History Museums*. Yardley, Penn.: DBR Publications, 1991. 260 pp.
Rigby, Douglas, and Elizabeth Rigby. *Lock, Stock and Barrel: The Story of Collecting*. Philadelphia: Lippincott, 1944. 570 pp.
Saarinen, Aline B. *The Proud Possessors: The Lives, Times, and Tastes of Some*

Adventurous American Art Collectors. New York: Random House, 1958. 395 pp.
Savage, George. *Forgeries, Fakes, and Reproductions: A Handbook for Art Dealer and Collector.* New York: Praeger, 1964. 312 pp.
Williams, David. *A Guide to Museum Computing.* Nashville, Tenn.: American Association for State and Local History, 1987. 187 pp.

The Museum as Conservation

Fall, Frieda Kay. *Art Objects: Their Care and Preservation . . .* LaJolla, Calif.: Lawrence McGivey, 1973. 332 pp.
International Council of Museums. *Museum Security.* Edited by Robert G. Tillotson and Dinah D. Menkes. Washington, D. C.: American Association of Museums, 1977. 256 pp.
_____. *Problems of Conservation in Museums.* London: George Allen and Unwin, 1969. 222 pp.
Keck, Caroline K. *A Handbook on the Care of Paintings.* Rev. ed. Nashville, Tenn.: American Association for State and Local History, 1967. 136 pp.
_____. *Safeguarding Your Collection in Travel.* Nashville, Tenn.: American Association for State and Local History, 1970. 80 pp.
Keck, Caroline K., and others. *A Primer on Museum Security.* Cooperstown, N.Y.: New York State Historical Association, 1966. 85 pp.
MacLeish, A. Bruce. *The Care of Antiques and Historical Collections.* Rev. edition of Per E. Guldbeck's *The Care of Historical Collections: A Conservation Handbook for the Non-Specialist.* Nashville, Tenn.: American Association for State and Local History, 1987. 248 pp.
McGiffin, Robert F., Jr. *Furniture Care and Conservation.* Nashville, Tenn.: American Association for State and Local History, 1983. 255 pp.
Menkes, Diana. ed. *Museum Security Survey.* Paris, France: International Council of Museums, 1981. 116 pp.
National Committee to Save America's Cultural Collections, Arthur W. Schultz, Chairman. *Caring for Your Collections.* New York: Harry N. Abrams, Inc., 1992. 216 pp.
Oddy, Andrew. ed. *The Art of the Conservator.* Washington, D. C.: Smithsonian Institution Press, 1992. 208 pp.
Organ, Robert M. *Design for Scientific Conservation of Antiquities.* Washington, D. C.: Smithsonian Institution Press, 1968. 497 pp.
Plenderleith, Harold J. and A. E. A. Werner. *The Conservation of Antiquities and Works of Art: Treatment, Repair, and Restoration.* 2d ed. London: Oxford University Press, 1971. 394 pp.
Thomson, Garry. *The Museum Environment.* 2d ed. London: Butterworth, 1986. 308 pp.
United Nations Educational, Scientific and Cultural Organization. *The Conservation of Cultural Property with Special Reference to Tropical Conditions.* Paris: UNESCO, 1968. 344 pp.

The Museum as Research

Borhegyi, Stephan F. de, and Irene A. Hanson, editors. *The Museum Visitor: . . . Visitor Reaction to Exhibits in the Milwaukee Public Museum.* Milwaukee: MPM,

1968. 187 pp.

International Council of Museums. *Museums and Research: Papers from the Eighth General Conference*. Munich: Deutsches Museum, 1970. 126 pp.

Loomis, Ross J. *Museum Visitor Evaluation: New Tool for Management*. Nashville, Tenn.: American Association for State and Local History, 1987. 320 pp.

Melton, Arthur W. *Problems of Installation in Museums of Art*. Washington, D. C.: American Association of Museums, 1935. 269 pp.

Neustupny, Jiri. *Museum and Research*. Prague: National Museum of Czechoslovakia, 1968. 160 pp.

Nicol, Elizabeth H. *The Development of Validated Museum Exhibits*. Washington, D. C.: Office of Education, 1969. 114 pp.

Parr, Albert E. *Mostly About Museums: From the Papers of A. E. Parr*. New York: American Museum of Natural History, 1959. 112 pp.

_____. *Selected Papers, 1959–1967*. Privately assembled reprints with bibliography, 1926–1967. New York, 1967. c. 450 pp. separately numbered.

Royal Ontario Museum, Toronto. *The Museum Visitor*. By D. S. Abbey and Duncan F. Cameron. 3 vols. Toronto: ROM, 1959–61. 66 pp.

Screven, C. G. *The Measurement and Facilitation of Learning in the Museum Environment: An Experimental Analysis*. Washington, D. C.: Smithsonian Institution Press, 1974. 91 pp.

Shettel, Harris H., and others. *Strategies for Determining Exhibit Effectiveness*. Pittsburgh: American Institute for Research, 1968. 244 pp.

Taylor, James B., and others. *Science on Display: A Study of the United States Science Exhibit, Seattle World's Fair, 1962*. Seattle: Institute for Sociological Research, 1963. 184 pp.

Wells, Carolyn H. *Smithsonian Visitor: A Survey . . . in the National Museum of History and Technology and the National Museum of Natural History . . .* Washington, D. C.: Smithsonian Institution, 1969. 97 pp.

The Museum as Exhibition

Ames, Kenneth L., Barbara Franco, and L. Thomas Frye, editors. *Ideas and Images: Developing Interpretive History Exhibits*. Nashville, Tenn.: American Association for State and Local History, 1992. 344 pp.

Bayer, Herbert. *Herbert Bayer: Painter, Designer, Architect*. New York: Reinhold, 1967. 211 pp.

Brawne, Michael. *The New Museum: Architecture and Display*. New York: Praeger, 1965. 208 pp.

Carmel, James H. *Exhibition Techniques: Traveling and Temporary*. New York: Reinhold, 1963. 216 pp.

Dorner, Alexander. *The Way Beyond "Art": The Work of Herbert Bayer*. New York: Wittenborn, Schultz, 1947. 244 pp.

Favretti, Rudy J., and Joy P. Favretti. *Landscapes and Gardens for Historic Buildings*, 2d ed., revised. Nashville, Tenn.: American Association for State and Local History, 1991. 216 pp.

Gardner, James, and Caroline Heller. *Exhibition and Display*. London: B. T. Batsford, 1960. 191 pp.

Lohse, Richard P. *New Design in Exhibitions: 75 Examples . . .* Zurich: Erlenbach,

1953. 260 pp.
McLuhan, Marshall, Harley Parker, and Jacques Barzun. *Exploration of the Ways, Means and Values of Museum Communication with the Visiting Public . . .* New York: Museum of the City of New York, 1969. 82 pp.
Neal, Arminta. *Exhibits for the Small Museum: A Handbook*. Nashville, Tenn.: American Association for State and Local History, 1976. 169 pp.
_____. *Help! for the Small Museum: A Handbook of Exhibit Ideas and Methods*. Boulder, Colo.: Pruett Press, 1969. 200 pp.
Nelson, George. *Display*. New York: Hill and Wang, 1953. 190 pp.
Royal Ontario Museum, Toronto. *Communicating with the Museum Visitor: Guidelines for Planning*. Toronto: ROM, 1976. 498 pp.
Seale, William. *Recreating the Historic House Interior*. Nashville, Tenn.: American Association for State and Local History, 1978. 270 pp.
United Nations Educational, Scientific and Cultural Organization. *Temporary and Travelling Exhibits*. Paris: UNESCO, 1963. 123 pp.
Witteborg, Lothar P. *Good Show! A Practical Guide for Temporary Exhibitions*, 2d ed. Washington, D. C.: Smithsonian Institution Traveling Exhibition Service, 1991. 184 pp.

The Museum as Interpretation

Alderson, William T., and Shirley Payne Low. *Interpretation of Historic Sites*, 2d edition, revised. Nashville, Tenn.: American Association for State and Local History, 1985. 202 pp.
American Association of Museums. *Museums and the Environment: A Handbook for Education*. Edited by Ruth N. Oliver. New York: Arkville Press, 1971. 261 pp.
Bay, Ann. *Museum Programs for Young People: Case Studies*. Washington, D. C.: Smithsonian Institution, 1973. 282 pp.
Collins, Zipporah W. ed. *Museums, Adults and the Humanities: A Guide to Educational Programming*. Washington, D. C.: American Association of Museums, 1981. 425 pp.
Harrison, Molly. *Learning Out of School: A Teacher's Guide to the Educational Use of Museums*. London: Ward Lock Educational, 1970. 80 pp.
Karp, Ivan, Christine Mullen Kreamer, and Steven D. Lavine. *Museums and Communities: The Politics of Public Culture*. Washington, D. C.: Smithsonian Institution Press, 1992. 672 pp.
Karp, Ivan and Steven D. Lavine. *Exhibiting Cultures: The Poetics and Politics of Display*. Washington, D. C.: Smithsonian Institution Press, 1991. 480 pp.
Larrabee, Eric, editor. *Museums and Education*. Washington, D. C.: Smithsonian Institution Press, 1968. 255 pp.
Low, Theodore Lewis. *The Educational Philosophy and Practice of Art Museums in the United States*. New York: Teachers College, Columbia University, 1946. 245 pp.
Metropolitan Museum of Art, New York City. *The Metropolitan Museum as an Educational Institution*. By Barbara Y. Newsom. New York: MMA, 1970. 128 pp.
Newsom, Barbara Y., and Adele Z. Silver. *The Art Museum as Educator*. Berkeley:

University of California Press, 1978. 800 pp.

Pitman-Gelles, Bonnie. *Museums, Magic, and Children: Youth Education in Museums.* Washington, D. C.: Association of Science-Technology Centers, 1981. 263 pp.

Russell, Charles. *Museums and Our Children: A Handbook and Guide.* New York: Central Book Co., 1956. 338 pp.

Tilden, Freeman. *Interpreting Our Heritage.* Chapel Hill: University of North Carolina Press, 1967. 120 pp.

Winstanley, Barbara R. *Children and Museums.* Oxford, England: Basil Blackwell and Mott, 1967. 125 pp.

Zetterberg, Hans Lennert. *Museums and Adult Education.* London: Evelyn Adams and McKay, 1968. 89 pp.

Zucker, Barbara Fleisher. *Children's Museums, Zoos, and Discovery Rooms: An International Reference Guide.* Westport, Conn.: Greenwood Press, 1987. 278 pp.

The Museum as Cultural Center and Social Instrument

American Association of Museums. *Museums: Their New Audience.* Washington, D. C.: AAM, 1972. 112 pp.

Harvey, Emily Dennis, and Bernard Freiberg, editors. *A Museum for the People: Neighborhood Museums—A Report from the Brooklyn MUSE Seminar.* New York: Arno Press, 1972. 86 pp.

International Council of Museums. *The Museum in the Service of Man: Today and Tomorrow—The Museum Educational and Cultural Role; Papers from the Ninth General Conference.* Paris: ICOM, 1972. 195 pp.

Low, Theodore L. *The Museum as a Social Instrument.* New York: Metropolitan Museum of Art, 1942. 71 pp.

Newark Museum. *A Survey: 50 Years.* Newark, N. J.: Newark Museum, 1959. 136 pp.

The Museum Profession

American Association of Museums. *America's Museums: The Belmont Report.* Washington, D. C.: AAM, 1969. 81 pp.

_____. *Museum Accreditation: A Handbook for the Institution.* Washington, D. C.: AAM, 1990. 90 pp.

_____. *Museum Ethics.* Washington, D. C.: AAM, 1991. 39 pp.

_____. *Museum Studies: A Curriculum Guide for Universities and Museums.* Washington, D. C.: AAM, 1973. 28 pp.

Association of Art Museum Directors. *Professional Practices in Art Museums.* New York: AAMD, 1971. 28 pp.

International Council of Museums. *Training of Museum Personnel.* London: Hugh Evelyn, 1970. 242 pp.

_____. *ICOM Statutes and Codes of Professional Ethics.* Paris: International Council of Museums, 1990. 28 pp.

Smithsonian Institution, Office of Museum Program and International Council of Museums, Committee for Training Personnel. *Museum Studies International.* 5th ed. Washington, D. C.: 1988.

Index

[As a convenience to readers, this index lists in two ways most of the museums, botanical and zoological gardens, and historic sites mentioned in the text. Each is listed alphabetically, by name, and again under the name of the city where it is situated.—Editor]